24 $\underline{50}$

Habermas and the Dialectic of Reason

HABERMAS
and the
DIALECTIC
OF REASON

DAVID INGRAM

Yale University Press
New Haven and London

Designed by Nancy Ovedovitz and set in
Palatino type by Eastern Graphics. Printed in
the United States of America by BookCrafters,
Inc., Chelsea, Michigan.

Library of Congress Cataloging-in-Publication Data
Ingram, David, 1952–
Habermas and the dialectic of reason.
Bibliography: p.
Includes index.
1. Habermas, Jürgen. 2. Habermas, Jürgen. Theorie
des kommunikativen Handelns. 3. Sociology—Philo-
sophy. 4. Rationalism. 5. Social action. 6. Communi-
cation—Philosophy. 7. Functionalism. I. Title.
B3258.H234I54   1987   301'.01   86-22394
ISBN 0–300–03680–9 (alk. paper)

The paper in this book meets the guidelines
for permanence and durability of the
Committee on Production Guidelines for
Book Longevity of the Council on Library
Resources.

10   9   8   7   6   5   4   3   2   1

For Julia

Der Ethiker muß immer von neuem zur Welt kommen. Der
Künstler ein für allemal
      —Karl Kraus, *Vom Künstler*, in *Werke*, ed. Heinrich Fischer
                  (Munich: Kosel Verlag, 1952), vol. 3, p. 239.

Engel (sagt man) wüßten oft nicht, ob sie unter
Lebenden gehn oder Toten. Die ewige Strömung
reißt durch beide Bereiche alle Alter
immer mit sich und übertont sie in beiden
            —Rainer Maria Rilke, *Duino Elegies*, ed. J. B. Leishman
            and Stephen Spender (New York: Norton, 1939), p. 24.

CONTENTS

PREFACE

Since 1978, the year in which Thomas McCarthy's pioneering study *The Critical Theory of Jürgen Habermas* was published, no major synoptical treatment of Habermas's work has appeared. To appreciate the significance of McCarthy's endeavor, one need only recall the relative ignorance of German philosophy among Anglo-American thinkers at the time—one compounded in Habermas's case by his dense style and seeming obliviousness to the needs of potential readers, most of whom were unfamiliar with the broad range of problems, disciplines, and figures presupposed in his work. McCarthy's main achievement was to provide English-speaking readers with an accessible, sympathetic, yet critical introduction to Habermas's thought.

There would be no need to attempt another explication of Habermas's thought in English were it not for the changes that it has undergone during the past eight years. Of course, much of what is contained in McCarthy's commentary is still valid, and much of Habermas's work prior to 1978 sheds light on his most recent research. It is also clear, however, that the scope of issues and arguments has been expanded—mostly in response to the growing mass of secondary literature—to include new topics in aesthetics and poststructuralism, as well as problems in first-generation critical theory that had hitherto been neglected. Most important perhaps, the conception of critical theory that began to emerge in Habermas's writings in the late seventies marked a departure from the earlier program of ideology critique. That this new development has not yet been fully appreciated in the English-speaking world is to be attributed presumably to the fact that none of his most recent works—*Theorie des kommunikativen Handelns* (1981), *Moralbewusstsein und kommunikatives Handeln* (1983), *Der philosophische Diskurs der Moderne* (1985), and *Die neue Unübersichtlichkeit: Kleine politische Schriften V* (1985)—has yet been translated in its entirety.

The aim of this study is twofold: to provide a brief commentary on *Theorie des kommunikativen Handelns* (hereafter abbreviated *Theorie*) and to evaluate it in the light of Habermas's more recent writings on modernity, politics, and aesthetics. There are several reasons for the first undertaking. Not only does *Theorie* advance the first major defense of Habermas's program in its entirety, it also constitutes a major reassessment of its function. Critique of ideology is supplanted by a holistic criticism of social reification, a shift that is related to a global reappraisal of first-generation critical theory and deficiencies in the philosophy of consciousness. What emerges is the clearest statement yet of Habermas's philosophy of communication and the bilevel lifeworld-system model of society implicated in it. *Theorie* also represents an attempt on Habermas's part to settle his differences with the classical sociological tradition. Indeed, one can legitimately read it as a grand synopsis of the entire sociological tradition extending from Marx to contemporary ethnomethodology and cybernetics. No major school of thought is ignored, and commentaries on such towering figures as Weber and Parsons comprise virtually self-contained, book-length studies in their own right. These magnificent forays into the history of social theory (*Theoriegeschichte*) are interspersed with digressions (*Zwischenbetrachtungen*) in which Habermas develops his own theory in response to the possibilities and limitations of the tradition as a whole. I cannot hope to capture in a brief study the richness of a book whose scope spans more than eleven hundred pages, but I would like to think that I have succeeded in outlining its major contours and summarizing the not inconsiderable secondary literature.

As for the second undertaking, I believe that Habermas's conception of rationality is far more complex than most of his critics have realized. Habermas has conceded for some time now that reason can no longer be grounded transcendentally, as if it were necessary for the possibility of human experience and communication. But it is only very recently that he has acknowledged that reason, such as it exists for modern man, is aesthetic as well as communicative. *Theorie* presupposes a holistic conception of rationality that cannot be adequately articulated by a formal notion of procedural justice, one that implies an intuitive integration and dialectical harmonizing of substantive values. If I am not mistaken, Habermas's conception of aesthetic rationality constitutes a significant effort to reinvest his theory with hermeneutic content, thereby bridging the gap between discursive reflection and lived experience that has bothered so many of his critics.

With regard to hermeneutic methodology, the dialectical mode of presentation is a trademark of some of Habermas's earlier monumental studies, most notably *Zur Logik der Sozialwissenschaften* (1967) and *Erkenntnis und Interesse* (1968). Like many German philosophers who have come under the influence of hermeneutics by way of Hegel, Habermas realizes that the concepts that inform current debates in the human sciences possess meanings that have evolved historically and contain their own sedimentation of past interpretations. Unlike theories in the natural sciences, social theories draw their categories and problems from everyday concerns and therefore stand in a particularly intimate relationship to their subject matter. The validity of a general theoretical paradigm is never decided solely on the basis of empirical evidence but is in part determined by its capacity to encompass the distinct interpretative contributions of the tradition in ways that give rise to new possibilities of meaning for society today.

It is my hope that this book will address the needs of the novice as well as the veteran Habermas scholar. For the benefit of the former I have included an introductory chapter designed to acquaint the reader with the pertinent issues and influences shaping Habermas's thought from 1960 to 1970. I have not hesitated to refer to the earlier writings or to remarks by commentators and critics in clarifying the present argument. In general, however, my policy has been to locate the more detailed aspects of my exegesis as well as critical asides of lesser import in the notes and to confine my own critical observations to the concluding sections of each of the four main subdivisions. Finally, I make no claim to absolute interpretative originality. My own vision owes much to the work of Thomas McCarthy, Fred Dallmayr, Richard Bernstein, and scores of others, cited and uncited. Where I differ from them is chiefly in my stress on the aesthetic dimensions of Habermas's thought.

It is impossible to acknowledge all those who have helped make this book possible. But first I must express my deepest gratitude to my wife, Julia Ingram, to whom the book is dedicated, for providing an intellectual sounding board for many of my ideas. Special thanks are also due to Fred Olafson, mentor and friend, whose unflagging support helped me to survive my darkest moments as a graduate student, and to Herbert Marcuse, who spent many hours patiently explaining Hegel to me. Among those whose comments have been most helpful in revising the manuscript are Fred Dallmayr, Benjamin Gregg, and Richard Bernstein. I am also indebted to Martha Reinecke and other members of the Philosophy and Religion Department at the University of Northern Iowa, not to mention my students, for their valuable criticism. Special thanks are due to John Downey and Ruth Ratliff of the University of Northern Iowa for research funding during the summer of 1983. I am especially grateful to my editor at Yale University Press, Jeanne Ferris, for her enthusiastic support of this project. I am indebted to Cynthia Wells, Jean van Altena, and Meighan Pritchard for their assistance in the production and editing of the book, Betty Seibert and Chris Seres for typing earlier drafts of it, and to Beacon Press and Thomas McCarthy for permission to quote from their translations of Habermas's work. I would also like to acknowledge *Praxis International* and *The Philosophical Forum*, which published some material from this book in article form.

A BRIEF OUTLINE OF THE BOOK

This book documents the struggle of a great thinker to come to grips with the central paradox of modern life: the loss of freedom, meaning, and respect for human life. The seeds were planted early, when, as a doctoral student still in his mid-twenties and very much affected by the postwar trauma, Habermas discovered the writings of the early Marx and the early Lukács. At the time, he was absorbed in writing a dissertation on Schelling's transcendental reconciliation of nature and spirit, which was deeply rooted in Jewish and Christian mysticism and which figured predominantly in the ontological critique of Cartesian dualism advanced by Heidegger. However, the discovery of Marx, Lukács, and the Young Hegelian critique of speculative philosophy by way of Löwith's masterpiece *From Hegel to Nietzsche* soon convinced him that the spiritual fragmentation and alienation afflicting the modern age had social rather than metaphysical causes. It was the dawning of this awareness that drew him to the Frankfurt school. As an assistant to Adorno from 1956 to 1959 he immersed himself in the study of Marxist economics, Freud, and the sociological tradition of Weber, Durkheim, and Parsons. The influence of Gadamer's philosophical hermeneutics and Apel's communicative pragmatics in the early and mid-sixties sparked a further interest in the analytic philosophy of language and science, American pragmatism, structural linguistics, and developmental psychology. More important still, it was during this period of ferment that Habermas rediscovered the seminal essays of the *Zeitschrift für Sozialforschung* published by the Frankfurt school during the thirties. The need to develop a systematic grounding of societal rationality that would realize the original aim of critical theory while avoiding a dialectic of reason of the sort that later proved so tempting to Adorno and first-generation members of the school inspired him to publish in 1979–81 a series of programmatic sketches culminating in a theory of communicative action.

I do not intend to examine in detail the various influences shaping

Habermas's career.[1] The first chapter attempts to sketch in rather broad strokes the maturation of Habermas's thought from the early to the late sixties, however. After introducing the problem of understanding by way of a brief look at the eighteenth-century quarrel between the ancients and the moderns (Vico, Descartes, Bacon, and Hobbes), I discuss in the following order Habermas's critique of Popper in the "positivist dispute" of the early sixties, his early analysis of the structural transformation of the public sphere, his Hegelian appropriation of Marx, the influence of philosophical hermeneutics and early critical theory on the development of his thought (Heidegger, Gadamer, and Horkheimer), and his first systematic effort to ground social critique in a theory of knowledge-constituting interests. Habermas's rejection of some of the formulations concerning the relationship between theory and practice underlying *Knowledge and Human Interests* sets the stage for the remainder of my commentary. I wish to defend the thesis that since the late seventies, Habermas has developed a more sophisticated—and more problematic—way of conceiving this relationship, one that is torn between a discursive conception of practical reason and a conception incorporating intuitive elements.

Chapters 2–5 consist of a commentary on Part 1 of *Theorie*. Chapter 2 lays out Habermas's theory of rationality and action and briefly summarizes his defense of the evolutionary superiority of Occidental rationality over mythopoeic modes of thought. Winch, Lukes, Popper, Jarvie, and Piaget are among those who make their entrance in this chapter. Chapter 3 expands on the relevance of the preceding analysis for hermeneutic methodology in the social sciences and defends the possibility of objectivity and rationality in interpretation. This defense of hermeneutic sociology, which goes beyond anything Habermas has previously said on the subject, is followed by a section on linguistic philosophy that systematically surveys the contributions of various schools of thought to the development of a theory of communicative action: the speech pragmatics of Bühler, Wittgenstein, Austin, and Searle; the generative linguistics of Chomsky, and the truth-functional semantics of Carnap, Dummet, and others. Here I show how Habermas's recent reflections on the nature of perlocutionary and locutionary speech acts constitute his first significant attempt to justify the primacy of communicative over strategic action. Having established this primacy, Habermas can proceed to argue that the normative expectations regulating ideal speech—reciprocity and freedom from constraint—are implicit in the *telos* of communication as such and therefore constitute a prima facie refutation of ethical skepticism.

Chapter 4 introduces the concept of modern, "rational" society by way of an extended commentary on that solitary thinker who has contributed more than anyone to its problematization, Max Weber. Weber's conception of social rationalization raises questions about the capacity of Habermas's theory of communicative action to refute his diagnosis of modern society as necessarily tending toward a struggle between opposing factions of value and rationality. Here I present some of Habermas's recent ideas on aesthetic rationality, which seem to suggest a broadening of the category of communication. Chapter 5 continues the preceding discussion in a higher register: the appropriation of Weber's sociology by Lukács and first-generation critical theory. The synthesis of Weber, Marx, and Freud effected by the first generation had the consequence of naturalizing reification, thereby undermining its original emancipatory intent. This paradoxical identification of reason and domination is traced by Habermas to the subject-object dualism informing the philosophy of consciousness. To resolve the paradox, he proposes a paradigm shift of the sort that he himself has already undertaken. Doubts persist, however, as to whether a narrowing of communicative rationality to discourse can succeed where an ontological aesthetic has failed.

At this juncture, I have interjected a lengthy excursis on Habermas's most recent works, *Der Philosophische Diskurs der Moderne* and *Die Neue Unübersichtlichkeit*, since they address the preceding concerns from the standpoint of the problematic role of aesthetics in the current debate over the relative merits of modernity and postmodernity. Accordingly, chapter 6 begins with a cursory glance at the major themes in this debate and then summarizes the positions of Habermas on the one side and Hegel, Nietzsche, Heidegger, Derrida, Bataille, and Foucault on the other. The remarkable convergence between Habermas's communication theory and Schiller's aesthetics is a clear indication, I believe, that Habermas might be willing to extend the concept of communicative rationality to include a prediscursive moment of practical reason (*phronēsis*).

Chapters 7–10 continue where chapter 5 left off and are principally devoted to clarifying the distinction made in *Theorie* between lifeworld and system and to explaining their pathological dynamic. Chapter 7 addresses the contribution of communication to the symbolic reproduction of society: cultural reproduction, social integration, and socialization. Mead and Durkheim are the major figures here, Mead providing the link between communication and identity formation, Durkheim the normative foundation buttressing social solidarity. The next chapter situates Habermas's differentiation between lifeworld and system within his theory of social evolution and concludes with a brief discussion of some of the secondary literature generated by his reconstruction of historical materialism and a critique of the residual "intellectualism" implicit in his theory of ego development. Chapter 9 is concerned with Habermas's complicated relationship to the systems theory of Talcott Parsons. After introducing the concept of system and outlining Habermas's earlier debate with Niklas Luhmann, I summarize Habermas's own lengthy exegesis of the Parsonian corpus.

Chapter 10 begins with an analysis of the various interchanges between lifeworld and system and then shows how this model illuminates the social pathologies that Habermas believes to be indigenous to advanced capitalism. Colonization of the lifeworld and the splitting off of elite subcultures are contrasted with the forms of legitimation and motivation crisis discussed in his earlier studies, thereby setting the stage for the dramatic settling of accounts with first-generation critical theory over such diverse issues as bureaucratic socialism, the nuclear family, and mass culture. The final section weighs the strengths and weaknesses of Habermas's diagnosis of advanced capitalism, focusing on the role of radical politics in effecting social change, the limits and possibilities of social democracy, and the potential of critical theory for addressing the peculiar needs of women and workers. The concluding chapter returns to the relationship between theory and practice introduced at the outset and examines the recent change in Habermas's understanding of the proper function of critical theory. I contend that the transition from ideology critique to holistic criticism is closely related to Habermas's budding interest in aesthetics and his attempt to strike a balance between everyday understanding and discursive critique.

Habermas and the Dialectic of Reason

CHAPTER ONE

*The Historical Foundations
of the Theory of
Communicative Action*

Aside from its impressive range and mastery of sources, the most striking feature of Habermas's published work from the past two decades is its sense of moral purpose. In an age when technology and science reign supreme and the life of the individual is increasingly fragmented, this may seem somewhat academic. However, although science and technology can help us to evaluate the consistency of our goals, our chances of realizing them, and the means by which they can be pursued most efficiently, they cannot help us determine which goals are intrinsically worthwhile or even morally obligatory. To clarify ethical questions concerning social justice, political authority, and the good life, Habermas turns not to the methodology of the exact sciences, but to the hermeneutic, or interpretative, methodology of the human sciences (*Geisteswissenschaften*). The distinction that we make today between the exact sciences, humanities, and the fine arts grew out of the dissolution of the medieval curriculum. Science came into its own with the removal of theology from the academic realm and the discovery of experimental method. In the wake of these developments, Francis Bacon criticized traditional prejudice and ordinary language; eliminated theology, metaphysics, history, and poetry from the study of nature; relegated questions of right conduct to the province of divine revelation; and proposed basing ethics and politics, shorn of any normative predilection, on the method of induction.[1] Bacon's rejection of tradition as a source of moral inspiration in favor of investigation of the laws of nature for purposes of technological mastery had a profound influence on his amanuensis, Thomas Hobbes, who was the first to undertake

1

the scientization of politics. Hobbes essentially redefined the scholastic doctrine of natural law by ridding it of its normative, teleological meaning and reinterpreting human nature in accordance with the principles of Galilean mechanics. In effect, his theory of political sovereignty constitutes a defense of Bacon's assertion that the sole aim of political science is to teach those who wield power "how to frame and subdue the will of men."[2]

Several centuries before Bacon wrote his treatises, humanists such as Leonardo Bruni, Leon Alberti, and Vittorina da Feltre had rebelled against the arid metaphysical speculation of the scholastics and had sought to revive academic interest in classical studies, rhetoric, and civic virtue.[3] But it was not until the eighteenth century, after Newtonian physics had made its impact that Giambattista Vico ushered in a new and decisive phase in *la querrelle des anciens et des modernes* by insisting on the importance of historical understanding for the attainment of true self-knowledge.

Vico started out as a Cartesian but later rejected the Cartesian claim that only ideas possessing absolute certainty and demonstrability warrant the title of truth. He attacked this view on both theoretical and practical grounds. He maintained that geometry is known with certitude only because it is based on agreed-upon conventions created by the imagination, not because it conforms to the inner reality of nature—a view that presages his radical thesis in *Scienza Nuova* (1725) that we can know only what we ourselves have made (*verum et factum convertuntur*).[4] Knowledge involves understanding the purposes of things, but because God created external nature, only he can understand its true purpose. The natural sciences can explain *how* reality operates, but not *why*. But with the languages, myths, institutions, and actions of mankind, it is different, since they are themselves human creations. As an ethicist, Vico saw that analytic rationality could not provide guidance in the areas of life that matter most, since exercise of moral judgment depends on the proper formation of character and the cultivation of common sense, imagination, and memory, and moral education consists primarily in learning the languages, traditions, and exemplary ideals of past cultures.[5]

The pedagogical value of understanding as a kind of dialogue with the past was also appreciated by early nineteenth-century German romantics, including Hegel, who elevated dialectical reason (*Vernunft*) above analytic thought (*Verstand*). Hegel maintained that it is only by carrying on an interpretative dialogue with past or alien cultures that one is stimulated to reflect on one's own situation and thereby overcome the limits of one's own parochial understanding, thus achieving freedom from traditional constraints. Seen in this light, spiritual formation (*Bildung*) is not acquired by way of a skeptical bracketing of traditional assumptions, but through the interpretative preservation and critical enrichment of assumptions already operative.

THE POSITIVIST CONTROVERSY AND
THE SCIENTIZATION OF POLITICS

The domain in which Habermas has continued the debate between the ancients and moderns is that of the social sciences, the disciplines that, having once claimed undisputed title to the field formerly dominated by classical political thought, now aspire to the status of exact sciences. In the *Positivismusstreit* of the early sixties, Habermas sought to justify the primacy of a critical social science against the methodological hegemony espoused by Karl Popper and other neopositivists.[6] In seeking to capture the nature of scientific knowledge, Popper had recourse to the covering-law model, which presupposes that the proper aim of any scientific discipline is to predict particular events —to be able to derive a description of any event *E* from a singular statement of initial conditions *C* and a conditional law statement of the form, "If (whenever) *C*, then *E*." Predictions of this sort are valid if the universal laws from which they are deduced are experimentally corroborated—a notion that Popper sees as best captured in the principle of falsifiability, according to which the empirical value of a general law is proportional to the number of predictions to which it gives rise that could be falsified on the basis of factual observation. A social science based on the covering-law model would therefore refrain from passing judgment on the overall goal of history or of a given society, since neither unconditional teleological predictions nor evaluations are susceptible to empirical falsification. The practical worth of such a social science would be gauged by its capacity to produce behavioral laws permitting the discovery of efficient means for engineering incremental changes in social institutions.[7]

Habermas's rejoinders to Popper focused on both the methodological and philosophical limitations of his position. Methodologically, it has been noted by Weber, Collingwood, and others that statistical uniformities . . . "constitute 'sociological generalizations' only when they can be regarded as manifestations of the understandable meaning of a course of action." One cannot explain *why* a given action has occurred by appealing to how often it happens. One must also appeal to the intentions of the actor. Indeed, one has already begun to explain the intentional causes of an action when one has understood its meaning.[8] Habermas cited William Dray's objections to the covering-law model as particularly apposite in this regard. Dray argues that for a behavioral law to be valid, it must be either so general as to apply to any action whatsoever, in which case it is too trivial to provide sufficient explanation, or so specific that only the action in question counts as an instance of it, in which case it succeeds only by sacrificing its nomothetic generality.[9] In any case, appeal to observed behavior can at most allow an observer to adduce a *functional* meaning, extending no further than objectively postulated "aims" of biological survival. But actions to procure the basic necessities of life are undertaken in accordance with cultural values that define a standard of living considerably higher than that of mere subsistence. The meaning of an agent's action is symbolically constituted with respect to shared meanings; therefore it cannot be described adequately without some participatory understanding of the network of communicative action sustaining these meanings. But participatory understanding requires that the objectifying, value-neutral standpoint of an impartial observer give way to the subjectively open, value-committed attitude of an interlocutor in a shared practice.[10]

Although Habermas offers a defense of hermeneutic social science on strictly methodological grounds, he is more concerned to establish an ethical basis for his position. He believes that behavioral social science can "be called upon as an auxiliary science in rational administration" only if it is supplemented by a hermeneutic social science that elucidates the rational ends and interests to be served.[11] He has devoted considerable effort to examining the ethical implications of social engineering and the scientization of political life. Political philosophy as Aristotle understood it was an extension of ethics that aimed to cultivate moral character and to further the attainment of the good and just life. Since Hobbes, however, its scope has gradually narrowed to the technical resolution of social problems, thereby contributing to another—the nihilism wrought by a scientization of life.[12] In his early study *Strukturwandel der Öffentlichkeit* (1962), Habermas traced the emergence of an enlightened, politicized public realm in the eighteenth century and its gradual emasculation under advanced capitalism. Whereas in feudal society the public saw itself as passively representing a divinely preordained political order, with the rise of capitalism a public sphere emerged, composed of private citizens who sought to limit the authority of the state and affirm the principle of public accountability.[13] The state was regarded as legitimate as long as it implemented the general interests of the public under conditions of free association and free speech; thus government proceedings were to be made public, and the press was to be allowed to form and articulate a critical public opinion.[14]

Although Habermas recognizes that this liberal phase of the bourgeois public sphere was not entirely free of contradictions, in that the great mass of workers and peasants were excluded from membership and private interests often supervened in what was ostensibly a rational articulation of the public interest, he nonetheless appreciates the principle of democratic self-determination and critical accountability that it embodied.[15] With the development of modern capitalism, however, the conditions that nurtured the bourgeois public sphere —homogeneous class interests and a relatively high level of education and material affluence—disappeared. The intensification of class conflict in the nineteenth century and the concomitant expansion of the press beyond its original bourgeois base were accompanied by both a decline in disinterested discussion and a rise in propaganda wars between competing private interests.[16] The dissolution of public life into naked power struggles between self-interested economic classes presaged the absorption of the market into the protective orbit of the welfare state in the twentieth century. This "refeudalisation of the public sphere" stems from the need of the state to make controversial decisions vital to the management of a class-based economy without fear of public reprisal and to plan policy without regard to public demands for accountability. But this requires depoliticizing the public sphere and making it malleable to the state's designs. This is accomplished by artificially orchestrating public opinion so as to promote the illusion of a profusion of competing interests. The assumption that such interests are rationally irreducible indirectly justifies the right of the state to intervene in the role of arbitrator.[17] It also contributes to the further dissemination of "technocratic consciousness," for, if economic interests cannot be decided rationally, then public policy planning geared toward the technological maintenance of steady economic growth must be directed from above by trained bureaucratic elites.[18]

THE MARXIAN AND HEGELIAN LEGACIES

Although Habermas sees Popper's position as symptomatic of the scientific-technological obsession of modern society, he does not advocate a return to the natural law doctrines of classical political philosophy, much less a return to what Popper, thinking of Hegel and Marx, calls historicism. Nevertheless, it is these latter thinkers who supply him with much of the inspiration for his own critical theory. For Marx, the aim of social theory is to enlighten people about their true interests, so that they can plan their historical destinies in a rational manner. Marx believed that the natural life process (*Naturwüchsigkeit*) of prebourgeois societies, rooted as it is in the dark sediment

5

of preconscious traditions and parochial prejudices, would gradually be eroded in the process of secularization initiated by the industrial revolution. Still, he was aware that the acquisitive, self-serving behavior of competing entrepreneurs in an unregulated market would produce fortuitous events at the macroeconomic level. The only solution in his view was the revolutionary overthrow of class domination and the establishment of a socialist society spearheaded by an enlightened proletariat. But what Marx envisaged as rational conduct was not the enlightened egoism of Adam Smith but rather presupposed the attainment of a superior consciousness of human sociality.[19]

The major obstacles to achieving class consciousness, Marx believed, were ideology, which involves the manipulation of the cultural superstructure for the purpose of legitimating exploitative class relations, and commodity fetishism, which creates the illusion that social relations among persons are natural and invariant.[20] Although Marx believed that labor organizations would engender authentic feelings of solidarity, he was well aware that isolated enclaves of proletarian militancy would be vulnerable to fetishism and parochial prejudice. Subsequently, he came to believe that the critique of political economy which he undertook in *Das Kapital* was indispensable for raising proletarian class consciousness. By exposing the lie of equal exchange in the production of profit and by showing that accumulation of capital was ultimately contingent on the labor of dispossessed producers, *Das Kapital* shattered bourgeois illusions of equality, freedom, and justice, as well as the fetishistic reification of society.[21]

The critique of ideology was the dominant motif in Habermas's vision of a social theory prior to the present decade. Much of his work during this period involved reformulating Marx's method of ideology critique and recasting the philosophical foundations of his theory of historical materialism.[22] Because he failed to anticipate governmental regulation of the economy, Marx discounted the tenacious hold of authoritarian patterns of thought on individuals in bourgeois society. But the authoritarian personality was later recognized by members of the Frankfurt school, following their discovery of Freud, to have its roots in basic psychological drives. Moreover, their recognition of the inability of the nuclear family to provide strong parent-child role identification, the intransigence of ideology conceived as a mass cultural phenomenon embracing the linguistic base of social consciousness as such, and the transference of legitimation functions from the economic sector to the political sphere in post-liberal capitalism led them to eschew the critique of political economy in favor of *Kulturkritik*.

Habermas followed first-generation critical theorists such as

Adorno, Marcuse, and Horkheimer in removing the locus of ideology critique from the economy to language and culture. But in so doing, he, perhaps more deliberately than they, sought to recover the seminal inspiration of critical theory in Hegel's philosophy. The early Marx had also returned to Hegel, but in a rather different way. For him, Hegel's account of the master-slave dialectic in *The Phenomenology of Spirit* brings into relief the moment of self-objectification in which the slave achieves self-confirmation in an external form. Here, Marx believed, was the true basis of practical reason, for every act of self-objectification is simultaneously a reflection on the self objectified, so that the latter is changed along with the object. But every satisfaction of a need generates a new need. Seen in this light, labor overcomes nature's resistance to human fulfillment while making satisfaction of the needs of others a necessary condition for the satisfaction of one's own needs. The entire motivation for Marx's materialism is summed up in the transference of rational Bildung from the ethereal plane of abstract philosophical contemplation—as in Hegel's mature political philosophy—to that of concrete practice.

Habermas takes exception to this assimilation of Bildung to labor, claiming that it led to Marx's equation of rationalization with scientific and technological progress. To defend the integrity of critical theory, he turns to Hegel's early Jena philosophy of mind,[23] in which *Geist* (spirit or social life) is seen as the intersection of family, language, and labor. Whereas language is the primary vehicle of social integration, communication being the medium in which individuals come to share a common moral identity based on reciprocal expectations, labor, the medium of need gratification (desire), enables one to achieve a sense of security with respect to nature.[24] Hegel further addresses the relationship between language and identity in his description of the criminal whose abrogation of an ethical totality leads to the suppression of the moral bond linking criminal and victim and to a later overwhelming compulsion to atone. In Habermas's opinion, the alienation of the criminal from society exemplifies the peculiar "causality of fate" that occurs when the reciprocity between social classes is violated. The ideological suppression of open communication invariably produces identity crises, anomic social relationships, and political strife. Hence the Bildung of humanity is a dual struggle for emancipation: from the material constraints imposed by economic scarcity and the communicative constraints imposed by domination.[25]

PHILOSOPHICAL HERMENEUTICS AND CRITICAL THEORY

Gadamer's philosophical hermeneutics is indebted principally to Heidegger's notion that understanding—here conceived as the disclosure of meaningful experience, the aperture onto the world through which we have any world worth speaking of—is an integral aspect of human existence (*Dasein*). Heidegger likens it to projecting a net of familiar meanings in light of expectations. Reading is a case in point: the meaning of each word unfolds in anticipated completion of the sentence, just as the meaning of each sentence unfolds in anticipated completion of the text. The interdependence of part and whole is analogous to the contextuality of practical and perceptual experience. Perceptual phenomena are not disclosed initially as "things" possessing substantive properties such as weight and extension, but as pragmata capable of facilitating or obstructing action. They are thus identified with respect to a meaningful totality of assignments and functions that refers ultimately to the intentions, aims, and interests of the agent. Thus the throwing into relief of a particular idea or interest against a horizon of possible meaningfulness (world) is always relative to practical expectations that are themselves shaped by the cultural presuppositions determining identity.[26]

The subject and object of understanding are thus related to one another in a kind of ontological circle. What first seems meaningless or unfamiliar calls forth a special effort of reflection, thereby provoking a revision of expectations. What was at first merely implicit—the preunderstanding of the interpreter and the alien grammar of the subject matter—is made explicit; thus the identity of each term in the relationship is changed. It is as if the subject matter becomes part of the interpreter and vice versa, or, better, as if subject and object are subordinate aspects of a single continuum of meaning (being).[27] Understanding is thus characterized by a kind of historical continuity, or historicity (*Geschichtlichkeit*), by means of which the cultural heritage that forms part of the interpreter's identity is continually being reinterpreted.[28]

Gadamer's *Truth and Method* (1960), whose controversial critique of scientific method became something of a cause célèbre among both radical and conservative German intellectuals opposed to positivism, developed Heidegger's theory of understanding in a way that proved to be particularly seminal for Habermas's critical program in *Erkenntnis*. Gadamer's primary aim was to discredit the empathetic model of understanding deriving from the romantic tradition of Schleiermacher, Ranke, and Dilthey. Although this tradition started out as a reaction against the Enlightenment, it discarded neither the subject-object dualism nor the methodological glorification of value-freedom that were its Cartesian trademarks. Although some of its later exponents, including Weber and Emilio Betti, acknowledged the irrefutable link between values and understanding (*Wertbeziehung*), they still held that understanding was a kind of psychological reliving (*Nacherleben*) of thought processes. Therefore, understanding culminating in the correct "correspondence" between subject and object of interpretation required putting in abeyance one's own cultural presuppositions and immersing oneself in the alien *Weltanschauung* of the subject matter.[29]

Gadamer submits that the subject-object dichotomy embraced by romantic hermeneutics is controverted by the ontological continuity of historical life. Psychological empathy (*Einfühlen*) and reenactment (*Nacherleben*) are confused with true understanding, which involves deciphering the meaning of a nondatable, publicly communicable message. Once the message is understood, it acts as a bridge linking interpreter and text. Far from effacing the interpreter's assumptions and interests, the attempt to reach an understanding (*Verständigung*) brings them into play, generating in the process a critical interplay of questions and answers. Because it is assumed that a text's message is potentially true and coherent, understanding issues is a practical dialectic or mutual critique, whose "truth" is at once the fusion and expansion of distinct horizons (*Horizontverschmelzung*).[30]

By demonstrating that all forms of knowledge and experience are interpretative in the deepest sense, Gadamer's philosophical hermeneutics undercuts the shibboleth of value-neutrality and presuppositionlessness that lies at the center of positivism. Science does not mirror reality; it interprets it as a measurable spatiotemporal field of matter and energy in accordance with its own methodological assumptions. Habermas is in agreement here; he also sees Gadamer's critique of romantic hermeneutics as explaining why deep ethical currents run through the human sciences. Every successful understanding applies new meaning to the current situation of the interpreter, thereby revealing new possibilities for action.[31]

Although in his work prior to the mid-sixties Habermas stressed the dependence of critical reflection on historically situated understanding, he returned eventually to a more orthodox, transcendental approach to philosophizing, of the sort practiced by neo-Kantians such as Rickert, Windelband, and Dilthey. In this reorientation, first articulated by Habermas in his 1965 inaugural address, we detect a concern with system building and critical methodology. This break with philosophical hermeneutics chiefly hinged on dissatisfaction with its deference to tradition. Philosophical hermeneutics assumes that the possibilities of understanding self and society are circumscribed by prevailing tradition, and that although we can question any given cultural belief, such questioning will necessarily be relative to some more fundamental, unquestioned assumption. Hence any

9

criticism of an entire tradition is precluded. Because of the obvious implication of this posture for ideology critique, Habermas came to reject the ontological identification of tradition and understanding just as strenuously as he had earlier repudiated the positivistic equation of science and knowledge.[32] However, if neither the human sciences, whose primary aim is the preservation of tradition for its own sake, nor the exact sciences, whose principal aim is the technical domination of objective nature, provide adequate models for critical social science, then what science or methodology does?

Max Horkheimer addressed this problem in his 1937 manifesto "Traditional and Critical Theory." He saw modern science as a continuation of traditional metaphysics, rather than its negation, for both science and metaphysics construe objective reality as an eternal "given" that comes to be known through disinterested contemplation or value-neutral measurement. Traditional metaphysics, with its system of beliefs mirroring eternal laws, is "uncritical" in two senses in Horkheimer's judgment: not only does it uncritically accept the status quo, but it fails to examine the validity of its own presuppositions. As for science, its presuppositions are linked to the "advance of the bourgeois period," with its demand for technically exploitable knowledge.[33] The emergence of capitalism is not the ultimate raison d'être of the exact sciences, to be sure; nevertheless, it provides the societal framework necessary for the methodological articulation of what is otherwise an anthropologically entrenched interest in domination. But insofar as that domination is extended over social relations, there arises a counter interest in emancipation, whose corollary is the method of reflection peculiar to critical social science. The latter delimits the validity and scope of particular branches of knowledge while freeing the social agent from the ideological integuments of tradition.[34]

The main difficulty facing Horkheimer and other members of the Frankfurt school was that of establishing a legitimating warrant for critical reflection that would be as securely grounded in social life as that for technical knowledge. This has also been a central preoccupation of Habermas, whose efforts have been largely designed to rectify the failures of his predecessors. Habermas maintains that past attempts ran aground largely because they were based on the assumption of a culturally immanent critique of ideology and therefore, like philosophical hermeneutics, could not avoid the pitfalls of historical relativism. Horkheimer's claim that the emancipatory aim can be variously recognized as a "force in history," "an expression of cultural creations," or "goals of human activity . . . immanent in human work" are, in Habermas's opinion, hopelessly vague and rely entirely upon the validity of contingent historical interpretations and expressions.[35]

KNOWLEDGE AND HUMAN INTERESTS

In his inaugural address Habermas paid tribute to Horkheimer's hypothesis regarding cognitive interests by suggesting that critical theory need not derive its standards from fortuitous traditions but could establish a transcendental warrant for its endeavors that would be universally valid. Three years later he published his first systematic treatise on the subject. *Erkenntnis* is an ambitious attempt to renew the critique of knowledge first undertaken by Kant and subsequently radicalized by Hegel and Marx. In his *Critique of Pure Reason* (1781) Kant sought to uncover the necessary conditions for the possibility of experiencing objects. Its critical function lay in confining the valid epistemic deployment of reason to the sensory fields of space and time, its positive intent in refuting Hume's skeptical animadversions concerning causality, substance, and other principles underlying Newtonian mechanics, through a transcendental proof of their objective validity. Habermas's project radicalizes Kant's critique in the direction of Marx's social theory by taking up anew Hegel's phenomenological metacritique of transcendental epistemology. Hegel appeals to the dialectical element implicit in Kant's transcendentalism—that the only meaningful objective reality is that constituted by the knowing subject—in order to refute the idea of a nature existing independently of consciousness. By the same token, he rejects the notion of transcendental subjectivity, because it ignores the conditioning of consciousness by society and history. Because individual consciousness is determined by society and culture, knowledge (of what is) and judgment (of what ought to be) are mutually interdependent.

Hegel's metacritique runs aground, however, in its Schellingian postulation of an absolute identity of subject and object. Not only does his concept of absolute knowledge contradict his own account of the open dialectic of experience, but his ontological assimilation of experience to conceptual thought excludes material aspects of social being that condition thought from without.[36] Marx's appeal to labor as an invariant anthropological structure marks a return to Kant's transcendental philosophy and its postulation of an irreducible element of external contingency (nature-in-itself). By stressing that life is conditioned by its own objectifications, Marx initiates the final transition from idealistic metacritique to materialistic ideology critique. Because it must now incorporate reflection on the social evolution of the human species, epistemology must aspire to the rank of critical social theory.

11

Although Habermas accepts Marx's critique of German idealism, his own use of the category of cognitive interest to tie together action, knowledge, reason, and emancipation is wholly indebted to Kant's notion of a practical interest in reason. Pursuing the penetrating line of inquiry pioneered by Charles Peirce, Habermas argues that scientific method, understood as a procedure for attaining a progressive consensus about reality, ultimately derives its validity from the natural trial-and-error revision of beliefs that accompanies the success or failure of adaptive behavior.[37] When the need for technological enhancement of economic productivity arose during the Renaissance, this feedback circuit was gradually institutionalized in the form of modern experimental science. For Peirce, both the validity and the meaning of scientific knowledge are ultimately traceable to behavior necessary for survival.[38]

Habermas maintains that once the instrumental activity necessary for survival is institutionalized under the aegis of science, it becomes a social learning process mediated by a different kind of activity, communication. He regards ordinary communication as an epistemological action-interest framework that founds the hermeneutic methodology of the human sciences. Drawing on Dilthey's post-psychological writings and their hermeneutic appropriation of the Hegelian category of life, Habermas notes that the part-whole circle intrinsic to narrative understanding has its basis in one's personal experience. The stability, coherence, and identity of this autobiography is sustained by acquiring general, intersubjectively recognized categories of meaning that connect one to the community. Underwriting the social sciences is the aim of maintaining a historical continuity of meaning and identity, first and foremost at the level of communal life and second, by implication, at the level of individual biographical life. The survival of a society as a distinct entity possessing its own identity not only depends on securing harmonious interaction among its members based on universally accepted norms, but also requires sustaining a sense of moral purpose over generations, a function for which history and philology are particularly well suited.[39]

Operational behavior and communicative action comprise two distinct aspects of social life, corresponding roughly to labor (the instrumental satisfaction of material needs) and language (the establishment through communication of a shared sense of meaning and value). It is because labor and communication make distinct contributions to social life (facts and values) that political and economic domination, the third determinant of social life, can ideologically disturb the formation of culture and tradition below the threshold of linguistic understanding—hence the need for critical theory. The interest governing such theory is explicitly emancipatory in that it aims to strip the social agent of deeply engrained patterns of thought that constrain self-understanding.

Unlike the technological interest in controlling nature and the practical interest in sustaining social harmony, the emancipatory interest is not coeval with society; nor does it constitute reality from a particular transcendental perspective. With the advent of modern class society, however, it has increasingly become a survival interest. As Habermas puts it, the interest in emancipation develops "to the degree to which repressive force, in the form of the normative exercise of power, presents itself permanently in structures of distorted communication."[40] Because technological and moral progress requires unconstrained discourse, there is a sense in which all knowledge is related to an emancipatory interest. Habermas's understanding of this relationship is chiefly indebted to Fichte, for whom a practical decision to free oneself from all unquestioned presuppositions was a necessary condition for achieving insight into the universal conditions of knowledge. Although Habermas criticizes Fichte for his neglect of political struggle, he nonetheless accepts his principal thesis that in emancipatory reflection, our practical interest in becoming free, universal moral agents coincides with our theoretical interest in gaining knowledge about the natural and social conditions that shape us.[41]

Habermas recommends psychoanalysis as a methodological paradigm for critical reflection, first, because the aetiological profile of neurosis is similar to that of ideological delusion, and second, because the combination of causal explanation and *sinnverstehen* succeeds in steering a middle course between the objectivism of the behavioral sciences and the subjectivism of a purely hermeneutic approach.[42] On this model, ideological delusion stems from a censoring process in which the need defended against is denied expression in language, action, and culture; but repressed needs continue to influence behavior subconsciously, compelling the neurotic to act compulsively. Similarly, in a society in which individuals no longer feel satisfied with the rewards attendant on fulfilling ideological expectations, all the symptoms of social disintegration (identity crisis) —apathy, alienation, anomie—manifest themselves. In this case sublimation is accompanied by displacement of need gratification to substitutes such as religion, art, entertainment, and economic consumption. Although Habermas agrees with Freud that every society that has existed hitherto has needed to rechannel libidinal drives away from reproduction in order to satisfy the exigencies of work and consumption, he also believes that the degree of sublimation that is socially necessary in a given society is inversely proportional to its level of material affluence.[43]

Psychotherapy also appears to strike a good methodological balance between the distancing and participatory approaches of the behavioral and hermeneutic sciences. Although Freud tried to explicate the assumptions inherent in psychoanalysis in terms of a physicalistic tension-reduction paradigm, he later came to realize that classical philology offered a more perspicacious comparison, since it too involved the hermeneutic restoration of a mutilated text.[44] Psychoanalysis aims at restoring the full text of a patient's life by reincorporating repressed contents into the stream of consciousness. Following Alfred Lorenzer, Habermas characterizes this process as a reinsertion of paleo-symbolic contents into public language. In contrast to philological interpretation, which relies on the etymological connection between living and dead language to fill in textual gaps whose meaning has been obscured due to the passage of time, psychoanalysis is called on to dispel misunderstandings whose origin has nothing to do with changes in meaning brought about by the evolution of language, but stems instead from the repression of meaning caused by extralinguistic conflicts. To understand the meaning of a neurotic episode, one must *explain* its *cause*, which has its origin in some event in childhood involving a subconscious conflict between the id (the unconscious agency of desire) and the superego (the introjection of parental authority).[45]

The theoretical basis of psychoanalytic depth interpretation consists of general interpretations of psychodynamic development that specify lawlike phases (oral, anal, phallic, and genital) of object identification, conflict, and conflict mastery. Like theories in the natural sciences, general interpretations permit the deduction of invariant causal relationships between specific types of conflict and specific pathological modes of conflict resolution. Unlike theories in the natural sciences, however, the lawlike succession of developmental stages retains a hermeneutic and teleological dimension, for the ego is like an actor in a drama, struggling to achieve full moral identity, autonomy, and self-understanding. The reflective integration of concealed motives breaks the pathological link between the repressed motive and a particular behavior. Finally, unlike scientific predictions, general interpretations cannot be demonstrably falsified, since the normal behavior that they predict upon completion of treatment depends entirely on whether the patient successfully completes the process of reflection provoked by the analysis.[46]

14

KNOWLEDGE AND HUMAN INTERESTS RECONSIDERED

Although *Erkenntnis* continues to stimulate discussion among scholars, Habermas has largely abandoned the attempt to ground critical social theory in cognitive interests. His reasons, some of which are mentioned in his "Postscript to *Knowledge and Human Interests*" (1973) and in the introduction to the second edition of *Theorie and Praxis* (1971) do not relate to the soundness of the program, but only its execution. First, there are obvious difficulties in trying to explain the peculiar status of a cognitive interest, which "is not meant to suggest a naturalistic reduction of transcendental logical categories to empirical ones."[47] It is not an interest that is productive of individual happiness, yet, despite the fact that such interests are implicated in the survival of the species, they do not possess the invariant *habitus* of biological instincts or drives. "Cognitive interests," Habermas insists, "mediate the natural genesis of mankind with the logic of its cultural development."[48] However, the precise sense in which "human interests . . . derive both from nature and from the cultural break with nature" remains obscure. Occasionally Habermas suggests that these interests are inextricably tied to a cultural notion of self-preservation commensurate with the emergence of the emancipatory interest in achieving the good life. But if so, the theory of cognitive interests moves perilously close to historicism and its reduction of the transcendental to the empirical. Moreover, as McCarthy remarks, it is faced with the same conundrums that have plagued German idealism from Kant onward. For, if the interest in technological control constitutes our experience of nature under the auspices of mechanistic science, how can it also be understood as having evolved empirically as part of humanity's natural history? Habermas's appeal to nature-in-itself (*natura naturans*) as a quasi-teleological ground of cultural evolution appears to be wholly speculative and indefensible in view of the nonteleological conditions under which nature, understood as a domain of objects (*natura naturata*), appears to us.[49]

A more serious problem is Habermas's conflation of philosophical and emancipatory reflection. As K.-O. Apel and Dietrich Böhler have pointed out, it is no more possible to identify an interest in impartial philosophical analysis with a commitment to engage in risky political struggle than to equate transcendental reflection on the necessary and universal conditions of knowledge with the sort of emancipatory reflection apposite to psychoanalysis and ideology critique.[50] In the years since the publication of *Erkenntnis*, Habermas has conceded that his attempt to ground critical social theory in epistemic interests was flawed by his ambiguous usage of the word *reflection*. Philosophical reflection, or rational reconstruction, is a pure form of theoretical knowledge that is motivated by neither technical, communicative, nor emancipatory interests but is "generated within a reflexive attitude."[51] As such it abstracts from particular historical contexts and has no immediate practical consequences.

This distinction between rational reconstruction and emancipatory reflection coincides with a revision in Habermas's conception of the relationship between theory and practice. In redefining this relationship, he expanded his original conception of knowledge to include a new taxonomy consisting of two distinctions: between truth and intersubjectively accepted belief and between discourse and action. The former is necessary because universal cognitive interests alone are not sufficient grounds for establishing the possibility of true, rationally justifiable belief (knowledge in the strong sense), however entrenched they may be in forms of action that "constitute" intersubjectively accepted or objectively valid belief. The intersubjective acceptance of belief means only "that everybody can count on the success or failure of certain actions. The truth of a proposition . . . means that everybody can be persuaded by reasons to recognize the truth-claim of a statement as being justified."[52] Such a distinction, Habermas insists, is a necessary postulate of the sciences. Just as critical theory must distinguish between ideologically induced consensus and authentic solidarity, so too the natural scientific distinction between objective experience and scientific knowledge helps to explain why the commonsense view of reality as a spatiotemporal continuum of sensory things, though scientifically false, possesses a practical validity that is rooted in patterns of operational behavior common to all historical cultures.[53]

The distinction between truth and objective validity corresponds to that between discourse and action. Discourse is a form of pure communication that, in a manner reminiscent of Husserl's phenomenological *epoché*, hypothetically brackets the validity of all existential and normative assumptions for purposes of rational examination. Purged of the external and internal constraints associated with everyday action, it seeks true statements and right prescriptions and is motivated solely by the force of the better argument. By contrast, action is guided by conventional attitudes that are intersubjectively compelling in a dogmatic sense. Thus discourse is bound by counterfactual reasons, action by factual constraints.

Using these distinctions, Habermas reinstated the categorical separation of theory and practice by relegating philosophical reflection to the realm of discourse, emancipatory reflection to the therapeutic dialogue between party intelligentsia and rank-and-file membership. Although such dialogue is dependent on the particular historical context, it cannot provide guidance for prospective political action. Thus questions of political strategy remain theoretically undecidable. The willingness of a political constituency to act on the interpretations offered by party intelligentsia furnishes indirect confirmation of critical social theory, though failure to do so, given the potential risks of political praxis, does not falsify it.[54]

In retrospect, the difficulties encountered by Habermas in his effort to ground critical theory in cognitive interests led to two major revisions in his thinking. First, the distinction between rational reconstruction and emancipatory reflection corresponded to a new conception of the relationship between history and theory. The "natural history of the human species" presupposed by *Erkenntnis* was not only epistemologically question-begging, but appeared to bind the validity of critical theory to contingent historical reflection. Since the early seventies, Habermas has attempted to avoid historical relativism by reconstructing the social evolution of human beings on the basis of genetic structuralist studies of the sort undertaken by Piaget and Kohlberg. This approach ostensibly avoids the reduction of developmental structures to actual historical processes.

Second, the epistemological grounding of critical theory, though not strictly transcendental in a Kantian sense, was still burdened by transcendental paradoxes associated with the old philosophy of consciousness (*Bewusstseinsphilosophie*). To avoid these problems, it seemed advisable to locate the validating basis of critical theory in something other than knowledge, nature, or history. Habermas had already announced a way out of the impasse in the inaugural address:

> The standards of self-reflection . . . possess a theoretical certainty. The human interest in autonomy and responsibility is not a mere fancy, for it can be apprehended *a priori*. What raises us out of nature is the only thing whose nature we can know—*language*. Through its structure, autonomy and responsibility are posited for us. Our first sentence expresses unequivocally the intention of a universal and unconstrained consensus . . . only in an emancipated society whose members' autonomy and responsibility had been realized, would communication have developed into the non-authoritarian and universally practical dialogue from which both our model of reciprocally constituted ego-identity and our idea of true consensus are always implicitly derived. To this extent the truth of statements is based upon anticipating the realisation of the good life.[55]

The idea that critical theory finds its justification in communication has been the chief inspiration for Habermas's research since the late sixties. What remained on the agenda was the philosophical reconstruction that would support this contention. If there is a serious question about the tenability of this project, it is whether it reintroduces the kind of gap between theory and practice that Habermas has always sought to avoid. Little in this program bears witness to the classical conception of the *summum bonum*. Not only is there no attempt to relate societal happiness to rational discourse, but there is a lingering suspicion that this program is not as critical as it first appears. If rational reconstruction is essentially detached from the immediate concerns of social life, then does it not represent a return to traditional theorizing? The vindication of critical theory from this charge and the reaffirmation of its practical intent is the paramount aim of *Theorie*. It remains to be seen, however, whether Habermas's monumental effort to elucidate the relationship between reason and historical understanding, structure and process, system and lifeworld, succeeds and, if so, at what price.

CHAPTER TWO

Rationality, Reality,
and Action

In the foreword and introduction to *Theorie*, Habermas reminds us of the provisional nature of his undertaking. Although it shares the traditional philosophical aim of subsuming the various realms of thought under a single umbrella, it follows modern philosophy in forsaking absolute knowledge of the whole. It thus eschews the ontological agenda of traditional metaphysics and of contemporary proponents of identity theory, while remaining ever mindful of the subjectivist impasse of Kant's critical philosophy. It continues the line of research pioneered by Habermas in his earlier studies of communication, whose common aim was the defense of practical reason against positivistic abridgement.[1] But, most important, it reformulates the problem of rationality at three levels of analysis. The metatheoretical level situates the relationship between action and reason within a developmental account of rational learning capacities. This proves to be indispensable at the methodological level, where the understanding of meaningful social action is shown to presuppose rational critique. Third, the theory of rationality establishes at the empirical level a critical basis for identifying progressive and regressive features of modern society.[2]

RATIONAL ACTION

Theorie begins with a provisional conceptual analysis of rationality and its relationship to action and language, premised on the idea that rational action is inextricably linked to argumentation. Since Plato, philosophers have held that the distinction between correct opinion and true knowledge hinges on the role of reasoned justification in permitting us to hold a belief with confidence. Appealing to our implicit understanding of rational action as behavior that is guided by knowledge, Habermas argues that the function of practical reason is to provide arguments supporting the beliefs underwriting decisions to act. This inference is not as straightforward as it might at first seem, for much of the knowledge guiding our actions consists in aptitudes, skills, and competencies—in other words, tacit know-how—that we would have difficulty describing and explaining, let alone justifying. But for Habermas, a considerable portion of habitual knowledge must be susceptible to such explicit, propositional formulation if the action in question is to be seen as rational. A rational action, then, is one about which an agent could entertain rationally justifiable beliefs. Habermas's paradigm case involves a person who undertakes some goal-oriented action; such action may be highly adaptive, but unless it can be justified in terms of beliefs about means and ends founded on verifiable causal regularities, it cannot be considered rational.[3]

Habermas thus reminds us that reasoning proper unfolds within the fundamentally different frame of reference of communication. Whereas persons acting alone are rational to the extent that they efficiently satisfy their private needs, social agents, who are accountable to others, are rational only to the extent that they resolve potential conflicts through argumentation. But willingness to be persuaded by reason implies, among other things, that agreement is constrained solely by the force of the better argument.[4] In avoiding the pragmatist confusion of rationality with instrumental adaptation, Habermas reaffirms the phenomenological insight that the environment to which we adapt is already a linguistically articulated world of shared—and to that extent, public and objective—experience.[5]

Of course, some of the beliefs underlying the rationality of our actions are nonfactual. In order to be fully rational, an action must be morally and legally right; it must sincerely express the authentic feelings and desires of the agent and be oriented toward the shared values of the given community. Thus rational action is guided not only by factual beliefs whose claims (*Geltungsansprüche*) to truth can be argued, but also by normative, expressive, and evaluative beliefs with their claims to rightness (*Richtigkeit*), sincerity (*Wahrhaftigkeit*), authenticity (*Authentizität*), and appropriateness (*Angemessenheit*).[6]

It is important to note that the conditions of argumentative discourse vary according to the type of validity being claimed. With regard to a factual belief, we expect arguments to be forthcoming that would convince anyone of its truth. But Habermas insists that such an expectation of universal assent obtains mutatis mutandis in the case of claims to moral, or normative, rightness as well. It would be irrational for me to believe that I ought to perform some act while not believing, ceteris paribus, that anyone else in a similar situation ought to perform it also. I would be applying a general rule inconsistently if, while holding that there were no morally relevant differences between my situation and that of another, I bound myself to a moral precept that I did not recognize as binding for that other person. Here Habermas follows Kant in holding that the deontological force of moral obligation prohibits exceptions, that we are always required to set aside our selfish interests when they conflict with the universal interest.[7]

It is noteworthy in light of Habermas's ultimate goal of providing a unitary model of rationality that his two major exceptions to the model of theoretical and practical discourse—therapeutic and aesthetic critique—deviate in important respects from the pragmatic logic of argumentation. In the first, consistency of behavior, rather than argumentation, is the decisive factor in rationally determining the sincerity of a person's intentions; moreover, canons of discourse are just as inapplicable when the person in question is suffering from self-deception. Therapeutic dialogue—psychotherapy in the case of individual neurosis and ideology critique in the case of mass delusion—may appeal to argumentation, but the latter is necessarily circumscribed by the clinical setting, which is fundamentally incompatible with the reciprocity conditions required for an unconstrained, impartial effort to reach agreement.[8] The second, aesthetic critique, although in other respects abiding by the canons of discursive impartiality, departs from the expectations of strict universalizability implicit in theoretical and practical discourse.

It is only since 1976 that Habermas has ascribed to art a unique claim to appropriateness, and his decision to do so is somewhat obscured by his tendency to identify art with claims to success, authenticity, and harmony (*Stimmigkeit*) as well. Aesthetic disputes resist adjudication vis-à-vis objective principles (either cognitive or moral); yet, unlike expressions of a purely personal, sensual gratification, judgments of taste claim an "exemplary necessity and universality." For Kant, this means that aesthetic judgments are instances of a rule grounded in a transcendental *sensus communis*, or prediscursive a priori agreement; for Habermas, that they are instances of discursive interpretations of the good life—and therewith the needs appropriate to that life in its authenticity and integrity (*Stimmigkeit*)—with respect to specific cultural values indigenous to given historical communities.[9] The irreducibility of aesthetic rationality to the formal pragmatic conditions of argumentative discourse is further reinforced by Habermas's most recent pronouncements regarding the mediating function of art, which "reaches into our cognitive interpretations and norma-

21

tive expectations and transforms the *totality* in which these moments are related to one another."[10] This "cognitive" function of art plays a key role in Habermas's new critical program, as we shall see later.

Habermas devotes considerable attention to the presuppositions underlying theoretical and practical discourse, since these provide the most important rationale for social critique. His analysis of argumentative discourse is greatly indebted to Stephen Toulmin's attempt to capture "the force of the better argument" in terms of general structures of consensually oriented dialogue.[11] Some of these structures involve familiar elements of argumentation: the conclusion to be grounded, the grounds cited in support of the conclusion, the warrant connecting the grounds to the conclusion, and the backing for the warrant itself. This model permits a radicalization of reflection that renders disputes over competing theoretical paradigms resolvable by appeal to practical reason, whereas political disagreements over common interests lead in extreme cases to a therapeutic critique of needs.[12]

Habermas follows Aristotle's triadic division of argumentation into logic, rhetoric, and dialectic. The most important structures defining theoretical and practical discourse are those extralogical conditions that capture the counterfactual notion of validity, or rational persuasion, since it is precisely these that possess an explicit ethical content. As products of logic, arguments must exhibit both internal and external consistency among interlocutors over the meanings of terms. As a rhetorical process, however, argumentation is governed by formal conditions of procedural justice—what Habermas calls "the ideal speech situation"—by which the rationally motivated attempt to reach agreement is protected from internal and external repression, and everyone has an equal chance to proffer reasons and rebuttals. As a dialectical procedure, argumentation is characterized by a "special form of interaction" in which validity claims can be hypothetically criticized independently of everyday pressures to succeed, so that interlocutors can recognize one another as sincere and rationally accountable.[13]

THE MYTHIC VERSUS THE MODERN VIEW OF REALITY

The preliminary analysis of rationality purports to show that the rationality of an action is a function of the extent to which it can be justified. Actions either implicitly or explicitly raise validity claims to truth, moral rightness, appropriateness, sincerity, and comprehensibility. These claims refer to criticizable beliefs that, however tacit, are capable of being articulated in language. Linguistic utterances explicitly refer to items of experience—facts, norms, intentions, and so forth—that constitute the world in which action takes place. Without agreement about this world, social action would be impossible. Descriptions assert the truth of relations between datable, localizable things in an *objective* world. Prescriptions assert the rightness of obligations and norms that make up a *social* world. Expressive utterances assert the sincerity of intentions, desires, and feelings—the dispositions of the speaker's *subjective* world. And evaluations assert the social appropriateness of the speaker's *subjective* value preferences. In critically evaluating the rationality of descriptive, prescriptive, expressive, and evaluative utterances, one must have recourse to items of reference in three different worlds.[14]

The relation between referentiality and rationality is decisive for Habermas's comparison of modern and mythic ways of understanding. He is especially concerned to show that the modern, decentered understanding of the world uniquely merits the title of rationality, because it makes possible the most extensive and progressive form of learning. This concern is provoked by cultural relativists who argue that occidental rationality merely reflects the peculiar standpoint of scientific culture and is therefore neither preferable to, nor more valid than other forms of understanding. Habermas intends to refute this view by showing that the relativist cannot criticize rationalism without presupposing its superiority.

He concurs with anthropologist Evans-Pritchard that the difference between mythic and modern thought is not one of formal logical aptitude. The Azande, Evans-Pritchard notes, are just as capable of drawing inferences and recognizing inconsistencies in reasoning as Westerners. If there is a difference, it resides in the fundamental conceptual grid in terms of which the two interpret the world.[15] Relying on the structuralist studies of "primitive" cultures undertaken by Levi-Strauss and Godelier, Habermas characterizes the mythic world as a seamless totality in which any one item of experience is metaphorically or metonymically associated with every other item through the binary relations of sameness and difference. In the words of Godelier, myth "constructs a giant maze of mirrors in which the opposing images of man and world are infinitely reflected in each other and the relations of nature and culture are continuously separated and united as in a prism." This associative nature of mythic understanding is diametrically opposed to the analytic sundering of objective, subjective, and social domains of reference fundamental to modern rationality.[16]

The "confusion," as Habermas puts it, between objective and subjective reality is reflected in the mythic conceptualization of nature as spirit (animism). Natural relations are not subsumed under the category of causality but are conceived as personal relations among unpredictable wills. The inner realm of subjective imagination is projected outward; dreams, for example, are regarded as possessing veridical, prognostic import. Conversely, because subjective and social realities are "naturalized" in such a way as to conceal their human origin, values and codes of conduct remain all but impervious to critical revision. Since personal identity is no more differentiated from society than society is from nature, behavior, too, is rigidly bound to stereotypical patterns whose origin is regarded as being located in the immutable order of the cosmos.[17]

The concretizing aspect of mythic thought—that is, its inability to abstract or distinguish general attributes of things from the things themselves—is symptomatic of its associative modus operandi. The confusion of objective and social nature explains, for example, the curious hybrid nature of ritual magic, which combines an instrumental understanding of cause and effect (teleological action) with incantations, invocations, and supplications of the sort found in interpersonal communication. The fusion of semantic and causal relations is evident in even the simplest acts of denotation and explanation: names, for example, are said to possess the powers of the things to which they refer. The ethical and practical implications of concretization are particularly striking. Since intentions and motives are not sharply distinguished from the consequences of actions, instrumental failures are occasions for assessing moral blame. Validity and efficiency remain undifferentiated. In the final analysis, the binary categories of mythic thought must be seen as stemming from the reciprocity structures of kin systems and relations of exchange, from the ambivalence of active agency and passive nature, and above all, from the need to explain away the powerlessness of the individual in the face of a capricious world.[18]

As recounted above, the mythopoeic understanding of reality seems deficient and irrational in comparison to our own. Habermas argues that the confusion of domains of reference and the lack of reflexivity inherent in mythopoeic understanding have also been observed in infants and juveniles in so-called advanced Western societies. Although he is cognizant of the concerns voiced by Steven Lukes, Peter Winch, and others who defend the historicist position regarding the dangers of ethnocentrism, he argues that ethnocentrism can be combated only by assuming the superiority of the modern standpoint.

Lukes observes that to understand the meaning of behavior requires that one refrain from prejudging it in light of one's own standards of rationality. But this principle of charity commits one to accepting the standards of natives as no less valid than one's own. Habermas does not dispute the methodological importance of the charity principle; since the meaning of an action is logically related to the reasons for undertaking it, its explication will necessarily appeal to standards of normalcy (rationality) indigenous to that culture. Furthermore, he recognizes that mythic knowledge and standards of conduct may be more functional than their modern counterparts in preserving cultures with relatively simple needs. But these considerations in no way rule out the possibility of ranking forms of understanding logically.[19]

The problem confronting the non-historicist is that of coming up with an inventory of criteria that would be ideally valid for all cultures—a futile undertaking according to Winch, whose social theory is inspired chiefly by the linguistic philosophy of the late Wittgenstein, according to whom the limits of one's language determine the limits of one's world. "Language games" delimit acceptable conduct while cognitively filtering possibilities for understanding reality. Insofar as they present differing but similarly valid perspectives of a single reality, they are less like true or false propositions and more like right or left profiles of portraits. Armed with this conception of language, Winch attacks Evans-Pritchard's claim that the modern view of the world is more rational than the mythic view of the Azande.[20]

Habermas objects to Winch's analogy between portraits and linguistic world views on the grounds that the cognitive worth of a world view is properly conceived as a function of the number of true assertions that it is capable of generating, rather than its picturing capacity. As Evans-Pritchard notes, the witchcraft of the Azande issues in contradictory oracles that seldom materialize, thereby indicating inadequate criteria for truth claims. When pressed, the Azande themselves admit to finding their oracles dubious, yet such absurdities abound in their world view.[21] Even if it is inappropriate to construe the Azande world view as a quasi-scientific theory that seeks to put forward testable predictions, one can still criticize it, *pace* Robin Horton, because, by refusing to countenance alternative modes of explanation, it precludes any critical self-evaluation whatsoever and thus prevents any progressive acquisition of knowledge.[22]

Winch has responded to these objections by noting that the worth of a world view cannot be measured solely in terms of its capacity to promote instrumental knowledge. It depends also on the extent to which it makes sense of the truly universal, existential experiences of birth, death, sickness, guilt, love, solidarity, and loneliness. A mythic world view possessing an abundance of religious and aesthetic meaning may offer more to its adherents than the disenchanted world view of modernity offers us. To hold the Azande to the standards of logical consistency characteristic of modern thinking is to misclassify their beliefs as explanatory theories and to misrepresent the people as pressing their ways of thinking about witches to a point at which they would be involved in contradictions.[23]

Habermas accepts Winch's argument as a valid criticism of the kind of scientistic ethnocentrism that limits rationality to the cognitive-instrumental domain, but he rejects his identification of happiness (aesthetic harmony) with rationality. Horton, by contrast, operates with a communicative conception of rationality that stresses the importance of critical reflection and dialogical openness for learning. Habermas appeals to this model to show that the relativist is implicated in a kind of bad faith when the world view defended as no less rational than the modern one does not permit the openness and reciprocity acknowledged to be necessary for real understanding.[24]

The contrast between closed and open world views provides the key to Habermas's defense of the superior rationality of the modern view. To be sure, the force of his argument is qualified by the fact that one is committed to recognizing certain standards of rationality only if one takes dialogue and argumentation seriously. The tu quoque strategy, in other words, does not show that the discursive attitude is unconditionally valid.[25] To justify the claim of the modern understanding of reality to universal validity, Habermas must show that it is logically superior in learning potential to mythopoeic and religious-metaphysical world views.

But this task requires nothing less than a systematic theory of social evolution. Habermas's theory takes the observed stages of learning and arranges them hierarchically so that higher phases logically presuppose and incorporate lower ones, thereby constituting a cumulative advance in learning potential. It also distinguishes empirical learning mechanisms and contingent boundary conditions from the sequential logic of structures. Whereas the historical teleologies implicit in, for example, Hegel's philosophy of spirit and some orthodox Marxist interpretations of historical materialism construe historical events as the inevitable, irreversible outcome of a prior developmental logic, Habermas's theory of social evolution, like Kant's universal history, binds actual developmental advances and regressions to contingent historical praxis.[26]

The theory accomplishes two things. First, by assuming isomorphism between phylogenesis (social evolution) and ontogenesis (individual maturation) and accepting the empirical claim advanced by

Piaget, Kohlberg, and other structural psychologists that "every child who passes from one (cognitive or sociomoral) stage of thought to the next can be brought by maeutic means to explain why his or her way of judging things is now able to solve given problems better than at the previous stage,"[27] it enables Habermas to justify the privileged rationality of modern thought. Second, it provides structural reference points for social critique that explain why modern societies are unable to solve their economic and administrative problems.[28]

At this juncture, Habermas is less concerned with elaborating the details of his theory than with articulating its general contours, especially those bearing on Piaget's genetic structural account of child maturation. Piaget's theory concentrates on those structures of thought and action by which children gradually learn to adapt to an objective world of things and to a social world of norms, relationships, and people. Cognitive and moral development involve acquiring the capacity to decenter one's understanding of reality away from an egocentric perspective and see things from another person's point of view. This process of decentration, Habermas contends, also underlies social evolution. Although he is cognizant of the imperfect fit between ontogenesis and phylogenesis, he steadfastly insists that there are "abstract reference points" for comparing ego development and world view development.[29] Indeed, the internally related cognitive, linguistic, and moral-practical "structures of consciousness" that comprise world views are nothing more than repositories of individually acquired learning abilities that have become embedded in culture.[30]

Using Piaget's research as a base, Habermas distinguishes four stages of child development. At the symbiotic stage, children are incapable of distinguishing themselves as corporeal subjects from primary reference persons (that is, parents) and the physical environment. At the egocentric stage, they are able to differentiate themselves from the environment but not yet to distinguish between physical and social reality, and they continue to perceive and judge situations solely from their own, body-bound perspective. Once children begin to initiate concrete operations and to distinguish perceptible and manipulable things and events from understandable subjects and actions, they enter the sociocentric stage. By the seventh year they are typically able to distinguish subjective fantasies and impulses from objective perceptions and social obligations. With the onset of adolescence there begins a universalistic stage of development, in which they are able to reflect critically on existing values and assumptions in light of hypothetical alternatives, thereby breaking out of the parochial constraints of tradition.[31]

27

Applying this model to social evolution, Habermas speculates that the transition from mythopoeic to cosmological, religious, metaphysical, and modern forms of understanding likewise exhibits a moral and cognitive decentering. The mythic world view collapses objective and subjective reality into a collective, totemic identity in much the same way that objective and social domains of reference merge in the subjective world of the child. With the transition from archaic to developed civilizations (*Hochkulturen*), a decisive rupture occurs, and narrative accounts are replaced by explanations that can be justified through argument. Monotheistic religions subsume reality under a single, unifying principle, thereby exhibiting a strong impulse toward universalism and logical consistency. Although the Judeo-Christian and Greco-Roman heritages gave rise to legal and theoretical innovations that paralleled the moral and cognitive structures typical of the universalistic stage of development, they retained religious and metaphysical residues redolent of less mature, precritical stages. With the advent of modernity, the highest principles (God, Being, or Nature) surrender their status as first principles to the formal principles of discursive reason.[32]

RATIONALITY, ACTION AND REFERENCE

We have already noted that a person can be said to act rationally only if he or she is guided by justifiable beliefs of a factual, normative, evaluative, or expressive nature. Validity claims refer beliefs to various domains of reality; claims to truth refer to the world of spatiotemporal objects, claims to rightness and justice to the world of social norms, and claims to sincerity and authenticity to the world of a person's own feelings and desires. The connection between validity claims and objective, social, and subjective domains of reference becomes clear once the types of statements that articulate these claims are examined. Thus, part of the very meaning of a descriptive statement—indeed, that part of it which is explicitly intended—depends on a referential relationship between the statement and some spatio-temporal entity.

The relationship between meaning, reference, and intentionality has been of great interest to philosophers since Brentano and has been taken up by Habermas in greater detail in his theory of language. Here it suffices to note that, for Habermas, action—as distinct from mere corporeal movements and operations—is inherently meaningful, because it expresses an agent's intentions vis-à-vis reality. This is important, because some philosophers and social behaviorists have attempted to explain the meaning of action in purely operational terms, with no reference to the intentionality, or meaning-giving activity, of the agent. But, severed from an intentional relationship to objective, social, and subjective reality, action loses whatever cognitive, normative, and expressive content would accrue to it and can no longer be evaluated critically.[33]

Habermas's discussion of the three worlds, or referential domains, underlying meaningful action was largely inspired by I. C. Jarvie's application of Popper's theory of three worlds to sociology. Popper's distinction of three worlds—of physical objects, subjective events, and objective thought contents—was intended as an ontological distinction among different kinds of entities. The major strength of Popper's model, in Habermas's opinion, is its mediation of the first and second worlds by the third world of objective spirit. The entities that inhabit the third world are symbolic creations in the broadest sense: social institutions, works of art, scientific theories, languages, machinery, and implements. Though they are themselves products of the subjective thought processes of individuals, once they have become embedded in an objective substrate, they take on a life of their own, tacitly harboring problems whose existence is prior to, and independent of, human agency. Insofar as the third world functions as an interpretative nexus of problematic concerns that conceptually structures the perception of objects and the discovery of causal uniformities, the relationship between subject and object is pragmatic and intentional.[34]

Jarvie conceives the third world as the "social landscape" on which individuals map out optimal strategies for pursuing ends. The ideal meanings and values that comprise this map provide explicit guideposts, expressible in terms of truth claims, which agents use, more or less consciously, to orient themselves to persons and things around them. When these values and meanings no longer prove efficacious, they are revised in a critical process of truth testing.[35] Although application of the theory of worlds to social life marks an important advance in conceptualizing intentional action, it still conceives the interaction between subject, nature, and objective spirit instrumentally; cultural values are revealed to cognitive consciousness as objectifiable means for facilitating action that may be more or less successful but are neither morally right nor wrong.[36] This objectification of culture, Habermas contends, raises several problems. First, it obscures the distinction between performative and hypothetical-reflective attitudes toward culture. In everyday life, people coordinate their actions around definitions of situations that are taken for granted; only when there is dissension do the underlying meanings and values become objects of conversation. A hypothetical-reflective attitude toward culture may be implicit in everyday communicative action as an ideal limit, but it is approximated only in those institutionalized fields of endeavor encompassing the various arts and sciences.[37] By construing culture as an embodiment of propositional truth claims, Popper's model cannot explain the counterfactual power of culture to compel interaction.

Habermas proposes the following emendations to Popper's theory. First, since each world is defined as the intentional correlate of a certain attitude—objectifying, valuating, or expressive—it designates a formal mode of schematization rather than a material classification of an object domain. The objective world of facts is no more to be confused with nature than the social world is to be equated with society or culture. Persons and norms can be regarded either as observable facts to be taken into consideration in a strategic calculation or as meaningful values commanding respect. Second, Habermas advocates a distinction between world (the domain of reference that is explicitly attended to) and lifeworld (the complementary background of preunderstandings). Third, rejecting the cognitive one-sidedness of Popper's model, Habermas refers the elements of the second and third worlds to validity claims other than truth, thereby allowing for legal and artistic, as well as scientific, domains of objective spirit.[38]

The neo-Kantian division of validity claims, referential domains, and value spheres elaborated above grounds Habermas's division of social action into communicative, strategic, normative, and dramaturgic types. Like their Weberian prototypes, these categories must be understood as exemplifying certain features of action that normally occur together. Habermas defines teleological action as action undertaken by a single person who seeks to realize some goal.[39] He calls teleological action "strategic" when the decisions and behavior of at least one other person are included in a means-end calculation.[40] Teleological action is rational to the extent that a person calculates the most efficient means for bringing about the desired end. According to this model of rationality, actors in the strategic mode relate to other persons as objectifiable means or obstacles to the attainment of their aims.[41]

Habermas characterizes normative action as social action in which the primary intention of the parties involved is to fulfill reciprocal expectations by conforming their behavior to shared norms and values. The pursuit of personal goals may then be overridden by social duties or canons of taste.[42] Those engaged in normative pursuits must also calculate the objective consequences of their actions for others of course. Prima facie, normative action is rational as long as it conforms to socially acceptable standards of conduct, but these standards must advance the general interests of those affected if the action is to be rational in an ideal sense.[43]

The third type of action mentioned by Habermas has as its principal aim self-presentation, or the projection of a public image. His introduction of the concept of dramaturgical action is chiefly inspired by Erving Goffman's pioneering use of theatrical role playing to illuminate social encounters. The term *role playing* here refers less to action in conformity with socially mandated forms of behavior than to the free, selective self-expression of one's own personality.[44] There is a sense in which even the simplest of actions is imbued with the personality of its agent. Conversely, every dramaturgic action is implicitly strategic, intended to elicit a desired response from an audience. In the theater of life it is assumed as a condition of mutual trust that the roles played by the actors are congruent with their true characters. Accordingly, for performances to be rational in a nonstrategic sense, they must be sincere, and the intentions expressed must be authentic—that is, they must not be ones about which the actor could be deceived.[45]

The final, communicative category of action is, as one might expect, the most important one in Habermas's work. Communicative action occurs when two or more persons expressly seek to reach voluntary agreement (*Verständigung*) on their situation for the sake of cooperating. Although persons relating to one another in other kinds of action may engage in communication for purposes of coordinating their efforts, they need not do so with the expressed aim of reaching an uncoerced settlement. Persons acting strategically, for example, may force others to comply with their aims by issuing commands, threats, lies, and other manipulative statements. Likewise, persons acting dramaturgically or normatively may use language without expressly intending to reach agreement over problematic claims. Since these kinds of action are distinguished from strategic action in tacitly presupposing some agreement over mutual expectations, they are sometimes classified by Habermas as subsidiary forms of communicative action. Properly speaking, however, communicative action involves an explicit concerted effort to reach agreement on the entire spectrum of validity claims (simultaneously thematizing all three domains of reference) and therefore transcends the other, more limited and less reflexive, types. Because "stability and univocity are . . . exceptions in everyday practice," communicative action is always an immanent possibility.[46]

CHAPTER THREE

Understanding and Language

Since the Positivismusstreit, the debate over the merits of sinn-verstehen as a method of social research has taken new directions. Philosophers of science, led by Kuhn, Lakatos, Feyerabend, and Hesse, have become increasingly disillusioned with the traditional boundaries separating the natural and the human sciences. Taking their cue from hermeneutics, they have argued that changes in scientific paradigms should not be acclaimed as indications of progress toward mirroring a mind-independent reality. Science interprets reality by setting forth data in a prior theoretical language. Because each paradigm describes its subject matter in a language that is incommensurable with other languages, there exists—so goes the most extreme version—no common standard of reality in terms of which the veridicality of competing paradigms could even be assessed.[1] Habermas's critique of positivism, by contrast, sharply distinguishes between natural and human sciences, which, because of their distinct cognitive interests, give rise to very different methodologies. Unlike the natural sciences, the social sciences are doubly hermeneutic, in that they not only subsume data under theoretical languages for purposes of explanation, but also interpret them as a means of gaining access to them.[2]

For Habermas, "the same problematic of rationality that we run into in the investigation of sociological concepts of action reappears from another angle when we pursue the question concerning what it means to understand social action. The basic concepts of social action and methodology hang together."[3] The meaning of an action must be made comprehensible in light of the interpreter's own assumptions about rational conduct. Furthermore, it must be supposed that these assumptions about rationality are shared by agent and interpreter alike, for the rationale behind an action is essentially related to the kinds of reasons and arguments that the agent could marshal to justify it as the most appropriate thing to do under the circumstances.

Suppose that we are trying to explain the behavior of a stockbroker who is bidding for shares. Such bidding is a means of maximizing gains and minimizing losses and approximates a strategic type of social action in that it considers the decisions of other persons in a means-ends calculation. Given an understanding of the rules governing the stock market that is shared by broker and interpreter alike, the interpreter constructs an ideal train of reasoning corresponding to the broker's action. In reconstructing the broker's rationale, he makes sense of the broker's action by showing that it was the reasonable thing to do under the circumstances.

It is important to note that implicit in this process is a phase of critical evaluation, for the course of action undertaken by the broker is compared with the one that would have been undertaken by an ideally rational agent, and only if there is a reasonable correspondence can the action be said to be comprehensible. In the case of what appears to be irrational behavior, the interpreter's own assumptions about the intentions and circumstances underlying the broker's activity would have to be critically reexamined. If the preunderstanding of the situation bears up under close scrutiny, then the interpreter is entitled to judge the action as irrational. Perhaps the broker was remiss in following through the prescribed strategy, bungled the calculation, or neglected to include all relevant factors in making a decision. If expressed intentions do not jibe with behavior, the interpreter may be forced to consider the psychological disposition of the broker, but only after this impasse has been reached.[4]

The same process of critical evaluation applies mutatis mutandis to normative, dramaturgical, and communicative types of action. Thus, one explains normative action by showing that it conforms to legitimately recognized norms which express generalizable interests. Should the action violate such norms or conform only to norms of doubtful legitimacy, there would be prima facie reasons for suspecting its rationality. This procedure is slightly more problematic in the case of dramaturgical action, in which the interpreter must first make sure that the action in question is not in fact strategic. Assuming that it is not, its meaning can be garnered from conventional patterns of expression and the person's past behavior. Only if the express intentions of the agent do not jibe with the observed behavior do we suspect that the action is strategic, insincere, or pathologically compelled.[5]

It has been assumed that the interpreter and the agent share the same canons of rationality—a situation that might not obtain if the agent belongs to a different culture. In the case of an agent belonging to a culture that conflates distinct types of action, the would-be interpreter has three options: to refuse to conceive of the action as meaningful and treat it as brute behavior; to recur to depth-hermeneutic, structuralist, or developmental methodologies that attempt to establish an internal link between mythic and modern rationales surrounding psychosexual taboos, binary linguistic codes, or logical phases of learning; to interpret the action as if it were rationally motivated. Only the second option avoids the dual dangers of behaviorism and ethnocentrism. However, the social scientist must relinquish his privileged position vis-à-vis the native speaker when both have the same level of rational competency.[6] The interpreter then becomes a participant in communicative action who is accountable to native speakers.[7] For the participants of communicative action—including now the interpreter—the meaning of a situation is not arrived at until agreement is reached over the facts of the case, the operant normative expectations of the situation, or the sincerity of the speakers. But even when the speakers agree on terms, there is no guarantee against self-deception, and hence the peculiar status of the social scientist as both participant and critic.[8]

Habermas discusses the problematic role of the participant-critic in conjunction with phenomenological, ethnomethodological, and hermeneutical theories of understanding. Heading the list of theories is the perceptual theory of meaning developed by Hans Skjervheim. Skjervheim attempts to resolve the problem by appealing to a distinction between two kinds of attitudes: an objectifying attitude, which schematizes social life as a field of measurable facts, and a performative attitude, which schematizes it as a network of shared values and meanings. The social scientist, Skjervheim suggests, somehow manages to relate to utterances and actions in both modes simultaneously.[9] Habermas does not find this convincing, for not only does Skjervheim fail to explain how the social scientist can achieve this dual stance, but the reduction of an action to an objective sequence of measurable movements and sounds would appear to suppress its meaning altogether. A better solution, Habermas maintains, is to conceive of the social scientist as a *virtual* participant who relates to two different frames of communicative action simultaneously. Whereas people engaged in communicative action seek mainly to coordinate their individual plans of action, social scientists seek only to understand what is going on. The communicative activity of the scientific community is motivated solely by a theoretical interest in reaching an unconstrained consensus, whereas that of social agents is motivated by a practical interest to succeed under less than pressure-free conditions.[10]

But this account raises another problem, for, in reconstructing the meaning intended by the actors in accordance with ideal standards that are recognized by them only obscurely, if at all, isn't the interpreter twisting it? This caveat identifies the meaning of an action with the psychological intentions of its agent—a view that is challenged by ethnomethodology and philosophical hermeneutics. Ethnomethodology is indebted very largely to the phenomenological sociology of Alfred Schutz, who sought to ground the categories of social science in the everyday world. He correctly saw that the perspective of the disinterested observer is achieved by breaking away from the natural stance of a historically situated member of a society and assuming the attitude of the social scientist, who hypothetically brackets the validity of presuppositions that are normally taken for granted.[11] The problem of clarifying the phenomenological perspective was bequeathed to ethnomethodology, which is the study of the interpretative procedures (ethnomethods) by means of which actors negotiate a mutual understanding of their world. The profusion of incomplete utterances, as well as the high incidence of indexical and deictic terms (I, you, here, now, this, that, and so forth) in everyday conversation testifies to the importance of the lifeworld as the shared background against which utterances take on definite meaning. The continuity of the lifeworld over against the fragility and evanescence of negotiations is itself a product of these creative reinterpretations.

However, as an active participant, the sociologist alters the context of social life, destroying the possibility of any neutral understanding. This fact may be used to good advantage when criticizing positivistic assumptions about the objectivity of statistical measurements and questionnaires, but it seems to undermine any hope for elaborating an objective theoretical framework.[12] Some ethnomethodologists, such as Harold Garfinkel, have attempted to remedy this situation by seizing on the structural invariances of speaker-hearer relationships.[13] Garfinkel follows Schutz and Husserl in holding that the individual phenomenologist gains an undiminished understanding of the true meaning of lived experience by suspending the performative attitude. Once the lifeworld of the interpreter's biographical ego has been "reduced" to the status of a purely immanent phenomenon of consciousness, a process of imaginative variation can be made to yield an eidetic intuition of necessary, universal structures. The problems of such a reduction were exhaustively detailed by Habermas in his earlier study of the logic of the social sciences.[14] For our purposes it suffices to note that aside from the enormous methodological difficulties attendant on bracketing presuppositions and confirming intuitions, the restriction of intentional analysis to the sphere of transcendental consciousness contradicts the cardinal ethnomethodological tenet that meaning is an intersubjective accomplishment grounded in contingent performative contexts. Phenomenological sociology, Habermas concludes, appears to set ideal structure against everyday performance.[15]

In Habermas's judgment, it is philosophical hermeneutics that comes closest to articulating the sense in which ideal structures of rationality are located in everyday understanding. For Kuhlmann and Gadamer, understanding can only aspire to the status of an objective undertaking when it is conceived as a process of reaching agreement.[16] This process is guided by what Gadamer calls an expectation of perfectibility (*Vorgriff auf Vollkommenheit*): the assumption that the text is a coherent whole embodying an ideal claim to validity. Corresponding to this expectation is the notion of an unlimited speech community representing an ideal consensus toward which all opposing interpretations of a text converge. The relationship between the ideal speech community and its historical permutations is essentially dialectical, everyday conversation activating a process of reflection that elevates it to the level of rational dialogue.[17]

Habermas praises Gadamer's understanding of the way in which ideal structures are reflectively generated within the historical processes they govern but voices reservations about his tendency to subordinate the critical moment opened up by the temporal distance separating the interpreter from the subject matter to the conservative moment of renewing the authority of tradition. He claims that Gadamer regards the interpreter as an actual participant in practical conversation, so that understanding tradition is equated with assenting to its validity and rationality in an ideal sense. By construing interpretation as an application (*Anwendung*) of a living truth to the practical concerns of the present, the conservative intention underlying the philological preservation of the classics, the juridical extension of legal precedent, and the theological proclamation of biblical authority is elevated to the rank of an ontological principle.[18]

ACTION AND LANGUAGE

Although Habermas presents his theory of language as an intervening consideration (*Zwischenbetrachtung*) in his discussion of Weber's social theory, it is convenient to discuss it at this juncture, since it rounds out the metatheoretical analysis of rationality. Weber's theory of action involves an ambiguity that elucidates some of the problems associated with contemporary theories of meaning. In Weber's great posthumous work *Wirtschaft und Gesellschaft* social action is said to include any action that is meaningfully "oriented toward the behavior of others" or involves some reciprocity, such as mutual respect for private property.[19] If reciprocity is taken as the defining feature of social action, then social engagements of a relatively intransitory nature would presuppose at least some communicative agreement, and the meaning of action would accordingly refer to a public accomplishment rather than a private episode in the mind of the actor. However, Weber goes on to illustrate his theory of social action with several examples that are predominantly strategic in nature (including the case of two cyclists trying to avoid a collision). Moreover, his own descending ranking of social action—purposive-rational (*Zweckrational*), value-rational (*Wertrational*), affectual, and traditional—stresses the superior rationality of instrumental action, thereby prejudicing the interpretative enterprise in favor of a psychological divination of strategic intentions. The rational approach, by contrast, goes hand in hand with the theory of meaning developed in twentieth-century philosophy of language.[20]

The organon model of linguistic signs introduced by Karl Bühler provides a convenient point of departure for Habermas's survey of linguistic philosophy. Bühler's semiotic analysis of language isolated three functions common to all signs: a cognitive function (the sign as symbol of reality), an expressive function (the sign as a symptom of the sender's inner experience), and an appellative function (the sign as a signal aimed at influencing the receiver's behavior).[21] What is required in addition to Bühler's semiotic analysis of isolated sign functions, Habermas maintains, is a syntactic analysis of rules governing the construction of well-formed sentences and a semantic analysis of the relationship between meaning and validity.

Habermas believes that the theories of language developed by Carnap, Wittgenstein, Davidson, Dummet, Austin, and Searle have largely succeeded in remedying these deficiencies. Working within the formalist tradition, Carnap identified the sentence, not the isolated word, as the primary vehicle of meaning. He maintained that for sentences to be meaningful, they must satisfy formal rules of grammatical construction. Thus, meaning is held to be a function of the capacity of sentences to designate objective states of affairs.[22] The truth-conditional theories developed by Frege, early Wittgenstein, and more recently Davidson and Dummet are basically inspired by the same idea—namely, that the meaning of a sentence is reducible to the conditions under which it is true. The major contribution of truth-conditional semantics is its recognition of the internal link between meaning and validity. Its major drawback, Habermas contends, is its tendency to assign linguistic meaning exclusively to the cognitive operation, thereby consigning expression and evaluation to the status of strategic devices for influencing behavior.[23]

Habermas mentions two important movements that challenge this imbalance. The first, exemplified by Dummet's verificationist theory of meaning, exposes the limits of truth-conditional semantics from within. The old verificationist theory of meaning associated with the Vienna school assumed that the truth conditions of so-called protocol sentences about observable objects were amenable to conclusive testing. Dummet points out, however, that natural language abounds with meaningful statements about temporally and spatially inaccessible events that cannot be verified. He therefore recommends that the verificationist principle be reformulated in such a way that the verification of propositions comes to be seen as involving the proffering of counterfactual reasons. In Habermas's opinion, Dummet tacitly binds verification and meaning to the pragmatic conditions of formal argumentation, in which validity is also seen as a function of satisfying normative and expressive validity claims.[24]

The tradition of ordinary language philosophy associated with Wittgenstein, Austin, and Searle is even more radical in its repudiation of classical truth-conditional semantics. For Wittgenstein, the meaning of sentences is tied to their use in everyday speech, or to be more precise, to rules specifying their socially acceptable usage. By tying meaning to rules governing social interaction, he inaugurated the transition from truth-conditional to communicative semantics.[25]

Habermas's universal pragmatics combines the communicative semantics of Wittgenstein, with its emphasis on the intersubjectively criticizable nature of utterances, and the functional semiotics of Bühler, which holds that every sign simultaneously combines representational, performative, and expressive functions. In earlier statements, Habermas sought to clarify this synthesis by appealing to the generative linguistics of Noam Chomsky and the speech-act theories of Austin and Searle. Chomsky attempts to reconstruct the "depth grammar," or necessary and universal formal-syntactic rules, underlying linguistic competence, the latter understood as an innate capacity to produce phonetically and semantically correct sentences. Habermas's universal pragmatics is intended to carry out a similar program with respect to *communicative* competence, necessitated by the fact that the conditions for producing meaningful utterances are not reducible to the innate capacities of isolated speakers to form grammatical sentences but also involve mastering the performative rules of social interaction and the reciprocal role qualifications of speaker and hearer that are part of them.[26]

Universal pragmatics aims at disclosing the universals of dialogue that a person must acquire in order to participate in a speech situation. The most important concern the use of performative verbs, which, unlike nonperformative verbs which facilitate the reporting of information, occur only in a speech setting, where they serve the exclusive purpose of proposing a social engagement.[27] Taking the speech-act theory of Austin as his point of departure, Habermas analyzes the kinds of assertion in which performative verbs occur (speech acts) in terms of a first-person expression addressed to a second-person direct object of the form "I promise (assure, request, know, etc.) that," followed by a propositional clause containing a referential term and a predicate. Habermas regards this standard form as properly depicting, if not the typical form of speech acts, at least their essential structure.

Unlike Austin, who referred meaning exclusively to locutionary (propositional) content, Habermas endorses the view that the *illocutionary*, or performative force of speech action, no less than the locutionary content, constitutes a bona fide category of meaning. Together, these levels of meaning comprise a double structure, or dual intentionality, which is inherent in every speech act. At the illocutionary level, speech is guided by a performative attitude oriented toward an intersubjective relationship; at the locutionary level, by an objectifying attitude oriented toward a world of objects. These two levels are reflexively related to one another, the locutionary level referring to objective boundary conditions, the illocutionary level to conditions under which truthful reference and right action are agreed on.[28]

Besides incurring social obligations and transmitting information about the objective world, speakers express their intentions.[29] The perlocutionary effects of such expressions of intention serve to coordinate action strategically; they are not announced explicitly in the utterance itself and are entirely dependent on the context. Although social action is often coordinated through perlocutionary effects, Habermas insists that communicative, not strategic, action is the principal medium of cooperation, since perlocutionary effects depend on a prior trust based on communicative expectations. A warning of impending danger, for example, can have the intended effect of frightening the hearer into a certain course of action only if the warning is taken seriously.

After noting that speech acts simultaneously raise claims to truth, rightness, and sincerity, Habermas classifies them into four major

39

groupings (see table 3.1).[30] Regulative speech acts, which explicitly raise a claim to rightness, prescribe, command, or proscribe. Expressive speech acts disclose the speaker's feelings, desires, and dispositions.[31] Declarations and statements of intent, though referring to actions in the objective world, fundamentally raise claims to sincerity. Perlocutionary and power-backed imperative speech acts primarily raise claims to success or effectiveness. Unlike normatively authorized commands such as "No smoking on board the plane," which are regulative in nature, genuine commands openly declare the strategic intentions of the speaker in conjunction with some threat. Constative speech acts, which raise claims to truth, represent, describe, assert, or deny some objective state of affairs.[32] Habermas completes his analysis of the pure types of linguistically mediated interaction by relating his taxonomy of speech acts to his theory of social action.[33]

The abstractness of his model raises serious doubts about its value for empirical research. Speech acts seldom occur in standard form; many are institutionally bound (nongeneralizable); actual conversations often combine strategic and communicative types; and people who are on good terms with one another sometimes forego speech when coordinating their actions.[34] Furthermore, it remains unclear why a formal pragmatic analysis of speech action is needed in the first place.[35]

Although Habermas admits that many speech acts, especially those that approximate the institutionally unbound, ideal type, possess a meaning that can be captured literally in standard form, he concedes that there is always a residue of meaning that is exclusive to the particular context.[36] This need not be seen as casting aspersions on the theoretical reconstruction of those formal structures of rationality that govern the lifeworld as a whole.[37] Nevertheless, since it is undeniable that many of our communicative negotiations occur within institutionally bound settings circumscribed by legal sanctions and hierarchies of power, in which speakers are motivated to accept one another's offers on the basis of authority or custom or out of fear of punishment, the assertion that communicative action is logically linked to structures of rational discourse may seem odd.[38] Strictly speaking, institutionally bound speech acts such as arbitrating, contracting, marrying, and christening are either strategic in nature (as in the case of legally sanctioned arbitrations and contracts) or are embedded in ritualistic contexts governed by religious custom and civil authority (as in the case of marrying and christening). Institutionally unbound speech acts, by contrast, constitute a repertory of illocutionary offers that may appear in any context.[39]

Unbound regulative, expressive, and constative speech acts, such

Table 3.1. *Pure Types of Linguistically Mediated Interaction*

Types of action	Characteristic speech acts	Functions of speech	Action orientations	Basic attitudes	Validity claims	World relations
Strategic Action	Perlocutions Imperatives	Influencing one's opposite number	Oriented to success	Objectivating	(Effectiveness)	Objective world
Conversation	Constatives	Representation of states of affairs	Oriented to reaching understanding	Objectivating	Truth	Objective world
Normatively regulated action	Regulatives	Establishment of interpersonal relations	Oriented to reaching understanding	Norm-conformative	Rightness	Social world
Dramaturgical action	Expressives	Self-representation	Oriented to reaching understanding	Expressive	Truthfulness	Subjective world

Adapted from Jürgen Habermas, *The Theory of Communicative Action*, vol. 1, trans. Thomas McCarthy. Introduction and translation copyright © 1984 by Beacon Press. Reprinted by permission of Beacon Press.

as claiming to know something, promising, prescribing, expressing a desire, and so on, are those in which speakers premise their acceptance of one another's offers on the mutual expectation that the validity claims raised could be justified rationally. Consequently the rational accountability of everyday speakers is logically wedded to ideal conditions of discourse. This connection grounds Habermas's refutation of ethical skepticism by arguing that unconstrained social interaction carries with it a practical commitment to procedural justice that is not open to voluntary rejection or acceptance. The skeptic engaging in communicative action cannot repudiate this commitment without being convicted of either gross insincerity or outright inconsistency.

Classical philosophy from Plato to Hegel regarded dialogic analysis as only one aspect of rationality, the other being an intuitive power of unification. Understood in its universalizing capacity, reason has certainly lost the prestige it once enjoyed as a method of speculative thought. Still, one wonders whether the restriction of rationality to the province of formal discourse is not purchased at the cost of practical reason. As Habermas admits, implicit in practical life is a prediscursive moment of hermeneutical reflection that crosses the formal boundaries separating cognition, action, and expression. It is related to an intuitive know-how, or preunderstanding of life in its totality, that enables us to generate an indefinite number of improvisations on the basis of a finite repertory of general rules. What Plato calls *poēsis*—the metaphorical capacity to discern likenesses between heterogeneous experiences, to subsume diverse particulars under unitary ideas, or, what is the same thing, to generate novel applications out of a prior unity—has much in common with Aristotle's notion of phronēsis, the application of general rules of conduct in everyday practice. Both involve art as well as taste—the mimetic emulation of exemplary models of speech and virtue that the Greeks took to be essential for the aesthetic cultivation of character. If this, the most substantial part of our practical lives, is to be accorded the dignity of reason, then Habermas's provisional analysis of rationality will have to incorporate a countervailing moment of aesthetic reflection.[40]

CHAPTER FOUR

Weber's Theory of Rationalization

It was with great irony that Weber and first-generation critical theorists concluded that the cage in which contemporary man, bereft of any cosmic meaning and moral dignity and subject to the impersonal whims of bureaucracy, ekes out his monotonous existence, was nothing less than the tragic fulfillment of an aspiration born in an age in which reason was still regarded as the universal guarantor of a kingdom of autonomous subjects.[1] What seems scandalous about this diagnosis today has less to do with its outright dismissal of "scientific progress"—a chimera of which we ought to have been thoroughly disabused anyway by now—than with its sweeping indictment of everything rational. Who, least of all a social scientist professing moral scruples, would dare cast doubt on his credentials as a practicing member of the free, enlightened community of *Kulturmenschen*? And yet Weber's "deconstruction" of reason—to paraphrase the paradox in contemporary jargon—is far from being the sort of innocent ruse that intellectuals delight in visiting upon themselves *pour épater les bourgeois*. It is the continuing allure of Weber's critique of rationality for neoconservatives and radicals alike that makes it of such vital concern to Habermas.

RATIONALITY

Weber uses the concept of rationality in a wide variety of contexts to refer to certain aspects of action, decision, and systematized world views.[2] As a feature of action, rationality may refer either to the purposive-rational calculation of ends with respect to given preferences (decision rationality) and efficient means (instrumental rationality) or to the value-rational "formulation of the ultimate values governing action and the consistently planned orientation of its detailed course to these values."[3] Sometimes Weber juxtaposes the cold formalism of pure purposive rationality, which always involves an impersonal and largely quantifiable calculation of consequences, with substantive, highly personal value-rational commitment, which is "determined by a conscious belief in the value for its own sake of some ethical, aesthetic, religious, or other form of behavior, independently of its prospects of success."[4] However, when discussing the legitimating potential of value-rational, as distinct from affectual (emotionally motivated) and traditional (habitually motivated), types of action, or when addressing the "infinite number of possible value scales" for "substantive goal rationality," Weber strongly implies that pure value rationality consists in the logical deduction of practical maxims from universal—and to that extent formalizable or procedural—principles of equity and justice of the sort articulated, for example, in natural law.[5] It must be noted, of course, that Weber never went as far as to equate either natural law or an ethic of ultimate ends with purely procedural forms of rationality, nor could he have done so, given his unwavering belief in the subjective status of value commitments generally.[6]

Rationality becomes a definitive feature of action only after it has been incorporated in personality structures, cultural interpretations, and social institutions.[7] *Rationalizierung* ("rationalization") is the term used by Weber to designate the process by which this transformation is brought about. At the risk of oversimplifying, one might say that cultural rationalization denotes a complex ensemble of events encompassing the progressive differentiation, formalization, and grounding (what Weber calls *Wertsteigerung*, "value intensification") of value-related spheres of activity, the most fundamental of these gravitating around the Kantian triad of truth (knowledge), right or goodness (morality and law), and beauty (art and taste). The distinctive features of secular culture—abstract art, science and technology, individualistic ethics and formal law—represent domains of inquiry that are guided by a single value. Corresponding to the growing emancipation (*Verselbständigung*) of each value sphere from the constraints imposed by their former amalgamation under unitary religious world views is a parallel process of self-reflection whereby each form of inquiry is grounded with respect to its own peculiar principles.[8] If experimental method is the purposive-rational quintessence of scientific cognition, universalizability would seem to be the heart and soul of value-rational pursuits in the normative field of ethics, politics, and jurisprudence undertaken in the name of justice.

In the West, cultural rationalization was synonymous with the secularization of the Judeo-Christian world view. Weber is careful to point out that secularization encompassed much more than the systematic elaboration of this world view into a consistent cosmology; for the disenchantment (*Entzauberung*) of nature as a purely objective setting for humanity's redemption vis-à-vis a transcendent ethical deity—the feature that ostensibly sets the Judeo-Christian tradition apart from its Asiatic counterparts—already prefigured a differentiation of cognitive, practical, and aesthetic value spheres. Secularization must therefore be construed as the great liberating force that paved the way for modern, "emancipated" society. Just as the development of technology enabled entrepreneurs and administrators to conduct their respective activities on the basis of impersonal calculations independent of religious and moral considerations, so too the liberation of art from the dominion of the Church hastened its entry into the marketplace, thereby permitting untrammeled pursuit of materialistic ideals. By the end of the nineteenth century, *l'art pour l'art* became the rallying cry for an avant-garde counterculture that had all but rejected naturalistic, market-oriented conventions in favor of abstract styles of expression based on highly refined techniques.[9] But the single most decisive event paving the way for modern society was undoubtedly the separation of ethics and law from one another and from religious custom (*Sittlichkeit*).

By elevating faith above "good works" in the achievement of personal salvation, the Reformation succeeded in translating diffuse inner feelings into what later became an individualistic ethic of conscience and responsibility. Conceptions of moral autonomy also figured in social contract theories of law, for, by shifting the burden of political legitimation from traditional authority to formal procedures of consent, such theories increasingly made the serving of justice an impartial affair. This is reflected in both the delegation of authority for the enactment, application, and execution of statutory law to office-holders who have attained their position through election, appointment, examination, or some other impersonal means and in constitutional limits to the exercise of authority itself. The accountability of office-holders and, therewith, the judgment of their policies in terms of their effectiveness in serving the commonweal, was further augmented by the establishment of democratic institutions embodying rules of procedural justice.[10]

The rational core of Judeo-Christian culture can be fully articulated only within the institutional confines of universities, academies, and professional organizations, all of which require public recognition. Society undertakes to subsidize these costly ventures only when the potential for rationalization embedded in culture is infused into personal motivations and social orders. Corresponding to this phase of cultural institutionalization or social rationalization is a process of differentiation, formalization, and grounding that in many respects parallels that discussed above. In modern—which for Weber means capitalist—society, the economy, the state, and private households are segregated into relatively autonomous domains with their own distinctive values. With the institutionalization of private property and contractual law, a market economy comes into being whose primary organizational unit, the business firm, disposes over purposive-rational methods of accounting, management, and production in the calculated pursuit of profit. The organizational core of the modern state, the bureaucratic administration, uses the same techniques of rational accounting and management to secure its monopoly over the use of force in maintaining law and order. Both government and business administration are regulated internally by formal procedures for delegating authority, processing information, and organizing the flow of communication from department to department within an overall economy of efficiency, though in the former the purposive-rational exercise of power remains circumscribed by considerations of legitimacy.[11]

The nuclear family, by contrast, is the vehicle by which value-rational orientations are instilled in the individual personality. In Weber's view, the most important normative factor shaping the consciousness of Western civilization is the Protestant work ethic, which combines an acquisitive, purposive-rational orientation toward success with value-rational sentiments concerning individual responsibility and familial-occupational loyalty, thereby forming the basis of that "methodical" life-style peculiar to vocationalism. Emerging as a reaction to this ascetic emphasis on self-improvement through hard work is a competing life-style that embodies the hedonistic values commonly associated with an artistic counterculture.[12]

THE EMERGENCE OF MODERN STRUCTURES OF CONSCIOUSNESS

The fundamental question animating Weber's inquiry can be formulated accordingly: Why does the developmental logic inherent in all religious world views reach its zenith only in the Judeo-Christian tradition? Weber addresses the cultural rationalization of religious world views in his comparative study of the three great world religions: Confucianism/Taoism, Hinduism/Buddhism, and Judaism/Christianity. In keeping with his dual materialist-idealist method of explanation, Weber sought to trace the emergence of these religions back to the theodicy problematic, which is concerned first and foremost with cosmic justice and key existential experiences centering on human mortality.[13]

Weber classifies the major world religions with respect to how they treat the theodicy problem. Judaism and Christianity, exemplifying the theocentric strategy, posit the existence of a personal deity—variously characterized in anthropomorphic and abstract terms—who exists independently of the created world. Suffering is interpreted as a fall from grace, salvation as a gift from God. The ethos of the Judeo-Christian world view requires action in accordance with divine moral commands. Oriental religions, by contrast, conceive salvation as participation in a cosmic order and eschew action in favor of knowledge, thus resonating more with the life experiences of Mandarin bureaucrats (Confucianism) and beggar monks (Buddhism) than with those of the masses.[14]

Weber also classifies world religions with respect to their evaluations of the world. Confucianism and Taoism affirm the "here and now" and therefore advocate a life-style of passive acquiescence to the status quo. Judaism and Christianity and Buddhism and Hinduism posit a dualism between the temporal world and ultimate reality and accordingly advocate active transcendence of the former in thought and action. For Weber, a religion's potential for rationalization depends on its capacity to represent phenomenal reality objectively, as pure nature, or ethically, as a realm of ultimate ends. He contends that only the Judeo-Christian world view possesses an internal structure that both sets objective nature against ethical teleology, thereby forcing a turn inward, and represents a transcendent imperative governing the resolution of social conflict. Denial of the world is necessary, but not sufficient, for ethical rationality, and the contemplative "flight from reality" characteristic of the Hindu and Buddhist response to the cleavage between existence and essence is a withdrawal from, not a mastery of, moral conflict. The demythologization of nature and the subsumption of social action under a moral order condition one another.

Habermas accepts most of Weber's sociology of religion but regrets its neglect of theoretical intuition as a necessary condition for cognitive rationalization. Weber surmised that religions with cosmocentric, world-affirmative world views possessed the least potential for rationalization, but in fact, it was within the cradle of Greek religion that *bios theoretikos* was born. Taken separately, neither Greek nor Judeo-Christian world views possess the structural prerequisites necessary for ethical and cognitive rationalization. It is Habermas's belief that it was the confluence of these two world views in Europe during

47

the High Middle Ages that provided the catalyst responsible for the rise of experimental science and the Protestant work ethic.[15]

THE LEGAL AND ETHICAL FOUNDATIONS OF RATIONALISM:
WEBER'S DIAGNOSIS OF THE PRESENT

Weber's book *The Protestant Ethic and the Spirit of Capitalism* provides the bridge between the analysis of cultural rationalization given above and the media by which it is invested in social institutions. In it he sought to explain how the occasional profiteering of economic adventurers that had existed throughout history could have become institutionalized in a market system supported by a methodical, vocational life-style. He traced this development to an "elective affinity," or structural attraction, between the ascetic life-style of members of certain Protestant sects and the methodical life-style of entrepreneurs, an attraction rooted in the psychological need for confidence in one's own salvation and self-improvement through hard work.[16]

In his study of modern law, Weber stressed the parallel emancipation of individual moral conscience from ethical custom. For the first time ever, civil law appears as something posited, the legitimacy of which is tied to notions of sovereign consent (the social contract) institutionalized in democratic rules of procedural justice. It no longer requires the adoption of any particular moral or religious attitude, but only outward compliance with respect to behavior. In other words, it procures a realm of individual freedom in which it is permitted to do anything that is compatible with a like freedom for others.[17]

Our sketch of rationalization so far has focused on its liberating effects. Scientists, artists, jurists, administrators, and members of the business community are relatively free to ply their respective trades unencumbered by religious constraints. But although freedom of conscience is now protected from social and political encroachment, it comes to play an increasingly marginal role in everyday life. Even the desire for a meaningful view of the cosmos would seem to have been progressively satisfied by the success of modern science. Yet Weber's diagnosis of modernity reveals precisely the reverse phenomenon: an ineluctable erosion of freedom and meaning.

The logical move would be to try to blame these disturbances on factors other than rationalization, but Weber, strangely, declines to take this path. He maintains that loss of meaning in the wake of the disintegration of religious world views into opposed "ultimate ideas" is inevitable, since a logical contradiction necessarily ensues, compelling the corresponding orders of life to "drift into tension with one another." The explanatory poverty of science is merely the most glaring manifestation of rational differentiation and specialization. As he rather ingenuously remarks, "Wherever rational empirical knowledge has consistently brought about the disenchantment of the world and its transformation into a causal mechanism, a definitive pressure arises against the claims of the ethical postulate that the world is a divinely ordered, that is, somehow ethically meaningful cosmos."[18] If science is incapable of addressing our existential concerns—of answering what, for Tolstoy, is the only important question: What shall we do and how shall we live?—then this must be taken as symptomatic of a deep fragmentation of reason into irreconcilable value spheres.

> Scientific pleading is meaningless in principle because the various value spheres of the world stand in irreconcilable conflict with each other. . . . And since Nietzsche, we realize that something can be beautiful, not only in spite of that aspect in which it is not good, but rather in that very aspect. You will find this expressed earlier in the *Fleurs du Mal*, as Baudelaire named his poems. It is commonplace to observe that something may be true although it is not beautiful and not holy and not good. Indeed, it may be true in precisely those aspects. But all these are only the most elementary cases of struggle that the gods of the various orders and values are engaged in. I do not know how one might wish to decide 'scientifically' the value of French and German culture; for here too, different gods struggle with one another, now and for all times to come.[19]

Intrepidly pursuing this line of argument, Weber concludes that what applies to each of the major spheres of value applies equally well to the sciences; the values of technical efficiency, health, and justice that respectively authorize physics and chemistry, medicine, and jurisprudence "can by no means be proved." In other words, no scientific appeal to facts or consequences can answer the question of "whether the existence of these cultural phenomena have been and are *worth while*."[20] In the face of scientific demands for rational justification, all values, including those of science itself, are devalued as meaningless. Weber is convinced that the world must "appear fragmentary and devalued in all those instances when judged in the light of the religious postulate of a divine 'meaning' of existence. This devaluation results from the conflict between the rational claim and reality, between the rational ethic and the partly rational, and partly irrational values."[21]

It is not the least bit surprising that the main casualty of the rational devaluation of values turns out to be the ethics of responsibility and its principle of universal reciprocity. The extension of one's "brethren" to encompass the whole of humanity was already undermined by the purposive-rational thrust of the Protestant ethic. "Puritanism,"

Weber remarks, "accepted the routinization of the economic cosmos. . . . This meant in principle to renounce salvation as a goal attainable by man, that is, by everybody. It meant to renounce salvation in favor of the groundless and always only particularized grace (*Gnadenpartikularismus*)."[22] He then shows that the value-rational substance of the Protestant ethic is also incompatible with political, aesthetic, erotic, and intellectual spheres of life. The use of violence in territorial pursuits can no more abide by the tenets of such an ethic than can the demand for artistic freedom in the name of subjective sovereignty, the glorification of the purely sensual, or the cosmopolitan relativization of values by connoisseurs of culture (*Kulturmenschen*).

With the withering away of religious sentiment, Weber believed that the value-rational aspect of a principled ethic would be eclipsed by the purposive-rational demands of ascetic vocationalism. "Limitation to specialized work, with a renunciation of the Faustian universality of man which it involves, is a condition of any valuable work in the modern world; hence deeds and renunciation necessarily accompany each other."[23] The loss of freedom entailed in such renunciation is most telling for the professional bureaucrat, who "is only a single cog in an ever-moving mechanism which prescribes to him an essentially fixed route of march."[24] Paradoxically, the mechanization and dehumanization of office life in which decisions are imposed from the top down owe their raison d'être to legal formalization and democratization. As Weber points out, "the position of all 'democratic' currents, in the sense of currents that would minimize 'authority'"—bureaucratic authority included—is "necessarily ambiguous":[25]

> Equality before the law and the demand for legal guarantees against arbitrariness demand a formal and rational "objectivity" of administration, as opposed to the personally free discretion flowing from the "grace" of the old patrimonial domination. If, however, an "ethos"—not to speak of instincts—takes hold of the masses on some individual question, it postulates *substantive* justice oriented toward some concrete instance and person; and such an "ethos" will unavoidably collide with the formalism and rule-bound and cool matter-of-factness of bureaucratic administration.[26]

Though formal law and bureaucracy impose an unfreedom of their own—and it need hardly be mentioned that Weber was acutely sensitive to the "injustices" perpetrated on "the propertyless masses" by a system of formal law—any attempt to reinstate "popular justice" based on substantive ethical principles of social democracy "crosses the rational course of justice and administration just as strongly. . . as the 'star chamber' proceedings of an 'absolute' ruler.[27]

Bureaucracy may be the most obvious example of the renunciation exacted by rational asceticism, but it is not the driving force that sustains it. For, lurking behind the "specialist without spirit" (*Fachmenschen ohne Geist*) is the proverbial "sensualist without heart" (*Genussmenschen ohne Herz*), and herein is revealed that mutual affinity between ceaseless toil and insatiable consumption that is so pervasive in capitalist society. The irrational confluence of asceticism and consumerism is brilliantly captured by Weber in the memorable denouement of the *Protestant Ethic*:

> The Puritan wanted to work in a calling; we are forced to do so. . . . In Baxter's view the care for external goods should only lie on the shoulders of the saint "like a light cloak, which can be thrown aside at any moment." But fate decreed that the cloak should become an iron cage. . . . Since asceticism undertook to remodel the world and to work out its ideals in the world, material goods have gained an increasing and finally inexorable power over the lives of men as at no previous period in history. Today the spirit of religious asceticism—whether finally, who knows?—has escaped from the cage. But victorious capitalism, since it rests on mechanical foundations, needs the support no longer.[28]

Thus, value-rational orientations continue to recede in importance until "the pursuit of wealth, stripped of its religious and ethical meaning . . . become[s] associated with purely mundane passions."

Habermas does not dispute Weber's observation that Western society has witnessed a progressive erosion of meaning and freedom, and he concedes that some of this is undoubtedly the result of cultural and social rationalization. Feelings of alienation and despair invariably follow demythologization, mechanization of production, and bureaucratization, regardless of the degree to which the latter accompany a rational increase in moral and cognitive learning capacity. But, for Habermas, the loss of freedom and meaning engendered by these developments is more than compensated by the enhancement of individual autonomy vis-à-vis tradition and by the emergence of new possibilities of meaning as a result of modern art and the democratic ethos of communicative humanism.[29] Moreover, insofar as this process is at all pathological, it is the result of a one-sided selective institutionalization of rationality—what Habermas calls the "colonization of the lifeworld"—that stems from the peculiar dynamics of advanced capitalism.

The path to a clear understanding of social pathology is closed to Weber because of the metatheoretical and methodological narrowness of his approach. First, Habermas contends, Weber conflates rational society with capitalism. In his study of world religions, he distinguishes between the necessary and universal features intrinsic to any process of cultural rationalization and the specific, historical forms that such a logical potential has assumed in the course of social institutionalization. But this distinction becomes blurred in his later analysis of the religious and juristic roots of capitalism. Second, Habermas maintains that Weber's inability to escape the tendrils of philosophy of consciousness and its postulation of an opposition between subject and object led him to mistake purposive rationality for reason tout court. Lacking an understanding of the communicative basis of formal reciprocity or democratic procedural justice, he quite naturally concluded that value rationality and its correlative mode of political legitimation would eventually be overshadowed along with the religious ethic to which it was substantively linked.[30] Third, by prematurely rejecting sociological functionalism as a naturalistic aberration, Weber was forced to restrict his sociological explanation to the action-theoretical plane of sinnverstehen. But Habermas contends that to focus narrowly on the agent's subjective understanding of his or her action, including whatever cynicism he or she may entertain about the meaningfulness and freedom-enhancing virtues of the values that the action embodies, gives the impression that cultural rationalization itself is responsible for social pathology and altogether neglects those unintended (and uninterpretable) consequences of action resulting from the irrational functioning of economy and state. A bilevel model of society incorporating a systems-theoretical analysis of these objective constraints would properly reinstate the source of social pathology in a contradiction between the action-theoretical (communicative) infrastructure of a meaningful lifeworld and the systems-theoretical (functional) goals of a managed capitalist economy.

As Habermas notes, Weber's late essays "Politics as a Vocation" and "Science as a Vocation" and the famous Zwischenbetrachtung included among the studies on sociology of religion, "Religious Rejections of the World and Their Directions," convey the impression that the loss of freedom is logically entailed by the loss of meaning. In the Zwischenbetrachtung, Weber connects each of the three cultural value spheres (cognitive, normative, and aesthetic) with corresponding interest positions, or orders of life, that regulate the possession of ideal goods (science/knowledge, religion/morality, and art/taste) and material goods (economy/wealth, politics/power, counterculture/ love).[31] The resulting conflict between the religious ethic of love of neighbor and the other orders of life is attributed not to particular, nonrational value preferences (contents), but to the logical irreducibility of universal, rationalizable value spheres (formal structures). So construed, none of the three rationality complexes is capable of exerting a structure-building influence on society as a whole; as a consequence, value-rational orientations are entirely uprooted from their religious base and are replaced by instrumental and hedonistic modes of conduct. The resulting loss of freedom is in part symptomatic of the disappearance of moral autonomy (in the Kantian sense), but, to complete the image of society as an iron cage, Weber must further assume that modern law can be detached from natural law, its legitimating anchor, and can be rationalized in accordance with the instrumental logic of statutory proceduralism. What emerges is a model of selective rationalization in which society, culture, and personality are overburdened with integration problems while at the same time being threatened with absorption into the combined economic-bureaucratic apparatus.

Habermas does not deny that the freedom to adopt differing attitudes toward the three domains of reality "can become a source of conflict as soon as different cultural value spheres *simultaneously* penetrate the same institutional domains, so that rationalization processes of different types compete with one another in the same place." He adds, however, that "cognitive-instrumental, moral-practical, and aesthetic-expressive orientations of action ought not to become so *independently* embodied in antagonistic orders of life that they overburden the personality system's average capacity for *integration* and lead to permanent conflicts between lifestyles."[32] The paradoxical conclusion that such conflicts are logically necessitated by cultural rationalization stems from confusing the particular *contents* of cultural traditions with those universal *standards* of value. This confusion is especially apparent in "Science as a Vocation," in which Weber compares "the most elementary cases of struggle that the gods of the various orders and values are engaged in"—namely, between truth, goodness, and beauty—with the problem of deciding "scientifically" the relative worth of French as opposed to German culture. Even more revealing is the passage alluded to earlier in which Weber underscores the irrationality of *all* vocations:

> Whether life is worth living and when—this question is not asked by medicine. Natural science gives us an answer to the question of what we must do if we wish to master life technically. It leaves quite aside . . . whether we should and do wish to master life technically. . . . Consider a discipline such as aesthetics. . . . It does not raise the question whether or not the realm of art is perhaps a realm of diabolical grandeur . . . in its core hostile to God and, in its innermost and aristocratic spirit, hostile to the brotherhood of man. . . . Consider jurisprudence. It establishes what is valid according to the rules of juristic thought, which is partly bound by logically compelling and partly by conventionally given schemata. Whether there should be law and whether we should establish just these rules—such

53

questions jurisprudence does not answer. . . . Consider the historical and cultural sciences. They teach us how to understand and interpret political, artistic, literary, and social phenomena in terms of their origins. But they give us no answer to the question, whether the existence of these cultural phenomena have been and are *worthwhile*.[33]

Habermas's interpretation of this passage merits further scrutiny, since it provides unique insight into the problems besetting his own theory. Of all the vocations mentioned above, only medicine, Habermas submits, articulates a particular value content.

Here we have a case of the value-oriented application of natural scientific knowledge, that is, of the rationalization of services in the framework of a professional practice that, as the practice of healing, is directed to a specific value content—the health of patients. Empirically, this value is almost universally accepted; nevertheless, it is a matter of a particular pattern of values that is by no means internally connected with one of the universal validity claims. This is, of course, not true of medicine as a scientific discipline; qua research it is oriented not to particular values but to questions of truth. The situation is similar with aesthetics and jurisprudence insofar as they are considered as scientific disciplines. These disciplines can also be transposed into professional practices, for example, aesthetics into art criticism, jurisprudence into the administration of justice or legal journalism. They thereby become components of cultural systems of action: the artistic enterprise or the administration of justice. These systems, however, unlike the professional practice of medicine, are not oriented to particular values, such as "health" but to systems of knowledge that have been differentiated out under one or another of the universal validity claims.[34]

Habermas maintains that "the unity of rationality in the multiplicity of value spheres rationalized according to inner logics is secured precisely at the formal level of the argumentative redemption of validity claims."[35] Given his admission that "arguments play different roles with different degrees of discursive binding force" depending on whether they are cognitive, normative, aesthetic, evaluative, or therapeutic, such a claim can hardly be expected to carry much conviction. Moreover, his more recent attempts to develop a holistic model of social criticism centering on the unifying forces of aesthetic rationality are not easily reconcilable with his assertion that health is a particular value. For if health is a balanced interplay and interpenetration of vital functions, as Habermas sometimes suggests it is, then it is essentially related to that integral aesthetic harmony or rationality of everyday experience celebrated by Dewey and first-generation critical theorists—a notion whose significance is revealed only in light of Habermas's theory of selective rationalization.

HABERMAS'S THEORY OF RATIONALIZATION

The rational decentering of consciousness that allows actors to adopt different attitudes with respect to different domains of reality provides Habermas with the reference points required to construct a nonselective model of social rationalization. Such a model depicts those rationalizable action systems that must not be "subordinated to laws intrinsic to heterogeneous orders of life" if the institutionalization of the three value spheres is to proceed toward healthy equilibrium. By contrast, a selective mode of rationalization results when "(at least) one of the three constitutive components of cultural tradition is not systematically cultivated (*bearbeitet*) or when (at least) one cultural value sphere is insufficiently institutionalized without a structure-building effect for the whole society or when (at least) one sphere of life prevails so far that it subordinates other orders of life under its alien form of rationality."[36] Now there are six spheres of cultural life—what Habermas calls "rationalization complexes"—in which cognitive-instrumental, moral-practical, and aesthetic-expressive types of knowledge are stabilized in permanent, cumulative learning processes, and these demarcate value spheres possessing their own inner logics and capable of being organized into professional discourses. Habermas "deduces" them in the following way. Since each world may be reflexively dissociated from the attitude in which it originates and may be thematized from the perspective of any of the other attitudes (for example, we can factually report the content of prescriptive and expressive statements), the three worlds and attitudes can be cross-tabulated to yield nine possible formal pragmatic relations.[37] The three original formal pragmatic relations (shown in table 4.1) of cognition and instrumental action (1.1), social obligation (2.2), and feeling and self-expression (3.3) can be linguistically articulated in assertions, regulatives, and expressive utterances and then rationalized in the context of theoretical, practical, and aesthetic (evaluative or therapeutic) discourses. These relations and their corresponding modes of discourse can be extended to underwrite strategic action (1.2), moral self-control and autonomy (2.3), and aesthetic taste (3.1), respectively. Only cognitive-instrumental (1.1/2), moral-practical (2.2/3), and aesthetic-expressive (3.1/3) relations are singled out by Habermas as founding areas of social life susceptible to rationalization. These rationalization complexes (shown in table 4.2) roughly correspond to the three cultural value spheres of Weber.[38]

Difficulties arise if one tries to conceive each of the above complexes as "cumulative," "continuous," and "institutionalizable" in ex-

Table 4.1. *Formal-Pragmatic Relations*

Basic attitudes	1. Objective	2. Social	3. Subjective
1. Objectivating	Cognitive-instrumental relation	Cognitive-strategic relation	Objectivistic relation to self
2. Norm-conformative	Moral-aesthetic relation to a nonobjectivated environment	Obligatory relation	Censorious relation to self
3. Expressive		Presentation of self	Sensual-spontaneous relation to self

Adapted from Jürgen Habermas, *The Theory of Communicative Action*, vol. 1, trans. Thomas McCarthy. Introduction and translation copyright © 1984 by Beacon Press. Reprinted by permission of Beacon Press.

actly the same sense.[39] Moreover, it is unclear why Habermas thinks that relations 1.3, 2.1, and 3.2 cannot be rationalized. His denial that anything "can be learned in an objectivating attitude about inner nature qua subjectivity" (1.3) puts empirical psychology and utilitarian ethics beyond the realm of rationalizable undertakings. The idea of a hedonistic calculus has long been held suspect by philosophers, but the success of experimental psychology and psychopharmacology can hardly be doubted.[40] Although Habermas acknowledges that "we can indeed adopt a performative attitude to external nature, enter into communicative relations with it, have aesthetic experiences and feelings analogous to morality with respect to it" (2.1), he concludes that "there is for *this* domain only one *theoretically fruitful* attitude, namely the objectivating attitude of the natural-scientific experimenting observer"—a view that has been challenged by McCarthy, Whitebook, and Ottmann, who in different ways have sought to retrieve a teleological reflection on nature.[41] The reason given by Habermas for excluding an expressive-aesthetic attitude toward the social world (3.2)—perhaps the most revealing of the three formal-pragmatic relations deemed not to be rationalizable and indisputably the most significant as far as the argument of this book is concerned—is that "expressively determined forms of interaction (for example, countercultural forms of life) do not form structures that are rationalizable in and of themselves."[42]

We must turn to Habermas's difficult and highly ambivalent discussion of modern art to fathom the arcane meaning of this sentence.

Table 4.2. Rationalization Complexes

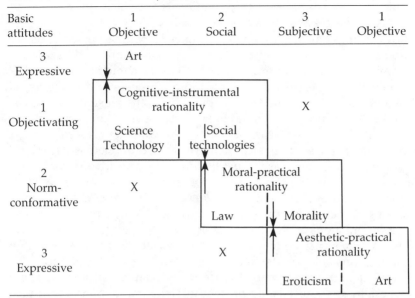

Basic attitudes	1 Objective	2 Social	3 Subjective	1 Objective
3 Expressive	Art			
1 Objectivating	Cognitive-instrumental rationality Science Technology | |Social technologies		X	
2 Norm-conformative	X	Moral-practical rationality Law | Morality		
3 Expressive		X	Aesthetic-practical rationality Eroticism | Art	

Adapted from Jürgen Habermas, *The Theory of Communicative Action*, vol. 1, trans. Thomas McCarthy. Introduction and translation copyright © 1984 by Beacon Press. Reprinted by permission of Beacon Press.

The cognitive—and, for Habermas, essentially critical—value of modern art is that it nourishes "a counterculture, arising from the center of bourgeois society itself and hostile to the possessive—individualistic achievement- and advantage-oriented—life-style of the bourgeoisie."[43] This new view reflects the influence of Habermas's mentor, Adorno; however, in singling out modern art as the aesthetic medium of critical reflection par excellence, Habermas seems to be advocating a view held by Adorno's chief rival, Walter Benjamin. Modern art—exemplified, for Benjamin, in the poetry of the French symbolists and by such avant-garde movements as Dadaism, surrealism, and futurism—is art that has been stripped of the cultic, ideological illusion (aura) of beautiful repose as a result of a technical decontextualization and juxtaposition of images in photographic, lithographic, and cinematographic reproduction and montage. It is precisely through the combination of conflicting images that society is exposed as a reified, fragmented totality and that new possibilities of synthetic perception are revealed: "The *purification* of the aesthetic from *admixtures* of the cognitive, the useful, and the moral, is mirrored . . . in the surrealistic celebration of illumination through shock effects with its ambivalence of attraction and repulsion, of *bro-*

ken continuity, of the shudder of profanization, of agitated disgust: in short in the reflection on those moments in which the bewildered subject 'transgresses his boundaries' as Bataille puts it."[44]

The rather cavalier manner in which Habermas tosses together modern art, with its shocking violation of convention and its uncompromising hostility toward the affirmative, harmonious illusion of the beautiful, and aesthetic claims to appropriateness and harmony, is disconcerting, to say the least. Explication of the tension involved in this juxtaposition can be found in Habermas's criticism of surrealism, in which he claims that dispersion of the contents of desublimated meaning arising from the destruction of form is not necessarily emancipatory and, in any case, must be linked to a positive mediation of cognition, evaluation, and expression at the level of everyday communication. But if so, why does *Theorie* deny counterculture *any* stabilizing, structure-building effect on society? And why does it assert that autonomous art is rationalizable, even though it putatively "has just as little structure-forming effect on society as a whole as do the shifting, unstable countercultures that form around this system"?[45]

Despite these disclaimers, the idea of an aesthetic structuring of social reality is unmistakably present in Habermas's more recent pronouncements, in a Hegelian rather than a Kantian vein, concerning the "potential for truth" of works of art. The following statement by Albrecht Wellmer is cited by Habermas in support of this contention:

> Neither *truth* nor *truthfulness* may be attributed unmetaphorically to works of art, if one understands "truth" and truthfulness in the sense of a pragmatically differentiated everyday concept of truth. We can explain the way in which truth and truthfulness—and even normative correctness—are *metaphorically* interlaced in works of art only by appealing to the fact that the work of art, as a symbolic formation with an aesthetic validity claim, *is at the same time an object of the lifeworld experience, in which the three validity domains are intermeshed.*[46]

On this reading, art's potential for truth would denote a kind of learning process, based, if you will, on a mediating, or dereifying, reflection "in the sense of a concentrically expanding, advancing exploration of a realm of possibilities," rather than "in the sense of an accumulation of epistemic *contents*." In contrast to Benjamin's notion of modern art as "concentrated distraction" or social critique that "remains unassimilated in the interpretative achievements of pragmatic, epistemic, and moral mastery of the demands and challenges of everyday situations," artistic truth articulates the intention of "redeeming a promise of happiness" whose "superabundance radiates beyond art."[47] Here we find Habermas affirming the other side of Benjamin's "rescuing criticism," whose aim was to preserve the primal power of nature in language, its allegorical relationship to mundane suffering and happiness (Nietzsche's eternal return of the same), and to release it from the bondage of esoteric, autonomous art.[48] As against the "false *Aufhebung* of art into life" effected by the precipitous "liquidation of appearance" contained in so much surrealist art, the determinate negation, or mediation, of artistic truth "reaches into our cognitive interpretations and normative expectations and transforms the *totality* in which these moments are related to each other. In this respect, modern art harbors a utopia that becomes a reality to the degree that the *mimetic powers* sublimated in the work of art find resonance in the *mimetic relations of a balanced and undistorted intersubjectivity of everyday life.*"[49] I shall later argue that the critical task which Habermas now sets for himself can no longer be justified independently of this aesthetic sensitivity.

CHAPTER FIVE

From Lukács to Adorno:
Rationalization
as Reification

Weber was so imbued with the idealistic spirit of Southwest German neo-Kantianism that he could not have interpreted the nihilistic tendencies at work in modern capitalism as other than a logical consequence of cultural rationalization. Marx, by contrast, saw the dehumanization and fragmentation of life under capitalism as symptomatic of the reduction of labor to an exchange value. Beginning with Lukács, later critical theorists—most notably persons affiliated with the Frankfurt School of Social Research—appropriated Marx's theory of value in order to articulate the socioeconomic implications of Weber's analysis of rationality. It is Habermas's contention that, despite their success in redefining Weber's paradox in terms of a contradiction between the economic imperatives of capitalism and the emancipatory needs of a rationalized lifeworld, they did not succeed in extricating themselves from the peculiar assumptions—rooted in the subject-object model of consciousness indigenous to German idealism—that spawned the paradox in the first place. In the following discussion we will focus on the implications of this model vis-à-vis critical theory—an aspect of Habermas's settling of accounts with his former teachers that is best dealt with independently of his critique of their diagnosis of advanced capitalist society, which is treated in chapter 10—and consider the extent to which the subject-object model of consciousness obstructed the justification not only of critical theory but of reason itself.[1]

THE IMPORTANCE OF WEBER IN THE TRADITION OF
WESTERN MARXISM

As far as Habermas is concerned, the reception of Weber by Western Marxism is nowhere more clearly documented than in Georg

Lukács's *Geschichte und Klassenbewusstsein* (1922). Lukács postulates a logical connection between formal rationality, understood as a global "form of objectivity" (*Gegenständlichkeitsform*) penetrating consciousness and social reality, and the reification of human relationships —what Marx called commodity fetishism.[2] In the first volume of *Das Kapital* Marx wrote that "the mysteriousness of the commodity form thus consists simply in this, that it reflects to men the social character of their own work as the objectified character of the products of labor itself, as social-natural properties of things."[3] In traditional societies, labor is coordinated by customary norms which regulate standards of production, occupational roles (usually inherited), conditions of exchange, and so on. It is closely interwoven with social identity and, in addition to procuring a livelihood, also serves communicative needs of self-expression and role reinforcement.[4] With the advent of capitalism, labor is no longer aimed solely at preserving the social and material well-being of the worker but becomes a commodity, or exchange value, that is reducible to a monetary equivalent. As such it is regulated in accordance with the impersonal, functional laws of supply and demand. The emancipation of labor from its former embeddedness in communicative action affords greater opportunities for its strategic deployment. Yet freedom to sell one's labor to the highest bidder is purchased at the price of one's individuality and humanity. Freedom gained is freedom lost, since by surrendering control over the production process, one is beholden to conditions of production that vitiate one's creativity, sociality, and rationality. Even the freedom to sell one's laboring capacity is illusory inasmuch as it is constrained by the need to survive and so depends on the employment opportunities made available by the fortuitous laws of the market.

Lukács found in Weber ready confirmation of his thesis that the commodity form had thoroughly penetrated all orders of life. After all, it was Weber who had observed that the form of organization characteristic of public administration was identical with that of the business firm. If Lukács could be said to surpass Weber in his understanding of contemporary social pathology, it was because of his recognition that the reification associated with the commodity form stems from a deeper contradiction between the functional exigencies of a market economy and the practical needs of everyday life. His diagnosis is still wedded to a critique of scientific, or formal, rationality, however, and inasmuch as formal rationality analyzes what is originally a dynamic totality into discrete, lifeless abstractions and oppositions, it is itself symptomatic of reification. Lukács later recanted this idealistic and somewhat romantic critique of natural science under threat of expulsion from the Hungarian Communist party. Not the least of the party's concerns was Lukács's decision to embrace a dialectical conception of reason that not only claimed to penetrate the illusion of reification by restoring the subjective dimension of social reality, but also catapulted the rank and file into a privileged position that threatened the notion of an elite cadre, or vanguard leadership.

Although he did not have the benefit of Marx's early writings, Lukács was sufficiently steeped in the writings of Hegel and the later Marx to recognize the importance of labor as a process of self-transformation and raising consciousness; the location of the proletariat at the point of *production* ostensibly enables it to perceive the contradiction between its potential sovereignty as a spontaneous social form and its perverse actual debasement to a mere appendage of the machine—or what is the same thing—between social reality (society as a dynamic totality of meaningful interrelationships rooted in social labor) and social appearance (society as a static juxtaposition of isolated things and events governed by the external laws of the market). The underlying assumption that social theory is already anticipated in practice recalls a long-standing problem in German idealism. Lukács noted that Hegel's attempt to resolve the theory-practice, determinism-freedom antinomy posed by Kant led him to seek a reconciliation of subject and object in a higher, speculative reason— Absolute Spirit. Since Hegel conceived Absolute Spirit in terms of religious, artistic, and philosophical contemplation of ideas, he quite naturally interpreted history (the realm of freedom) as itself the dialectical resolution of logical contradictions between ideas (the realm of necessity). However, because of his conviction that the logical progression of ideas could be grasped only theoretically, in retrospective philosophical reflection, Hegel concluded that prospective practice aiming at historical change must remain blind to the real meaning, necessity, and consequences of its action. But Lukács, like Marx, concluded that the antinomy of theory and practice could be resolved by locating reason on the side of practice rather than theory.[5]

Lukács's revolutionary optimism belied the rise of totalitarianism and the deterioration of the labor movement in European politics. The assumption underlying all praxis philosophy, that there exists an immediate practical unity of subject and object, action and knowledge, Habermas darkly suggests, may even have contributed to Lukács's willingness to sacrifice the integrity of social theory to the advancement of the strategic aims of the party—an abuse particularly prevalent among intellectuals who condoned Stalinist repression in the name of historical necessity.[6] But, for Habermas, as we have already seen, theoretical knowledge (truth) cannot be regarded solely as a function of action without jeopardizing the autonomy and pure reciprocity of discourse. Later critical theorists seeking to avoid both the contemplative objectivism of traditional metaphysics and the pragmatic subjectivism of science and political praxis were thus faced with a dilemma. By rejecting ultimately both conceptual (objective) and practical (subjective) attempts to unify theory and practice, they put the legitimacy of their own program in doubt. Repudiation of "identity thinking" in all its manifestations reintroduced a cleavage between theory and practice that was enlarged further by a willingness to take the theory of reification to its utmost extreme. In Habermas's view this was nowhere more clearly expressed than in the later writings of Horkheimer and Adorno.

> Horkheimer and Adorno stand before the following problem. On the one hand, they contest Lukács's premise that the complete rationalization of the world finds its limit in the formal character of its own rationality; they contest it empirically by pointing out the manifestations of a penetrating reification of culture and inner nature, and they contest it theoretically by demonstrating that even Hegelian-Marxist objective idealism merely continues the line of identity thinking and reproduces in itself the structure of reified consciousness. On the other hand, Horkheimer and Adorno radicalize Lukács's critique of reification. They regard the complete rationalization of the world as not merely an "appearance" and they thence deploy a conceptual device which permits them to denounce the whole as nothing less than the false. They cannot reach this goal by way of an immanent critique of science, for the conceptual device which could fulfill their desideratum advances a claim that still remains at the level of the grand philosophical tradition. This tradition, however—and this is the Weberian thorn in the side of Critical Theory—simply cannot be renewed in its systematic claim; it has "outlived" its own claim and in any case cannot be renewed in the form of philosophy.[7]

THE CRITIQUE OF INSTRUMENTAL REASON

Horkheimer's critique of instrumental reason betrays a close affinity to some of the central themes raised by Weber.[8] Like Weber, Horkheimer saw the emergence of formal rationality as signaling the demise of the "objective" rationality that had informed the Thomistic world view of medieval Christianity, which united cognitive, practical, and aesthetic values under a divinely preordained, objectively preexisting summum bonum. With the sole exception of truth, the various value domains were consigned to the imprimatur of subjectivity—private conviction or faith in authority—thereby establishing a link between the irrational fanaticism of Protestant sectarianism (*Glaubensfanatismus*) and later historicism (*Bildungstraditionalismus*). The logical outcome of this de-objectification of reason, the degradation of ultimate ends and values—extending eventually to truth

63

itself—to mere means in the struggle for self-preservation, culminated in the convergence of formal, instrumental, and subjective reason.[9] On the one hand, Horkheimer noticed that cultural rationalization issues in a progressive loss of meaning symptomatic of the fragmentation of society into isolated, self-interested egos lacking the moral fiber, the shared sense of value and purpose, necessary for imbuing personality and character with distinction. Thus, "the increasing formalistic universality of reason, far from signifying an increasing consciousness of universal solidarity, expresses the skeptical separation of thought from its object. . . . The triumph of nominalism goes hand in hand with formalism."[10] The abstraction of the individual as an egoistic subject of universal formal rights, on the other hand, epitomizes for him the loss of freedom emanating from social rationalization—the totalitarian hegemony of technological domination over passive objects. As Marcuse, writing at the same time as Horkheimer, put it: "In this manner, the various professions and occupations, notwithstanding their convergence upon one general pattern, tend to become atomic units which require coordination and management from above. The technical democratization of functions is counteracted by their atomization, and the bureaucracy appears as the agency which guarantees their rational course and order."[11]

Like most first-generation critical theorists, Horkheimer amplified Weber's thesis by means of insights drawn from Freudian psychology. The "rational" suppression of vital instincts for the sake of societal preservation is inherently dialectical. The internalization of repressive social authority in the form of an overzealous superego issues in a "revolt of nature," clinically manifested in an uncontrolled release of aggressive drives of the sort commonly associated with paranoid and manic behavior. Taking this as a model for understanding the mass psychology of fascism (the authoritarian personality), Horkheimer saw the reconciliation of seemingly antithetical tendencies —the annihilation of individual freedom in deference to the total authority of the state and the uncontrolled release of lawless behavior and violence—as "a satanic synthesis of reason and nature." Fascism appeals to precisely those classes who, perceiving themselves to be victims of modern society's legal protection of minorities, labor unions, and other formerly disenfranchised groups, seek a return to a monolithic order based on social homogeneity and unquestioned obedience to authority.[12]

The theory of mass culture—the term *culture industry* was later introduced by Horkheimer and Adorno to emphasize that consumer preferences were manipulated by publicity managers "from above" rather than democratically integrated "from below"—also linked social integration with the suppression of vital instincts. Adorno maintained that the sadomasochistic tendencies at the root of fascism are also operative in the consumption of cultural commodities. The consumption of art in capitalist society is geared toward providing release from the repressive regimen of work. The kind of pleasure afforded by the entertainment industry, however, is essentially anaesthetic—one is invited to "possess" momentarily the superficial thrills and luxuries denied one in everyday life as compensation for accepting the ascetic self-renunciation required by the discipline of production and consumption. Destruction of the formal unity of work that enables it to transcend fragmented social conditions likewise issues in a regression of aesthetic appreciation to the level of precognitive, sensual distraction.[13]

In *Dialectic of Enlightenment* (1947), Adorno and Horkheimer advanced what is perhaps the most radical version of the reification thesis. Not content to equate formal rationalization with the rise of capitalism, they speculate that the need to forestall gratification of basic drives to secure survival requires rational objectification of and control over self and nature. The principal thesis of this remarkable tour de force is that "myth is already enlightenment and enlightenment reverts to mythology," or simply, "power and knowledge are synonymous."[14] If myth constitutes a reaffirmation of the primal powers of collective fate, it is equally true that it enables the self to differentiate itself from, and thereby rationally control, those very same forces.[15] Enter Odysseus, the "prototype of the bourgeois individual," who practices that quaint deception of getting more out of his bargain with Polyphemus and Circe—by far the most treacherous of primal forces—than was originally stipulated.[16] But this cunning extrication from passion is purchased at the cost of incurring a new debt. Accordingly, we read that Odysseus is "delivered up to the mercy of the waves," whence he is forced to "recklessly pursue his own self-interest."[17] What Freud called the return of the repressed—the power of primal instincts to resurface in neurotic episodes—is here joined with the anarchy of production imputed to capitalism by Marx and the bureaucratic reification of political life imputed to rationalized society by Weber to produce a global dystopia in which the gods of reason devour their own children. The rational bifurcation that the autonomous self inflicts on itself in the course of individuation (self-consciousness as self-objectification) is not an isolated incident but is symptomatic of a far-reaching disenchantment that extends to nature in its entirety.

It was Nietzsche, not Weber, however, to whom Adorno and Horkheimer turned in explicating the reversion to arbitrary power as the ultimate source of valuation—albeit, not without reservations. Nietzsche's panegyric to the agonal culture of Homeric civilization, especially its glorification of natural beauty and strength, was seen by them as a harbinger of fascism. At the same time, however, they conceded that "the realization of Nietzsche's assertions both refutes them and at the same time reveals their truth."[18] Thus, they could agree with Nietzsche that the task of enlightenment—"to make princes and statesmen unmistakably aware that everything they do is sheer falsehood" and to show how even in democracy "the reduction and malleability of men are worked for as 'Progress'" was fundamentally ambiguous.[19] As Nietzsche so eloquently put it: "What an enormous price man had to pay for reason, seriousness, and control over his emotions—those grand human prerogatives and cultural showpieces! How much blood and horror lies behind all good things!"[20]

Just how much finds ample testimony in the rational "interiorization of the instincts" whereby the "soul"—what Nietzsche calls that "wild beast hurling itself against the bars of its cage"—is born.[21] The recurring motifs of Nietzsche's genealogy that resonate in *Dialectic of Enlightenment*—the relationship between exchange, justice as equivalence-retribution-revenge, guilt, punishment, responsibility, rational calculation, domination, and asceticism—are indeed ambivalent monuments to a protean will to power which can just as easily affirm life as deny it. Once again, the reversion to power as the ultimate source of valuation and, by implication, identity formation, reminds us that only a short distance separates the self-imposed legal domination of the categorical imperative from the explosive sexual violence of Sade's *Juliette*.[22] For Nietzsche, the will to power enshrined by Socratic rationalism and subsequently inscribed in modern science and Judeo-Christian morality more often than not expresses resentment toward time, a craving for eternal repose in the empty oblivion of the transcendent, and inevitably issues in a devaluation of values.[23] In response to this purely negative (passive) nihilism Nietzsche proposes a positive (active) nihilism whereby the possibilities of the past are creatively recycled in a continuous transvaluation. In place of skepticism, conformism, utilitarianism, and fanaticism—all symptoms of modern subjectivism that stifle creativity and breed weakness—Nietzsche offers a life-affirmative vision of aesthetic modernity: a Dionysian self-forgetfulness wherein linear time is suppressed through the celebration of creative spontaneity.

Heidegger maintained, however, that Nietzsche's will to power doctrine brought to its culmination the very tradition that it sought to overcome—the nihilistic subjectivism of Western metaphysics.[24] The

Frankfurt school, accordingly, could not have acceded to Nietzsche's decision to enthrone the taste and dazzling power of the artist as the measure of value, nor could they have swallowed his genealogical estimate of the superior—because more creative and original—power of the older nobility as compared to the degenerative morality of the herd. Their negative assessment of his will to power doctrine did not deter them, however, from appropriating what they took to be the core of his aestheticism—a mimetic reconciliation with nature free of domination. In the aesthetics of Benjamin, Adorno, Marcuse, and Habermas, this venerable relic of German idealism is combined with that other Dionysian trait commonly associated with the countercultural aspirations of the avant-garde—the destruction of formal unity—in a synthesis that, as Jean-François Lyotard has pointed out, could hardly be more problematic.[25]

Horkheimer's and Adorno's diagnosis of civilization thus resonates with Freud's, for the possibility of an ego possessing an identity distinct from outer and inner nature is predicated on the instrumental domination of both.[26] Having once conceded that reason, be it formal or dialectical, is impelled by a need to dominate, however, Horkheimer and Adorno were at a loss to account for the rationality of their own emancipatory critique. For, as noted earlier, Horkheimer saw modern science and its exemplification of instrumental reason as having certain important features of the metaphysics, or objective reason, that it replaces. Logical positivism and neo-Thomism are distinguished from critical theory by their acceptance of an ahistorical correspondence between conceptual system and objective reality.

Adorno's *Negative Dialectics* (1966) develops this idea further by arguing that even the dialectical rationality advocated by Lukács and other neo-Hegelians as a reference point for criticizing formal rationality is not immune to the reification syndrome. Adorno advances what in Habermas's opinion amounts to an existentialist critique of dialectical rationality. This form of rationality ostensibly abolishes the difference (nonidentity) between subject and object, universal and particular, that is necessary for maintaining the dual autonomy of human agency and nature. In some of his earlier writings Adorno had already criticized the ontological presuppositions of Heidegger's notion of historicity, Kierkegaard's concept of repetition, and Bergson's identification of lived time with *durée*, all on the grounds that to reduce human understanding to a quasi-natural regeneration of tradition—that is, to insert it in an oppressive historical continuity—deprives it of the critical distance necessary to effect a radical disclosure of revolutionary possibilities.[27] The same sentiment was expressed even more strongly by Benjamin, whose "Theses on the Philosophy of History" extolled, in Nietzschean terms, the messianic retrieval of past images which "blast open the continuum of history."[28]

In many of their later writings Horkheimer and Adorno seemed to play off instrumental (subjective) and dialectical (objective) conceptions of rationality against one another: reconciliation of spirit and nature was often invoked to offset the reifying abstraction of instrumental reason, while, conversely, the nonidentity of subject and object was enlisted in the effort to expose ideological reductions of thought and being. This approach is similar to the "self-reflection of the science" undertaken by Habermas in *Erkenntnis*, but it remains caught in an oscillation between subjectivism and objectivism. Because there was no longer any point in developing a rationally grounded theoretical system of the sort proposed by Horkheimer in the thirties, critical theory had to remain satisfied with taking aphoristic jabs at the establishment from outside the ambit of discursive reason. Nevertheless, Horkheimer and Adorno refused to follow Nietzsche in relinquishing the idea of critical rationality altogether. The paradox of such a stance was not lost on Adorno, who once conceded that "the only philosophy we might possibly engage in, after all that has happened, would no longer be free to credit itself with power over the absolute. It would have to forbid itself to think the absolute, lest it betray the thought—and it must not allow itself to be gulled out of any of the emphatic concepts of truth. This contradiction is its element."[29]

Critical theory must live disconsolately with the knowledge that its truth is ungrounded. Inherent in this situation is a contradiction insofar as the privileged status of those who proffer enlightenment to those who have fallen under the sway of ideology is itself without argumentative warrant. Subsequent attempts to establish autonomous reference points for critical rationality in a nonobjectifying, aesthetic adaptation (*Anschmiegung*) of man and nature—an endeavor that harks back to the early Marx's proposed reconciliation of naturalized humanity and humanized nature—are, Habermas notes, even more problematic.

> The paradox in which the critique of instrumental reason is entangled and which obstinately opposes even the most supple dialectic, consists in the fact that Horkheimer and Adorno would have to put forward a *theory* of mimesis, which according to their own concepts, is impossible. So it follows that the "universal reconciliation" is allowed to stand, not as Hegel still sought to explain it, as the unity of the identity and non-identity of Spirit and Nature, but rather as an almost life-philosophic (*lebensphilosophisch*) cipher.[30]

For Adorno and Horkheimer, the fact that "there is no longer any available form of linguistic expression which has not tended toward accommodation to dominant currents of thought" means that social criticism must find its inspiration in prediscursive reflection. Habermas has traced this repudiation of discursive thought back to deep undercurrents of cabalistic mysticism—such as the distinction between sacred and profane speech—which insinuated themselves early on into German idealism, most notably by way of Jacob Böhme and Jacobi's resurrection of Spinoza.[31]

This is especially apparent in Benjamin's early belief that language mediates the original, creative word of God with human understanding by elevating the lower strata of material being to the level of meaningful existence. Even after Benjamin converted to historical materialism, he continued to hold that the natural substratum of language—that is, primitive cries and gestures of animal origin—constitute a primal storehouse of meaning from which language derives its own expressive power, thus indicating a basic *correspondance* (Baudelaire) between nature and spirit. Benjamin's early fragment on the mimetic faculty, however, suggests that language is more like writing than speaking, more like a static tableau of semiological resemblances exhibiting the timeless unity of all things, than a dynamic process of communication.[32] Benjamin's influence on later critical theorists in their attempts to locate the origin of meaning and truth in the unconscious and to construe art as a kind of palimpsest, or mimetic refraction of nature through the lens of the unconscious, cannot be underestimated. According to Horkheimer, "Philosophy is the conscious striving to bind all of our knowledge and insight into a linguistic structure in which things are called by their right names."[33] This idea also appeared in *Dialectic of Enlightenment:*

> Even though laughter is still the sign of force, of the breaking out of blind and obdurate nature, it also contains the opposite element—the fact that through laughter, blind nature becomes aware of itself as it is and thereby surrenders itself to the power of destruction. This duality of laughter is akin to that of the name, and perhaps names are nothing more than frozen laughter, as is evidenced now in nicknames—the only names that return something of the original action of name giving.[34]

Finally, as Adorno notes, it is this subterranean life force which, living on in the unconscious, provides artistic inspiration with the utopian image of prelapsarian innocence, of a freedom undefiled by any need for domination.

> Authentic works of art . . . have always stood in relation to the actual life-process of society from which they distinguished themselves. Their very rejection of the guilt of a life which blindly and callously reproduces itself, their insistence on independence and autonomy, on separating from the prevailing realm of purposes, implies, at least as an unconscious element, the promise of a condition in which freedom were realized.[35]

Habermas remarks that the mimetic thought (*Eingedenken*) that is simultaneously of and in nature comes perilously close to the ontological aesthetic espoused by the later Heidegger, for whom it is being, rather than man, who speaks through poetry. This tendency is especially pronounced in the writings of Marcuse, who retained a fundamental interest in ontology from his studies of Heidegger in the late twenties and early thirties. Marcuse staunchly maintained up until his death in 1979 that reason could not be divorced from the erotic drive toward sensual (aesthetic) gratification without becoming a destructive force in the service of an unregenerate death instinct. Thus he too came to look on the mimetic mirroring of self in another that is exemplified in the erotic images of Orpheus and Narcissus as reinscribing speculative reason within the parameters of the unconscious imagination.[36]

The attempts by first-generation critical theorists to account for the legitimating warrant underlying their critical *aperçus* were never satisfactory. The school's conception of ideology critique, developed in the thirties, seemed to be trapped in an invidious historicism. Horkheimer followed the early Marx in holding that the standards of critique were immanent in existing social reality, especially as manifested in the concrete ideals of bourgeois culture. But Habermas, while accepting the Young Hegelian assumption that the ideal is implicit in the real, explicitly distinguishes between developmental logic and historical dynamic, formal conditions of rational communication and concrete, prescriptive contents, thereby circumventing historicism, at least in principle. The bitter writings of the postwar era, by contrast, seem to downplay the emancipatory kernel of the Enlightenment heritage, identifying rationality with technological domination. The total subsumption of the individual under the system of domination proves to be paradoxical, for not only are social pathology and resistance to the system left unaccounted for, but reification and social conflict are themselves seemingly elevated to the stature of rational norms.[37] The deployment of ad hoc forms of social criticism to combat the effective identity of freedom and domination was thus deprived of legitimating warrant. This was the contradiction to which Adorno alluded—a contradiction reflected in the school's hostility to both instrumental and dialectical forms of rationality.

Despite their persistent criticism of "identity thinking," first-generation critical theorists were ineluctably drawn to the higher ground of ontology, where the unconscious powers of mimetic imagination reminded them that nature could also issue in a free play of faculties quite different from the freedom born of dominating it. It is this mimetic impulse that Habermas will locate in his theory of communicative rationality—albeit shorn of its original status as a prediscursive niche for primordial reason.[38] Habermas's examination of Mead's theory of symbolic interactionism will show that the mimetic act of role playing is the principle means by which children grow into a language and achieve the competence necessary for mutual recognition, individuation, and emancipation from stereotypical role playing. Moreover, as we shall see in the next chapter, aesthetic rationality, which Habermas has hitherto described as a kind of mimesis, is rather intimately linked with communicative rationality; for it is the possibility of a rhetorical blending of distinct validity claims and domains of discourse that enables heterogeneous disciplines to "communicate" with one another in the medium of philosophy, art, literature, and everyday language.

That Horkheimer and Adorno were driven to denounce the legacy of the Enlightenment which figures so decisively in the tradition of Western Marxism was, Habermas submits, because, like Marx, Weber, and other social thinkers influenced by the subject-object model of consciousness, they could not have conceived formal rationalization on any model other than that of purposive rationality. Since Descartes, philosophers have been accustomed to explaining cognition in terms of a relationship between an isolated subject and its object. Because Descartes construed this relationship in terms of the mind's ability to adequately *represent* clear ideas possessing objective reference, he was unable to appreciate the pragmatic relationship between self-preservation, causal knowledge, and instrumental intervention that has become the cornerstone of epistemology since Francis Bacon. In considering the problem of self-preservation, German idealists extended it to include the reflexive maintenance of self-identity. The preservation of self and society cannot be achieved merely by the egoistic satisfaction of material needs, for the coordination of productive efforts necessary to sustain a level of culture also requires the normative reproduction of shared values and mutual expectations linking social and personal identity.[39]

Where German idealism went astray was in its continued reliance on a subject-object model of consciousness that conceived social and personal identity as products of self-objectification—a model whose weaknesses, Habermas submits, are well illustrated by the philoso-

phy of Dieter Henrich.[40] Henrich argues that the existential dilemma
that informs the modern struggle for self-preservation is impelled by
a spiritual need to acquire confidence in, and rational understanding
of the conditions underlying, one's existence as a knowing and acting
subject.[41] Self-certainty is achieved once one recognizes that reality
rationally comprehended by the self and stripped of its "otherness" is
reality "owned" by the self. Mind conscious of reality is mind conscious of itself; or, the act whereby an object is constituted as a rational unity of appearances perduring through change is the same act
that produces a self-identical subject of possibilities, for objectivity
and subjectivity mutually condition one another.

Henrich's attempt to eliminate this circularity by postulating an original selfless consciousness, or prereflexive locus of identity, is patently question-begging, Habermas claims, since the possibility of a
transcendental subjectivity whose identity is not constituted by objectifying reflection is unaccounted for. Such a transcendental consciousness could be understood only as a selfless process of boundary
maintenance of the sort characteristic of self-regulating systems.[42]
It was the young Hegel, Habermas reminds us, who, in criticizing
Kant's notion of transcendental subjectivity, first ventured on a communicative paradigm of consciousness. Corresponding to this shift in
paradigm is a parallel shift in the nature of action and rationality.

> The knowledge of an objectified nature and the *act whereby it is rendered use-*
> *ful* are no longer themselves taken as the phenomena needing explication,
> but rather the intersubjectivity of possible *agreement*—on the interpersonal
> as well as on the intrapsychic plane. The focus of research thereby shifts
> from *cognitive-instrumental* to *communicative rationality.* On the latter model
> of rationality, the relation of isolated subjects to something in an objective
> world that can be represented or manipulated is not paradigmatic, but
> rather the intersubjective relation which subjects capable of speaking and
> action take up when they reach agreement with one another about
> something.[43]

Mutual recognition, adoption of the other's point of view, becomes
the primary phenomenon underlying consciousness and knowledge,
replacing instrumental manipulation and self-objectification; freedom
and reconciliation supplant domination and antagonism as the definitive features of rational self-preservation. As Habermas says, "The
utopian perspective of reconciliation and freedom is adumbrated in
the condition of a communicative socialization of individuals (and) is
already built into the reproduction mechanism of the species. . . ."

As in the case of his metatheoretical and methodological exposition
of rationality, Habermas's treatment of rationalization, as contained

in the sections devoted to Weber and critical theory, is provisional. Although mention has been made of the differentiation of cultural value spheres and the concomitant differentiation of spheres of action, nothing yet has been said about the systemic differentiation of economy and state from private household and public domain—the uncoupling of media-steered contexts of instrumental action from the communicative structures of the lifeworld—necessary for reformulating and resolving the paradox of rationality. However much the commentary on Weber and Weberian Marxism succeeds in showing how the classical statement of the paradox rests on a narrow conception of rationality, it remains to be seen whether the change in paradigm celebrated by Habermas is sufficient to placate concerns about the capacity of formal rationality to provide a unitary basis for social critique. In any case, the rigid insistence on separating theory, practice, and aesthetic mimesis that informs this discussion—a bifurcation that accords well with Habermas's restitution of the rights of formal rationality against its dialectical counterpart—marks a reversion to neo-Kantian thought that is just as problematic for him as it was for his predecessors.

Habermas's account of the six rationality complexes implicit in the concept of a rational society rules out the possibility of a rationalizable aesthetic attitude toward social reality. But if the aesthetic element in social life is subsequently proclaimed to be irrational from a practical standpoint or to be merely a function of subjective expression, then the province of practical reason would appear to be reduced to that of moral argumentation. If, however, the aesthetic element in practical life is deemed to be an essential part of practical reason, then the concept of rationality would have to be expanded to include an intuitive element of taste. So construed, practical reason would involve a hermeneutic preunderstanding which, while relating to the whole of life, would not be reducible to speculative thought. The concept of aesthetic rationality, or mimesis, that Habermas has alluded to in some of his more recent writings, may well mark an attempt to break out of the subjectivistic impasse that plagues his account of aesthetics in *Theorie*.

This brings into stark relief Habermas's deviation from classical and neo-Hegelian Marxism. Classical Marxism maintains that critical theory must not be divorced from revolutionary practice, a doctrine that finds its quintessential articulation in Marx's *Theses on Feuerbach* and in the praxis philosophy of the Yugoslavian school, but one that also appears in the early writings of Horkheimer and Adorno. Yet, by and large, critical theorists have remained skeptical of attempts to locate practical reason in labor or political praxis in that these modes of action remain sullied by instrumental and strategic residues. Despite Habermas's expansion of the category of practical rationality to incorporate communication, he too seems to share this view of action.

As we have already seen, Habermas is critical of praxis philosophy because it undermines both the autonomy of theory formation (the disinterested search for truth) and the autonomy of action (the freedom to commit oneself to risky, unpredictable ventures). But he also objects to the aesthetic reconciliation of man and nature proposed by Horkheimer and Adorno as a reversion to precritical metaphysics. Only a concept of practical reason that can be fully articulated independently of action, with its inevitable strategic constraints, and aesthetic intuition, with its quasi-speculative, contemplative preunderstanding of totality, suffices for him as a possible basis for critical theory. In attempting to grasp the two horns of this dilemma, however, Habermas seems to have assimilated practical reason to communicative rationality—and more specifically, to discursive, theoretical reason.

Now if one assesses the contributions of Weberian Marxism in light of the relationship between aesthetics and practical reason discussed at the end of chapter 3, that is, the role of taste and sound judgment in evaluating particular situations, then this tradition's cool reception of formal rationality comes across in a rather different light. Horkheimer may well be right about the subjectivistic consequences of formal rationalization. Certainly, what Habermas says about the relativity of particular value contents would tend to confirm this assessment. Nevertheless, Habermas has not endorsed a more objective aesthetics of the sort that might help mediate reason and action. If Horkheimer's formulation of the problem is valid, then his solution is not as implausible as Habermas would have us believe. For Marcuse, pursuing a line of thought extending back to Schiller, the solution involves mediating reason and feeling, theory and practice, freedom and nature in aesthetic cultivation. In this respect it shares with the post-Kehre writings of Heidegger an awareness that practical reason is intimately connected to that poetic thought to which I referred earlier. On this reading, practical reason would incorporate that network of dispositions, competencies, and preunderstandings that comprise the totality of our lifeworld—a problematic that is first broached in the second half of *Theorie*.

CHAPTER SIX

*Discourse on
Modernity:
A Philosophical
Interlude*

When Horkheimer and Adorno abandoned Marxist social theory for a total critique of the Enlightenment, they were marching in step with very different philosophical tendencies—foremost among them conservative Heideggerian philosophy, with its proposed "destruction of metaphysics," and the radical Cercle Communiste Démocratique founded by Georges Bataille. These too drew inspiration from Nietzsche's critique of occidental rationality, but differed from critical theory in their rejection of the bourgeois ideal of emancipation and self-realization. That the new critics of modernity often ignore this difference is distressing enough to Habermas, but even worse, in his opinion, are the political symptoms of their wholesale rejection of reason: cynicism, apathy, narcissism, superficiality, lack of seriousness, and resignation to the rhetoric of power and conflict—symptoms prevalent among intellectual youth in Germany during the last decade.

Habermas's classification of French poststructuralism under the rubric of neoconservatism has drawn considerable fire from critics, since many proponents of this school expressing sympathy with postmodernism often regard themselves as further to the left than defenders of modernity such as Habermas. In order to disentangle some of the complexities of this dispute, we will begin with a brief examination of the connection between modernism and postmodernism on the one hand and postmodernism and poststructuralism on the other.

The term *postmodern* dates back to the late fifties, but it was not until the seventies, when it became a stylistic catchword in architecture, dance, theater, painting, film, and music, that it gained widespread currency outside literary circles.[1] It is often used to designate a break with classic high modernism, the essence of which Clement Greenberg once defined as residing in "the use of the characteristic methods of a discipline itself, not in order to subvert it, but to entrench it more firmly in its own area of competence."[2] The modernist program, as Hal Forster puts it, "pledged to maintain the high quality of past art in current production, to stem the reduction of art in general to entertainment, to ensure the aesthetic as a value in its own right; and to ground art—the medium, the discipline—ontologically and epistemologically."[3] The postmodern rebellion against the idea of formal purity and its disdain for mass culture—if one can call it that—began with the emergence of a pop counterculture in the sixties. This opposition, however, was continuous with the high modernism of the European avant-garde—especially Dadaism and surrealism—and, like them, set great store by technical advances. By the seventies, this iconoclastic revolt—exemplified in the pop culture of rock'n'roll—had begun to run its course. The new postmodernism was typified, Andreas Huyssen tells us, "by an ever wider dispersal and dissemination of artistic procedures all working out of the ruins of the modernist edifice, raiding it for ideas, plundering its vocabulary and supplementing it with randomly chosen images and motifs from premodern and non-modern cultures as well as from contemporary mass culture."[4] Conceptual art, photorealism, neo-expressionism, computer video art, *le nouveau roman*, and neoclassical music are all manifestations of this new trend, but it is in the field of architecture that its effects are most evident.

Practitioners of the International Style (Le Corbusier, Wright, Gropius, and van der Rohe) sought to revolutionize social space by opposing the aesthetics of architectural design to the decaying fabric of the inner city. Venturi, Jencks, and other exponents of the postmodern credo maintain that this modern functionalism overly reflected the image of cold, efficient, standardized production. In particular, they rail against what they perceive as an elitist denial of the past in the sculpted monumentalism of glass high rises overshadowing older, urban neighborhoods. The postmodern alternative that they promoted, by contrast, constructs out of regional vocabularies a more environmentally balanced pastiche of baroque, rococo, classical, and high modern styles—a "schizophrenic mixture," as Jencks would have it, of slow-changing traditional designs and fast-changing fashionable designs. Its monuments range from Philip Johnson's AT&T high rise, which combines a neoclassical midsection with Roman colonnades at street level and a Chippendale pediment at the top, to the fast-food consumer landscapes and billboards of Las Vegas.[5]

The defense of postmodern architecture is obviously linked to political concerns in the broadest sense. The problem of sorting out the various ideological postures of those who identify themselves as modernists or postmodernists is further complicated by the difficult question of the relative continuity or discontinuity of the modern and the postmodern. Nonetheless, Fredric Jameson has succeeded in identifying four major stances. In the pro-postmodernism/anti-modernism camp one can discern a conservative disinclination toward innovation (Tom Wolfe) as well as a progressive, populist tendency (Jencks). Lyotard, whose critique of Habermas will be discussed in the last chapter, defends a pro-postmodernism/pro-modernism position that sees the postmodern as preceding and reinvigorating the antirepresentational, sublime aesthetic of the modern. By contrast, Manfredo Tafuri takes an anti-postmodernism/anti-modernism position on the grounds that these movements substitute cultural politics for political praxis. Finally, the anti-postmodernism/pro-modernism posture identified with Habermas has its conservative counterpart in Hilton Kramer's bourgeois critique of the pop culture of the sixties.[6]

The complexity of the issue is compounded when it is recalled that postmodernism also embraces a philosophical Weltanschauung. This is where poststructuralism enters the picture. As a political movement, it struggles against the totalitarian impulse to subordinate and assimilate dissident subcultures to the dominant scientific culture. At the same time, it is opposed to many of the things Habermas criticizes: bureaucratic control, economic growth at the expense of environmental aesthetics and self-expression, and compartmentalization and disciplinary specialization. As a philosophical movement, however, poststructuralism blames this impulse toward systemic closure and social homogeneity on the rational demand for unity, purity, objectivity, universality, and ultimacy. In its endeavor to combat these "metaphysical illusions," poststructuralism has wholeheartedly embraced the method of literary deconstruction developed by Derrida.[7] But the deconstruction of rational distinctions between subject and object, knowledge and power, and validity and success, Habermas claims, undermines poststructuralism's own claim to truth.

In certain respects poststructuralism must be regarded as an outgrowth of aesthetic modernism. As Andreas Huyssen notes, "it is as if the creative process of modernism had migrated into theory and come to full consciousness in the poststructuralist text—the owl of minerva spreading its wings at the fall of dusk."[8] To be sure, its sub-

77

stitution of the text for the work of art, playful transgression of boundaries, and denial of subjectivity and history favors an aesthetic that is far removed from the high aesthetic modernism espoused by Adorno. But the same could be said of its relationship to aestheticism generally, modern or postmodern. The stylistic eclecticism of postmodernism is somewhat analogous to the deconstruction of binary oppositions, but the underlying humanism, historicism, restoration of representational art, and celebration of the signature style of the artist-architect that inform so much postmodern thinking are clearly at odds with the major thrust of poststructuralist philosophy.[9]

Having looked at the confusion that currently reigns in the modern-versus-postmodern debate and the ambiguous role played by poststructuralism, we shall now turn to Habermas's interest in the matter. Habermas distinguishes two major schools of postmodern thought whose conservatism is distinguished by its lack of reverence for the simplicity and stability of traditional society. One consists of neoconservatives such as Arnold Gehlen, who argue that the cultural values underlying modernization, subjective freedom, and democratic self-determination are exhausted, and that only the social consequences—accelerated technological advance and economic and administrative growth—remain. The other is made up of young conservatives who deny this separation of cultural enlightenment and social rationality, but insist nonetheless that the linkage between subjective freedom and reason conceals a will to power that ultimately binds the individual to the technological apparatus. Although both camps see modernization as threatening to absorb the individual in the economic/administrative system, they differ over what, if any, countervailing tendencies exist to offset this trend. Neoconservatives accept the accelerated growth of the system at the expense of social democracy and look to religious tradition and premodern artistic models to provide the meaning and dignity required for self-identity, whereas young conservatives place their hopes in the resurgence of an anarchistic, aesthetic avant-garde *à la* Nietzsche.

The challenge that these schools of thought pose for Habermas's defense of modernity are serious enough to warrant a closer look at the relationship between subjectivity and rationality. Are these two items contingently related as the neoconservatives maintain? Or are they intertwined in a dominant will to power of the sort claimed by the young conservatives? Or are they related to one another through the medium of communication? And, if the latter, what is the role, if any, of aesthetics in counteracting the fragmentation and subjectivism of modern society? For Habermas, any clarification of these issues must take its point of departure from Hegel's philosophy of Spirit.[10]

HEGEL AND THE PROBLEM OF MODERNITY

Modernity is defined by a consciousness of novelty, and it is this awareness that forms the cornerstone of Hegel's philosophy. For Hegel, the most recent stage of history, beginning with the Reformation and continuing with the Enlightenment and the French Revolution, enjoys a special preeminence insofar as the principle that it brings to explicit articulation, freedom, is the motor force of history (novelty) itself. Hegel realized that a new epoch such as this could not derive its legitimacy from the past but would have to do so from within. Habermas claims that la querelle des anciens et des modernes in eighteenth-century France over the status of artistic standards anticipated the direction that this problem would take in Hegel's philosophy. Does the model prescribed by Aristotle's *Poetics* provide a standard of criticism for all ages, or is the conception of a beautiful work of art relative? Writing after Hegel, Baudelaire grasped both horns of the dilemma. The authentic work of art, he submits, is bound to the present yet somehow breaks through the transitoriness of everyday life to satisfy, if only for a moment, the desire for eternal beauty.[11]

According to Habermas, it was Walter Benjamin, more than any other contemporary philosopher, who clarified the historical consciousness of modernity by recourse to what, in retrospect, could be described as a postmodern aesthetics of fashion. This approach to the legitimation of the modern age is diametrically opposed to that of Hegel and therefore provides a good reference point for understanding the latter. Benjamin believed that the legitimacy of the modern age was rooted ultimately in the past: "The French Revolution viewed itself as Rome incarnate. It evoked ancient Rome the way fashion evokes costumes of the past."[12] The modern age does not rigidly imitate the past from which it derives its legitimacy, nor does it appropriate the past with a view to solving the problems of the present. Rather, the past is creatively invoked to counteract "homogeneous and empty time," the evanescence of the everyday, the oppressive continuity and normalcy of the routine, in a revolutionary correspondence with the unredeemed hopes of former generations. This "redemptive criticism," so at variance, it seems, with the emancipatory thrust of ideology critique, combines a messianic suspension of time, in which past, present, and future come together (eternity as "now"), with a surrealistic disruption of objectified relations.

Benjamin condemned historicism and evolutionism (philosophy of history) for viewing the past as a series of discrete events without contemporary meaning and worth. But he also protested against the

79

self-serving appropriation of tradition characteristic of conservative *Wirkungsgeschichte*. Emancipation of the present age from the past —or, what amounts to the same thing, atonement of the present generation for its complicity in benefiting from the injustices inflicted on past generations—can occur only, Benjamin believed, through recollection (*anamnēsis*) of and thoughtful identification (*Eingedenken*) with the hopes of those whose sacrifices have paved the way for the future.[13]

For Hegel, Benjamin's view of history would constitute an unacceptable reversal of principles. Its repudiation of the idea of progress casts aspersions on the concept of modernity and renders the principle of freedom suspect. And yet Hegel was forced to admit that the idea of progress through freedom was no longer as self-evident as once it had been. The romantics had a point. The sundering of spirit and nature, freedom and necessity, faith and knowledge, feeling and reason, implicit in Kant's system of subjective idealism—for Hegel an accurate barometer of the rational differentiation that the modern spirit was then undergoing—could not be ignored. The principle of subjective reason seemed invalidated by its very opposition to the objective orders of God, nature, and society.

The young Hegel regarded subjectivism and ethical positivism as expressing polar aspects of one and the same phenomenon of separation. By stressing deference to authority and adherence to law, ethical positivism merely expressed Spirit's alienation from the very substance—universal reason—that sustained its life. Repelled by a legal necessity imposed from without, Spirit withdraws from social existence into the inner recesses of subjective faith. Spirit should overcome this alienation and become both social substance and free subjectivity in the course of secularization, and indeed, there is evidence that religion itself evolves into a more rational, humane, and worldly entity. Christianity freed itself from the legal positivism of Judaism, Protestantism eliminated the cultic fetishism of Catholicism, and Kantian rational religion overcame the dogmatism of sectarian faith. Still, reason initially appears as the negation of religion, not its fulfillment. Religion and enlightenment grow apart, so that community confronts the emancipated subject like an objective destiny. Like Rousseau, Hegel hoped that a civic (folk) religion combining reason and feeling and lending subjectivity a visible presence in the public sphere would establish at a higher level the harmonious community of the Greek *polis*.[14]

In the early theological writings reason is conceived as a positivistic power of self-objectification that subsumes particular drives and natural feelings under the repressive regime of universal moral law. Hegel subsequently extended the concept of reason, conceived in terms of the analytic faculty of understanding (*Verstand*), to incorporate a higher, speculative rationality, an intuitive power of unification (*Vernunft*). The Jena philosophy of 1804–06 developed this Schellingian conception of intellectual intuition in a decidedly new direction. The ethical totality is construed as an original unity, or intersubjectivity. If alienation occurs, it is because the communication wherein both the oppressor and the oppressed achieve freedom and identity in mutual reflection is disrupted. This resolution of the problem of modernity — grounding subjectivity in communicative reflection rather than reflexive self-objectification — was not pursued any further by Hegel. Perhaps, as Habermas suggests, the ethical community reminded him too much of the Greek polis, whose conception of political life conflicted with that of the political economists he was then studying.[15]

In any case, Hegel refused to follow the lead taken by Schiller, Schelling, and Hölderlin in developing an aesthetic alternative to religious reconciliation. He proposed instead to legitimate modernity by way of a dialectical critique of its own rational principle. Kantian philosophy postulated a subjective identity of subject and object, culminating in Fichte's idea of an abstract ego imposing its moral will on an objectified nonego. Properly conceived, the absolute ground of experience and reality is both subject *and* substance — that is, it is a process of reflection whereby Spirit *practically* (objectively) distinguishes itself from nature, only to later reappropriate it *theoretically* (subjectively) as its own. Philosophy, religion, and art merely exemplify in descending order the levels at which this truth, the dual objective-subjective unity of thought and being, is made known.[16]

It is worth noting how Hegel proposed to translate the accomplishments of aesthetic intuition and religious imagery into his *Geistesphilosophie*. In Germany the debate between the ancients and the moderns was first framed in the language of aesthetics. Schiller observed a tension between the Greek ideal of the beautiful and the ideal of the sublime, which, despite its romantic exaltation of untamed nature, testified, he believed, to a distinctly modern appreciation of the dignity of subjective freedom and progress. In the naive artist of antiquity, rapprochement between the material, sensuous impulse and the formal, active impulse occurred spontaneously; whereas in the sentimental artist of modernity it is posited only as an infinite ideal to be striven for. The supreme principle of antiquity was beauty (freedom within nature), that of modernity the sublime (freedom above nature). For Schiller, the aim of aesthetic education is to reconcile the two principles, the one aesthetic and immanent, the other moral and transcendent.

81

Like Schiller, Hegel extolled the spiritual superiority of romantic over classical art, while acknowledging the latter's unsurpassed beauty, its harmony of form and content. Romantic art is too subjective to find adequate material expression and hence transcends the sensuous medium of art in the direction of philosophy. The same movement of sublation can be seen in religion. Philosophy preserves the content of religion, the moment of reconciliation and redemption, while transcending its form, sensuous imagery. The preservation of religion is thus mediated by the subjective form of modernity, whose supreme expression is philosophical reflection.[17]

The same solution to the conflict between antiquity and modernity, Habermas notes, surfaces in Hegel's political philosophy. Modern society is still defined by a cleavage between civil society (the sphere of particular interests) and the state (the sphere of universal interests); however, Hegel does not regard civil society as the dissolution of ethical totality, since he sees the pursuit of private interests as working for the benefit of all. This optimistic assessment of modern life is qualified somewhat by Hegel's frank admission that civil society is also a sphere of trenchant social antagonisms pitting rich against poor. The destructiveness of this conflict, which threatens the property basis of subjective freedom, can be kept under control only by restricting political representation to propertied classes and balancing the legislature with a strong, impartial bureaucracy spearheaded by a monarch.[18] Reconciliation among hostile parties is achieved only at the level of philosophical reflection, where the necessity of these arrangements is seen to work for the benefit of all.

Habermas remarks that Hegel's decision to ground his conception of Spirit in self-objectifying subjectivity rather than communicative intersubjectivity may well have dictated his choice of ethical community. His model of rational society—as involving a strategic conflict of interests held in check by a bureaucratic administration—resolves the problem of modernity by devaluing everyday life and minimizing social critique; subjectivism is criticized philosophically, while people's needs for democratic community go unheeded.[19] It is this residual philosophical idealism that the Young Hegelians later sought to extirpate from Hegel's system.[20]

What began as a critique of orthodox Christianity at the instigation of David Strauss soon inspired an examination of the sensate (Feuerbach), socioeconomic (Marx), and existential (Kierkegaard) bases of religion. Like their mentor, the Left Hegelians believed that Absolute Spirit (philosophy, religion, and art), was rooted in historical practice.[21] But whereas Hegel invoked this belief conservatively, his radical followers took it as an invitation to change reality in accordance with the rational demands of the age. The practical realization of philosophy, they maintained, would require nothing less than the transformation of civil society into an ethical community held together by universal interests.[22] They rejected establishment of any community centered on folk religion, since they viewed religion, with its creeds possessing dogmatic authority, as a sphere of alienation. Accordingly, some Young Hegelians agreed with Bruno Bauer that atheism should be made a prerequisite for the possession of political rights. Marx and Hess went even further. Criticizing Bauer's espousal of universal atheism as but another form of idealism, they argued that what was required was nothing less than a revolutionary overthrow of the entire social order.[23]

In his Feuerbachian critique of Hegel's *Philosophy of Right* Marx claimed that Hegel's concept of the state was merely an illusory projection of humanity's own social essence. Citizens experience alienation not only as a conflict of interest between their particular nature and an oppressive universal Spirit standing opposed to it, but also, internalized, as a split between their true, social essence, which lacks concrete reality, and their egoistic existence as property-holders in civil society, which lacks the social formation of character necessary for self-realization. Thus, they relate to the state as Christians relate to God. State and civil society, "citizen" and "man," cease to be mere appearances or abstractions and become real, once the cleavage between them is overcome—that is, once civil society is transformed into a democratic association of social producers united by common interests. In his critique of Bauer, Marx made it clear that this change would require going beyond political emancipation or the securing of civil and democratic rights; indeed, the modern state would cease to exist as soon as its raison d'être, commercial activity (money) and private property—in short, the entire sphere of civil right, warranting freedom from outside interference and exclusion of others—was abolished.[24]

Habermas remarks that the antimodern blueprint for human emancipation outlined above rests on a communicative paradigm of rationality. Like the young Hegel, though, Marx subsequently abandoned this blueprint in favor of a subject-based philosophy.[25] We have already seen in chapter 1 how Marx's concept of labor transferred the process of self-cultivation from thought to work. In the *Paris Manuscripts* (1844) work is imbued with aesthetic content; by denying the worker any control over the product and process of labor, capitalism breaks the cycle of self-objectification and reflexive appropriation required for the free, creative realization and expansion of capacities and needs.[26]

83

There is no need to repeat the discussion of Habermas's criticism of Marx's conception of praxis presented in chapter 1, but three objections raised by him in the present context have a bearing on the problem of modernity. First, the concept of praxis straddles the line separating instrumental activity, which condones unlimited growth of social technocracy and domination, from aesthetic expression, which opposes it. Second, it implies that alienation is overcome once objectified labor is transformed into something personal and immediately identifiable; but this ignores the fact that in complex societies, social production has unintended side effects that invariably give rise to impersonal economic and administrative structures. Third, the normative grounding of praxis in philosophical anthropology or existential phenomenology proves unsatisfactory.[27] If by *praxis* one understands the production and consumption of goods apart from any communicative interaction, it is hard to conceive how this alone could generate norms regarding access to production and distribution. Moreover, the only normative goals that could be derived from productivity pure and simple would be an increase in human needs, an expansion of technological knowledge, and a heightened division of labor—criteria that are compatible with unemancipated society.[28]

Now it was precisely these structural consequences—the separation of economic and administrative subsystems from the personal relationships of the lifeworld and the heightened stratification and differentiation of functions—that the Old Hegelians defended as rational. Though expressing concern over the potential for social conflict in bourgeois society, Rosenkranz, Hinrichs, Gans, Haym, and Oppenheim had grave doubts about the viability of radical reforms. Moreover, their confidence in the power of the state to maintain order in the face of social disintegration, Habermas remarks, later found its limit in the collapse of the Weimar Republic and the rise of fascism.[29]

Contemporary neoconservatives such as Joachim Ritter attempt to retrieve the basic spirit of the Hegelian Right without deluding themselves regarding the regenerative powers of the state. They defend both the claims to exclusive validity of technological science and the relative autonomy of civil society, while assigning the state a limited role in the management of the economy. According to Ritter, the stability and progress of modern society are sustained by technological growth in production and management. This dynamic is totally detached from the historical transmission of tradition and in effect severs the relationship between past and future. Although Ritter believes that citizens owe their subjective freedom to their historical uprootedness, he concedes that they would lose their freedom and identity by being entirely absorbed into the economic or administrative system were it not for the compensatory, meaning-preserving role of religion and premodern art. This combination of scientism and traditionalism deprives social critique of any legitimating warrant and condemns modern forms of culture—avant-garde art and moral universalism —on the grounds that they are inherently destabilizing.[30] Habermas finds Ritter's ascription of a compensatory power to tradition paradoxical in view of the dynamics of modern society. If science alone possesses validity, and this validity is defined in terms of the technological success of scientific method, then the human sciences would be prevented by their own objectifying procedures from carrying out their assigned task, the preservation of tradition in the face of mounting historicism.[31]

FROM NIETZSCHE TO DERRIDA

Hegel and his followers sought to defend modernity by invoking rational substitutes for the loss of religious reconciliation. The various and sundry appeals to speculative thought, praxis, state administration, and premodern tradition were bound to fail, Habermas concludes, because they presupposed the subject-object standpoint of philosophy of consciousness. It is hardly surprising, therefore, that Nietzsche rejected these substitutes as symptoms of the very subjectivism that they were intended to combat. Like the Young Hegelians, Nietzsche believed in the power of history. In *The Uses and Abuses of History* (1873) he criticized the methodological objectivity of historicism for its emasculation of the past as an antiquarian possession of a sovereign subject. In *The Birth of Tragedy* (1871) he combined his antiquarian interest with a philological approach in an attempt to recover the mythic, Dionysian powers of regeneration capable of exploding the nihilistic indifference of the modern age. Strangely, it is not archaic tradition, but modern art that is supposed to reawaken the utopian possibilities of archaic experience. Postmodernity is modernity taken to its limit; a heightened subjectivity leads to an overcoming of subjectivity in which the *Volk*, rather than the individual, becomes the artist.[32]

At first glance, Nietzsche's celebration of Dionysus and art seems romantic rather than postmodern. Schiller had already conceived aesthetic education as a means for restoring nature and ethical community to the overly rational, overly subjective individual of modern society. Schelling's *System of Transcendental Idealism* (1800) went even further by proclaiming art (*poesie*), with its mythic reconciliation of opposites, to be the very goal of any philosophy seeking to overcome the one-sidedness of subjective idealism. It was Friedrich Schlegel

85

who set the stage for the romantic counterenlightenment. Upholding the radical autonomy of art, Schlegel questioned Schelling's postulation of an aesthetic identity of truth, beauty, and goodness. Schlegel's "new mythology" was not to be conceived as an aestheticization of rational ideas, but rather as a return to the archaic sources of social integration—the "original chaos of human nature." It was in this context that Hölderlin's resurrection of the Dionysus myth took place.[33] Seen from this vantage point, Habermas's claim that Nietzsche's originality resided less in his linking the birth of tragedy to the Dionysian chorus than in his repudiation of the romantic link between Dionysus and Christ makes sense. Whereas the romantics wanted to rejuvenate modern society, to fulfill the messianic promise of Christianity as promulgated in the Reformation and the Enlightenment —the realization of subjective freedom in solidarity with the Holy Spirit—Nietzsche rejected the two sides of this equation, transcendent God and subjective freedom, entirely.[34]

Nevertheless, Nietzsche continued the Romantic's purification of the aesthetic by identifying it with an ecstatic experience of primal nature. This heightening of subjectivity beyond the objective boundaries of reason and social convention—a transgression of values leading to the overcoming of selfhood generally—should not be confused with the nirvanic self-annihilation proposed by Nietzsche's mentor Schopenhauer, who located the death of the individual will in aesthetic contemplation. For Nietzsche the will to power, the metaphysical force that lies behind all world appearance, is essentially a creative, aesthetic potency that finds supreme expression in an artistic avant-garde and projects its own values and interpretations on experience that would otherwise be chaotic. Whatever order and meaning reality has is entirely dependent on the differing perspectives of valuating subjects. There is no reason or divine text to ground these perspectives; truth and falsity, good and evil, are distinctions that rank orders of knowledge and action solely in accordance with the criterion of life, augmentation of power. However, Nietzsche thought that the fictive projection of a world of objects, values, and subjects existing in themselves and possessing stable identities—all metaphysical illusions of science and morality—had lost whatever life-affirming value it formerly had. Having masochistically consumed itself in willing these worn-out shibboleths of modern society, the ascetic will to power can will only its own undermining. Arising from the ashes of rationalism, the creative will to power inscribed in the superman learns to rejoice in the eternal recurrence of the same, without hope of otherworldly redemption or cessation of suffering, thereby reconciling itself to the pure, selfless ecstacy of valuation for the sake of valuation.[35]

Habermas contends that Nietzsche's critique of reason is enmeshed in a self-referential paradox. If the value-creating taste of the artist is enthroned as the ultimate arbiter of true and false, good and bad, and if, moreover, it is located in archaic experience, then it cannot legitimate itself rationally. Only two strategies are possible: either philosophical critique of metaphysics and scientific objectivism, or what appears to be an opposite approach, deployment of a scientifically grounded genealogy of enlightenment that unmasks the will to power behind all values. Heidegger and Derrida adopt the first, Bataille and Foucault the second.[36]

Heidegger's "destruction of metaphysics" is of interest to Habermas in that it attempts to renew Nietzsche's Dionysian messianism but without the paradox of a self-referential critique of reason. (Heidegger credits Nietzsche with having traced the nihilistic subjectivism of the modern age back to Western metaphysics without having overcome it himself.) To do this, Heidegger had to return to the grand tradition of German philosophy and ground his critique of subjective reason in an ontological conception of truth.[37]

Heidegger's first major attack on Western metaphysics, *Being and Time*, is discussed in some detail by Habermas. Heidegger's ontological critique of subjective reason, published at the time of decline of neo-Kantian thought as a result of vitalistic (*lebensphilosophisch*) attempts to situate transcendental subjectivity within prior contexts of embodied, historical life, proceeds in three steps. First, the transcendental problem of knowledge—that is, of the subjective constitution of objects (beings)—is shown to be derivative, since scientific knowledge and objective referentiality are founded on a prior, nonobjectifying preunderstanding of a world horizon (Being) situated in concrete existence (*Dasein*). Second, the phenomenological method developed by Husserl is transformed into an ontological hermeneutic. Phenomena do not directly show themselves as they are in themselves, as Husserl thought, nor can their essence, their universal structure, be directly intuited and grounded in apodeictic evidence. On the contrary, the "thing" that is directly perceived by a theorizing subject appears initially as something embedded in a pragmatic context of possible teleological assignments. Because this referential context can never be fully thematized or made an object of knowledge but can be interpreted only as a text with inexhaustible layers of meaning, phenomenological description must be supplemented with existential analytic; for only a being that already questions its own existence can question being generally. Here the practical problem of self-deception—the need to protect against objectifying concealment, to tear away the layers of self-rationalization—becomes a methodological problem as well. The hermeneutic concept of truth is thus inextricably interwoven with that of authenticity.[38]

It is the problem of authenticity, Habermas claims, that later proved fatal for Heidegger's attempt to overcome subjectivism. Heidegger situates the problem of self-identity—the "I" as a continuous subject of experiences—within the intersubjective horizon of social interaction but does not conceive this horizon as an original sphere of communicative reciprocity. According to Habermas, he regards Being-with-others as an inauthentic mode of existence in which the "who" of *Dasein* is submerged by the "they" of *das Man*. By contrast, he sees authenticity as presupposing a radical separation from everyday social life, in which the self seizes on its mortality as a possibility for resolutely choosing its own unique identity. Socialization and individuation are thus radically opposed. In Habermas's opinion, the foundation of fundamental ontology, the authentic self, is ultimately revealed as none other than the pure spontaneity, or freedom, of the transcendental ego. The self grounds itself, and the social world, as in Husserl's *Cartesian Meditations*, is reduced to an objective field constituted by the intersecting intentions of solipsistic egos.[39]

In his later writings, Heidegger reacted against this subjectivism. First, he abandoned the project of self-grounding; being is no longer seen as referring to a transcendental structure but is associated with a contingent event that can be narrated but not grounded. Second, the historicity of *Dasein* is seen as a function of the historicization of Being itself, an "event of truth" combining disclosure and concealment. The history of Western metaphysics merely reflects this ontological fatalism; the historical fate of a society is predetermined by its collectively binding ontological preunderstanding—its metaphysics, if you wish—rather than by the freely chosen projects of its constituent members. Thus, the global domination and nihilism of Western society is attributed both to the assimilation of truth to subjective certainty, in which beings are disclosed for the first time as quantifiable matter, and to the dissimulation of Being itself, the self-concealment of a mysterious God.[40]

This raises an issue of decisive importance for Habermas: does the self-forgetfulness of Being in the technological objectification of beings signal an end or completion of metaphysics, and if so, what might this end portend? The end of an age, Heidegger proclaims, announces an apocalyptic arrival of the utterly new, whose messenger is Being itself. Habermas likens this return to an archaic experience of selflessness to Nietzsche's resurrection of Dionysus: "Just as Nietzsche once hoped for the tiger's leap into the future past of Greek tragedy from Wagnerian opera, so too, Heidegger wants to spring back to the pre-Socratic origins of metaphysics of the will to power."[41] But the destruction of metaphysics on which this critical vision is predicated cannot be grounded in discursive thought or reason, since Heidegger identifies even the subject-predicate structure of conceptual language with an objectifying will to power. The event of truth conceived in terms of disclosure that simultaneously conceals provides no criterion for resolving the problem either.[42]

The problem of grounding is traced by Habermas to the question of Being itself, which remains within the theoretical ambit of a transcendental philosophy of consciousness. The ontological problematic is tied ultimately to the epistemological problematic, which privileges truth (disclosedness) as the primary mode of experience over inter-subjectivity. This has three consequences. First, by regarding the religious need for ethical community as an ontological need for Being, Heidegger depreciates the communicative praxis of the lifeworld, which he sees as a domain of objectification and self-forgetfulness. Second, the poetic thought of the philosopher that harkens to the call of Being necessarily bypasses the empirical and normative questions raised by the social sciences. Consequently, Heidegger's critique of *das Man*, the dictatorship of public opinion, mass society, and technology, becomes just one among many dogmatic declamations belonging to the "repertory of opinions held by German mandarins."[43] Third, the poetic transcendence of the ontic, of propositional truth and conceptual thought, means that the fate of Being must be left wholly undetermined, a difficulty that is compounded by Heidegger's pseudo-sacral terminology, which identifies Being with the experience of the Holy, man with the shepherd of Being, and so on.[44]

Perhaps no philosopher has tried harder to rid Heidegger's destruction of metaphysics of its residual ontotheological transfiguration of Truth, Being, and Presence than Derrida. In his later work Heidegger often referred to language as the "house of Being," but it was Derrida, Habermas maintains, who first saw the possibility of recasting the critique of metaphysics in the nonsacral terminology of structural linguistics. Derrida is convinced that the metaphysical postulation of a transcendent ground underlying a rational explanation (*logos*) is linked to the privileging of speech over writing. Logocentrism is implicit in phonocentrism, since it is the simultaneous presence of utterance (signifier), object of denotation, and concept (signified) in the act of speech that leads to the illusion that language is a transparent medium of Being in which subject and object coin-

89

cide. Writing, by contrast, is detached from its original context and lacks a concrete situation that would guarantee an unequivocal identity between meaning and objective reference. Writing survives as the trace of an absence become desideratum; the text, like the eternal word of God, is preserved only in its lack of self-identity—that is, through its being interpreted differently in different contexts. The interweaving of texts within a changing context and the contextuality of all signs within a changing system of binary resemblances and differences means that meaning itself is elusively deferred in a play of associations. Like Nietzsche, Derrida links the self-understanding of modernity with an absence of certainty—the decentering of the subject—reflecting if not the death, then at least the absence of God. Like Heidegger, he regards truth, or revelation of meaning, as a concealment, so that every text implies its own subtext, every fragment of meaning its nonsense, every literary construction its deconstruction, and every identity its difference.[45]

What Derrida calls *grammatology* has as its principal aim the reversal of the priority of speech over writing as a model of language. Derrida defends this reversal in conjunction with his critique of Husserl's theory of meaning. In the second volume of *Logical Investigations* (1901) Husserl distinguished between signs (*Zeichen*), which possess an ideal linguistic meaning, and signals (*Anzeichen*), which are psychologically or conventionally associated with certain experiences. Signs can be expressed in propositions referring to objects; signals, which remain bound to the pragmatic context of speech, cannot. Communication is conceived as an exchange of information in which signs and signals are interlaced. The interlocutors let one another know through signals what psychic acts are intended, then intuit the meaning of the signs designated by these acts in the interior monologue of transcendental consciousness. Meaning is thus a function not of intersubjectively shared, pragmatic rules, but of private intuitions of ideal essences.[46]

Derrida criticizes Husserl's Platonism for its metaphysical equation of meaning and truth (verification), contending that Husserl's attempt to guarantee identity of meaning through intuitive evidence founders on his own theory of inner time consciousness. The simple presence of an object corresponds to an act of making present in time, an act, however, that is itself so temporal it continually loses its own identity in the constant experiential flux of protensions (that which is coming to pass) and retensions (that which has just passed). Insofar as the act of intuition is temporalized, presence is necessarily interwoven with absence, since the present overflows into a past that is no longer and a future that is not yet. Thus, within every act of identification there is a passive act of becoming other, or differentiation (Derrida's play on the homophonic words *différence* and *différance* underscores the fact that every act of identifying something as distinct (differentiation) is continually deferred or frustrated by its own temporal modification. A better basis for identity is the written word, which lies outside the temporality of transcendental consciousness. Yet it is precisely the written signifier become signified that, for Derrida, best exemplifies the differential structure of meaning.[47]

Derrida turns to Saussure and structural linguistics to further explain how all modes of expression can be regarded as forms of writing. Like Saussure, he holds that the relationship between signifier (grapheme/phoneme) and signified (concept) is arbitrary. He diverges from Saussure, however, in denying the priority of speech over the system of signifiers, by means of which each is related to all the others, as the primary context of semantic determination. This ideal, but open, system of signifiers constitutes a kind of original "arche-writing"—Derrida's expression for that *supplement*, or indefinite storehouse of excess meaning from which the traces of spoken and written language are derived. Yet, despite the structuralist substitution of writing for transcendental subjectivity, Derrida's deconstructive project remains thoroughly ensconced in a subject-based philosophy in Habermas's view. In place of Heidegger's fate of Being, one finds a retreat from public communication to an arbitrary play of signifiers, in which interpretation remains ultimately arcane: an act of private revelation, or at most, an esoteric discourse with a hidden God.[48]

Derrida's deconstructive method has the further consequence—of special interest to Habermas—of leveling the distinction between philosophy and literature, for, like Adorno's negative dialectics, it elevates rhetoric over logic. The discovery of supplementary meanings that contradict the express meaning of texts is related ultimately to the intertextuality of all texts. This repudiation of the autonomy of the text is based on three assumptions: that literary criticism is itself literature and therefore conforms to the rhetorical standards of its subject matter rather than the logical precepts of science, that there is no absolute distinction between literature and philosophy, and that there is no absolute distinction between everyday communication and fiction.[49]

Habermas objects to this leveling of logic and rhetoric, of course, and opposes the reduction of critical and communicative functions to the poetic. Because Derrida aestheticizes language, he underestimates the normative dependence of critical interpretation, cultural transmission, individuation, social integration, and acquisition of knowledge on consensually oriented speech.[50] Moreover, he fails to appreciate the complex relationships that obtain among everyday communication, the technical language of specialists, and literary criticism and philosophy, which serve to mediate "expert cultures" and lifeworld. Just as literary criticism raises specific claims to artistic truth that refer in a critical way to the lifeworld, so philosophy raises theoretical claims to truth that function in the same way. Philosophy and literary criticism accomplish their mediating task "to the degree that they rhetorically expand and enrich their special languages . . . in order to connect indirect messages to the manifest contents of utterances."[51] Habermas's belief that the rhetorical function predominates more in philosophy and literary criticism than in everyday communication is tantamount to expanding communicative rationality—which he has hitherto compared to scientific discourse in its theoretical emphasis on transparent argumentation—to include, in however subordinate a role, a poetic moment of deconstruction.

THE GENEALOGICAL PATH TO POSTMODERNITY:
BATAILLE AND FOUCAULT

We have seen that for Habermas the critique of occidental rationality undertaken for the sake of destroying metaphysics founders on a religious fetishization of Being and language. The genealogical path taken by Bataille and Foucault attempts to circumvent this idealism by scientifically tracing the cultural achievements of modernity back to their material basis in erotic experience and corporeal power relations. Bataille's general economics no doubt provided the model for subsequent explorations in this field, and its sharp divergence from the philosophy of Heidegger is amply registered in its Dionysian celebration of sacrilege.

Like Derrida, Bataille was a champion of avant-garde art and leftist politics, but unlike Heidegger, he was interested in the ethical rather than the cognitive implications of social rationalization—an interest manifest in his early study of the psychological structure of fascism (1933). Bataille sought to trace the appeal of charismatic leaders to a release of suppressed destructive energies (the heterogeneous) that he, a Marxist influenced by the functionalist sociology of Durkheim and Mauss, believed to be incorporated in a sacral realm of unproductive expenditure consisting of refuse and excrement, dreams, erotic temptations and perversions, luxuries, ecstatic experiences, violence, and madness. These subterranean forces, he adds, are exploited by the state for purposes of generating solidarity; but because they are hostile to a profane realm of productive labor and delayed gratification, they also undermine its weaker, but more rational, capacity for homogeneous, or systemic, integration. Hence, these forces must be suppressed in proportion to the rationalization of production. The "imperative form of heterogeneous existence" (sovereignty) harnesses the unconditioned freedom of divine agency to the sadistical excesses of lower life functions. Whereas prerationalized forms of sovereignty are maintained in and through the excesses of the monarch, which are directed against the lower life functions associated with the masses, the rational sovereignty of the modern democratic state is characterized by an exclusion of all heterological elements; the state therefore succumbs to anomic disintegration. Herein resides the novelty of fascism, which Bataille sees as capable of fusing homogeneous and heterogeneous elements in a manner combining the discipline and deference to authority necessary for coordinating rational production with quasi-religious feelings of exuberance and freedom. The idea that the charismatic legitimation of authority consists in such a fusion of lower nature and reason was, as we saw earlier, a major tenet of the Frankfurt school's analysis of anti-Semitism and the authoritarian personality. But whereas the members of the school continued to believe in the possibility of a mimetic fusion of nature and reason free from domination, Bataille could conceive such a unity only as an explosive synthesis of extreme excess and extreme repression. Thus Habermas remarks that Bataille's unwillingness to countenance a "happiness without power" made it next to impossible for him to distinguish the subversive, anti-authoritarian violence of socialist revolution from that peculiar to fascism, and hence Bataille's observation of "the numerous connections between them and even a kind of profound complicity."[52]

In a treatise on conspicuous waste written at the same time, Bataille implicitly criticized the Marxist equation of exchange and production, labor and self-realization. For him, production for the sake of the life of the worker is radically opposed to the production and consumption of basic goods in which subjectivity is objectified and preserved. Bataille shared Marx's conviction that for labor to become a freedom-enhancing vehicle of self-expression, it must be freed from the exigencies of biological survival. By this notion of praxis, he meant, however, waste expended on jewelry, games, wars, cults, sexual acts, and other cultural superfluities, in which subjectivity, within the sovereign freedom of its own unlimited expressivity, consumes itself. The self-objectification that occurs in labor, by contrast, is construed by him as a form of self-reification.

Bataille saw secularization as progressively excluding sacral elements from the domain of rational production. It is true that all forms

93

of religious, political, and economic domination exploit the residues of sovereignty by aligning them with the repressive function of domination within the system of social labor. But history also reveals a tendency toward social democratization in which excess is purged from the system of social labor. The rationalization of productive forces is a mixed blessing; on the one hand, it issues in the progressive reification of productive relations; on the other, the separation of heterogeneous and homogeneous elements undermines the Protestant work ethic by depriving it of its religious sanction. This contradiction, whereby the system of rational production undermines its own raison d'être, is resolved in socialist society, in which rational production is transformed into a collective vehicle for the sovereign expression of superabundant powers.[53]

The expectation that a total reification of productive life will issue in the resurrection of pure sovereign power is explained by the dialectics of general economics. In his anthropological studies of the potlatch cults of Northwest American Indians, Bataille observed that all forms of historically embodied sovereignty bear within themselves a contradiction since they require the suppression of freedom of production for the sake of freedom in consumption. In the earliest societies, taboos against death and sex, the sovereign excesses of nature, set boundaries for individuation. The obligatory social force of these de-individuating energies of destruction and copulation is derived, ironically, from the sanctioned object itself, thus giving rise to the intense desirability and repulsiveness of the sacral. The world religions remove this ambiguity from the Holy by gradually extruding all erotic and destructive accretions, thereby paving the way for ethical and cognitive rationalization. Rational acceleration of economic growth creates a new problem, however, for creation of surplus value engenders energy in excess of what can be consumed in procreation and dying, and this energy threatens to explode in catastrophic forms of wasteful consumption—war, civil violence, environmental devastation—unless a form of society emerges that will free its wealth for sovereign waste.[54]

Habermas concludes that Bataille, like other postmodernists, was ensnared in the paradox of a totalizing self-referential critique—a fact that in all likelihood led him to prefer the mysticism of poetic writing to the discursiveness of scientific treatises. Foucault blamed this lack of methodological coherence on Bataille's failure to pursue the scientific enterprise far enough. Although Foucault admired Bataille's criticism of subjectivity and his estimate of the expressive powers released in the transgression of rational boundaries—indeed, his own *Madness and Civilization* (1961) sought to vindicate the "truth" of madness along these very lines—he later rejected the depth-hermeneutic recovery of meaningful life as unscientific.

As Habermas notes, the structuralist reduction of meaning to objective differences between elements of discursive systems and the quasi-functionalistic reduction of rules of discursive formation to relations of power undertaken by Foucault shortly thereafter were already anticipated in that early work. For Foucault the dialogue between madness and reason that existed during the Renaissance was redefined by the rules of exclusion underwriting the classical age. The rational exclusion of madness from the domain of truth not only reflected a change in discursive topography, it brought with it a new set of practices—the doctor–patient relationship, surveillance, confinement, therapeutic treatment, the objectifying constitution of subjects, and so forth—that were themselves linked functionally to new constellations of power associated with nascent capitalism. In Foucault's later work reason is said to dominate the entire need structure of the organism, as well as the body politic in general. This objectivistic treatment of meaning and validity as functions of a power-based structural exclusion once again raises questions about the possibility of a scientific critique of science.[55]

Citing Nietzsche's transvaluation of the monumental, antiquarian, and critical uses of historiography, Foucault characterized his own genealogical method in terms that left little doubt as to his anti-Platonic sympathies. "The first (historical sense) is . . . directed against reality, and opposes the theme of history as reminiscence or recognition; the second is dissociative, directed against identity, and opposes history as continuity or representative of a tradition; the third is sacrificial, directed against truth, and opposes history as knowledge."[56] Nothing could be more contrary to the spirit of idealism and its fable of humanity progressing from victory to victory until it arrives at universal reciprocity than genealogical historiography, which traces the noble accomplishments of reason—liberty, justice, truth, and logic —back to a *pudendo origo*, the arbitrary installation of violence in systems of rules serving the interests of class domination.[57]

"We wished to awaken the feeling of man's sovereignty by showing his divine birth; this path is now forbidden, since a monkey stands at the entrance."[58] Nietzsche's parody of the historical subject as a sovereign being is taken up by Foucault in his treatment of man as a subject-object, transcendental-empirical doublet. The aporias endemic to humanism and the modern epistemē generally have their basis in the "analytic of finitude" first expounded by Kant, which proclaims that man is sovereign by virtue of his limitations. As a transcendental-empirical doublet, man is at once causally predetermined

95

object and spontaneous source of meaningful reality.[59] This duality is articulated further in that peculiar tension between the *cogito* and the unthought wherein the modern impulse aims at neutralizing the coercive effects of language, work, tradition, and instinct in the self-transparency of objectifying reflection without depriving itself of worthwhile motivations.[60] Humanism, finally, is caught between a retreat from and a return to primordial origins. The prelapsarian innocence of the beginning, which for Nietzsche, Heidegger, and the authors of *Dialectic of Enlightenment* antedates the Western understanding of being and truth, remains forever elusive.[61]

The image of man adumbrated above incorporates in a striking way some of the features developed by Adorno in *Negative Dialectics*, save for one difference: whereas Adorno consciously affirmed the contradiction just mentioned as the only authentic expression of a reason deprived of social legitimation, Foucault rejected it and sought to undercut its methodological presuppositions by double-bracketing meaning and validity. His first venture in this direction, entitled *The Archaeology of Knowledge* (1969), sketched out a structuralist methodology that would show how, for any discursive formation or field of knowledge, the selection of possible true, meaningful statements is a function of a system of rules determining semantic-denotative transformations and exclusions. Because the notion of "regulative function" deployed in the text played on the transcendental-empirical, prescriptive-descriptive ambiguities inherent in the image of man, Foucault seemed to recognize a need even then to supplement discourse analysis with genealogical explanation.[62] By viewing discourse against a prior background of cultural practices, the regulative function could be ascribed solely to the empirical effects of power relations, without having recourse to ideal significations of "right," "wrong," "essential," or "necessary."[63]

Foucault's methodology thus enabled him to rethink the notion of political sovereignty independent of rationalistic conceptions of legitimation and functional adaptation. Neither the liberal conception of a rationally accountable chain of command grounded in a social contract nor the Marxist conception of a hegemonic system of production is adequate for grasping the nature of political sovereignty, since normative and functionalistic perspectives invariably invoke global rationalizations of power.[64] From the nontheoretical standpoint of the genealogist, power appears as something wholly anonymous and pre-ideological that insinuates itself in corporeal habits and micro-technologies of a local nature, such as the religious confessional, the clinical examination, and the military exercise.[65] It was the fortuitous overlapping and cross-fertilization of these techniques in the nineteenth century that produced the peculiar "capillary effect" whereby power was intensified, concentrated, and extended in the more advanced strategies of detention, surveillance, behavioral conditioning, statistical measurement, classification, and therapy associated with modern "carceral" society.[66] This new type of domination—what Foucault calls "bio-power" utilizes accounting, statistics, demographics, therapeutics, and other methods to mold individuals into productive self-monitoring subjects who collude in their own manipulation as objects.

The behavioral sciences, which have played such a decisive role in the reform of penal institutions, drew upon the objectifying techniques of normalizing judgment, hierarchical observation, and examination that, already deployed in hospitals and monasteries, soon spread to schools, factories, and ultimately households.[67] The hermeneutic sciences, especially psychoanalysis, reflected the Victorian bourgeois family's preoccupation with hysteria, masturbation, eugenics, and perversion. By utilizing techniques developed in the confessional, psychoanalysis furthered the constitution of persons as subjects possessing a hidden and dangerous sexuality that needed to be brought to light, interpreted, and controlled.[68] It is largely owing to the introduction of psychotherapy into the judicial process that punishment has become detached from the juridical process of retribution or rectification of an objectively determined criminal act and made over into a highly discretionary instrument for evaluating, reforming, and thereby preempting the "deviant tendencies" indicated by the case histories of "delinquents"—a regression from formal legality that in certain respects parallels the breakdown of the German justice system as recorded by Otto Kirchheimer and other members of the Frankfurt school during the thirties.[69]

We have seen that Foucault's genealogical method enabled him to avoid inserting an empirical description of power relations in a normative conception of reason. However, a perusal of his writing shows that it is charged with such value-laden expressions as "domination," "subjugation," and "the carceral archipelago," which clearly have critical implications. Moreover, it is plain from numerous interviews and from his involvement in political struggles that he was a staunch advocate of civil libertarian and democratic reform. Nevertheless, he refused to justify this partisanship in the name of reason, preferring to situate his appeal within the counterknowledge discourse of prisoners, mental patients, homosexuals, and other social pariahs. In effect, this strategy amounted to fighting fire with fire—to mobilizing largely isolated enclaves of dissent with the aim of dismantling, overthrowing, or transforming the dominant centers of power responsible for their social outcast status. Reversing Clausowitz's famous nostrum to read "Politics is war continued by other means," Foucault left no doubt as to the true vocation of the radical reformer: not the elimination of domination per se, but its transformation into a more tolerant and democratic form.

For Habermas, who is just enough of an "old European rationalist" to bristle at the thought of might making right, the refusal of the genealogist to ground his critique in reason presents a trenchant dilemma. The genealogist is either trapped in the dialectic of humanism or, like a true positivist, is guilty of neglecting the normative dimension of social life. The supplementation of archaeology by genealogy does not dispel the transcendental-empirical, prescriptive-descriptive ambiguity that plagued Foucault's earlier account of the structural rules of exclusion, but simply pushes the problem back further by transferring the transcendental force of validity claims to empirical power relations. Moreover, if Foucault really wants to avoid "transcendental historicism" by returning to a positivistic suspension of meaning and validity, how, Habermas asks, can his work presume to claim any critical significance?[70]

Habermas is less concerned with the insouciance of a self-proclaimed antiscience that would wrap itself in the dignified mantle of established authority than with the misguided assumption that a methodological bracketing of meaning and validity will somehow assure objectivity. Marshaling Gadamer's well-known objections to historicism, Habermas argues that as long as the historian's historicity, or participation within a continuous horizon of shared meaning, remains bracketed and the interpretation of traditional validity claims is bypassed in favor of a description of their effects, the conditions necessary for a dialogue in which the historian's own prejudices are checked and the autonomy of the past preserved will be lacking.

Habermas regards his methodological reliance on philosophical hermeneutics as what enables him to avoid the paradoxes of man and reason that haunted Foucault and first-generation critical theorists. Social reification and a suspect subject-object model of knowledge have contrived to make it appear that reason is so truncated that one can achieve individuation and autonomy only by withdrawing into the inner recesses of one's subjectivity and dominating the objectifiable forces that threaten constraint from without. That Foucault and the others failed to grasp the dynamics of individuation and socialization must in part be attributed to their neglect of the communicative structure of the social lifeworld, which resists assimilation to the instrumental rationality of economy and bureaucracy. Because critics of modernity from Nietzsche to Derrida reduce the logic of communication to the rhetoric of poetic creativity and deconstruction, they end up subordinating social solidarity to creative self-assertion.[71]

Habermas is convinced that the communicative paradigm of rationality circumvents the paradoxes associated with both the image of man and the concept of reason. As for the transcendental-empirical ambiguity inherent in the image of man, he agrees with Foucault that it is language, not some trans-historical subjectivity, that provides the "transcendental" conditions for the possibility of meaningful experience. These conditions change over time, and their emergence and continuing efficacy are dependent on empirical processes. Even the universal validity claims underwriting communicative action in the modern world can be shown to have evolved in response to historical events and to have had their efficacy sustained, in large part because humanity has hitherto consented to abide by them. Because they are directly constitutive of actual speech in much the same way that rules of everyday speech constitute the logical meanings of words, their "transcendental," or "normative," force is often ignored and is by no means immune to the vicissitudes of changing custom. The paradox of man as both free and conditioned, creator and created, is likewise dissolved once it is understood that freedom and individuation are achieved only through communicative insertion within ever expanding horizons of shared meaning. Such horizons can never become fully transparent to consciousness, but always retain the implicit sense of performative competencies, or "know-how," that escape our control.[72]

THE NEW OBSCURANTISM

The philosophical discourse on modernity has as its real-life correlate the political debate over the future of the welfare state and modern culture generally. This debate is rife with ambiguities and inconsistencies—a fact that in Habermas's view is amply borne out by shifts that have occurred in the traditional boundaries separating conservatives, liberals, and radicals, the lack of clarity being nowhere more evident than in the wave of new conservatism sweeping Europe and North America.

In the United States this new conservatism began as a response by New Deal liberals to what was widely perceived at the time of the cold war to be the threat of global Communist hegemony.[73] But this defense of democratic pluralism gradually evolved into a hybrid program favoring the strengthening of executive power vis-à-vis "ungovernable" legislative bodies, resurrection of a war economy linking the military-industrial complex to governmental support, and promotion of traditional values and traditional authority as a bulwark against a new class of intellectual cynics, coupled with a supply-side economic agenda relieving the government of the need to satisfy competing demands for distributive justice. The willingness of neoconservatives to expand economic freedom and executive privilege at the expense of social equality and legislative self-determination, as well as to restrain newspapers, leftist intellectuals, decadent artists and writers, and protesters advocating civil disobedience puts them squarely on the side of those who oppose democratic pluralism, Habermas argues.[74] Even liberals like Daniel Bell who resist the totalitarian, antidemocratic thrust of the new conservatism are conservative in their acceptance of the traditional values of discipline and achievement orientation underlying the work ethic, which they feel has been eroded by the hedonism of modern culture.[75]

The idea that modern culture has exhausted itself in one-sided hedonism, formless anarchy, and cold, functional planning is addressed by Habermas in several essays on modern architecture and art. Aesthetic modernism culminated in the emancipation of art from the cognitive constraints of representation and the conventional constraints of religion and morality. However, in its most extreme form—surrealism and Dadaism—it came to question its own autonomy. Surrealists and Dadaists sought to illuminate the subconscious meaning of everyday life by shattering distinctions between form and content, reality and appearance, fiction and praxis, artifact and object for use.[76]

As we have seen already, architecture has been one of the major battlegrounds on which the modern-versus-postmodern debate has been fought. Habermas sympathizes with postmodernists who lament the utilitarian coldness of modern architecture because it violates the organic rhythms of the surrounding natural and social environment. Romantics such as Ruskin and Morris, he notes, had also complained about the purely functional, anaesthetic living spaces of factory and city in the nineteenth century. Early twentieth-century architectural movements such as art nouveau and Bauhaus reacted strongly against the dysfunctional ornamentalism that followed, which juxtaposed powerful—usually neo-Gothic or neo-baroque —exteriors and relatively banal interiors. But, Habermas adds, the organic functionalism that they advocated has since run its course, or so the critics of cultural modernity claim.[77]

According to Habermas, rejection of cultural modernity on the grounds that it is incapable of reconciling life and art is rooted in two ambiguities. First, since modern architecture straddles the line separating art from everyday life, it falls under two competing imperatives: the functional imperative to adapt form to the utilitarian exigencies of conventional, routine life, and the aesthetic imperative to adapt form to the unconventional, expressive demands of cultural modernism. Second, what is functional is itself debatable; it can refer to what meets individual need or to what best serves the economic and administrative system. Wright, Loos, Le Corbusier, Gropius, and other exponents of modern architecture took it in the former sense, so that for them, as for Plato and Dewey, what functions well also exhibits aesthetic form and vice versa.[78]

The crisis in modern architecture, Habermas submits, has its source in the conflict between life and systems functions, a conflict that is to some extent unavoidable. City planning, for example, is largely a systemic concession to modern complexity that runs counter to more traditional models of urban life. Elsewhere, however, the conflict results from a one-sided rationalization or hyperextension of the economic-administrative system into local neighborhoods. The pollution of residential areas by billboards, airports, freeways, and unsightly commercial buildings not surprisingly calls forth an antimodernist reaction, whose attempt to conceal dreary stucco interiors behind Tudor façades, for example, more often than not imitates the traditional eclecticism of the late nineteenth century. A consistent modernism, by contrast, would seek ecologically balanced styles that would harmonize organic function and form without degenerating into a superficial play of neon lights and flashy commercial strips.[79]

Can communicative rationality counteract the fragmentation of life into an aesthetic lacking social and cognitive significance, a morality detached from subjective need and objective reality, and a science bereft of feeling and moral purpose, without succumbing to a premature mediation of art and life of the sort typified by either totalitarian functionalism or formless hedonism? An answer to this question may be found in Habermas's discussion of the problem of modernity in German idealism.

The transition in German philosophy from Kant to Hegel was largely fueled by Schiller's Aristotelian reading of Kant's *Critique of Judgment* (1790).[80] According to Kant, judgments of taste raise claims to universal validity that rest on a feeling of pleasure arising from a harmonious, imaginative play of sensory and ratiocinative faculties in disinterested contemplation. In aesthetic reflection, a particular object is contemplated as an end in itself, without regard to any purposes it might serve. Its form alone seems purposive, or especially designed to elicit pleasure from us, but this is because it is seen as exemplifying a universal freedom that is not theoretically or practically necessitated by our perception or use of it. The universality exemplified in the formal representation is reflected in our expectation that

101

others will agree with us. Kant grounds this presumption of shared standards of taste, of the possibility of unanimity among all "culti-vated" persons, in a common sense existing a priori in the mind of the critic. This "psychological" interpretation of the aesthetic was seen by Kant's successors as symptomatic of Kant's general inability to re-solve the oppositions in his system between individual and society, freedom and nature, and private moral duty and public ethical life. However, it was plain to them that something like his conception of reflective judgment (involving the intuition of a universal exemplified by a particular) provided the link between these opposed moments, since, as Kant himself recognized, individual moral freedom had to be cultivated in a rational constitutional republic. Moral autonomy, they reasoned, should not be opposed to ethical community, in which everyone seeks fulfillment and self-realization. Living a life of ethical virtue implies moderation and the exercise of sound judgment in finding the universal principle that best fits the particular instance (Aristotle's *phronēsis*), but taste, not being innate, presupposes the cultivation of character. Such cultivation, however, involves partici-pating in a public community of shared values—a common sense shaped by discursive and prediscursive, or mimetic, communicative behavior.

It is in the context of this Aristotelian inscription of aesthetic judg-ment in practical life, Habermas believes, that Schiller's contribution to the discourse on modernity must be assessed. Schiller did not ad-vocate an immediate aestheticization of life but rather a restoration of an ethical totality that would protect the moral and expressive auton-omy of individuals from the atomizing, dehumanizing tendencies of bourgeois society.[81] For Schiller, the aesthetic cultivation of character and the establishment of a rational society are mutually implicative, and both, Habermas adds, are dependent on a prior framework of communicative interaction.[82]

In his writings on the philosophy of history, Kant had suggested that diffident, natural inclinations could be thought of as tending to a higher end—the development of rational faculties culminating in perpetual peace among nations—and that this harmony would be the accomplishment of a constitutional republic guaranteeing formal rights. In Schiller's opinion, however, such a constitutional republic would leave intact the division of labor and the split between civil so-ciety and state, private inclination and moral duty, nature and free-dom, a split similar to that criticized by the young Marx as well. The polarization of life into prereflective, *naturwüchsig* subcultures on the one hand and specialized enclaves of scientific reflection on the other results in double tyranny for the individual: physical coercion of the material impulse (*Stofftrieb*) over the rational striving for moral autonomy and legal coercion of the formal impulse (*Formtrieb*) of reason over the natural need for self-fulfillment. Schiller concluded that this alienation from self and others ultimately frustrates the development of faculties and invariably leads to social conflict.[83]

In ancient Greece, Schiller found what he thought was an alternative: true freedom and individual fulfillment mediated by public art, whose play impulse (*Spieltrieb*) shared in both the natural, mimetic proclivity toward beautiful harmony characteristic of the material impulse and the rational, reflective striving for sublime freedom typical of the form impulse.[84] In a rational society, labor would be transformed into recreation, thereby permitting the full realization of all faculties. This would not involve an aesthetic de-differentiation of society, since the division between physical and mental activity, labor and management, could be eliminated in accordance with an exchangeability of functions that would still permit a division of labor. At the political level, harmony of personal and public aims would be achieved through aesthetic education, or communicative interaction, in which individuals would confront one another in the mimetic play of response and counter-response. Communicative rationality would then have to be understood as including in addition to formal presuppositions of ideal argumentation the prediscursive, metaphorical play of diverse value spheres and realms of discourse in cognitive, practical, and aesthetic judgment—a rhetorical extension of language and communication that, as we saw earlier, is particularly apropos of philosophy as Habermas has recently come to understand it. To be sure, this deconstructive moment—if one can call it that—goes against the grain of the rational differentiation of value spheres exemplified in *Theorie*. But as Hohendahl, Misgeld, and others have pointed out, it is hard to see how the truth claim of autonomous art can illuminate everyday experience *and* provide insight into the proper balance among rationality complexes conducive to the good life without extending the concept of communicative rationality in this direction. Contrary to Habermas's assertion that deconstruction is merely a literary approach of a specialized discipline that has no bearing on solving problems in the lifeworld, I would argue that it constitutes that middle term in communicative rationality that, as Schiller puts it, shares in the material impulse of prediscursive life and the form impulse of reflective discourse without being reducible to either.[85] In the concluding words of Habermas, "The sociable character of the beautiful and of taste should alone prove that art conducts everything which has been sundered in modernity—the system of unfettered needs, the bureaucratic state, the abstractions of rational morality, and the science of experts—'under the open heaven of common sense.'"[86]

CHAPTER SEVEN

From Purposive to
Communicative Action
in the Social Theories
of Mead and Durkheim

The second half of *Theorie* is concerned with the function of self-preservation that was appealed to in the discussion of the paradigm shift from philosophy of consciousness to philosophy of communication discussed in chapter 5. The remainder of Habermas's treatise is devoted to examining this aspect further. Although the conclusion of Part 1 anticipates a functionalist treatment of communication in its passing reference to the peculiar contributions of language to securing the survival of self and society, functionalism, properly speaking, abstracts from the shared values, goals, and meanings that anchor these contributions. Actions, or rather systems of action, are conceptualized as objective structures whose unintended consequences are causally related to the global maintenance of the social organism via feedback control mechanisms. Part 2, subtitled "Critique of Functional Reason," may thus be understood as an attempt to develop a bilevel conception of society that assigns to the hermeneutic and functionalist approaches equal but limited roles in explaining social action.

COMMUNICATIVE FOUNDATIONS OF THE SOCIAL SCIENCES

The chief defect of philosophy of consciousness is its location of the original source of valuation and cognition in an isolated subject, thereby ignoring the significance of communicative interaction. This subjectivism was criticized at the turn of the century by linguistic philosophy and behavioral psychology, both of which are indebted to pragmatism, which conceives action and knowledge in terms of observable, shared practices. Neither movement by itself could account for the richness of social behavior; classical behaviorism neglected the inherent meaningfulness of action, whereas linguistic analysis ignored the pragmatic dimension underlying speech action. These disciplines were first combined in a single theoretical perspective in the symbolic interactionist theory of George Herbert Mead.[1]

For Habermas, Mead's theory of language constitutes a clear advance over the behaviorist semiotics developed by Charles Morris, in that it conceives identity of meaning as a function of role playing, rather than as consistency of outward responses to verbal stimuli. Mead argued that interaction based solely on instinctive responses to stimuli—what he called the "conversation of gestures"—is meaningful only in a derivative sense. The "natural" interpretation ascribed to the behavior of dogs biting one another—that they are defending themselves against attack—is not accessible to the dogs themselves but is something that might occur to a spectator seeking to relate the observed behavior to functional prerequisites for their survival. The gestures only become truly "significant" once the dogs themselves internalize them.[2]

Mead mentions two higher stages in the evolution of symbolic interaction, signaling and propositional communication, both involving the internalization of meaning. This internalization is explained as the outcome of a reflexive act whereby the self comes to understand the meaning of its own behavior as it is reflected in the behavior of others. What is decisive here is the interpretation of the other's behavior as expressing needs and interests analogous to one's own. The primitive positioning that occurs in the use of single-word exclamations, cries, and sounds (signaling) enables speakers to anticipate responses on the basis of a prior internalization of similar behavior and listeners to respond in ways that conform to the expectations of others. The advance from mechanical (stimulus-response) interaction to interpersonal relationship therefore presupposes not only the internalization of speaker and listener roles, but also the ability to distinguish communicative action (in which one addresses an alter ego) from strategic action (in which one causally influences an object). Signaling, in which a person "calls out the response in himself that he calls out in another," is not sufficient to account for this distinction, however. Only at the level of propositional communication, in which meaning is conventionally fixed by norms, can identical meaning arise.[3]

But Mead, Habermas submits, because of his reliance on a subject-object model of interaction, never distinguished sharply between the quasi-strategic manipulation of behavior that occurs in signaling and

105

the communicative coordination of action that occurs in propositionally differentiated speech. In signaling, behavioral expectations reflect prognoses founded on empirical generalizations; in differentiated speech, they reflect demands founded on intersubjectively recognized norms. The logical relationship between meaning and intersubjective validity is illustrated by Habermas with the hypothetical example of a tribe whose members have not yet advanced beyond the state of signaling. If one of them yells "Attack" in the company of the others and they do not respond in the expected way, they cannot be criticized for not having done so. The behavioral expectations of the signaler tied to this call are predictions that they *will* react in a certain way, not that they *should* do so. In the absence of such normative expectations, the meaning of the command will be understood differently by different members of the tribe.[4]

Habermas underscores the logical relationship between norm and meaning by appealing to Wittgenstein's conception of language as rule-governed activity. Wittgenstein argued that the idea of a private language is meaningless, since it would be impossible for its inventor to know with certainty whether he or she was using an expression consistently, for he or she would have only subjective feelings and memories to fall back on in deciding the issue. Without an independent criterion for testing one's beliefs—that is, without the possibility of someone else confirming or disconfirming one's use of terms— there is no way of judging consistency. And since the meaning of an expression is logically determined by its regular usage, there is thus no way of determining whether the meaning currently intended is that intended in earlier uses.[5]

Mead realized that language was the primary vehicle of socialization and coordination of action. He did not fully appreciate, however, the importance of consensual communication as the mechanism underlying these processes[6] and, consequently, was never able to account for the possibility of normative action. Nevertheless, Habermas finds his attempt to account for the possibility of socialization and coordination of action from a social psychological perspective illuminating because of its conception of the formation of personal identity and moral autonomy as a function of internalizing social roles in symbolic interaction.

Mead's discussion of the ontogenetic formation of selfhood presupposes a normative solidarity between speaker and listener. In Habermas's opinion normative solidarity precedes rational obligation (illocutionary force) and, in conjunction with the instrumental constitution of a field of objects and the subjective expression of basic needs, comprises one of three prelinguistic roots of communicative action. Although Mead never accounted adequately for the possibility of normative solidarity, he did offer explanations of the ontogenetic origin of objective perception and personal identity that Habermas finds plausible.

Mead's account of how children learn to perceive objects is similar to that of Piaget. Upon breaking away from the stimulus-response circuit, infants learn to identify properties with respect to the particular forms of resistance that they (the objects) offer in the course of manipulation. These properties are not yet fully objective, since young children have a tendency to transfer to things responses acquired in their dealings with persons. Whereas an adult usually reacts to a broken tool by casting an analytic glance over the parts, a young child may respond with feelings of anger or perhaps even betrayal. The degree of desocialization of perception is commensurate with the acquisition of language, since it is the ability to make verbal assertions that enables perceivers to acquire an objective distance from their environment.[7]

Habermas is interested chiefly in Mead's theory of socialization and its demonstration that mastery of communicative competence is necessary for the achievement of complete ego identity. Like Mead, he identifies the realization of selfhood with the progressive acquisition of reflexivity; indeed, he had alluded to the utopian dynamics of self-realization in his earlier commentaries on Hegel and Freud. Achievement of complete selfhood is not inevitable in any natural sense, and Habermas seems less sanguine today than he once was about its prospects. In *Erkenntnis* the ideal is described in terms of undistorted communication between the id and the ego—which amounts to a translation of the repressed life of the unconscious into the public language of consciousness.

Achievement of complete selfhood is thus contingent on the individual freeing him or herself from unconscious constraints through self-reflection. In turn, self-reflection presupposes a confrontation with potential critics in dialogue. Hence, the fully emancipated society is dependent on the rational institutionalization of democracy in two ways. First, people are rationally accountable for their collective destiny only to the extent that they have reflected on their needs and interests and subjected them to public critique. Only in this manner can aggressive, socially deleterious drives be controlled and freedom attained. Second, individual emancipation would seem to presuppose a nonauthoritarian, classless society, in which there is no social or political repression. For Freud and members of the Frankfurt school, such emancipation is problematic. To the extent that individuals learn to control their aggressive instincts consciously—or, as

Habermas, following Marcuse, puts it, to the degree that these needs are raised to the level of rational social needs—repression is unnecessary. But it remains questionable whether the diversion of erotic energy from reproduction to work can be effected without some social repression—a problem, I shall later argue, that bears on the relationship between reason, happiness, and the aesthetic reconciliation of freedom, nature, and society.

Before proceeding further, it will be helpful to look at how Habermas construes the relationship between socialization and personal identity.[8] The topic of personal identity is addressed in a lengthy digression, in which it is argued that the conditions required to establish the numerical identity of a person—what distinguishes him or her from others in space and time—are identical with those necessary for establishing personal identity. The numerical identity of persons is more complicated than that of physical objects, because other data regarding name, place of birth, family membership, nationality, and so forth are required. Such data refer to objective times and places, of course, but they are embedded in a personal life history whose narrative unity constitutes a vast web of interactions located in social space and time. Membership in an ethnic, national, or religious group refers to an extension that has no objectively measurable location but specifies rather a place within a social order. Similarly, one's history involves events that occur within the *narrative time* of a personal biography. Habermas concludes that this way of specifying personal identity also "permits the spatiotemporal classification of a person in a life-context whose *social* space and *historical* time are symbolically structured. . . . A person fulfills the conditions and criteria of identity on the basis of which he can be numerically distinguished from another when he is in a position to ascribe to himself the corresponding predicates."[9] Since the criteria for establishing a person's identity depend on the ability of the person in question to proffer self-identifications, they will depend on that person's communicative competence.

Prior to acquiring this competence, children possess only a natural identity based on "the time-conquering character" of the body.[10] Speaker and listener roles are acquired first through interaction with concrete reference persons (parents). In the course of maturation, children begin to identify with more abstract (universal) ethnic, national, and cosmopolitan roles, but until they begin to identify with specific vocational roles and universal moral principles during adolescence, their identity will consist chiefly of roles assigned to them by others. But once adolescents begin to take responsibility for their identity by critically evaluating role identifications that were accepted formerly without question, identity ceases to be solely a function of conventional ascriptions and becomes acquired. Differences between role and ego identity thus demarcate different criteria of personal identity. To inquire about a person's role identity is to ask what has happened to that person; to inquire into a person's ego identity, by contrast, is to ask who that person is and wants to be.[11]

Mead's theory of socialization explains the acquisition of role identity as a two-stage process. In the first stage, exemplified in play, children selectively utilize some of the responses they have learned by imitating others. By internalizing the repertory of behavioral expectations associated with specific roles, children learn to mold their feelings and interests in accordance with general norms. This marks the transition to the second, game phase, in which they learn to internalize not just the particular binary role expectations of seller/buyer, policeman/criminal, and so forth, but the point of view of all the other players. Through reciprocal rewards and punishments children acquire a social perspective (the so-called generalized other) that enables them to identify with a higher collectivity (the "we" to which both "I" and "thou" belong).[12]

Mead's theory of socialization adequately accounts for the achievement of role identity, Habermas believes, but falls short with regard to ego identity. The adolescent in whom expectations are inculcated by means of the threat of sanctions may come to affirm these expectations in an unquestioning way. The subconscious desire to avoid punishment that compels obedience is not yet purged of strategic motivations. A fully autonomous ego is one that acts solely on the conviction that such dictates could withstand rational critique.[13] Mead acknowledges this by postulating a continual expansion of role expectations that ultimately encompasses "a feeling for society in its entirety"—a notion analogous to Kant's conception of moral consciousness but interpreted in the idiom of communication.

But contrary to Kant, Mead argues that the universal validity attached to moral judgments cannot be accounted for by a formal demand for consistency, since a moral law that applied to everyone without exception might unjustly promote the particular interests of some persons over the interests of others.[14] Further, Mead rejects the sovereignty of individual conscience as the final judge of right and wrong. Practical reason is acquired, not innate. One cannot rise above egoistic particularity by bracketing in one's mind the very prejudices that have shaped one's conscience. On the contrary, expansion of one's moral outlook to encompass more universal perspectives is accomplished only through dialogue with others. The implied distinction between universal and particular interests thus leads Mead to the threshold of a communicative ethic like Habermas's, with its postulation of an ideal "universe of discourse" transcending the status quo and governed by formal procedures of equity as foundational for rational autonomy.[15]

In rational communication the social roles of "I," "thou," and "we" are transformed. The social "me" is constituted by the internalization of particular conventional roles, the "I" by the autonomous ego. Insofar as the "I" represents the unique repository of desires, feelings, and responses that distinguish one person from another, it is other than the "me," this otherness being manifested in moral autonomy and expressive creativity.[16] Yet the "I" is also dependent on the "me," first because the demand for rational moral autonomy calls forth the generalized other as an ideal consensus founded on universal interests, not just those of one's own culture, and second because the "me" and "I" denote for Habermas the complementary roles of speaker and respondent, the former proposing a speech act determined by a prior set of social expectations that the latter is free to reject.[17]

Mead's theory of the self amplifies Habermas's earlier utopian sentiments regarding the logical course of individuation, sentiments that are qualified in *Theorie*, in which it is now conceded that the capacity of the self to create its own life history is limited.[18] Our self-understanding is always refracted through the lens of an acquired role; the possibility of reflectively thematizing certain aspects of our personality requires that other aspects remain unquestioned. Furthermore, utopian self-realization is limited by economic and political constraints that condition the scope of communication from outside; language can never be a transparent medium of reflection. Finally, there may be some truth in Adorno's observation that complete freedom from the "compulsions" of acquired social identity would be purchased at the cost of "natural" spontaneity and happiness.[19]

THE NORMATIVE BACKGROUND OF COMMUNICATIVE ACTION

Mead's philosophy of mind sheds light on two of the prelinguistic roots of communicative action: the instrumental constitution of objectivity and the psychosocial formation of subjectivity, neither of which can come into being in the absence of social solidarity. Durkheim is the authority to whom Habermas appeals in tracing the formation of social solidarity. Like Kant, Durkheim equated morality with selfless obedience to impersonal authority. Based on a feeling of respect (*Ehrfurcht*), obedience commands that something be revered for its intrinsic worth and honor (*Ehre*), but at the same time dreaded for its awesome power (*Furcht*), an ambivalence which, as we saw in the discussion of Bataille, is seen in the religious separation of sacred and profane realms of life.[20] Although Bataille's interpretation of this ambivalence was heavily influenced by his reading of Nietzsche and Freud it was Durkheim's conception of the sacral, encapsulated concisely in Rudolf Otto's idea of the Holy as *mysterium tremendum et fascinans*, that led him to link sovereignty and religion. Durkheim saw this connection as problematic, however. Is religion the root of moral solidarity, or vice versa? Durkheim is unclear; the claim that religion expresses a "collective consciousness" symbolically representing society is patently circular.[21]

Habermas sees a more promising approach to the question of origins in Durkheim's ethnological studies of totemic systems, which indicate that religious symbolism and society are coeval. The most primitive religions, totemic cults, revolve around taboos against defiling in everyday usage certain objects (totems), such as plants, animals, stones, and emblems imputed to possess divine power. Such totems function as nodal points in connection with which diffuse social feelings are given concrete expression.[22] These feelings cannot exist apart from the original rites that celebrate the collectivity, since they do not represent a solidarity already in existence but actually contribute to its constitution.[23]

For Habermas, Mead's account of symbolically mediated interaction casts light on the mechanism whereby totemic rituals generate social expectations, Durkheim's theory of religious symbolism providing the key for understanding its underlying cohesiveness. Significant gestures are imbued with instinctual residues that limit their use to strategic adaptation. The differentiation of sacred and profane meaning enables symbolic interaction to break out of this adaptive circuit. Prelinguistic rituals already require postponement of immediate gratification for the sake of maintaining collective identity.[24] Individual moral autonomy, however, is a different matter altogether. Because Durkheim breaks with Mead in opposing individuation to socialization, he can explain individuation only as a function of corporeal peculiarities.[25]

Habermas attributes Durkheim's inability to account satisfactorily for individuation to his failure to make the shift from philosophy of consciousness to philosophy of language. If the emergence of propositionally differentiated language and communicative action should prove to be decisive for the possibility of a higher form of moral solidarity, then rationalization will have to be conceived as involving the elevation of symbolic interaction to the linguistic plane (*Versprachlichung*). Durkheim addresses only the legal ramifications of this process, however. According to him, the most primitive legal institu-

111

tions are in the realm of criminal justice and deal with violations of taboos. But the punishment of sacrilege is intended not so much to prevent future crimes as to restore cosmic order through the expiation of guilt—a sacral residue still seen in retributive conceptions of justice.[26] The situation is more complicated in the case of civil law, though here too compensation for damages aims at restoring a status quo ante. In archaic society access to property depends on one's standing in the community,[27] but with the advent of modern civil law a problem arises concerning how secular contracts between freely consenting individuals can be morally binding when they lack religious sanction. Durkheim finds the appeal to sanctions unsatisfactory, since it does not account for the voluntary compliance of those who, believing that they could break the law with impunity, nevertheless refrain from doing so. In such instances compliance is motivated by a sense of moral obligation sustained by a perception of justice. Durkheim follows Rousseau in construing the latter as an embodiment of a general will, definable in terms of formal democratic procedures.[28]

Durkheim's sociology of law, Habermas concludes, bears witness to the link between secularization and the evolution of language; the impartiality of religious sentiment lives on in formal legal institutions that are themselves based on discursive reason. Connections between individuation, rationalization, and propositionally differentiated language are implicit in Durkheim's examination of the structural transformation of social integration. The transition from a mechanical (segmentary) form of social solidarity, in which there is no significant division of labor, to an organic form is marked by a growth in individual moral autonomy and personal identity. In segmentary societies each individual or clan is a self-sufficient unit of production, and in the absence of economic interdependence the sole bond uniting these individuals and clans is a uniform code of conduct. The price of self-sufficiency is homogeneity, personal identity and autonomy being all but nonexistent in the single role identity of the collective. As the division of labor increases, so does the functional interdependence of members of the society. Contractual bonds linking diverse functional aggregates permit the freedom necessary for mastering complex vocational tasks. Still, functional interdependencies alone are incapable of generating solidarity without the support of a vocational ethic that presupposes the justice of contracts. Habermas proceeds to show that this moral solidarity can be given a functionalist reading with respect to propositionally differentiated language.[29]

Habermas's demonstration of the structural role of propositionally differentiated language in rational society serves to connect his earlier, universal pragmatic analysis of language with his functionalist theory of society. In particular it shows how the formal unity of cognitive, expressive, and practical speech functions is transposed into the grammatical unity of social reproductive functions: cultural transmission, individuation, and social integration. To begin with, a society's capacity to maintain a stable identity is secured only after norms and values have been abstracted from symbolic practices whose transmission is bound to ritual reenactments and have been converted into propositional knowledge capable of being preserved and modified through critical reinterpretation.[30] The possibility of a discursive testing of tradition freed from the context of action can be shown to presuppose an important structural asymmetry, which is reflected in the grammatical differentiation of language into assertive, regulative, and expressive functions. The ability to convert first-person performative utterances into third-person propositions is acquired in the learning of performative verbs; indeed, regulative and expressive utterances already contain a propositional component that makes this conversion possible. By contrast, assertive statements in the indicative mood cannot be converted into performative utterances without taking on an entirely different propositional sense.[31]

Cultural transmission is itself related to an advanced stage of individuation. The autonomy of the individual with respect to de facto tradition is likewise mirrored in a structural asymmetry. One can infer from a sincere expressive utterance what the speaker holds to be true or right, but one cannot infer from a true assertion or right prescription how the speaker feels about it or even whether he or she is sincere in uttering it. The grammatical asymmetry between what is publicly announced and what is privately intended opens up a gulf —necessary for creativity and critical reflection—between public and private realms of thought.[32]

Habermas concludes that cultural transmission and individuation are themselves dependent on a third communicative function: the consensual integration of action. We saw earlier that critical interpretation presupposes taking up a performative stance, and the preceding discussion of Mead has shown just how integral the mastery of speaker and listener roles is to the development of ego identity. The primacy that Habermas accords to consensual integration is an expression of a Kantian proclivity to elevate practical over theoretical reason, rationality being preeminently a function of accountability, of maintaining one's moral autonomy through self-reflection. "The practical self-consciousness retains in reflective self-relation a certain priority over epistemic and pathic self-consciousness. The reflective self-relation grounds the accountability of an action. . . . Although accountability is in essence a moral-practical category, it ranges over cognitions and expressions entrenched in the spectrum of validity (proper to) agreement-oriented action."[33] The primacy of practical reason has as its corollary the provenance of truth and sincerity in counterfactual moral obligation. Since no performative offer is announced openly outside the context of social expectations, propositional and expressive statements cannot of themselves motivate a hearer to accept the corresponding claim to validity. The performative meaning that transforms truth and sincerity into criticizable validity claims compelling acceptance supervenes at two levels. First, it serves to indicate that a validity claim of a certain sort can be appropriately raised, given the specific context of action; second, it announces that the claim so raised ought to be accepted, attaching to it a context-independent, counterfactual idea of validity.

Here a kind of cognitive reductionism intrudes that is every bit as invidious as the one that Habermas criticizes in Popper and others. Habermas has been content so far to trace the counterfactual sense of moral obligation to prediscursive modes of symbolic interaction. The provenance of moral obligation in symbolic ritualism is a promising point of departure for establishing the parity, if not primacy, of aesthetic mimesis as an element in practical reason. But here he chooses the reductionist path, arguing that rationalization transforms validity into a cognitive category. The demand for moral justification in its most radical form, Habermas argues, is not endemic to archaic societies, however much they may deploy a grammatically differentiated language. This radicalization is explained by Durkheim as a result of the idealizing tendencies inherent in the sacral. The ideal self-image that a society projects in its religious symbolism represents a counterfactual "agreement between minds"—the prototype of Plato's concept of truth, understood as a product of pure, impersonal dialogue. In this manner, the counterfactual category of moral validity is elevated to the cognitive status of discursively redeemable truth.[34] Simply stated, advances in cultural reproduction, action coordination, and individuation are set in motion once normative action is mediated by propositionally differentiated language. The corresponding de-immunization of religion vis-à-vis profane life subordinates theological interpretation to canons of logical consistency and truth. The discursive component of religious world views, coupled with the grammatical differentiation of language, then issues in the differentiation of cultural value spheres and in the formalization and generalization of ultimate principles constitutive of modern forms of social integration and personal autonomy.

CHAPTER EIGHT

System and Lifeworld

The second Zwischenbetrachtung is devoted to examining the distinction between system and lifeworld. The distinction is formally introduced in order to specify spheres of social reproduction (material and symbolic), which in turn designate functions of societal integration (system and social) embedded in different contexts of action (strategic and communicative). We are told that the system integrates diverse activities in accordance with the adaptive goals of economic and political survival by regulating the unintended consequences of strategic action through market or bureaucratic mechanisms that constrain the scope of voluntary decision.[1] The lifeworld, on the other hand, contributes to the maintenance of individual and social identity by organizing action around shared values, so as to reach agreement over criticizable validity claims. Given the importance of the distinction, one might expect a more definitive—and certainly less problematic—exposition of it than Habermas gives. Moreover, his tendency to identify each of the terms with specific institutions only complicates the issue. For lifeworld and system are viewed as belonging to absolutely separable realms of society, households and spheres of public access—cultural, social, and political—to the lifeworld, businesses and state agencies to the system.

The difficulties attending this interpretation of the distinction—and there are many—derive from assigning lifeworld and system to absolutely separable realms. But clearly one can no more dissociate material reproductive functions from the family than divorce symbolic reproductive functions from the business community. This overlapping of functions is acknowledged by Habermas; on his reading, the system is generated within the lifeworld as the unintended consequence of action and remains anchored to it in a normative sense. It might be best, then, to think of lifeworld and system as relating to logically distinct functions that overlap within institutions. This might comport better with the methodological way in which the distinction is sometimes made by Habermas, though it would not be equivalent to it. On the methodological reading, any action whatsoever can be viewed from two perspectives: that of social agents who participate in a communicative network of shared meanings and norms and that of an outside observer who views social behavior in terms of unintended consequences. Although this methodological distinction would entail neither logical nor ontological distinctions between spheres of integration, it would at least be compatible with them. Thus one could still hold that different domains of activity should be regulated more by one mode of integration than the other, and that the hegemonic extension of economy and state into areas of life primarily concerned with symbolic reproduction—family, school, public domain—ought to be avoided. But this line of thought presupposes the inherent rationality of an uncoupling of lifeworld and system, which is highly controversial and problematic, given Habermas's desire to recouple, if only in part, the economic-administrative system with the democratic ethos of the lifeworld. To further complicate matters, the differentiation of lifeworld and system is taken by Habermas to refer not only to a logical distinction between integrative functions carried out by all societies, but also to an evolutionary achievement—the ontological distribution of these functions to distinct frames of action—whose possibility is first established by the rationalization of the lifeworld. We will return to the difficulties that attend this Hegelian conflation of methodological, logical, ontological, and teleological aspects of the lifeworld-system distinction in chapter 10. For now we will take a closer look at the concepts themselves.[2]

THE LIFEWORLD

The lifeworld was defined earlier as the unthematized horizon of meanings that comprise the background against which particular items are thrown into relief. This background is not, as Husserl believed, constituted and unified by the intentional activity of a transcendental ego but consists rather of a preexisting stock of knowledge that has been handed down in culture and language. Like Humboldt and Wittgenstein before him, Habermas maintains that the structural limits and possibilities of language define the scope of possible understanding; the transcendental link between language and lifeworld prevents the latter from ever becoming an object of consciousness and likewise suffices to distinguish it from the idea of a formal world.[3]

A rationalized lifeworld possesses the linguistic structures that allow formal differentiation of objective, social, and subjective domains of reference. Persons relate to all three domains simultaneously; thus every action defines a complex situation, or system of references comprising objective facts, social norms, and personal experiences. Any situation is a "slice" of the totality of possible preunderstandings that have become relevant to the immediate interests of persons. The network of references may be more or less determinate, tending to either emerge from or recede into the diffuse anonymity of the lifeworld, depending on how directly they relate to the theme, goal, or plan of the situation. The relationship between situation and lifeworld is best illustrated by the process of reaching agreement on validity claims necessary for coordinating action.[4]

Prior to the emergence of grammatically differentiated speech, experience is thoroughly entrenched in performative preunderstanding; in other words, it consists of practical know-how rather than theoretical knowledge. Theoretical knowledge is born of the conversion of practical experience into propositional information for purposes of cultural transmission—a transition that presupposes an intermediate phase of understanding. Performative preunderstanding can be raised to the level of propositional knowledge without being entirely detached from the practical biographies of subjects by being woven into narratives. Narratives—including the most primitive myths—unify personal life histories around shared events, thereby contributing to the maintenance of social and individual identity. They are therefore integral to the communicative functions of cultural reproduction, action coordination, and socialization.[5]

These functions, which correspond to the structures of the lifeworld respectively designated by Habermas as culture (knowledge), society (legitimate order), and personality (individual identity), are complementary. Developmentally, they are rationalized to the extent that they permit greater structural differentiation, separation of form and content, and reflexivity. The differentiation of culture from society frees normative institutions from metaphysical-religious world views, whereas the differentiation of personality from culture and society allows individuals greater freedom with respect to the interpretative revision of tradition, participation in interpersonal relations, and self-realization. Meanwhile, domains of reference, cultural value spheres, validity claims, and procedures of argumentation are separated from the particular contents of historical cultures; formal principles of procedural justice are separated from concrete contexts of action and substantive values; and cognitive structures, competencies, and attitudes are separated from particular life histories. Finally, the need for more reflexive approaches to solving practical problems lends impetus to the emergence of specialized disciplines, to the replacement of authoritarian institutions by democratic forms of discursive policy formation, and to the de-parochialization of education.[6]

Rationalization of the lifeworld gives rise to three "illusions": that ordinary language is a transparent, veridical medium of knowledge, that communicative interaction is characterized by pure reciprocity, and that individuals are fully conscious of their motives, which function as counterfactual presuppositions underwriting communicative action. By not attending to the systemic constraints that condition life below the threshold of everyday understanding, hermeneutic sociologists, Habermas submits, succumb to the ideology that society *is* as we ordinarily *assume* it to be—a realm of unfettered freedom, individuality, solidarity, and openness. However, as long as society is equated with lifeworld, the symptoms of social crisis that pervade "rational" society—the loss of meaning, security, and identity normally afforded by culture; the lack of respect, solidarity, and motivation vis-à-vis norms, and the resurgence of nihilism, alienation, and neurosis—will remain enigmatic. To account for social pathology in terms of selective rationalization, one must first examine the genesis of those systems of economic and political action that, having broken free from the lifeworld, have come to dominate it from without.[7]

HABERMAS'S RECONSTRUCTION OF HISTORICAL MATERIALISM

We must consult Marx's theory of history before turning to Habermas's understanding of the dynamics underlying the uncoupling of lifeworld and system. Marx's theory is predicated on a logical ordering of primitive, asiatic, ancient, feudal, capitalist, socialist, and communist modes of production. A *mode of production* is defined as a definite stage in the development of productive forces and relations. Under the rubric of productive forces Marx includes the laboring power of producers, the instruments of labor, and the organization of production. By productive relations he means those forms of ownership that regulate access to the means of production and the distribution of wealth.[8]

Marx's theory is materialist insofar as it locates the dynamics of historical development in social labor. The most famous statement of this thesis occurs in the *Preface to a Critique of Political Economy* (1859), where it is introduced in conjunction with a distinction between social base and superstructure.

> In the social production of their existence, men inevitably enter into definite relations of production appropriate to a given stage in the development of the material forces of production. The totality of these relations of production constitutes the economic structure of society, the real foundation on which rises a legal and political superstructure and to which correspond definite forms of social consciousness. The mode of production of material life conditions general processes of social, political, and intellectual life. It is not the consciousness of men that determines their existence, but their social existence that determines their consciousness.[9]

Contemporary schools of Marxism disagree over the precise meaning of this passage. Orthodox Marxists generally interpret it as asserting a hierarchy of causal dependencies linking (in order of primacy) economy, polity, society, and culture. A weaker interpretation, that of Engels, states that the economic system places structural limits on changes occurring in the sociopolitical and cultural spheres. Neo-Hegelian Marxists such as Lukács, Korsch, and Adorno abandon the distinction between levels of causation (conditioning), interpreting the economic base as consisting of an essential structure that is coeval with the totality of its political, social, and cultural manifestations. Habermas rejects all three interpretations, noting that "it is not some ontological interpretation of society that is intended, but the leading role that the economic structure assumes in social evolution."[10] On his reading, "Marx introduced the concept of *base* in order to delimit a domain of problems to which an explanation of evolutionary innovations must make reference."[11] Such problems, which assume the form of a political struggle against the ancien régime, occur whenever the political and economic survival of the system is obstructed by outmoded norms.

At the heart of Habermas's reconstruction of historical materialism is a reconceptualization of the Marxian categories of social labor, productive forces, productive relations, and mode of production. To begin with, Marx sometimes seems to equate social labor with strategically coordinated action, thereby conveying the impression that revolutionary change is the outcome solely of cognitive-instrumental advances in science and technology.[12] For Habermas, on the contrary, the distinction between instrumental and communicative aspects of social labor—a distinction that is roughly parallel to Marx's separation of forces and relations of production—is necessary if social evolution is to be conceived as proceeding along the two interdependent, but logically distinct, axes of cognitive and moral rationalization. Without making this distinction, Habermas could not maintain that "advanced capitalism is certainly not characterized by a fettering of the productive forces" and that the elevation of science to discourse is "approximately" complete while denying that similar progress has been made in the moral and political arena. In his view, the reproduction of society duplicates this distinction:

> I prefer to introduce the concept of *life-world* as a complementary concept to communicative action as the same *medium* through which the symbolic structures of the lifeworld are *reproduced*. At the same time, instrumental actions, that is, interactions in the objective world, present themselves as the medium through which the material substratum of the lifeworld is reproduced, that is, through which the lifeworld develops processes of exchange with external nature. From the perspective of an outside observer who objectivates the lifeworld, these 'material exchange processes' can be analyzed as functional interconnections and as self-regulating systems.[13]

Habermas's reconceptualization of "mode of production" is somewhat more complicated. Rather than ranking modes of production solely on the basis of technological progress and organic complexity (division of labor), Marx preferred to assess them with regard to their productive relations—an approach that is congenial to Habermas's belief in the evolutionary primacy of practical rationalization. But since very few societies fall neatly into any of the seven categories listed by Marx, an alternate concept must be introduced—what Habermas calls an *organizational principle*—that is sufficiently abstract to capture four universal modes of social integration: kinship (social roles determined by gender and generation), lineage (social roles determined by family status), political office (social roles determined by general moral conventions tied to the legislative, judicial, and executive authority of a ruler), and formal law (social roles determined largely by individual preferences in conformity with formal law and procedural justice).[14]

Organizational principles, then, "consist of regulations so abstract that in the social formations which they determine a number of functionally equivalent modes of production are possible"—that is, organizational principles cannot be logically equated with determinate forms of ownership (property relations).[15] Such principles must be sufficiently precise, however, to circumscribe definite possibilities for utilizing and developing new productive forces and for increasing functional adaptation and system complexity. They determine "firstly, the learning mechanism on which the development of productive forces depends; they determine, secondly, the range of variation for the interpretative systems that secure social identity; and finally, they fix the institutional boundaries of possible expansion of steering capacity."[16] Social evolution thus involves two planes: progressive utilization of learning capacity within the institutional range of variation permitted by an organizational principle and progressive institutionalization of new levels of learning capacity.

In general, advances in moral learning condition advances in cognitive-instrumental learning, the latter, in turn, conditioning tertiary advances in the division of labor (system complexity). Only the moral and cognitive dimensions properly designate axes of "expanded problem solving potential," and even these cannot be said to issue in progress in any univocal sense, since advances in the instrumental organization of labor may be inversely related to advances in the moral sphere. As Habermas reminds us, "We cannot exclude the possibility that a strengthening of productive forces, which heightens the power of the system, can lead to changes in the normative structures that simultaneously restrict the autonomy of the system because they bring forth new legitimacy claims and thereby constrict the range and variation of goal values."[17]

Such a model of social evolution requires that certain revisions be made in Marx's materialist conception of history. The conflict between the forces and relations of production as Marx conceived it grows out of an internally generated need for technological and industrial expansion which outstrips the organizational limits mandated by existing property relations. This form of the dialectic, though valid in certain instances, is false when applied to the evolutionary advances that gave rise to European capitalism, Habermas contends.[18] In this case the development of productive forces followed, rather than preceded, the establishment of new social relations. The crisis that spawned capitalism stemmed from the inability of feudalism to permit implementation of an accumulated stock of technical knowledge necessary for solving chronic economic and political problems.[19]

Steering problems generated in the system are experienced in everyday life as identity crises. Nonstratified tribal societies are ultrastable; because they have little need to produce surplus wealth, they are under no pressure to force the principle of organization beyond narrowly circumscribed limits that permit "a seemingly ordered sequence of less fundamental innovations."[20] However, population growth, diminishing ecological resources, and the expansion of tribal boundaries through marriage and conquest may overload the integration capacity of such societies. Since their scope does not extend beyond the family unit, kin relations impose severe limitations on the degree to which an efficient, globally organized division of labor can develop. Social stratification based on lineage may provide temporary relief from problems related to population density and scarcity of land, but it remains bound to the kin system, and, as Habermas suggests, the unequal distribution of wealth that often accompanies the rise of prestige groups generates new problems of class conflict.[21]

Political organizations succeed in mobilizing the labor necessary for solving problems of scarcity, but only by increasing productivity through open repression of the laboring classes. The internal contradiction between feudal customs "which cannot explicitly permit exploitation" and "a class structure in which privileged appropriation of socially produced wealth is the rule" exacerbates the potential for class conflict.[22] Restrictions affecting occupational and residential mobility and the establishment of inflexible patterns of production and distribution hamper the development of technological and organizational innovations, and reliance on religious-metaphysical world views for ideological justification of the status quo likewise prevents the growth of cognitive-instrumental knowledge. Consequently production of surplus wealth inevitably involves a direct exploitation of labor through forced payments and conscription.

In the final analysis, class conflict can be contained only by depoliticizing the class relationship so as to conceal exploitation. This first becomes possible with the transition to a principle of organization based on bourgeois civil law. The modern state guarantees the general conditions of production by maintaining law and order, providing systems of education, transportation, and communication, and so on, while leaving inviolate the market as an autonomous mechanism of exchange and distribution. The freedom to dispose of personal property permitted by bourgeois civil law is conducive to the unfettered development of productive forces. At the same time the market relieves the political order of pressures for legitimation. Since Locke, natural law theorists have dispensed with appeals to divine authority by locating the conditions of universal freedom in the market exchange of equivalents. Bourgeois ideology thus succeeds in masking exploitation behind the impersonal façade of voluntary wage contracts.[23]

Class conflict is now displaced from the politicized arena of social interaction to the nonnormative, largely impersonal domain of market transactions. In both traditional and capitalist societies, class conflict reflects an underlying contradiction inherent in the organizational principle. In feudalism the contradiction appears primarily as a political struggle between groups who confront one another with incompatible claims to justice. In capitalism, by contrast, it appears primarily as a systemic crisis that only secondarily assumes the guise of class conflict. Thus the contradiction that formerly manifested itself as an antithesis between incompatible claims to justice now manifests it-self as an antithesis between incompatible system imperatives. The accumulation of capital is pitted against the conditions necessary for its production, consumer demand. Unlimited development of labor-saving, cost-efficient technologies leads to overproduction; accumulation of capital by fewer and fewer investors goes hand in hand with progressive impoverishment of unemployed consumers. Without able consumers willing to dispose of the surfeit of capital, the accumulation process cannot but reverse itself, the subsequent depression revealing the inherent injustice of the market and its pretension to be an impartial system of exchange. Without a functional analysis of the system of exchange (for Marx, having as its terminus a quo the labor theory of value), however, economic crises assume the fetishistic guise of natural, fated events.[24]

The dialectic of social progress outlined above presents us with a paradox. "The extent of exploitation and repression," Habermas observes, "by no means stands in inverse proportion to these levels of development." Though developmentally superior to kinship as a principle of social integration, political organization is regressive insofar as it requires class domination. Habermas refuses to identify progress with any asymptotic approximation to a summum bonum, since new levels of learning not only solve old problems but generate new ones.[25] The antinomy of reason and happiness that insinuates itself here is one that appears all the more paradoxical in light of Habermas's identification of nonselective rationalization with healthy social equilibrium, according to which, fully rational societies possess the most felicitous integration of culture, society, and personality.

Political organization solved problems arising from archaic society's powerlessness vis-à-vis nature, thereby generating the problem of maintaining legal security. Liberal bourgeois society evolved legal institutions to contain political conflict while fostering new system problems related to the expansion and distribution of value. Finally, state welfare capitalism may have succeeded in controlling economic crises only to have created new scarcities in the cultural meaning required for identity formation and motivation. It is possible, Habermas speculates, that a postmodern form of class society based on mass-psychological domination—similar to the feudal form, but "refracted" through the education system—may supersede our present society, which is based on the economic form of class domination. However, he concludes that the manipulation of behavior, motivation, and identity formation may well encounter limits in the socialization process itself; increased administration may well generate new needs for democratic participation that will serve to check it.[26]

UNCOUPLING LIFEWORLD AND SYSTEM

What remains to be said about the developmental logic connecting forms of social integration and levels of system complexity is worked out in conjunction with an analysis of the uncoupling of lifeworld and system. In his study of the division of labor Durkheim distinguished between mechanical and organic forms of social solidarity, which he correlated with segmentary and functional forms of system differentiation respectively. Unlike their mechanically integrated counterparts, modern societies are not beholden to any normative solidarity of the sort associated with a monolithic collective consciousness but are functionally integrated vis-à-vis the organic interdependence of occupations and social orders—a view in keeping with Spencer's conception of modern societies as unconscious organisms whose equilibrium is governed by the market. Durkheim disputed Spencer's claim that the stability of modern societies could be entirely accounted for by contractual relations among mutually dependent, enlightened egoists, concluding that it must be anchored in an occupational ethic whose integrating power emanates from a rational, normative consensus.[27]

One can read Habermas's explanation of the uncoupling of lifeworld and system as a vindication of Durkheim's belief that the system must be anchored in an autonomous lifeworld. Durkheim clearly perceived a tension between system and lifeworld, attributing the anomic tendencies of modern society to the inability of formal principles of morality and law to counteract the disintegrating effects of the market. To expand this thesis in the direction of his own theory of lifeworld colonization, Habermas situates Durkheim's analysis of the division of labor within the broader orbit of a theory of social evolution of the sort alluded to above.[28]

As we have seen, Habermas's theory of social evolution is based on the structural similarity between the stages of learning through which children must pass in order to solve personal conflicts and the stages of evolution through which societies must pass in order to solve social conflicts.[29] The key to understanding social evolution, as well as ontogenesis, is moral development. Typically, the moral development of a society, like that of an individual person, is uneven. Moral action and the capacity to resolve conflict may lag behind moral judgment and the capacity to handle normal interaction. Similarly, existing legal institutions and actual moral obligations may not keep pace with moral ideology or general structures of normal action. This is important to bear in mind when considering Habermas's theory of social evolution, for organizational principles are chiefly identified by means of their capacity to adjudicate conflict.[30]

In the preceding chapter we saw that there was a correspondence between levels of communicative competence and levels of role behavior. These levels, in turn, correspond to preconventional, conventional, and postconventional stages of moral development. The least developed organizational principle (kinship) corresponds to preconventional moral consciousness. Kohlberg mentions two levels of preconventional morality: that of obedience and punishment orientation, characterized by "ego-centric deference to superior power, or prestige," and that of instrumental hedonism, described as involving "orientation to exchange and reciprocity" ("You scratch my back, I'll scratch yours"). At this stage, the child has yet to distinguish between actions, motives, and consequences.[31]

Kinship institutions, which define social roles ranging over gender, generation, and lineage, combine aspects of both levels. Prohibition of sexual intercourse between parents and children and between brothers and sisters (incest taboo) helps to contain strife, and kinship prescribes "amity" among kin. Owing to the flexibility of the mechanism, virtually anyone can be admitted to the privileged sphere of social intimacy, territorial and tribal boundaries notwithstanding. In this way exchange of women between different tribes establishes reciprocity and harmony. However, there are no independent legal, judicial, or executive institutions that can be called on to resolve conflict when it does arise.[32] Third-party arbitration, such as it is, does not extend much beyond restoring the status quo ante through restitution, with little regard for subtle distinctions between civil and criminal offenses, intentions, and consequences. Because the arbitrator's authority rests entirely on personal prestige, there is nothing to prevent further feuding in the absence of any voluntary settlement except for the departure of the numerically weaker party.[33]

Lineage does not represent an appreciable advance over kinship, save for its incorporation of a nonpolitical stratification of prestige groups. It seems to be cognate with the intermediary societies mentioned in Habermas's earlier essays that straddle the line separating preconventional morality from the "good boy" stage of conventional morality characterized by orientation toward approval by helping others and by social conformity.[34] Habermas speculates that under suitable conditions, such as construction of an irrigation project or a victorious mobilization of the population for purposes of conquest or defense, the privileges accorded temporarily to some persons or families due to lineage might have become permanent. On this reading, leaders could have been empowered "to adjudicate cases of conflict, no longer according to the concrete distribution of power, but according to socially recognized norms grounded in tradition."[35]

At the second stage of conventional morality characteristic of politically organized societies oriented toward law and order, motives are assessed independently of consequences, and reciprocity is elevated to the rank of customary duties enjoining obedience to authority. Political societies delegate authority on the basis of legitimate transfer of power rather than descent. Although criminal and civil law are distinguished, culpability is linked to intention, and punishment is regarded as retribution (justice), legal and executive powers not having yet been separated from ethical custom and the authority of the office-holder.[36] Only formal law embodying principles of postconventional morality manages to free itself from ethical tradition and political power and become an impartial framework guaranteeing individual freedom and popular sovereignty.[37]

The systemic complexity of institutional structures parallels the rationalization of the lifeworld—that is, the differentiation of culture, society, and personality. In societies integrated by kinship there is no uncoupling of lifeworld and system. Kinship not only determines the assignment of roles and tasks (the division of labor) within the domestic economy but also defines the nature of exchange between different social groups. This becomes evident upon examining the two mechanisms of systemic differentiation that occur at this level.[38] Tribal societies are economically self-sufficient; production is limited to what is required for basic consumption, and in general, no household can produce anything that others cannot also produce. Nevertheless, one can observe an incipient division of labor, stemming from the need to produce goods of high quality for exchange—a need rooted in social rather than economic exigencies. As population grows, the extension of tribal boundaries through intermarriage leads to a network of reciprocity in which goods are exchanged as proxies for women.[39]

By horizontally expanding the number of homogeneous units through marriage, exchange—the first mechanism of system differentiation—permits segmentary differentiation. Functional differentiation, by contrast, is impelled by the need to organize complex activities vis-à-vis vertical stratifications of power. The exercise of power—the second mechanism of system differentiation—initially devolves on persons by virtue of status, which is determined by lineage. Resting on personal prestige, such authority commands neither the recognition nor the means necessary for exercising effective political power. Though status represents the first step toward organizing society as a functional system, it too, ultimately, remains entrenched in the kin structures of the lifeworld.[40] Consequently, it does not yet constitute an independent systemic function of integration.

Uncoupling of lifeworld and system first occurs in politically stratified class societies organized around a state. Once positions of power are detached from the kinship system and annexed to political office—the third mechanism of system differentiation—legislative, judicial, and executive functions become organized formally. The state now requires ideological justification for a monopoly of power, the legitimate exercise of which is increasingly detached from the natural prestige of birth and is enhanced by distribution of political and economic privileges to loyal office-holders.[41] The uncoupling of lifeworld and system is complete under a regime of formal law. The freedom to enter into contracts for private gain has the unintended consequence of transforming capital and labor into monetary exchange media—the fourth mechanism of system differentiation. The market is thus elevated to the status of a self-regulating system that distributes commodities in accordance with the laws of supply and demand.[42]

Thus system integration is conditioned, but not necessitated, by the rationalization of the lifeworld. Prior to the emergence of a rationalized lifeworld, system integration is subordinated to social integration. With the advent of a class society, this relationship is reversed, at least in part, and the system becomes relatively independent of the lifeworld, increasingly imposing restrictions on it. Under advanced capitalism the lifeworld is gradually reduced to a satellite of the system.[43] Paradoxically, the mechanism by which whole areas of life are transferred to the system—what Habermas, following Parsons, calls *value generalization*—appears to be a direct outgrowth of rationalization.

Value generalization is the process by which moral and legal relations acquire an increasingly universal scope through formalization. The personal prestige that is decisive for securing compliance in egalitarian societies is generalized in hierarchical societies in the form of group status. Customs and legal edicts of the sort that accompany political office rise further still above the particularity of social factions, only to have their validity relativized by formal principles of procedural justice.[44] But Habermas sees two contrary tendencies stemming from value generalization. On the one hand, consensus-oriented communication becomes so general in its application that every interaction increasingly requires immediate justification and lengthy negotiation. But this proves impractical in many situations, since we are not always in a position to confront those with whom we communicate or to justify all the assumptions underlying our conduct. Communication can also frustrate interaction by making explicit potentially divisive assumptions. On the other hand, communication can be generalized through mass media in ways that serve to blunt this

127

tendency. In fact, communication is relieved of the constant danger of dissent by two mechanisms (*Entlastungsmechanismen*), one of which condenses consensual communication, the other of which replaces it with success-oriented action.[45] These in turn derive from two primitive ways of inducing compliance: through authority and prestige, which are a function of personal attributes, and influence, which is the function of the resources at one's disposal. These two can be used to motivate action strategically (empirically)—through strength or money, for example—or consensually (rationally)—through reliability and knowledge.[46]

Rational forms of prestige and influence condense but do not replace communicative action, for they rely on a potentially criticizable validity base to induce compliance. Rational certification of credentials may be temporarily suspended, as when a politician's reputation alone is sufficient to attract a loyal following; in such a case past performance is regarded as warranting a partial condensation of the formalities of consensual questioning that normally accompany communicative action. A similar situation obtains when the reputation in question is based on professional certification or scientific expertise. In these instances, the appeal to authority can telescope (*raffen*), if not replace, the lengthy process of discursive justification.

Generally speaking, rational appeal to authority underlies all forms of publicity, from the simple passing down of tradition to the relationship between a speaker or writer and his audience. The critical attitude is largely in abeyance, for example, when we read a newspaper. Indeed, since most of the information we rely on is based on second-hand knowledge acquired through one or more of the mass media, we are seldom in a position to challenge it. In this manner, the reach of the media is extended, or generalized, while their potential for critical dialogue is contracted.[47]

The invention of writing as an administrative tool was the first in a series of developments (including the advent of printing and electronic media) leading to the progressive emancipation of communication from specific contexts. This has had the effect of immunizing communication against the immediate risk of dissent; a message can be widely disseminated over an indefinite period of time without being directly challenged or interrupted. Mass media thereby facilitate the condensation of communicative action by promoting the possibility of specialized domains of action-independent discourse and hierarchies of authority and knowledge, thereby relieving us of the need to negotiate certain items of our cultural lifeworld ourselves. Instead, we simply take it for granted that certain problems have already been resolved by leaders, specialists, and others who are in a position to know.[48]

Habermas continually reminds us that such condensation of communicative action is a mixed blessing. Although it is indispensable for generating consensus in large, complex societies—indeed, the vitality of the public realm as a marketplace of ideas depends on it—it nevertheless harbors the potential for manipulative abuse. The potential for abuse is different in the case of empirical communication media of money and power, for the latter *replace* consensual with strategic interaction, shifting the burden from the validation of claims to the utilitarian calculation of costs and benefits. Still, the uncoupling of market and administrative transactions from normative communication is never absolute, since money and power can only function as generalized media once they have been normatively anchored in formal law.[49] There arises a mutual conditioning of lifeworld and system in which, as Habermas puts it,

> the [legal] institutions that anchor steering mechanisms such as money or power in the lifeworld either channel the influences of the lifeworld in the direction of formally organized realms of action or, conversely, channel the influences of the system in the direction of communicatively structured contexts of action. They function in the one case, as the institutional framework which subjects system maintenance to the normative restrictions of the lifeworld; in the other as the basis which subordinates and thereby mediatizes the lifeworld with respect to the systemic constraints of material reproduction.[50]

Although classical political economists from Smith to Mill appreciated the extent to which formal rights mediated the freedom of the lifeworld and the necessity of the market, it was Marx who first realized that the ideals of freedom and justice sanctioning the system of private property were severely compromised by their insertion within that system.[51] Habermas subscribes to the Marxist credo that ideological illusions can be diagnosed only when existing forms of social integration are understood as compromises between lifeworld and system. Functionalist theories, which reduce integration to adaptation, interpret cultural ideals as mechanisms for steering behavior. Such ideals can be functionally legitimated but not ideologically compromised by the system, and so they cannot serve as standards for criticizing the injustice of adaptive hierarchies of power and wealth. Conversely, hermeneutic theories which reduce integration to consensus are incapable of grasping how the ideals of freedom and equality underwriting civil and democratic rights are vitiated by the constraints of political and economic domination that lie "hidden in the pores of communicative action."[52]

Habermas introduces the notion of a form of consensual understanding (*Verständigungsform*) in order to designate the various types of systematically distorted, or *compromised*, communication and understanding (ideology) that have appeared historically. This notion is akin to Lukács's form of objectivity, except that it denotes the structuring of social life around the nonobjectifying aspects of consensual communication.

The four forms of understanding identified by Habermas—archaic, civilized, early modern, and modern—are ranked according to their rationality.[53] The susceptibility of a form of understanding to ideological distortion is a function of the disparity between levels of rationality that obtain in sacral and profane contexts. Although the archaic form exhibits an asymmetry between sacral and profane contexts, it is peculiar to tribal societies that have yet to evolve class distinctions requiring ideological justification.[54] The first class societies are those organized around a state, and the efficient organization of labor presupposes a higher form of understanding, in which profane communication has become fully rationalized. Although differentiation between communicative action and discourse is here incomplete—the critical exegesis of texts is still constrained to reinforce religious dogma—there nevertheless exists a differentiation (at the level of action) of attitudes, value spheres, validity claims, and domains of reference.

Containment of class conflict depends on ideological justifications that exploit the rationality gap between sacral and profane contexts. The sacral context of cultic practice and world interpretation permits a distinction between inner and outer reality, logical (normative) and causal (factual) relations, enchanted world above and disenchanted world here below. Such practices and interpretations lag far behind their profane counterparts in degree of internal differentiation, however, and hence do not advance validity claims that can be distinctly identified and criticized.[55] The distortion of communication that characterizes ideology, Habermas observes, is similar to that which occurs in ritual speech. The range of inflection, intonation, syntax, vocabulary, and style endemic to ritual speech is so narrowly circumscribed that validity claims that might otherwise be differentiated remain indistinct.[56]

Early modern forms of understanding typical of nascent economic class societies exhibit a high degree of rationalization, even though the secularization process has not yet fully penetrated the sacral realm. Everyday interaction normally features critical discourse; purposive-rational contexts of action governed by steering media have taken hold; and the search for truth is institutionalized in the secular sciences. Aesthetic and normative value spheres are still imbued with a religious aura, however. The sacral realm has progressed beyond sacramental praxis and the undifferentiated modes of world interpretation characteristic of the preceding form of understanding. The supreme elevation of contemplative imagination and reflection (*Vergegenwärtigung*) and religious inwardness and faith testifies to a differentiation of value spheres in which the enjoyment of art and the pursuit of moral conscience are encouraged. However, since the sacral realm does not yet permit a distinction between communicative action and discourse, bourgeois doctrines of natural right remain impervious to rational criticism. Such doctrines claim to be ontologically anchored in the absolute will of God rather than to be conventionally instituted.[57] With the disappearance of the sacral as a distinct domain of action, the mechanism underlying ideological distortions is deprived of its chief support. It remains to be seen whether a form of understanding that, in Habermas's judgment, is too rational to sustain ideological distortions in the strict sense of the term is vulnerable to distortions of a different kind, producing analogous results.[58]

The first two chapters of Part 2 attempt to situate what has hitherto been a highly abstract analysis of rationality and rationalization within a bilevel conception of society. Of the two levels, it is the lifeworld and its rationalization that set the stage for modernity. Two issues stand out in Habermas's treatment of the rationalization of the lifeworld: the first concerns the mediation of formal reason and everyday practice, the second the logic of social evolution.

We are told on the one hand that the formal differentiation of language makes possible the practical functions of cultural transmission, social integration, and socialization, and on the other, that the performative attitude sustaining rational reflection has its provenance in prediscursive cultic practice. Although Habermas underscores the contingency of reflection on practical presuppositions, he just as emphatically affirms the autonomy of reason. To be sure, levels of reflection mediating practice and reason are mentioned—performative, narrative, and discursive; nevertheless, one suspects that, more often than not, what appears to be mediation is really an assimilation of practical categories—such as validity—to theoretical ones—such as truth. As we saw in chapter 6, although the prediscursive horizon of validity, captured by aesthetic categories of judgment and taste, is a function of communicative action, it embodies a type of rationality which is distinct from that of formal argumentation. Yet it seems that Habermas all but identifies practical reason with competencies associated exclusively with the latter—the capacity to transcend one's parochial prejudices in reflection and ground one's judgments in first principles. This impression is reinforced by Habermas's commentary

131

on Mead's theory of socialization, in which he speaks of the social "me"—qua repository of traditional habits, roles, and mimetic competencies—as limiting, rather than enhancing, the ego's freedom. Concrete social roles are simultaneously held to be a condition of, and an obstacle to, personal identity. No attempt is made to situate discursive reason within a prior frame of practical preunderstanding construed as an intuitive complement to rational self-determination. This would require investing intuition with the dignity of reason. In striking contrast to Merleau-Ponty's somewhat extreme resolution of this problem, which conceives of the body as an original ensemble of dispositions, habits, and intentions possessing an intentionality and expressiveness pertinent to socialization, Habermas regards the body as a reactive, almost mechanical system of behavior.[59]

Habermas's theory of social evolution raises a number of issues, some of which concern the empirical status of developmental theories. How can any normative belief regarding preferred strategies of problem solving be confirmed by actual instances without committing the naturalistic fallacy of deriving "ought" from "is"?[60] Habermas defends Kohlberg's theory by claiming that the relationship between normative hypotheses and factual evidence is one of neither logical inference nor correspondence (verifiability or falsifiability) but is rather one of loose coherence; the reliability of a hypothesis is a function of empirical confirmation to the extent that preferences voiced by test subjects are based on rational comparisons.[61] Adopting McCarthy's recommendation, Habermas now regards confirmation as a function less of empirical observation than of critical dialogue among equally competent speakers, especially in cases involving comparisons between postconventional—utilitarian, Kantian, contractual, and communicative—moral schemas.[62]

No consensus over the ranking of these schemas is likely to emerge in the near future, but this has not prevented Habermas from asserting the superiority of postconventional over conventional morality or from rejecting moral skepticism as a dead end. Situated between conventional and postconventional (universalistic) morality, skepticism represents a transitional stage of reflection that is inherently unstable; dogmatic acceptance of conventions as a necessary condition in practice, coupled with a critical repudiaton of validity, creates a cognitive dissonance that cannot be resolved—least of all by refusing to engage in social interaction—without threatening the stability of an identity dependent on recognition by others.[63]

The controversy over the alleged superiority of postconventional moral schemas raises yet another question. Assuming that the end states postulated by Piaget and Kohlberg are confirmed in Western societies—an assumption that is far from universal acceptance—is there any evidence that they are valid for other societies? Might there not be, as McCarthy suggests, developmental paths that are "more adaptive in a given environment and more culturally valued" than those that have emerged in the Occident?[64] The fact that the competencies identified by Piaget as forming a unified ensemble develop unevenly and at different rates, depending on circumstances, suggests that the distinction between universal structure and culture-bound performance may not be valid.[65]

The pitfalls associated with developmental optimization remain, even when no particular normative end point is specified. Sometimes Habermas prefers to speak of evolutionary progress in terms of a general increase in problem-solving capacity rather than in terms of approximating specific ideals. The question then arises as to whether it would be possible to establish a universal index for evaluating problem-solving capacity. Weighing against such a possibility is the fact that the steering problems that societies face are not cross-culturally generalizable. The problems of advanced capitalism pertaining to the efficient production of surplus value and the democratic production of legitimacy are not the problems that beset archaic and traditional societies. Indeed, institutionalization of postconventional morality in the latter might prove detrimental to problem solving. But even if a universal standard for evaluating problem-solving capacity could be agreed on, we would be entitled to say only that, given differences in environment, some societies are faced with certain steering problems that are resolvable only if they institutionalize a higher problem-solving capacity, and not that the institutionalization of a higher problem-solving capacity would itself constitute social progress.[66]

Turning to Habermas's use of ontogenetic theories as models for reconstructing the developmental phases of social evolution, we detect problems of a rather different nature. Is the structural isomorphism between the two developmental schemas strong enough to justify this way of proceeding? The homology is strongest, Habermas observes, in the case of cognitive development, weaker in the case of moral development. In both one can observe roughly parallel paths of decentration. Nevertheless, there are places where the analogy breaks down. The pattern of individual development cannot mirror that of social evolution, since even the most primitive societies have institutionalized (at the adult level) relatively advanced interactive competencies involving reciprocity and generalized expectations. Again, the sorts of crises confronting the individual personality differ from those encountered by the social system and hence call for different developmental solutions. This asymmetry is itself a reflection of the complexity of traditional world views; not only do they contain particular, religious-metaphysical concepts that serve directly to stabilize individual and group identities; they also contain legal and moral ideas that guard against social disintegration.[67] There are also ways in which the analogy between personal and collective identity breaks down. Both secure continuity and recognizability, but social identity is not objectively bounded by birth and death, nor is it shaped by external encounters with others.[68] Nevertheless, Habermas talks as if there were a perfect correspondence between the rationality potential implicit in world views and in individual problem-solving capacities. As Michael Schmid notes, this leads to the erroneous impression that earlier societies did not evolve because of an alleged incapacity of individual members to engage in higher levels of reflection.[69]

Finally, it must be borne in mind that on Habermas's model of social evolution, cognitive and moral advances are not as closely allied as they are in ontogenesis. Given the uncoupling of lifeworld and system, it is possible for practical rationalization not to keep pace with cognitive-instrumental rationalization, however much the former may have originally set the pace for the latter. Practical rationalization—the extirpation of "those relations of force that are inconspicuously set in the very structures of communication and that prevent conscious settlements of conflicts, and consensual regulation of conflicts"—has as its end point the emancipation of the individual as a truly universal "species being."[70] As Marx recognized, an emancipated society would have to rise above the deep fissure separating particular and universal interests—a vision that finds eloquent testimony in the cosmopolitan, egalitarian doctrines of democratic socialism.[71] Such a vision raises important questions regarding the relationship between reason and tradition, individual autonomy and social necessity, and most important of all, regarding the limits of economic growth and management with respect to the lifeworld.

CHAPTER NINE

Talcott Parsons: Systems Theory

No other contemporary social theorist has influenced Habermas as much as Talcott Parsons. The vision of sociological tradition informing Habermas's theory and the cybernetic vocabulary in which his bilevel conception of society is couched are inspired largely by Parsons, and Habermas's defense of the methodological interdependence of critical theory and structural functionalism is undertaken chiefly with Parsons in mind. The extensive—and, as regards the corpus of Habermas's works, unparalleled—survey of Parsons's thought in *Theorie* traces the source of the difficulties frequently mentioned by detractors of a combined action-systems theory to a residual neo-Kantianism.[1] As one might expect, the solution that Habermas proposes involves transferring the action-theoretical framework from a purposive-rational to a communicative paradigm. Whether this solution is adequate is a question that will be addressed later.

THE FOUNDATIONS OF MODERN SYSTEMS THEORY:
FROM MALINOWSKI TO LUHMANN

The pioneers of sociological functionalism—Durkheim, Malinowski, and Radcliffe-Brown—were struck by the way in which societies, like biological organisms, maintain themselves as continuous living aggregates despite internal and external environmental changes. Malinowski took literally the analogy between biological organisms and social systems. He saw cultural institutions as instantiating values (the charter) that satisfy people's organic needs at the more complex, but instrumentally more efficient, level of economic, social, and spiritual interaction. On this reading, the social system maintains itself for the purpose of preserving the biological integrity of its members.[2] Malinowski believed that social facts were to be explained by "the part they play within the integral system of culture, by the manner in which they are related to each other within the system, and by the manner in which this system is related to the physical surroundings."[3] Fellow anthropologist Radcliffe-Brown went beyond Malinowski's simple organic functionalism by relating the idea of function to that of structure. According to him, societies organize survival functions around relatively constant patterns of social interaction (structures), such as kinship relations, which set limits on normal ranges of functioning, against which life-threatening deviations can be identified.[4]

Habermas's initial consideration of functionalism, in the sixties, took as its point of departure the methodological critique advanced by Hempel and Nagel.[5] Defending a positivistic approach to social inquiry, these philosophers challenged the logical irreducibility of teleological explanations. They maintained that without additional knowledge of the causal laws governing societies, the necessary conditions for formulating functionalist explanations could not be satisfied. More important, Nagel observed that a process could be proved to be functionally necessary for the maintenance of a system only if the boundaries of the system, the state in which it tends to maintain itself, the functions necessary for its maintenance, and alternate processes by which these functions could be carried out are empirically specified—conditions, he concluded, that could not be met in social systems.[6]

Social systems are not physiologically, geographically, or politically bounded, and their goal states cannot be equated directly with biological survival without reducing functional explanations to empty tautologies.[7] If one equates the goal state with the maintenance of structural continuity, there is still the difficulty that, in advanced industrial societies, structural changes of great magnitude occur without apparent loss of identity. Emendations to the structural-functionalist model proposed by Merton, Parsons, and others notwithstanding, Habermas submits that the difficulties surrounding the empirical determination of boundaries, goal states, and life-threatening changes are irremedial.[8]

> When systems maintain themselves through altering both boundaries and structural continuity (*Bestand*), their identity becomes blurred. The same system modification can be conceived of equally well as a learning process and change or as a dissolution process and collapse of the system. It cannot be unambiguously determined whether a new system has been formed or the old system has regenerated itself. Of course, not all systemic alterations in a social system are also crises . . . only when members of a society experience structural alterations as critical for continued existence and feel their

social identity threatened can we speak of crises. . . . Crisis states assume the form of a disintegration of social institutions.[9]

He believes that sociological functionalism cannot succeed in establishing conditions of structural continuity without first shedding its empirical-analytical cloak and acquiring the mantle of hermeneutically enlightened critical theory—hence the importance of Parsons's treatment of the problem, which seeks to incorporate meaningful cultural patterns in a system of functionally interdependent structures. The manifest meanings, values, and purposes explicitly intended by persons on the plane of social action are shown to possess latent meanings, to have unintended side effects on the system as a whole, which are understood as serving the functional purpose of maintaining it.

Parsons's concept of system is of a self-regulating organism that differentiates itself from its environment by maintaining stable boundaries.[10] Societies strive to sustain a preferred state of equilibrium (goal state), or level of self-sufficiency, along four general axes (pattern variables): pattern maintenance, goal attainment, adaptation, and integration.[11] Pattern maintenance (the function proper to the cultural subsystem) anchors action in shared values that secure social identity and legitimate social institutions. Goal attainment (the function proper to the political subsystem) provides the motivation for compliance with cultural patterns by allowing individuals to compete for political influence and its attendant rewards. Adaptation (the function proper to the economic subsystem) satisfies material needs through instrumental labor. Finally, integration harnesses the energy of the individual to cultural, political, and economic subsystems.[12] Changes in any one of the above functions and their respective subsystems necessitate changes in the other three, but Parsons adds that "a state of the system . . . may be described, relative to satisfactory points of reference, as 'farther along' or less far along on each of these dimensions," and advances need not be uniform.[13]

Parsons also distinguishes between structure and function. Social structures are empirically identifiable, relatively invariant, patterns of interaction. Social functions designate the contributions of structures to maintaining the system.[14] Cultural structuration defines social identity and membership; it demarcates the range of variations (normative boundaries) that the system can undergo without ceasing to exist. The cultural values of society thus determine the values of the four pattern variables that define the optimal equilibrium of the system.[15]

The amalgamation of information theory and functionalism found in Parsons's later conception of the social system is developed by Niklas Luhmann, who takes systems theory in new, and in Habermas's opinion not entirely desirable, directions. Unlike Parsons's structural functionalism, Luhmann's *functional structuralism* circumvents the problem of structural continuity by limiting the function of structures, conceived as dynamic processes, to that of reducing environmental complexity.[16] According to Luhmann, social systems maintain themselves by selectively registering a relevant portion of the world's complexity in symbolic systems of science, law, art, and literature, thereby imposing definite constellations of meaning on what would otherwise be an indeterminate horizon of possible experience. Raw experiential input from the external world is "processed" into information, whence it is "stored" in structures (institutions, norms, and so on).[17] These delimit a range of possible responses to environmental changes (output) and select possible interpretations. The process of reducing the complexity of the world to definite meaning is simultaneously a process of expanding the internal complexity of the system and its range of possible responses. Most important, it is a process by which challenges to the system are reflexively registered through changes in its own structures, so that the formation of structures is itself a result of selective adaptation.[18]

However much Habermas and Luhmann may agree in their terminology—both, for example, conceive of social evolution as a process of expanding problem-solving capacity through structural change—they disagree on the reducibility of structures to adaptive functions. Habermas contends that unless structural boundaries are defined independently of adaptive functions, there will be no way to determine goal states or criteria of system maintenance (identity), let alone whether increases in system complexity constitute advances in problem solving. Luhmann's model presupposes that problems of system complexity can be specified independently of social structures, as if the former were objective facts to which the latter must conform. However, the problems facing complex societies cannot be identified objectively in terms of mere biological survival. Luhmann himself concedes this point when he observes that the world and the peculiar challenges that it poses to the social system are not merely given but are already selectively preinterpreted with respect to structurally circumscribed ranges of possible meaning.[19] The survival of a society thus extends well beyond biological survival to include the preservation of culturally valued patterns of social interaction.[20]

Closely associated with this difficulty is that of establishing whether increases in system complexity constitute advances in adaptation. The expansion of internal complexity itself generates a second-order reduction problem when the profusion of information (for example, the growth of special interest groups and ideologies demanding representation) threatens to stifle decision-making processes. Luhmann claims that such debilitating overloads are reduced to a manageable size by establishing hierarchies of administrative control—what he calls *structurification*—that restrict democratic participation.[21] But on his model it is impossible to tell "when an expansion of alternative possibilities of action at the price of destructuring (processes of enlightenment) is functional and when the structurification of particular decisions at the cost of a contraction of the horizon of possibilities that is held (as in the case of dogmatization) is functional."[22]

But Parsons's empiricist assimilation of motivational factors to *institutionalized* cultural values is no more successful in specifying boundaries. Cultural values, Habermas reminds us, "not only serve to steer social systems, they also function within the system for goals which are not themselves reflected in them."[23] These goals refer to emancipatory interests which, denied authentic expression in institutionalized values, are nevertheless implicit in the preferred goal state of the system along with the nonnormative requirements of system integration.[24] A theory of social evolution is needed to establish the boundaries and goal states of systems, to specify ranges of structural variation (as determined by principles of organization), and to identify situations in which ruptures in tradition and attendant manifestations of social pathology are indicative of genuine, identity-threatening crises. Writing some fourteen years after his original assessment of Parsons, Habermas today finds it even more urgent that the structural-functionalist program avoid the neo-Kantian extremes of ahistorical idealism and uncritical empiricism.

THE ACTION-THEORETICAL FOUNDATIONS OF SYSTEMS THEORY

Parsons's systems theory grew out of an earlier analysis of social action that was indebted chiefly to neo-Kantian philosophy of consciousness and its corresponding model of purposive rationality. In *Structure of Social Action* of 1937 Parsons closely followed Weber in conceiving the action unit as an isolated actor seeking to bring about some end through the efficient deployment of some means. Action cannot be oriented toward efficient adaptation as its sole goal, he noted, but must also be oriented to ends that transcend immediate need gratification and survival—a view that harks back to Kant's identification of freedom and moral law.[25] Analysis of the action unit, then, must incorporate an analysis of the transcendent normative basis of social order (Durkheim). Parsons used Freud to explain how social norms that are internalized through fear of sanctions come to function as voluntary constraints; he elucidated the integration of needs and institutionally sanctioned values by adverting to Weber's theory of legitimacy, which ties voluntary compliance to the normative instantiation of universal interests. Parsons concluded that empiricist theories that reduce action to the purposive-rational pursuit of private ends are incapable of accounting for social integration founded on legitimate norms and reciprocity (the Hobbesian problem).[26]

For Habermas, the main difficulty with Parsons's theory of social action is that the primary analysis of the action unit, which is framed in teleological terms, stands opposed to the analysis of the action "system," which is characterized by communicative reciprocity. Given his methodological individualism, Parsons is forced to conceive of social interaction as doubly contingent on the mutual assent of ego and alter. This double contingency is not circumscribed by rational expectations that impose prior obligations on the actors, and this superimposition of social order on a teleological frame of reference leads to reduction of norms to the status of mere means. Without a foundation in communication, social interaction remains no more than a strategic engagement contingent on the morally unbound, unaccountable, and—in the Kantian sense—unfree decision (*Willkür*) of the actors involved.[27]

A second version of the social theory dates from the period 1951, the year of *Toward a General Theory of Social Action* and *The Social System*, to 1956, the year of *Economy and Society*, coauthored by N. J. Smelser. The evolution of this version began with the rejection of methodological individualism and culminated in a bilevel conception of society. As a result of his discovery of Freud's theory of personality and Malinowski's cultural anthropology, Parsons now conceived action orientation as a product of intersubjectively recognized cultural patterns that are institutionalized in society (in the form of binding values) and internalized in personality (in the form of permissible motivations). However, his failure to make the transition from philosophy of consciousness to theory of communication continued to frustrate any attempt to integrate the cultural, social, and personality components of his system.

The first stage of Parsons's revised action theory increases the number of action orientations from two to three. In addition to cathectic orientation (toward the attainment of goals) and cognitive orientation (toward the purposive-rational selection of efficient means), an evaluative orientation is introduced which binds motivation to cognitive, evaluative, and expressive patterns.[28] But, according to Habermas, this does not entirely succeed in showing how cultural patterns become binding for society and personality. Parsons treats culture as if it were an ideal realm of immutable objects distinct from norms and persons. The internalization of ideal values in role expectations and motives is problematic, since only role expectations and motives, as empirical elements of action, are causally efficacious. Parsons cannot explain the counterfactual force of institutionalized values, because he persists in regarding them as objects rather than as communicative conditions of possible action (validity claims). Social integration and socialization are functions of consensual understanding, not objective cognition and introjection.[29]

Parsons's own solution to the problem of the mediation of culture, society, and personality during this middle period led to his theory of pattern variables, according to which any action situation presents the agent with five problems. The first involves the dilemma of the private versus collective: Should one pursue one's own private interest or the collective interest? The second concerns gratification versus discipline (affectivity versus affective neutrality): Should one gratify one's desires immediately or postpone gratification until later? The third addresses the issue of transcendence versus immanence (universalism versus particularism): Should one transcend the particular circumstances of the immediate situation and evaluate it in light of universal standards, or should one concern oneself directly and intuitively with concrete circumstances? The fourth pertains to the issue of assessment of others (in terms of performance or personal qualities): Should one evaluate others on the basis of their achievements and their functions in social relations or on the basis of their intrinsic (ascribed) qualities? The final problem deals with the scope of interest (diffuseness versus specificity): Should one's interest in the object be of a global nature, focusing on the totality of the situation in all its complexity, or should it be specific in nature, singling out some analytic component for evaluation? These problems present the agent with five sets of possible choices, comprising a total of ten pattern variables. Cultural values are now seen as directly determining action by establishing preferences for one of the two possibilities given by each of the five patterns of choice.[30]

Despite the claims made for it by Parsons, the theory of pattern variables is not transcendentally valid for all action systems, Habermas contends, but designates choices that exist only for persons living in modern society or in transitional societies straddling *Gemeinschaft* and *Gesellschaft*. Compounding the problem of an absence of any hermeneutic sensitivity is Parsons's continued failure to take into account the role of communication in constituting action; cultural pat-

141

terns are seen as rigidly predetermining preferences, independent of the interpretative contributions of historical actors.[31]

The third stage of Parsons's reconstruction of action theory saw the introduction of a bilevel conception of society as consisting of a cultural action sphere on the one side and a functional system comprising social and personality subsystems on the other. The cultural sphere here consists of ideal meanings that are logically interrelated; the social and personality systems consist of empirical components (social norms and motives) that are functionally interrelated.[32] Culture, society, and personality make distinct contributions to social reproduction: social integration through the definition and coordination of personal motivations consistent with cultural values and functional adaptation and achievement through the effective mobilization of scarce resources. Although society and personality thus designate systems that contribute to adaptation and achievement respectively, they must also satisfy the requirements of consistency. Parsons concludes that "integration, both within an individual's value system and within the value system prevailing in a society, is a compromise between the functional imperatives of the situation and the dominant value-orientation patterns of society."[33] Conflicts between incompatible value systems are managed by relegating them to specific action contexts or by consigning them to the sphere of personal judgment. Special solutions are called for, however, in dealing with what Parsons calls "problematic facts," situations in which functional and cultural imperatives conflict with one another. The primary mechanism here is the ideological repression of dysfunctional values.[34]

Habermas argues that the neo-Kantian presuppositions underlying Parsons's bilevel conception of society render conflicts between cultural and functional integration inexplicable. Because the dichotomy between ideal values and empirical motivations prevents the former from having any effect, social integration must conform to functional imperatives, thereby negating any possible conflict between consistency and adaptation. Only if Parsons had conceived values as constitutive of communicative action could he have conceived the ideological compromise between social and system integration as a repression of ideal cultural values whose efficacy, however latent, would continue to surface in pathological symptoms.[35]

THE DEVELOPMENT OF PARSONS'S SYSTEMS THEORY

From the outset, the theory of action was incapable of integrating culture, society, and personality within a single paradigm. But the

142

second version of the theory, developed during the early fifties, anticipated what was later to become *the* solution to this problem by subordinating the action system in its entirety to a functionalist model of
society.[36] *Societies* (1966), perhaps the most succinct statement of
Parsons's mature systems theory, conceives of societies as action systems that achieve their highest level of self-sufficiency through functional differentiation. Every action is a point of intersection of mutually interpenetrating cultural, social, personality, and behavioral
subsystems: "Cultural systems are specialized around the function of
pattern maintenance, social systems around the integration of acting
units (human individuals or, more precisely, personalities engaging
in roles), personality systems around goal achievement, and the behavioral organism around adaptation." Each subsystem constitutes
an environment for the others and is linked to them by exchange relations (interchange media). Finally, there exists a cybernetic hierarchy
of control factors, descending from the cultural subsystem, and a corresponding reverse hierarchy of conditioning factors, ascending from
the behavioral subsystem. Subsystems that are high in the control hierarchy are relatively high in information, whereas those lower down
are relatively high in energy.[37]

Habermas mentions five steps taken by Parsons to strike a compromise between his cultural idealism and his functionalism. First, Parsons assimilates pattern maintenance to functional integration. He
continues to speak of the social system as a network of normative relations grounded in legitimate cultural patterns, the societal community, and the impression that the latter is integrated consensually is
reinforced by Parsons's use of such institutions as household and
church as illustrations.[38] Appearances notwithstanding, the societal
community remains a subsidiary environment of a larger, functionally integrated social system in which the domain of "norm-free sociality" (social relations governed by strategic exchange media) increasingly comes to preclude consensual processes.[39]

The second step of Parsons's synthesis of culture and social system
involves demonstrating the necessity and completeness of the four
system functions. It departs from the premise that system maintenance requires the solution of two distinct problems: the structural
delimitation of social identity (the maintenance of spatial boundaries
separating inner and outer environments) and the purposal-rational
securing of continued existence (the temporal process of extending an
initial state of self-sufficiency into the future). The spatiotemporal coordinate system of inner-outer and initial state–goal state allows Parsons to derive from the combination of cultural processes of boundary
maintenance and systemic processes of material production the four

143

functions known as the AGIL schema: (a)daptation (initial state versus outer environment), (g)oal achievement (goal state versus outer environment), (i)ntegration (goal state versus inner environment), and (l)egitimation (initial state versus inner environment).[40]

The third step consists of transferring the pattern variables from the evaluations and orientations of the isolated actor to the impersonal role definitions specified by the four system functions.[41] The fourth step eliminates the distinction between ideal values and empirical functions by treating the cultural sphere as an empirical action system in its own right. The theory of value realization (taken from Weber) is translated into cybernetic concepts so that cultural values now become control functions, or goal values of self-steering systems. There is still a residual trace of idealism in Parsons's postulation of a supramundane environment, or ultimate reality, which poses "problems of meaning." The steering power of cultural values, Parsons claims, devolves on them by virtue of their relationship to this (telic) system.[42]

The fifth and final step involves a transcendental deduction of the system of reality. The human condition is deduced by cross-tabulating cultural, social, personality, and behavioral subsystems with their respective poles of reference, a process that gives rise to telic, social, human, and natural domains of reality. Although Parsons follows Kant in regarding the world as humanly ordered and conditioned, he nevertheless commits, in Habermas's judgment, precisely the kind of transcendental category mistake that Kant repeatedly warned against; he conflates the necessary conditions under which objects are experienced—the telic system—with the objects themselves. In other words, he fails to see that the totality of linguistic meaning comprising the lifeworld is not a possible object of knowledge, but only the condition of possible knowledge.[43]

The fragility of Parsons's "compromise" between action and systems theory is nowhere more evident than in his supposition that strategic interchange media fulfill consensual functions. In the early sixties Parsons argued that money and power could be understood as specialized forms of linguistic communication. Money is a kind of code for sending and receiving information which presupposes a common set of expectations (defined by the cost-effective optimization of utility), a generalized value (utility), and the mutual freedom of buyers and sellers to influence one another's behavior through offers. Owing to its measurability, money can serve as a general lingua franca. Its claim redemption mechanism is further backed by the security of world banking institutions and the legal enforcement of contracts. Moreover, it constitutes an autonomous system (the market) which subsumes traditional relationships between household, state, and economy under a self-regulating mechanism of resource allocation.[44]

Power also involves influencing behavior on the basis of shared expectations (the optimization of efficiency through the unilateral exercise of sanctions). Power is not quantifiable, however; it can be measured only in terms of rank, and its circulation is therefore limited. Since it is not as readily disposable as money, it cannot be given to others or held in reserve without being wasted; power is sustained or augmented, as Nietzsche and Foucault would say, through exercise within adversarial contexts. It also lacks the system-building character of money; there is no market of power comparable to that of money, since concentration of power, unlike augmentation of buying power through credit, generates countervailing forces that tend to limit its steering potential.[45] Habermas attributes this failure of power to become a general exchange medium to the peculiar structure of its claim redemption mechanism. The exercise of power is essentially confined to an organizational setting; whereas the right to possess money gives its owner access to any number of markets commensurate with his or her financial worth, the right to exercise power confers on its possessor only certain privileges within a narrow chain of command. This brings to light a further difference between money and power: whereas contractors confront one another as equals who are free to accept or reject any offer, contingent on the mutual satisfaction of interests, subordinates can refuse the commands of superiors only on pain of reprisal. Because persons would not enter organizations were there no guarantee of mutuality, the successful exercise of power must rest on the rational accountability of executives and the legitimacy of their decisions.[46]

Given the normative conditions necessary for the organizational exercise of power, it is somewhat surprising that Habermas should continue to regard it as a strategic medium at all. Yet, he notes that, insofar as the claim redemption mechanism underlying monetary transactions is backed by legally established institutions of contract, credit, and property, its trustworthiness is also—albeit indirectly —related to considerations of legitimacy. If either of two contractors had reason to doubt the fairness of a contract as formally defined by provisions against fraud, theft, and other violations of equity, there would be no basis for entering into it. The legitimacy of such provisions, however, is ultimately tied to counterfactual principles of procedural justice mandating, among other things, equal representation and accountability in the legislative process. Consequently, strategic exchange media cannot entirely replace consensual mechanisms for coordinating action without endangering their own trustworthiness.[47]

PARSONS'S THEORY OF MODERNITY

Parsons's theory of modernity accords a decisive role to cultural rationalization, the four AGIL mechanisms of adaptation, differentiation, inclusion (social membership), and value generalization designating the salient features of this evolutionary process. Like Weber, Parsons saw the Renaissance and the Reformation as playing leading roles in implementing the "cultural code" of the Occident. Drawing on the heritage of antiquity, the Renaissance emancipated science, jurisprudence, and art as autonomous systems of action, whereas the Reformation made possible the secular ethics of conscience.[48] The institutionalization of these systems of action in distinct social subsystems of economy, polity, and culture, respectively, was spearheaded by the industrial, democratic, and educational revolutions and the development of English common and civil law, with the concomitant establishment of religious tolerance and wage labor in the sixteenth and seventeenth centuries contributing more than anything else to the anchoring of the capitalist system. Parsons sees the rise of a civil religion, in which inclusion within the broader moral community is stressed at the expense of denominational loyalty, as of key importance in providing the organic solidarity of modern society; his assessment of secularization is thus more positive than that given by Weber.[49]

By the end of the sixties, Parsons's theory of modernity had begun to show traces of biological evolutionism. Cultural development came to be seen as designating a change in the genetic code of occidental rationality, while the implementation of culture in social institutions was explained as a function of natural selection; the phenotypic characteristics selected from the total pool of cultural variants were those that, by and large, stabilized the adaptive functioning of the social system vis-à-vis environmental challenges.[50] The rationalization of the lifeworld (to use Habermas's terminology) was thus regarded as both necessary and sufficient for growth in system complexity. The structural differentiation of the lifeworld into society, culture, and personality was equated with the functional differentiation of the system into economy, polity, and culture.

The resulting collapse of action theory (the theory of cultural and social rationalization) into systems theory (the theory of biological evolutionism) proved auspicious for Parsons's diagnosis of modernity.

Parsons judiciously refrained from blaming occidental rationality for the symptoms of malaise plaguing modern capitalism, symptoms that he either overlooked or misunderstood. For him, conflicts between lifeworld and system, practical and functional rationality, democratic self-determination and bureaucratic manipulation, were viewed less as pathological expressions of trenchant identity crises than as temporary disequilibria accompanying adaptive readjustments. Accordingly, Parsons denied evidence of bureaucratic hyperextension, noting that "the main trend is not toward increased bureaucracy, but toward associationism." In response to the charge that the residential community had been "privatized" and that many relationships had shifted to the context of large formal organizations, he observed that "the whole system of mass communications is a functional equivalent of some features of *Gemeinschaft*." The desire for inclusion within the wider political community—more important in Parsons's judgment than the demand for power—was likewise thought to be satisfied by the opportunities for limited participation provided by formal democracy.[51]

In retrospect, Parsons's abandonment of structural functionalism in favor of functional structuralism can be seen to entail that social crises are conceivable only as systemic breakdowns in economic stability and political order:

> Only when relevant social groups experience structural changes that are systematically induced in a way that is critical for their existence and feel their identity threatened may the social scientist speak of crises. . . . Parsons does not have the conceptual means at his disposal to make this assessment; he deploys the concept of crisis independently of the experiences of the subjects in question without regard for identity problems—in the sense of a disturbance of intersystemic exchange relations. The recurrent crises in modern society can only be grasped by Parsons in terms of media dynamics; economic inflation and deflation serving as the model.[52]

Like Parsons, Habermas does not take subjective experiences of discontent caused by routine ruptures in tradition as indicative of social crises; they are only so when they reflect an objective contradiction between rational interests and systemic constraints. The directional evolution of rationality must be distinguished from the nondirectional growth of system complexity. Although an increase in system complexity can sometimes further social rationalization, it can equally well impede social rationalization by undermining cultural values that sustain it.[53]

147

CHAPTER TEN

From Parsons to Weber and Marx

In the late sixties and early seventies Habermas maintained that social functionalism could become viable only by being elevated to the rank of hermeneutically enlightened critical theory. The concluding Zwischenbetrachtung reaffirms this position; the positive yield of functionalism is to be obtained by retrieving the diagnosis of modernity advanced by Weber, but recast in light of Marx's analysis of ideology and commodity fetishism. Properly understood, the contemporary loss of freedom and meaning is not a manifestation of temporary disequilibrium or a pathology endemic to social rationalization but, rather, is symptomatic of a trenchant contradiction between normative conditions of social reproduction, which foster rational expectations of democratic participation, and functional prerequisites of material production, which necessitate the accumulation of capital under conditions of private appropriation. It was Marx who first perceived this contradiction—inadequately, to be sure, since he could not have envisaged the magnitude that it would assume in the twentieth century. What is needed today, Habermas submits, is a global analysis of reification in all its manifestations—economic, political, and cultural—which sees social pathology as the result of a compromise between lifeworld and system favoring a one-sided process of rationalization.

> My modifications of Weber's thesis . . . reduce the deformations studied by Marx, Durkheim, and Weber to neither the rationalization of the lifeworld generally nor the growth in system complexity as such. Neither the secularization of world views nor the structural differentiation of society per se have unavoidable pathological side effects. It is not the differentiation and subsequent, autonomous development of cultural value spheres that leads to the cultural impoverishment of the communicative

praxis of everyday life, but rather the elitist separation of expert cultures from the context of mundane communicative action. Likewise, it is not the uncoupling of media-steered subsystems and their forms of organization from the lifeworld that leads to onesided rationalization or reification of mundane communicative praxis, but just the penetration of forms of economic and administrative rationality into action domains which resist subordination [*Umstellung*] to media of money and power. . . . If we further assume that both the loss of meaning and the loss of freedom do not arise accidentally, but are structurally created, then we must try to explain why the media-steered subsystems unfold an inexorable dynamic all their own [*eine unaufhaltsame Eigendynamik*] which simultaneously causes the colonization of the lifeworld and its segmentation of science, morals and art.[1]

WEBER'S THEORY OF MODERNITY IN RETROSPECT

Contemporary loss of meaning and freedom, Habermas tells us, has its genesis in the extension of the economy and public administration into consensually integrated areas of life, not in the uncoupling of lifeworld and system per se.[2] The uncoupling of lifeworld and system is commensurate with the institutionalization of strategic media—contractual relations of exchange and organizational procedures of domination—in formal law. Although the process by which social relations come under increasing regulation by formal law (*Verrechtlichung*) is a primary index of systemic complexity, it should not be taken as a barometer of social pathology. Formal organizations may be impersonal, but they are not entirely detached from the lifeworld. It is only when the spread of formal organization threatens to undermine the communicative context in which it is normatively anchored that the loss of freedom and meaning assume identity-threatening proportions.[3]

Habermas discusses Weber's diagnosis of modernity in the context of a more detailed analysis of the various exchange relationships between formally organized economic and political subsystems and the institutional orders of the lifeworld.[4] The lifeworld is divided into public and private sectors. The private sector revolves principally around the institution of the nuclear family, which, having been relieved of its former economic function, is singularly well equipped to handle problems of socialization. Its major contribution to modern society lies in fostering conditions of intimacy and solitude, in which the personal reflection necessary for cultivating strong individual identity can occur independently of economic and political pressures. The institutional core of the public sector (*Öffentlichkeit*) comprises a network of cultural institutions in which public opinion is shaped and social identity cultivated. Its major contribution to modern society is its provision of the conditions of social dialogue necessary for generating the shared values and interests that undergird social integration.[5]

The distinction between private and public sectors arose out of the differentiation of lifeworld and system. The culmination of this process in the twentieth century has given rise to the welfare state, which has restricted the role these sectors play in modern society. As vehicles of socialization and social integration par excellence, households and local communities have surrendered whatever economic and administrative functions they may have had in the days when they were self-sufficient to formally organized subsystems of business and state, while remaining related to them. The relationship between household and business establishes both the economic input cycle required for production in which monetary income is exchanged for labor power and the economic output cycle (consumption) whereby money is exchanged for goods and services. Likewise, the relationship between public sphere and state establishes both the administrative input cycle whereby public services are exchanged for tax revenue and the administrative output cycle (policy formation) whereby officeholders make decisions that are favorable to their voting constituency in exchange for loyalty.[6]

The relationships involving input cycles crystallize around organizational roles—employee versus employer and client versus civil servant—that legally bind transactions to contractually predesignated terms. By contrast, the relationships involving output cycles crystallize around roles—buyer versus seller and elector versus office-holder—that are independent of any organization, consumers and electors being free to express cultural preferences and value orientations without being contractually bound in any way. It is no coincidence that bourgeois ideals of freedom gravitate around these latter roles; for, although they are fictive, they nonetheless resist legal formalization.[7]

Habermas takes issue with Weber's view that legal formalization necessarily issues in subversion of freedom and meaning. The transformation of concrete consumer preferences into abstract quantitative demand, the restructuring of public opinion around plebiscitary mechanisms for building mass loyalty, and the reduction of labor to exchange value are all consonant with the emancipatory ideals of rationality. Wherever such rationalization occurs, persons will initially experience a loss of freedom and meaning, but it will be more than compensated by the gain in rational autonomy. To be sure, such pathological tendencies as possessive individualism and consumerism seem to accompany the new freedom, but these can be attributed to an overextension of the economy, rather than to its institutional-ization. Similarly, the reideologization of political life can be under-stood as resulting from an overextension of public administration; un-der capitalism, controversial questions regarding distributive justice must be removed from the democratic process and dealt with as tech-nical problems requiring resolution by managerial elites. Habermas also attributes the impoverishment of culture to the inner dynamics of capitalist society, the depoliticization of the public sphere that accom-panies the welfare state's involvement in a capitalist economy being a prime example of such impoverishment. What still needs to be ex-plained, however, is why the selective mode of rationalization charac-teristic of advanced capitalism assumes the form of an overextension of steering media and a splitting off of expert cultures.[8]

MARX AND THE THESIS OF INNER COLONIZATION

Habermas believes that Marx's labor theory of value implies the kind of distinction between lifeworld and system requisite for critically exposing social pathology. The labor theory of value developed in the first volume of *Das Kapital* begins with simple commodity exchange between independent producers. The commodity possesses a dual character by virtue of its concrete utility (use value) and its transfera-bility (exchange value). Under capitalism, exchange of equivalents produces a surplus value for one of the parties, a surplus explained by Marx in terms of the reduction of living labor to the status of an ab-stract exchange equivalent. Like other commodities, labor power pos-sesses an abstract value that is the equivalent of the value of food, shelter, and clothing required to produce it. But unlike other com-modities, it is a living productivity that is capable of producing more value than is required for its own sustenance. The capitalist employer exploits the worker by appropriating the surplus value created by him or her. In addition to penetrating the ideology of just exchange, which masks the inequality and lack of freedom inherent in the wage relationship, Marx also examines the reification of social relations (commodity fetishism) that results from the organization of labor in-dependent of the needs and values of workers. Owing to the imper-sonal functioning of the law of supply and demand, changeable social relationships between free human beings thus assume the guise of immutable, law-governed relationships between things (commodi-ties). This creates a paradox: the increase in self-determination and self-realization promised by the capitalist social order is contradicted by the inexorable cycles and mechanical routines of production stem-ming from an aggregate of socially uncoordinated actions.[9]

Marx's critique represents a clear advance over Parsons's social theory insofar as it correctly identifies social disturbances as crisis phenomena arising from contradictory imperatives of social and system integration. Nevertheless, it suffers, in Habermas's view, from an overly romantic conception of society that defines any differentiation of lifeworld and system as an alienation to be overcome. According to Habermas, Marx's analysis of labor in *Das Kapital* correctly showed how the transformation of labor into an exchange value involved a process of "real abstraction" whereby labor was detached from its concrete form as a mode of self-expression and self-fulfillment, reduced to a quantitative value determined by the amount of time it involved, and confined to a uniform set of routine operations. However, because this analysis ultimately privileges a dialectical conception of reason, Marx did not fully appreciate the fact that the differentiation, purification, and formalization of action as such is inherently rational.

The analysis of real abstraction contained in *Das Kapital*, Habermas contends, remains bound to the categorical framework of Hegel's *Logic*, which equates truth with totality. On this model, any abstraction, or loss of unity, entails alienation and thus reflects an immature phase of social development. For Marx, the apparent realization of human freedom under capitalism implied in formal property rights and unfettered egoism—an illusion attributed by him to the mystification of class relationships—conceals the deeper truth of an essential unity. Marx's methodology compels him, in a manner reminiscent of the young Hegel, to view not only capitalism, but modern society in general, as a pathological sundering of an essentially classless, democratic community wherein state and economy no longer function independently of the collective planning decisions of united producers. At the same time, however, his dialectical methodology forces him to conceive of capitalist society as a false totality that has succcumbed entirely to reification. This assimilation of capitalist society to the category of "system," Habermas contends, justifies the self-proclaimed scientific (predictive) pretensions of Marx's social theory at the expense of its revolutionary thrust, which depends on an appeal to worker solidarity and class consciousness.[10]

The theory of value, Habermas adds, also fails to distinguish between pathological symptoms of reification and the nonpathological, but nonetheless painful, process of readjustment following the destruction of traditional life forms in the course of cultural rationalization. The theory of alienation proposed by the young Marx in the *Paris Manuscripts* of 1844 contrasts the essential freedom, sociality, and universal creativity inherent in human nature (*Gattungswesen*) with the distortion of same under capitalism. This ethical critique of capitalism was eventually repudiated by Marx, though traces of it linger in his account of the labor process in *Das Kapital*. The concept of alienation developed by Marx and Engels in *The German Ideology* of 1846 no longer appeals to a normative conception of human nature but still impugns the fragmentation of life wrought by the division of labor. Neither of the above conceptions of alienation, Habermas claims, distinguishes adequately between the normal costs of social rationalization and individuation and the pathological reification of the lifeworld. More important, Marx's analysis proceeds no further than the monetarization of labor, thereby all but neglecting the contribution of the complementary relationship between the state and the economy to bureaucratic reification.[11]

For a detailed statement of Habermas's understanding of this relationship, one must turn to *Legitimation Crisis*. Here, advanced capitalism is said to be characterized by extreme economic concentration (the rise of multinational corporations) and state intervention, both of which tend to limit, diminish, or replace market structures. The economic system in advanced capitalism is comprised of three sectors. In the public sector, which consists of state-owned businesses and privately owned firms dependent on government contracts, investment decisions are made without regard for the market. In the private sector, comprising competitive and monopolistic subsectors, the market is a factor, even if competition is tolerated only within very narrow limits. In liberal capitalism the administrative sector provides the minimum prerequisites necessary for the constitution and continued existence of the economic system, by securing property and contractual relations in a system of civil law, by protecting the viability of the market through antitrust legislation, labor laws, and so on, by providing for public education, transportation, and communication, by establishing trade and tariff policies, and by protecting foreign investments through military means.[12] It also complements the market in devising new legal arrangements in banking, business, and tax law. In advanced capitalism, government takes on the additional burden of regulating the economic cycle through national planning and creating and improving conditions for utilizing excess capital. National planning, which requires adjusting competing demands for steady growth, stable currency, full employment, and balance of trade through fiscal policy and regulation of investment and consumption by means of credits, price supports, subsidies, loans, income redistribution, and government contracts, does not interfere directly with the investment freedom of private businesses; it merely manipulates the boundary conditions for such investment. However, maintenance of conditions conducive to capital investment directly involves replacing market mechanisms by diverting capital into sectors neglected by the market, such as military hardware and space technology, improvement of transportation, education, health, and recreation facilities, the scientific intensification of labor productivity, and the compensation of the dysfunctional side effects of the capital accumulation process—unemployment compensation, welfare legislation, environmental control and restoration, and so forth.[13]

The repoliticization of the economic system under advanced capitalism also alters the class structure of society. Liberal capitalism succeeded in replacing the overt political class domination of feudal society with the covert economic class domination typical of the wage-capital relationship. But in advanced capitalism the state undertakes to control economic crisis tendencies before they assume politically volatile proportions—and does so, moreover, by acceding to the reformist demands of labor movements—with the result that the political anonymity under liberal capitalism is superseded by social anonymity, the difference between beneficiaries and victims no longer assuming the palpable form of a contrast between a few wealthy capitalists and a mass of impoverished workers.

Of special importance in this regard is the role of administratively supervised negotiations between unions and companies in establishing artificial wage scales and prices. Compromise between labor and capital in the monopolistic sector enables companies to maintain their level of profit by passing on increased labor costs to the consumer. The unresolved conflict between labor and capital, on the other hand, produces secondary side effects that are manifested in disparate wage scales between organized and unorganized sectors of the labor force, in permanent inflation, with its attendant redistribution of income, which always works to the disadvantage of workers and marginal groups, and in continual crises in government finances. Nevertheless, as long as the costs averting economic crisis are scattered over "quasi-groups" that straddle class lines—such as consumers, schoolchildren, and the elderly—or over identifiable social groups that remain unorganized—such as textile workers, hard-core unemployed, and single parents—social identity and class consciousness will remain fragmentary at most.[14] Most important, it is by institutionally neutralizing class conflict in abstract buyer-seller and client–civil servant roles that the state diffuses incendiary feelings of alienation and political antagonism stemming from concrete disparities in the social distribution of power and wealth; as compensation for being denied economic equality and effective political participation, worker-citizens are granted a high degree of material prosperity and security as consumers and clients.[15]

Habermas does not rule out the possibility that economic crises can be averted permanently. He is convinced, however, that the measures which must be taken by the state to forestall such crises merely displace the contradiction of socialized production for particular ends upward, thereby precipitating crises in rationality and legitimation at the level of the political system and crises in motivation at the level of the sociocultural system. Such tendencies must be distinguished from problems resulting from advanced capitalist growth, which include the problems of diminishing resources, the capacity of the environment to absorb heat due to energy consumption (the ecological balance), social integration (the anthropological balance), and thermonuclear warfare (the international balance), which are not specific to advanced capitalism. Nevertheless, given the internal limits of the system, which require that the production of surplus value be linked to continuous growth, that the coordination of action be detached from consensual processes through bureaucratic steering, and that the exploitation of new markets and resources be coupled with expansionist policies bolstered by government consumption of military hardware, it is unlikely that the state can resolve these problems in the long run. Yet it is only by maintaining constant economic growth that it can continue to siphon off the revenues necessary for underwriting opportunities for capital investment while also meeting the ever increasing demand for social services.[16]

Unlike the problems resulting from advanced capitalist growth, rationality, legitimation, and motivation crisis tendencies are endemic to advanced capitalism. Habermas examines each of these, in order of structural primacy. He dismisses two Marxist theories of economic crisis. He sees the orthodox theory, which holds that the advanced capitalist state remains subject to the imperatives of a self-regulating economic system (the law of value), as underestimating the extent to which the state can replace market mechanisms and alter the class structures under which surplus value is produced. Economic crises are not inevitable, since the tendency for the rate of profit to fall predicted by the law of value can be partially offset by government production of collective commodities that serve to heighten productivity.[17] Furthermore, the law of value is itself undercut by government fixing of wages and prices; because the value of labor then depends on political as well as cultural factors, the rate of exploitation is altered to the advantage of the best organized sector of the working class.[18]

According to the revisionist theory of economic crisis, which operates on the opposite assumption—namely, that the spontaneous working of economic laws has been replaced by centralized steering of the economic apparatus—the state acts as the agent of the collective interest of united monopolies, freeing investment decisions from

155

the market and repoliticizing the class relationship so that economic crises now assume a political form. Habermas sees this theory as overestimating the steering capacity of incompletely coordinated bureaucracies that are still beholden to conflicting interest groups for their power and ignoring the extent to which administration acts against such interests to preserve the economic status quo.[19]

Habermas concludes that a correct analysis of tendencies to economic crisis in advanced capitalism must be based on a notion of limited administrative planning that replaces market mechanisms without fundamentally altering the property relations circumscribing the accumulation of capital. For the state seeks to maintain productivity and growth and minimize the dysfunctional side effects of capital accumulation while procuring legitimation for itself through formal democratic means. In the final analysis, the capacity of the state to contain economic crisis tendencies depends on its ability to allocate tax revenue rationally (that is, to finance the social and environmental costs of production) without jeopardizing its standing with the masses, whose support is necessary for motivating compliance.

Rationality crises are precipitated when the state fails in the task of maintaining productivity. First, the welfare state is caught in a dilemma between sustaining constant growth, which requires concentration of enterprises and centralization of capital ownership, and compensating the dispossessed victims of such growth, which requires expropriation and redistribution of capital. This dilemma is exacerbated by the fact that the state cannot entirely avoid assuming responsibility for damages caused by a process for which it is in part responsible. It cannot proceed very far in satisfying one set of demands without at the same time deferring to the contrary set, thereby incurring mounting deficits.[20] Second, the government's capacity to read a compromise between competing claims is limited by the fact that it "has to investigate the *compromisibility* of interests without being able to bring up for discussion the generalizability of these interests."[21] Third, administrative planning in advanced capitalism generates "patterns of orientation" that are resistant to such planning. Government planning agencies cannot rely on market-based predictions of corporate behavior if the latter is oriented toward political patterns of valorization and decision. In transportation, health care, and housing, as well as in scientific and educational occupational spheres, work—especially professional work—is detached from market orientations. So too is the ever growing population of students, welfare recipients, and indigents who are not gainfully employed. Such people are unaffected by global planning strategies, which work by altering the monetary parameters of market exchange: rates of interest, taxation, inflation, and so on. Nevertheless, the detachment of large segments of the population from market orientations need not yield rationality deficits, Habermas concedes, if the state can motivate these segments to cooperate by other means. Whether or not this is possible depends in part on the capacity of the state to inspire loyalty.[22]

Thus, in advanced capitalism the state is confronted with contradictory steering imperatives; it is continually torn between underwriting the costs of economic growth and compensating its victims. This also raises a sensitive political problem, since the limited resources at its disposal are public revenues whose allocation for the benefit of private interests must be justified. Thus, although administrative crisis management against a background of class compromise may obscure the original boundaries of class conflict, it generates political conflicts that tend to contract the scope of government action. To avoid being undone by a crisis in legitimation, administration must be freed as much as possible from demands for legitimation. This is accomplished by concealing politically divisive issues behind a façade of symbolic gestures—such as appeals to nationalism, traditional values, side issues, subconscious prejudices, and so on—and ritual hearings, in which expert testimony is solicited to garner support for public policies.[23] Habermas believes that this strategy is counteracted by a disproportionate increase in demands for legitimation caused by the encroachment of the state on the cultural sphere. Administrative planning in education, health, and family life has the effect of repoliticizing areas formerly relegated to the private sphere. Traditions that were once accepted unanimously become topics of controversy that prompt demand for greater public participation. The state finds itself entangled in a new dilemma: it can neither yield to the pressure to reach consensus under conditions of class compromise nor ignore conservative and liberal-radical resistance to nonparticipatory planning.

Habermas thinks that legitimation crises can be contained as long as the population at large continues to prefer economic growth and material prosperity over democratic self-determination and to have faith in the capacity of technocrats to maintain it for everyone. Only if "expectations that cannot be fulfilled either with the available quantity of value, or generally, with rewards conforming to the system are systemically produced" can a legitimation crisis be predicted. Failure of administrative, educational, and occupational systems to provide incentives consistent with needs rooted in preexisting cultural traditions would be sufficient to instigate such a crisis, since these traditions cannot be torn from their natural context and artificially manipulated for steering purposes without losing their vital significance and power.[24]

Habermas gives two reasons for believing that a crisis in motiva tion may be endemic to advanced capitalism. First, the two cultural syndromes that contribute most to motivating compliance with the systemic goals of advanced capitalism—civil and familial-vocational privatism (here denoting a passive interest in administrative performance and a primary orientation toward consumption and leisure) and career achievement—are progressively eroded. Civil privatism is a hybrid product of bourgeois formal law, which promotes a belief in the accountability of government vis-à-vis a public composed of free citizens, and traditional and familial forms of political culture, which encourage deference to authority. Familial-vocational privatism likewise originates in a synthesis of bourgeois values (possessive individualism and utilitarianism) and religious traditions—most notably the Protestant work ethic, which is inculcated into the middle class in the form of uncoerced obedience to external authority and fatalistic acceptance of a conventional work morality.[25]

Habermas argues that the traditional values undergirding these two syndromes have not only surrendered their premier status to rationalization, but, thanks to the spread of "privatistic common consciousness," have succumbed to universal doubt. But those components of bourgeois ideology that comport with privatistic orientations, such as achievement ideology and possessive individualism, are also subverted by the system. Achievement ideology, which subordinates the natural—and from the standpoint of distributive justice, arbitrary—status assigned by birth to educational accomplishment under conditions of equal opportunity, becomes increasingly dubious as the connection between formal schooling and occupational success decreases. The ideology is further undermined by the fact that wages can motivate achievement in ungratifying occupations only if there is sufficient differential in income between workers and those unemployed—a differential that has largely disappeared as a result of governmental readiness to compensate the unemployed. Possessive individualism, which presupposes both that the common good is served by the preferences of private subjects and that these preferences reflect needs that can be satisfied through monetary rewards, has likewise lost its appeal. But in affluent societies, needs other than the minimal desire for individual subsistence are generated, which cannot be satisfied monetarily. And the expanded horizon of possible alternatives to existing institutionalized preferences raises social questions that can be decided only through collective discourse, and not through market decisions manipulated by public relations.[26]

Habermas observes that the deterioration in traditional and bourgeois values has been accompanied by the emergence of new normative structures that are unsuitable for reproducing civil and familial-vocational privatism. These normative structures, which crystallize around scientism, modern art, and universalistic morality, are tied to an irreversible logic that cannot be violated without severe psychological damage. Despite its affirmation of a positivistic common consciousness, scientism sets standards of critical discourse that not only undermine dogmatic attitudes but also provide a basis for criticizing its own dogmatic positivism. Modern art has given rise to a counterculture that renounces the life-style associated with achievement and possessive individualism. Finally, universalistic morality, which has its origins in bourgeois formal law, logically and unequivocally points in the direction of a communicative ethic whose guiding assumptions are at odds with the prevailing economic and political order of advanced capitalism. Not only do the universalistic presuppositions of a communicative ethic mandate the repoliticization and democratic resolution of conflicts of interest in a way that potentially threatens the class compromise worked out by the state, but the egalitarian conditions required for discourse stand in direct opposition to the disparities of wealth and power characteristic of class societies in general.[27]

Habermas concludes that "a legitimation crisis can be avoided in the long run if the latent class structures of advanced capitalist societies are transformed or if the pressure for legitimation to which the administrative system is subject can be removed."[28] The latter would amount to instituting a new form of socialization and integration uncoupled from normative justification. Supporting such a possibility are recent developments in the history of ideas: the widespread acceptance of cultural nihilism, as reflected in existentialism and positivism; the retrograde development of bourgeois political theory, which sees democracy more as a device for establishing compromises between ruling elites than as a participatory mechanism for reaching consensus over generalizable interests; and the conviction among many intellectuals that the notion of persons as autonomous individuals is but a relic of a passing phase in the evolution of the species that has been superseded by the objectivistic "technical-scientific self-reproduction of man."[29]

Speaking against the possibility of uncoupling socialization from normative integration is the stubborn need of human beings to overcome the contingencies of social existence through meaningful interpretations. With the passing of religious world views, modern humanity now lives "disconsolately" with those existential contingencies of guilt, loneliness, sickness, and death that resist rational justification. It is different, however, with the intensified suffering that results from uncontrolled societal processes. The norms of rational discourse anticipate the possibility of a community in which conflicting interests and needs are democratically and rationally adjudicated. It is not even idle speculation to suppose that the idea of God, denuded of personality, can be "transformed [*aufgehoben*] into the concept of a *Logos* that determines the community of believers and the real life context of a self-emancipated society," thereby serving as a counterweight to the positivistic "atheism of the masses" in which "the utopian contents of tradition are also threatened." Thus "the philosophical impulse to conceive of a demythologized unity of the world" holds open a promise of meaning that is compatible with scientific-technical rationality.[30]

Habermas's analysis of social pathology in *Theorie* is also premised on the embeddedness of social life in consensual communication. His analysis is an attempt to broaden the theory of social crisis developed in *Legitimation Crisis*. Symptoms of cultural impoverishment and the reification of the lifeworld caused by its assimilation to the economic-administrative system (inner colonization) are seen to constitute a crisis apart from other cultural crises.[31] Whereas motivation crises reflect input deficits in the economic system caused by dysfunctional cultural expectations, the loss of meaning, anomie, and mental illness symptomatic of cultural impoverishment and inner colonization reflect "deficiencies in the reproduction of the lifeworld" brought about by overextended economic and administrative subsystems. Systemic disequilibria resulting from contradictory steering imperatives produce legitimation and motivation crises centered in the societal component of the lifeworld. To stave off such crises, the state embarks on a strategy of ideology planning and civil depoliticization that, having as its focus those orders of life that directly impinge on the economy and public administration—education, health, welfare, and so forth—end up undermining the cultural and personality components anchoring the system.[32]

As we have seen, Habermas identifies the legal formalization of action as the mechanism underlying growth in system complexity. The first stage of formalization, which roughly coincided with the ascendance of the civil state (*bürgerlicher Staat*) during the period of political absolutism, saw the replacement of feudal economic relations by systems of contractual law guaranteeing universal economic freedom. During the second stage, public demands for legitimation compelled the state to subordinate its legislative power to the rule of law. Unlike the civil state, the constitutional republic (*bürgerlicher Rechtsstaat*) constitutionally guaranteed the freedom of its subjects from arbitrary state intervention as a matter of principle. In so doing, it took the first step toward anchoring the legal media of power—the administrative system—in the normative bedrock of the rationalized lifeworld. A further stage in the formalization of the political sphere was reached when the bourgeois revolutions of the nineteenth century succeeded in grounding the legitimacy of the state and its legislative apparatus in formal rules of participatory democracy. The fourth and final stage was precipitated by growing disparities in the social distribution of wealth. The economic freedom established by the first stage, unlike the extension of political freedom afforded by the second and third stages, was a mixed blessing as far as the proletariat was concerned, since it was purchased at the cost of great material deprivation. The ensuing struggle for workers' rights led to the legal establishment of the franchise followed by the creation of the welfare state. Whereas the constitutional republic and democratic state restrained the prerogative of the administrative system, the welfare state mitigated the inequities of the economic system.[33]

Laws that limit the workday, protect workers against recall, allow them to organize, and provide them with financial security result in a constitutional balance of power within the existing class structure that, at least from the perspective of their beneficiaries, unequivocally enhances freedom. This is not the case with all welfare legislation, however. Such legislation enhances freedom insofar as it establishes a legal claim to monetary compensation for loss of job due to old age, indigence, or recall; but the bureaucratic processing of such claims robs the beneficiaries of whatever freedom and dignity they may have gained from a guaranteed income. The paradox inherent in this type of legislation is that it promotes the social disintegration that it is designed to mitigate.[34]

What, precisely, is the source of this contradiction? Habermas tells us that it is not embedded in a juridical conflict between individual freedom (civil liberty) and collective self-determination (democracy), this opposition being artificial.[35] Nor is it endemic to a social conflict between strategic legal media (civil law), which detach economic and political systems from normative contexts, and legal institutions guaranteeing social integration (criminal, constitutional, and social law), which aim to reverse this process. Though legal media are anchored in legal institutions indirectly, the two do not normally operate within the same spheres.[36] The paradox of freedom-enhancing versus freedom-depriving legislation consists rather in the fact that social laws which aim to secure the material resources necessary for the exercise of equal civil and democratic rights can be effective only by formally organizing the private lives of dependent persons on a contractual, rather than a consensual, basis. When the state interferes in the private lives of citizens by threatening to withhold services unless they comply with the terms of a contract, they are made to feel less like persons and more like things in a calculus of liabilities and assets.[37] The legal formalization of reciprocal communicative relations vis-à-vis legal media that operate in accordance with strategic imperatives of system integration occurs throughout society in some subtle and not so subtle ways. Colonization of the lifeworld also encompasses that capillary network of economic, political, and cultural power effects detected by Foucault in the growing technical complexity of environmental management, the bureaucratic administration of nuclear waste disposal, the normalizing and stratifying features of education, and the systemic concentration and control of information. Its consequences range from the subsumption of leisure time, culture, and tourism under the laws of commodity production and mass consumption to the structural adaptation of the family to the imperatives of big business and the use of schools for distributing occupational opportunities and life prospects.[38]

THE PROBLEMS OF CRITICAL THEORY REVISITED

Armed with a bilevel theory of society, Habermas once again takes up the central problems of critical theory. With regard to the first problem, which concerned the social integrative achievement of national socialism, Pollack and Horkheimer were inclined to regard the totalitarian state as structurally isomorphic with the "state capitalism" instituted by the Soviet Union, in which both private property and the market are entirely controlled by a central party planning agency. Neumann and Kirchheimer demurred, insisting that the new regime relied on pseudo-democratic mechanisms for securing mass loyalty and thus provided an authoritarian buttress for monopolistic capitalism within the framework of the market.

In 1960 Habermas thought that the convergence of socialism and post-liberal capitalism "on the middle ground of a controlled mass democracy within the welfare state" should not be precluded, despite the fact that "the Soviet path to socialism only recommends itself as a method for shortening the process of industrialization in developing countries, one which is far removed from the realization of a truly emancipated society, and indeed at times has regressed again from the constituted rights attained under capitalism to the legal terror of Party dictatorship."[39] In his debate with Luhmann in the early seventies, however, he no longer spoke of such a convergence but instead saw both political systems as having replaced discursive mechanisms for adjudicating practical claims with technocratic means for procuring legitimacy: "Because the ideological forms of legitimation attendant upon growing system complexity become increasingly weakened, there arises in these systems . . . an increasing chronic need for legitimation."[40] Having considered the possibility that bureaucratic socialism was a distinct, post-capitalist social formation,[41] he is now inclined to regard it as a variant of the principle of organization (economic class society) characteristic of capitalism.[42]

The discussion of bureaucratic socialism in *Theorie* leaves no doubt that extant forms of capitalism and socialism are to be considered as having satisfied the initial conditions required for inclusion under the rubric of economic class society—namely, the rational differentiation of lifeworld and system. But, whereas, in capitalism, modernization is propelled by problems of economic growth that are independent of public administration, in bureaucratic socialism, public administration plays a direct role in rational planning and has achieved autonomy with respect to the economy and public spheres.[43]

Both types of society are fraught with crisis tendencies: "In bureaucratic socialism *crisis tendencies* arise from the planning administration, as they do in capitalism from the market economy, as soon as the administrative or the economic rationality of action orientations comes into contradiction with itself through unintended systemic effects."[44] Habermas draws on Arato's analysis of bureaucratic socialism in developing this thesis. According to Arato, economic crises under state socialism—typified by declining growth rates, consumer shortages, and lagging productivity—are caused by crises in management and information at the level of the administrative system. Management crises reflect the positive control of subsystems by a dominant system—in the case of bureaucratic socialism, of the economy to political, social, and ideological imperatives incompatible with economic goals.[45] Information crises stem from a superabundance of information vital to the economy (hyperinternal complexity), coupled with a lack of knowledge regarding consumer needs. It is interesting that the oscillation between policies predicated on the "self-healing powers" of the market and those involving state intervention that is regarded as characteristic of developed capitalism is even more pronounced under bureaucratic socialism. However, whereas the vacillation in capitalism is between regulation and deregulation of the market, that under socialism is between central planning and decentralization.[46] Pathological deformations of the lifeworld also arise, though here the points of incursion are not private households, as in advanced capitalism, but communicative media in the public realm:

> Here, too, a sphere relying on social integration, namely the political public sphere, is transferred over to system-integrative mechanisms. But the effects are different; in place of the reification of communicative relations, we

have the *shamming* of communicative relations in bureaucratically dessi-
cated, coercively harmonized domains of pseudo-democratic will formation. This *politicization* is in a certain way symmetric with *reification*. The
lifeworld is not assimilated to formally organized domains of action subject
to law; rather, the systemically independent organizations of the state are
fictively transposed back into the horizon of the lifeworld: the system is
draped out as a coercively integrated lifeworld.[47]

With regard to the second problem, which dealt with structural
changes in the nuclear family that contributed to the authoritarian
personality, it was thought that the authoritarian syndrome—typified by an emasculated ego and a corresponding compulsion to identify with surrogate superego figures—could be traced to a decline in
paternal authority caused by economic dependence. Members of the
Frankfurt school disagreed over whether instinctual drives posed
natural limits to authoritarian social structures—the view held by
Horkheimer, Adorno, and Marcuse—or were socially malleable
—the view held by Fromm.

Whereas his predecessors, under the influence of the Freudian
model of psychosexual development, with its emphasis on patriarchal authority and repressive introjection, saw the decline in paternal authority as indicative of a displaced identification with the state,
Habermas denies that the nuclear family has declined in importance
as an agent of socialization vis-à-vis the state. By transposing the purposive-rational model of psychosexual development onto the interac-
tional dynamics of language acquisition, it is possible, he thinks, to
explain freedom from the tyranny of the instincts in terms of dialogical accountability, rather than instrumental repression. On this reading, the decline in paternal authority would indicate a transition to a
higher, nonauthoritarian, nonrepressive form of socialization.[48]

The third problem, closely associated with declining proletarian
militancy and rising anti-Semitism, touched on the role of mass culture in modern society. Whereas Adorno, Löwenthal, and Marcuse
stressed the irrationality of mass culture, seeing it as a repressive
form of desublimation, Benjamin felt that the decontextualization of
mass-produced images would permit "profane illuminations" of a
critical nature.

If Habermas's estimate of the capacity of the family to withstand
the pressure of system integration is considerably more optimistic
than that of his predecessors, the same can be said of his opinions regarding the potential of mass culture for spawning political resistance
and social change. In the early seventies Habermas professed skepticism regarding the capacity of mass media to generate critical dialogue. Although he did not go as far as to espouse Adorno's and

Horkheimer's thesis that culture is nothing more than a commodity, he echoed their opinion that mass media serve predominantly as instruments of manipulation and social control. By contrast, the view set forth in *Theorie* underscores the ambivalent nature of mass media. To the extent that the public sphere has been colonized by the economic and administrative system, we may expect to find, as in the case of the family, certain contradictory features: the media must express competing interests in order to sustain a broad appeal, rather than be entirely homogeneous in conformity with mass consumer tastes (even trivial forms of popular entertainment contain critical messages); they are capable of disseminating ideology, but their effectiveness is limited by conditions of reception, intended messages being liable to critical inversion; and tendencies toward centralization are challenged by "video-pluralism" and "television democracy."[49]

Despite the decline, noted by first-generation critical theorists, in proletarian militancy, Habermas believes that the recalcitrance of family and public sphere to systemic pressures represents a considerable potential for political resistance. The "grammar of lifeworlds"—the quality of life, the social conditions for individual self-realization, and the extension of democratic participation and control to all aspects of life—is what is galvanizing the new protest movements. With the exceptions of the civil rights and the women's movements, the new movements bear a stronger resemblance to the anti-industrial and populist movements of the nineteenth century than to the emancipatory movements of the bourgeoisie and the proletariat. The mixed composition of these movements, albeit consisting predominantly of middle-class, young, college-educated people, comprises both conservative and progressive elements. However, like the class struggles of yesteryear, these new movements are directed against entrenched hierarchies.[50]

These movements protest the dependence of buyer-seller and employee-employer relationships, as well as the political dependence, passivity, and privatism fostered by client–civil servant and elector–office-holder relationships. Peace, antinuke, and ecological movements seem to have arisen specifically in response to the uncontrolled growth of the military-industrial complex. The need for public accountability becomes all the more urgent in view of widespread corporate and administrative indifference to the common welfare, as reflected in the growing arms race, the wanton polluting of human habitats by industry, and the disturbance of the organic and aesthetic harmony of the lifeworld that stems from sociotechnological engineering. What these movements seek above all is restoration of the public's right to decide how shared, nonrenewable resources are to

165

be disposed of. Habermas speculates that the desire for increased accountability of corporate and administrative bureaucracy might even lead to the emergence of new counter-institutions, such as informally organized economic cooperatives and participatory political organizations.[51]

If Habermas can be said to retrieve the emancipatory thrust of Marx's theory at all, it is in his attribution of the root cause of social pathology to economic and political domination. Not surprisingly, the path that he recommends for resolving the contradiction inherent in social production for private needs—namely, the institutionalization of a communicative ethic in which individual needs and decisions concerning the production and distribution of goods are subject to democratic review—has a distinctly egalitarian ring to it. But precisely how much credence is to be given to these utopian pronouncements, in light of his acceptance of rational management, is unclear. Habermas's synopsis of the progressive stages of legal formalization shows that the impulse to democratization arises in response to legitimation problems posed by the emergence of political and economic class stratification—a development that coincides with the anchoring of media-steered markets and bureaucratic organizations in bourgeois civil law. Because the power of individuals to influence the formation of public opinion in mass democracies depends on the material resources at their disposal, the push for equality must go beyond the establishment of formal rules permitting universal suffrage to include social welfare legislation. If the colonization of the lifeworld is not peculiar to post-liberal capitalism and bureaucratic socialism but obtains to some degree at least in any complex society in which the state has taken over the task of economic and administrative planning, then, short of retreating to simpler, smaller, and less developed forms of social organization—a possibility countenanced by Habermas only at the local level—it would appear that the tendency toward social rationalization is paradoxical after all.[52]

Assuming that the development of the social state is as irreversible as Habermas says it is, and that neither the radical goal of collapsing economy and state back into the pure democracy of an idealized lifeworld nor the conservative goal of depoliticizing economy and state in the direction of Luhmann's proposed uncoupling of system and lifeworld is a viable option, what sort of political agenda should critical theorists pursue? Habermas remains sufficiently radical to advocate the social democratization of the work place—compatible with the realities of efficient management, of course—as a worthwhile goal. But his Arendtean distrust of the Marxist subsumption of the political under the economic—a distrust born of the sobering experience of bureaucratic socialism—leads him to postulate a prior condition: reform of the political system itself.

Like other systems theorists, Habermas sees the political system as consisting of three subsystems: a bureaucratic state administration, which is made up of elected and appointed bureaucrats who implement authoritative decisions; a political party system, which generates mass support for the state through the competition of elected officials for administrative positions; and a public, which provides input and advocacy for general policies. Unlike systems theorists, however, Habermas opposes strict separation of the state from the public sphere, which he views as an extension of the lifeworld necessary for procuring legitimation. Though he regards mass political parties as indispensable for organizing and channeling diffuse input in complex, pluralistic societies, he harbors no illusions about their capacity to foster critical debate and democratic self-determination. In a recent interview he disparagingly remarks that party apparatuses "have become autonomous as large scale organizations and have migrated, as it were, into the political (administrative) system." The manipulative use of power takes on the eerie, surrealistic aspect of a postmodern nightmare in which traditional values are packaged in high-tech images and moral ideas are invested with the charismatic charm of "tinseltown" histrionics—"the waste dump of the refuse of civilization . . . dressed in plastic," as Habermas refers to it. Because he harbors grave doubts about the possibility of reforming the political party system, Habermas—who opposed the political organization of the Greens into a mass party—recommends that the party system and, with it, the state bureaucracy, be confronted by local, informal grass-roots groups. He says that "these autonomous public spheres would have to achieve a combination of power and intellectual self-limitation that could make the self-steering mechanisms of the state and economy sufficiently sensitive to the goal-oriented results of radically democratic will-formation." Raising the social state to "higher levels of reflection" would overcome the polarization of the public realm into nature-like, prereflective subcultures on the one hand and mass-organizational extensions of the state administration on the other, thereby challenging the boundaries separating system and lifeworld.[53]

Despite the social-democratic thrust of this proposal, doubts persist about the radicality of its scope. The most serious revolve around the system-lifeworld distinction. Can this distinction explain the interaction both inside and outside formally organized institutions, and is it compatible with a radical politics of emancipation? As we have seen already, Habermas is somewhat unclear as to the force of the distinction. Taken in a methodological sense as referring to dual perspectives from which any action whatsoever can be perceived, it does not justify the kind of categorical distinction between formal and informal organizations that Habermas claims it does. Taken as referring to analytic features that may be present in varying degrees in any domain of action, determination of whether such a domain falls predominantly under imperatives of social or system integration remains an empirical question. Habermas himself undermines the categorical nature of the distinction when he acknowledges that, even in formal organizations, superiors as well as subordinates are accountable for their actions. McCarthy adduces studies by William Buckley and Egon Bittner which confirm that procedural rules are often circumvented, selectively evoked, and subjected to continual reinterpretation and negotiation; and Dieter Misgeld has argued persuasively that market transactions do not so much replace consensual communication as narrow it. Money has a meaning to borrowers and lenders, buyers and sellers, that is rooted, however indirectly, in assumptions about fairness and reciprocity. Once again, the fact that the latent effects of an action—that is, its unintended objective consequences—are not recognized by the actor who undertook it does not mean that they are not present to another actor. Summarizing these findings, McCarthy concludes that one could just as easily reverse Habermas's claim that members of formal organizations act communicatively only with reservation and say that superiors in such organizations act authoritatively only with reservation.[54]

How compatible is the lifeworld-system distinction with social democracy? In his debate with Luhmann, Habermas opposed the idea of keeping systemic problems concealed, on the grounds that such structurification constituted a kind of counterenlightenment. This suggests that he would prefer an enlightened administration that would make such problems known to the public. But this could entail the sort of de-differentiation that Habermas, in his gloss of Marx, finds overly "romantic." Of course, in defense of such romanticism one might adduce McCarthy's observation that the extent to which democratic participation enhances or hampers global planning is an empirical question that cannot be decided theoretically.[55]

Given the difficulties regarding the viability of social functionalism that Habermas has detailed, one wonders with McCarthy whether it is at all defensible. It may be a plausible model for explaining the kinds of problems found in new technological industries in which effective task fulfillment is subordinated to considerations of structural flexibility. But Habermas seems to be wedded more to the theoretical rigor of the approach. In any case, the sorts of revisions involving the depth-hermeneutic determination of goal states that he recommends in *Legitimation Crisis* would not help in the present situation. Today Habermas relies more on a developmental logic in specifying the normative structures circumscribing the boundaries of social systems. But these abstract structures of justice are compatible with an indefinite number of possible goal states, and even if he were to return to the earlier hermeneutic approach of the sixties, he would have a hard time picking out the one valid conception of the good life from among those presently circulating among the various subcultures comprising our pluralistic society. Given the apparent vacuity of the ideal speech situation, it comes as no surprise to find Misgeld and McCarthy questioning Habermas's insistence on systemic rigor at the expense of historically situated culture critique.[56]

One of the major concerns of McCarthy and Misgeld is that the overly theoretical orientation of critical theory has severed its relationship with the concrete historical praxis of those progressive social movements whose aims and interests it was originally intended to clarify. Even Habermas has recently acknowledged this to be a problem. Pursuing this line of inquiry further, Nancy Fraser contends that the lifeworld-system distinction, as well as the institutional roles mediating these terms, conceal a gender-based subtext. Appealing to McCarthy's critique of the distinction, Fraser argues that to classify the nuclear family under the rubric of the lifeworld, the sphere of symbolic reproduction, is to ignore its material reproductive function as a sphere of unremunerated labor permeated by strategic decisions concerning control over income. Conversely, it ignores the degree to which the paid work place is structured by patriarchal forms of symbolic reproduction. Furthermore, if remuneration of domestic and institutional child rearing is a necessary condition for the emancipation of women, then it would appear on Habermas's model that the subsumption of this kind of activity under the wage relationship would issue in pathological side effects, although there is no empirical evidence to support this diagnosis.[57]

The institutional roles of worker, consumer, citizen, and client adduced by Habermas also conceal a gender-based subtext, which is passed over in his analysis. The role of worker is primarily masculine, since women are marginalized in "helping" professions in which they utilize their "motherly skills," or in part-time, low-paying, unskilled jobs, in which they supplement the incomes of their husbands. Whereas unemployment is regarded as an ego-shattering experience for men, who need to feel dominant, protective, and independent, it is regarded as the normal condition for women. The role of

169

citizen is also masculine. As one who defends country and home against aggressors, the citizen needs the analytic skills necessary for argumentation. Women's speech, by contrast, is systematically invalidated (when they say no, they mean yes). The passive roles of consumer and client, conversely, are predominantly feminine. Despite some recent changes in habits among men, women are the primary targets of advertising, and men seldom enter into the "phantasmatics of desire" without experiencing some cognitive dissonance. The client role is also "gendered" between workman's compensation on the one side and aid to families with dependent children on the other. Female heads of households claiming the latter do so not as individuals but as members of "defective households." Public patriarchy thus ends up replacing private patriarchy.[58]

Fraser concludes that male dominance is endemic to institutional roles under capitalism. Thus the major problem confronting women today, she submits, is not the colonization of the lifeworld by the system, but the reverse: the structuring of the system by patriarchal norms generated within the lifeworld. Whatever else it may require, the principal strategy for dealing with the ideological suppression of gender-based subtexts must be replacement of normatively secured contexts of agreement by problematizing discourse. This strategy may well require the kind of cultural separatism that Habermas has been hesitant to endorse.[59]

Commenting on other aspects of Habermas's separation of lifeworld and system, David Held has recently argued that the analysis of legitimation crisis overlooks the fact that "social integration, when tied to the generation of a shared sense of 'the worthiness of a political order to be recognized' (legitimacy) is not a necessary condition for every relatively stable society. . . . What matters is not the moral approval of the majority of a society's members . . . but the approval of dominant groups."[60] The broad mass of blue- and white-collar workers defer to the political order not because they find it worthy, but because they accept the necessity and rationality of coordination and management from above, and because in the absence of any real alternatives to the status quo they are inclined to resign themselves to the existing regime as necessary for securing their own well-being. The "dual consciousness" of many workers—which combines radical interpretations of social reality focusing on divisions between rich and poor, rulers and ruled, and so forth, with the conservative, privatistic attitudes mentioned above—may well have its source in the fragmentation of the work process rather than in precapitalist traditions as Habermas suggests.[61] To be sure, the analysis of the splitting off of elite cultures in *Theorie* encompasses the atomization of experience and knowledge caused by the hierarchical stratification of skilled and unskilled, mental and physical, labor. Habermas now agrees with Held that, in spite of a decline in culturally based privatistic orientations, a legitimation crisis can still be forestalled by the systemic "segmentation of the labor market and fragmentation of consciousness" in which "the need for normatively secured or communicatively achieved agreement is decreased and the scope of tolerance for merely instrumental attitudes, indifference, or cynicism is expanded."[62]

CHAPTER ELEVEN

The Theory-Practice Problem Revisited

Habermas's conception of the scope and function of critical theory has changed profoundly over the years. Early on, under the influence of Gadamer's hermeneutics, Habermas conceived of social life as a relatively undifferentiated sphere of action made up of the overlapping interpretative practices of individuals and groups. I say "relatively undifferentiated," because, despite his sensitivity to the ideological suppression of emancipatory interests, he continued to view this suppression as merely an effect of distorted self-understanding, one that could be vanquished through hermeneutical enlightenment. If a universalistic, systematically articulated tendency occasionally came to the fore during this period, it was never elaborated. The analytic differentiation and quasi-transcendental grounding of cognitive interests, disciplines, spheres of action, and social media propounded in his Frankfurt inaugural address of 1965 thus marked a significant departure from the hermeneutically conceived unity of theory and practice evident in his earlier work. Beginning with *Zur Logik der Sozialwissenschaften* of 1967, we find Habermas defending a combined hermeneutic-functionalist approach and with it an incipient conception of a bilevel model of society. To be sure, some of the distinctions hesitantly advanced in *Erkenntnis*—most notably that between empirical and transcendental structures—were soon discarded, if not always in practice, at least in theory. Others, however, were magnified. The new distinctions between rational reconstruction and emancipatory reflection, as well as those between discourse and action and among theoretical truth, critical enlightenment, and political strategy, signaled a further retreat from the relatively close interlocking of theory and practice still evident in *Erkenntnis*. Since 1973, however, there has been a softening of some of these distinctions. Although the threefold differentiation of cognitive interests has been "transformed in a new register within the theory of communicative action," as Richard Bernstein felicitously puts it, the cognitivistic bias informing that schema and the attendant implication of a subject-object model of interaction have not been retained.[1]

For all that it was hotly debated, the extent of Habermas's paradigm shift seems not to have been fully appreciated either by him or by his critics. If I am not mistaken, Habermas's recent expansion of communicative rationality to include a prediscursive, aesthetic moment reflects his growing conviction that the intention of modernity can be fulfilled only if the differentiation of specialized domains of rationality is somehow counterbalanced by their rational integration in the lifeworld. The dialectical expansion of communicative rationality beyond the narrow purview of ideal, argumentative speech also marks a profound change in the critical agenda. The shift from ideology critique to holistic criticism reflects a major reassessment of priorities; the Weberian emphasis on legitimation and motivation crises is now situated within a broader, more trenchant Marxist thematics of reification. The return to Marx by way of Parsons and Weber also raises new questions about the nature of rational society. Is societal institutionalization of a discourse ethic a sufficient condition for emancipation, or are there other conditions that must also be met? It seems that Habermas's negative response to the first question also implies a broadening of the category of reason. Neither practical nor social rationality can be grasped apart from aesthetic categories pertaining to the good life wherein harmony and integrity, self-realization and happiness, are achieved.

FROM IDEOLOGY CRITIQUE TO HOLISTIC CRITICISM

Marxist ideology critique departs from the premise that, to be palatable to the oppressed, relations of domination must be cloaked in universal interests.[2] For Marx, it was sufficient to show that so-called free exchange of equivalents in the market involved coercion, exploitation, and the promotion of class interests. But now that the state plays a leading role in manipulating the market, ideology critique can no longer take the form of a critique of the economy. Instead, it must focus on the legitimacy of political decisions that have been made through formal democratic channels. Justification for such a critique resides in the conviction that Western-style democracies fall short of the standards of rational dialogue—equal access to publicity, freedom from systematically distorted communication, and so on—that they ostensibly embody. The model of the suppression of generalizable interests that Habermas invokes to capture the failure of formal democracy in an otherwise undemocratic society assumes that what appear to be unresolvable conflicts between particular interests—for example, the antagonism between labor and capital—often belie common emancipatory interests. Whether democracy as it exists suppresses consensual discussion over generalizable interests behind the façade of pseudo-compromise or, what often amounts to the same thing, confers the dignity and title of "impartial policy" on class legislation can be determined only by penetrating the ideological veneer of consumerism, possessive individualism, and repressive asceticism.

First-generation critical theorists grounded ideology critique in subliminal sources of rationality contained in art or biological instincts.[3] While not denying that culture contains utopian intimations of emancipated life, Habermas has sought to distance himself from what he sees as the sometimes speculative, sometimes relativistic implications of these approaches, which rely all too heavily on a suspect philosophy of consciousness. The ideal speech situation thus offered itself as a less arbitrary—because universally justifiable—alternative, providing both a model of emancipated life and a method for hypothetically reconstructing the hidden interests of persons living in historical societies.[4]

It is a moot question whether deployment of the ideal speech situation avoids the speculative, relativistic implications of earlier methods of ideology critique.[5] Certainly the use of psychotherapeutic depth interpretation as a method of critique is hard to square with Habermas's recent pronouncements concerning the reciprocity existing between the social theorist and his or her peers—a difficulty that was pointed out earlier by Gadamer in their debate.[6] The debate also touched on the adequacy of the ideal speech situation as a model of rationality. Can practical rationality—in particular, the kind of sound judgment exercised in the application of general moral principles to concrete situations (phronēsis)—be reduced to argumentative discourse and emancipatory reflection? Is the cultivation of common sense that grounds the faculty of judgment not rather inserted in a different "game" of dialogue involving a "play" of questioning and answering, appropriation and emancipation, application and critique, that remains within the ambit of traditional prejudices? Indeed, is it not participation in concrete orders of ethical life that provides the limits of and possibilities for subjective choice in the first place; for without an intuitive, historically situated preunderstanding of the whole of life, could there be any understanding or any opening onto a meaningful world at all? Developing this critique of the Enlightenment's prejudice against prejudices further, Gadamer questioned the

174

extent to which society could do without certain forms of educational and political authority, especially those grounded in experience, tradition, and rhetoric. If some forms of authority constitute an ontological limit to social democracy and emancipatory reflection, then Habermas's conception of a rational society would seem dangerously abstract and anarchistic. A better conception, Gadamer averred, would be that of an organic totality that strives to achieve a dialogical balance between rational authority and communicative reciprocity, and therewith a balance between the arts and sciences and the everyday lifeworld.[7]

Aside from the issues of fairness—if Habermas did not always defer to the rights of legitimate authority and tradition during the debate, he has at least done so since then—Gadamer's critique raised important doubts about the viability of the ideal speech situation as a model of social rationality. These doubts were later echoed by Habermas himself, in his essay on Benjamin:

> Is it possible that one day an emancipated human race could encounter itself within an expanded space of discursive formation of will and yet be robbed of the light in which it is capable of interpreting its life as something good? The revenge of a culture exploited over millennia for the legitimation of domination would then take this form: right at the moment of overcoming age-old repressions it would harbor no violence, but it would have no content either. Without the influx of those semantic energies with which Benjamin's rescuing criticism was concerned, the structures of practical discourse—finally well established—would necessarily become obsolete.[8]

If an approximation to institutionalization of the ideal speech situation is not a sufficient condition for emancipation; if emancipation, narrowly conceived as liberation from dogmatic prejudice, must be counterbalanced by reinsertion within tradition—if, in short, the critique of ideology must be complemented by a redemptive critique of the present in light of the utopian possibilities of the past—then how is rational communication between persons and the life they share to be conceived? The "semantic energies with which Benjamin's rescuing criticism is concerned" do indeed point to a necessary interlocking of nature, happiness, tradition, and rational autonomy—a mimetic fusion, to be sure, which refrains from denaturing the primal stock of gestural meanings in the enervating limpidity of reflection —but this phrase does not capture fully the one-sidedness of the ideal speech situation. It was not until the late seventies that Habermas abandoned the idea that the ideal speech situation constituted a sufficient measure of global well-being and happiness and limited its scope to a single aspect of societal rationality—social justice. Because "it would be senseless to want to judge such a conglomeration as a whole, the *totality of a form of life*, under individual aspects of rationality," he saw the need to introduce a more holistic conception of societal rationality, along the lines proposed by Gadamer.

> If we do not wish to relinquish altogether standards by which a form of life might be judged to be more or less failed, deformed, unhappy, or alienated, we can look if need be to the model of sickness and health. We tacitly judge life forms and life histories according to standards of normality that do not permit an approximation to ideal limit values. Perhaps we should talk instead of a balance among non-self-sufficient moments, an equilibriated interplay of the cognitive with the moral and aesthetic-practical. But the attempt to provide an equivalent for what was once intended by the idea of the good life should not mislead us into deriving this idea from the formal concept of reason which modernity's decentered understanding of the world has left us.[9]

Habermas's reassessment of societal rationality reflects the diminished importance of ideology critique in his new agenda. Because the general trend toward secularization renders all ideological legitimations susceptible to critique, Habermas speculates that if rationalization were to proceed unhampered by systemic distortions, the modern form of communicative understanding (*Verständigungsform*) would become so transparent that "the imperatives of autonomous subsystems . . . [could] no longer lie concealed within the fissures of rationality separating sacred and profane spheres of action . . . inobtrusively penetrating and subsuming the action orientations of the lifeworld under intuitively inaccessible functional connections." Obstructing this trend, however, is the reification of consciousness caused by the splitting off of expert cultures and the colonization of the lifeworld. The splitting off deprives everyday consciousness of reflective capacities and opportunities for analyzing its experience (in terms of distinct cognitive, practical, and aesthetic standards) and reintegrating it in the form of a balanced life: "Everyday consciousness understands that it is dependent on traditions whose claim to validity has been suspended, and yet it remains hopelessly splintered wherever it would extricate itself from the influence of tradition. In place of *false* consciousness there today appears a *fragmented* consciousness which impedes an understanding of the mechanism of reification."[10] Habermas concludes that, "instead of serving the critique of ideology," critical theory should "explain the cultural impoverishment and fragmentation of everyday consciousness; instead of pursuing the scattered traces of revolutionary consciousness it would state the conditions for a recoupling of rationalized culture with everyday communication based on vital cultures."[11]

It may be wild speculation to suppose that, in light of the heavy costs of anomie, alienation, and reification, rational persons might prefer the self-indulgent gratification of sensuous appetites afforded by a higher standard of living to that halcyon bliss born of self-respect, communal solidarity, justice, and self-determination. But if it is true, it is not because an ideology critique of injustice tells us so. "There remains," Habermas tells us, "only the critique of deformations inflicted in two ways, on the life forms of capitalistically modernized societies: through devaluation of their traditional substance and through subjection to the imperatives of a one-sided rationality limited to the cognitive-instrumental."[12] It remains to be seen whether a procedural conception of communicative rationality can provide the basis for a critique of this sort, and whether it can ground the intention of the Enlightenment, which, as Habermas sees it, is to restore the rationality potential cultivated in separate, autonomous disciplines to everyday life.

HERMENEUTICAL REFLECTION AND AESTHETIC RATIONALITY:
BETWEEN NIHILISM AND DOGMATISM

From Kant's Third Critique to Husserl's *Crisis,* German philosophy has sought to defend a conception of rationality that would, as Habermas puts it, "preserve a relationship to the whole." Philosophy is assigned by Hegel the task of showing both that the mediation of distinct branches or levels of reason is a fait accompli, that reason is already a mediating force in social life, and that this potential, having not yet become fully actualized, remains problematic in an ideal sense. This way of formulating the problem was inspired originally by the dubious epistemic status of transcendental reflection in Kantian philosophy. By limiting knowledge to a causal understanding of spatiotemporal events and elevating the principle of analytic thought above speculative or dialectical reason, Kant could neither justify philosophy's unique claim to provide a system of a priori principles nor show how practical reason—a freedom from natural inclinations which the rational self "legally" imposes on itself—could be related to happiness. Habermas, who has thoroughly assimilated Hegel's critique of Kant, is nonetheless faced with similar, if not identical, difficulties.

Habermas believes that philosophy can fulfill both the tasks assigned to it by Hegel without resorting to a dialectical conception of reason that would overcome all categorical distinctions. Philosophy can demonstrate the de facto mediation of reason in the grammatical unity of speech. As we have seen already, this unity is exemplified, first, in the individual speech act, which simultaneously raises validity claims to truth, rightness, and sincerity, and, second, in the functional interdependence of different types of statements and thus of the communicative functions of cultural reproduction, normative integration, and personal individuation. Philosophy is also called on to articulate tendencies within the various human sciences that serve to counteract the formal fragmentation of reason:

> The *non-objectivistic* research program within the human sciences also brings to bear the standpoints of moral and aesthetic critique without endangering the primacy of questions of truth; only in this way is a critical social theory possible. The discussion concerning an ethic of responsibility and conscience and the more weighty consideration of hedonistic motives brings into play within universalistic ethics standpoints regarding the calculation of consequences and the interpenetration of needs, both of which lie within cognitive and expressive domains of validity. Here materialistic ideas find a secure niche within the moral sphere without violating its autonomy. Finally, post-avant-garde art is characterized on the one hand, by a reciprocity between realistic and action oriented (*engagierten*) directions, and on the other hand, by authentic continuations of that classical school of modern art which had revealed (*herauspräpariert*) the peculiar nature of the aesthetic. We thus see in the case of realistic and action-oriented art the coming together of cognitive and moral-practical moments within the sphere of the aesthetic. It appears as if in such countermovements the radically differentiated moments of reason aspire to a unity (*auf eine Einheit verweisen wollten*) which, to be sure, is not to be attained again at the level of worldviews, but rather only on this side of expert cultures, in a non-reified, everyday communicative praxis.[13]

However much it may contribute to a clarification of the real tendencies of rational mediation at work in everyday communicative praxis—tendencies that cannot be fully realized at the level of formally differentiated discourse, humanistic or otherwise—philosophy's highest office remains that of social critic. As social critic, the philosopher must defend the integrity of communicative praxis against systematic bureaucratization and economic reification. The formal conception of communicative rationality imputed by Habermas to inform the grammatical unity of cultural reproduction, normative integration, and personal individuation does indeed demarcate an absolute limit to socially engineered management of economic and political contradictions. Yet somewhere between the extremes bounding the spectrum of selective rationalization—total reification and total politicization (the binding of all social relations to mutually criticizable first-person speech acts)—there is an ideal balance of strategic and communicative action spheres that cannot be established formally. There are no criteria of rational argumentation to which we can appeal in disputes over how this balance, so central to our utopian understanding of the good life, should be construed. The problem, then, is to understand how and by what authority a proper state of equilibrium between heterogeneous orders of life can be discerned.

Of all discursive enterprises, philosophy seems especially well suited to performing this balancing act, since on Habermas's reading, the sort of rational reconstruction that it engages in manages to slide across the boundaries separating formally distinct spheres of rationality. Reconstructive hypotheses concerning formal-pragmatic speech conditions, cognitive and practical developmental stages, and so on are at once logical (normative), empirical (descriptive), and hermeneutic (reflexive).[14] Their validity is thus established with respect to theoretical, practical, and aesthetic discourse simultaneously; that is, they square with empirical data (truth), withstand questioning by reasonable persons in practical discourse (rightness), and satisfy aesthetic needs for coherence, unity, and simplicity—needs that underscore the fallibility of a program not anchored in a priori foundations. The universality of communicative structures is thus not transcendental, empirical, or logical but consists in a shared sense that regulates action while remaining contingent on the diverse, fluctuating interpretations of historical agents.

What enables philosophy to "communicate" with heterogeneous spheres of rationality, and in a manner that is not exclusively cognitive, normative, or aesthetic is something akin to what Gadamer calls "hermeneutical reflection."[15] In order to establish the rightful boundaries of each sphere, it is necessary to reflect on the whole range of human experience. This reflection, Habermas insists, can be articulated in language limited to a single validity claim, using a form of argumentation appropriate to a single discipline, but only if the contents of the reflection are expanded and enriched rhetorically so as to include indirect communications that refer back to everyday practice.[16] This enrichment of communicative rationality beyond the narrow purview of pure discourse, however, is still not sufficient to capture the peculiar rationality of critical theory.

As Habermas now envisages it, critical theory must go beyond a critique of ideology limited to questions of justice and legitimacy. The critique of reification proffers judgments about preferred states of equilibrium that are not unequivocally true, just, or authentic. These judgments cannot be justified in rational discourse limited to distinct validity claims. Are we to conclude, therefore, that they are irrational?

If we stick to the strong identification of rationality and discourse implicit in *Theorie*, the answer is yes. For if rationality is exhausted in such argumentation, then any claim that is indiscriminately factual, normative, and aesthetic would ipso facto be irrational. Moreover, as

179

Habermas's commentary on Weber shows, the value of health, which might otherwise ground the critique of reification, is not a rational value since it is irrelevant to the pragmatics of communicative action. That knowledge, legitimate norms, and trustworthy persons are all necessary conditions for any modern society is guaranteed solely by the direct role that cognitive, normative, and expressive validity claims play in the communicative reproduction of social life. By contrast, health, understood as a felicitous balance between strategic and communicative action spheres, designates something like the inviolable sanctity of communicative life as such.

It is ironic that the strict differentiation of discourses that threatens to undermine the global rationality of a critique of reification has as its complement a covert reductionism. On Habermas's reading, practical reason (*Moralität*) is virtually identical with the discursive justification of norms vis-à-vis counterfactual standards of universalizability. Conventional ethical life (*Sittlichkeit*), by contrast, is regarded as something motivated wholly by dogmatic and otherwise diffuse evaluations of the good life. However much the interpretative application of norms to concrete situations exhibits rational flexibility and openness, its uncritical acceptance of prior traditional authority stamps it as irrational.[17] But lest it be forgotten, Habermas's tendency to stretch practical reason to fit the procrustean bed of theoretical discourse is most evident in his overriding preoccupation with skepticism. Although he is much taken with Durkheim's attempt to trace the counterfactual concept of validity back to dogmatic—that is, habitual and affective—solidarity grounded in religious practice, he, like Durkheim, ends up as a Platonist, believing that rationality, be it theoretical or practical, is best captured by the notion of truth, conceived as unconstrained, universal consent. This imbalance is rectified, however, when we turn to Habermas's treatment of aesthetic rationality.

I shall argue that the kind of global rationality which guides the critique of reification is akin to the conception of aesthetic rationality which appears in Habermas's more recent writings. But first I shall return to Habermas's original discussion of aesthetic rationality in *Theorie*. One of that work's novel insights is that the rationality of aesthetic judgments resides in the objectification of a kind of knowledge in works of art that is different from the kind of knowledge objectified in theoretical and practical creations.[18] Habermas mentions two senses in which this is so. Following Weber and Adorno, he argues that art constitutes a separate domain of problems, one that exhibits a progressive technical mastery of materials—for example, the discoveries of perspective in painting and polyphony in music. More important, art embodies claims to authenticity, unity, and harmony. Rational are those persons who have interpreted their desires and feelings with respect to culturally established standards of value *and* who have reflected on the adequacy of these values as authentic expressions of an exemplary form of experience. Works of art embody such values, and it is the task of aesthetic criticism to show this, so that the work can "take the place of an argument and promote the acceptance of precisely those standards according to which it counts as an authentic work."[19] Learning takes place, and if the history of art does not show progress in actual achievement—it would be presumptuous to say, for example, that twentieth-century abstract expressionism is superior to, or more rational than, the representational art of the Renaissance—it at least issues in an "advancing exploration of a realm of possibilities for illuminating our familiar world in new ways."[20]

Aesthetic rationality is still a discursive enterprise that is primarily concerned with the raising of aesthetic claims to authentic experience, whether these be embodied in works of art or judgments of taste. This sort of rationality is attested to by an expectation of possible agreement. Like Kant and Shaftesbury before him, Habermas points to the presumed nonarbitrariness of aesthetic judgments as evidence for this claim: we do not dispute matters of personal preference—for example, which of two fragrances pleases most—but the fact that we do so dispute matters of taste indicates that a claim to intersubjective validity has been raised. The basis for our expectations of agreement is not, as it was for Kant, an unconstrained harmony of mental faculties common to us all, but rather a shared exemplar of experience. Although this exemplar is relative to concrete forms of social life and is therefore not judged to be universally binding for all cultures, in the way that claims to truth and justice are, it is nevertheless presupposed as "normatively regulating a common interest."[21]

As long as aesthetic rationality is defined in the narrow Kantian sense as discourse over expressive claims to authenticity—that is, as pertaining solely to the rationality of needs, desires, and feelings, it cannot be the global rationality for which we are searching. Indeed, as Habermas himself makes clear, the course of aesthetic rationalization would place this Kantian aesthetic in jeopardy. Aesthetic rationalization radicalizes the subjectivity of aesthetic experience to the point of undermining any rational basis in a shared community of values. Authentic aesthetic experiences "of which only a decentered, unbound subjectivity is capable" are "possible only to the extent that the categories of the patterned expectations of organized daily experience collapse, that the routines of daily action and conventions of ordinary life are destroyed, and the normality of foreseeable and accountable certainties suspended."[22] Having purified itself of all cognitive and

181

normative residues, avant-garde art withdraws ever further into the innermost regions of subjective experience—the unconscious, the mad, the fantastic, and the corporeal. It ceases to communicate, and its claim to authenticity is detached from any shared fund of values. Either art and art criticism become so specialized as to be totally alien to everyday experience—the problem besetting much esoteric autonomous art—or else, as in some of the more radical variants of modern art—surrealism in particular—the formal and semantic elements lose their peculiar expressive power by being absorbed into the unstructured, desublimated experience of everyday life. This explains why neither tendency, in Habermas's opinion, can have a structure-building effect for society as a whole. The esoteric expressions of an elite counterculture no more communicate authentic experiences to the average person than does the consumer propaganda of popular culture.[23]

This is not to say that Habermas rejects the critical intention of avant-garde art, only that for him it is less easily reconcilable with the model of aesthetic rationality developed in *Theorie* than bourgeois art. Autonomous bourgeois art has "taken up positions on behalf of the victims of bourgeois rationalization" by expressing those needs for "a mimetic relation with nature; the need for living together in solidarity outside the group egoism of the immediate family, the longing for the happiness of a communicative experience exempt from imperatives of purposive rationality and giving scope to imagination as well as spontaneity."[24] The illusion of beauty projected by bourgeois art contains direct reference to an anticipated agreement, inscribed in the desire for solidarity and undistorted communication, that is related to the sort of collective exemplary experience underwriting aesthetic rationality in *Theorie*. Modern art, on the other hand, shatters this illusion.

In his essay on Benjamin, Habermas took stock of the negative and positive yield of this development. On the negative side, the destruction of the aura potentially issues in the "degeneration of art into propagandistic mass art or into commercialized mass culture" and the loss of the primal mimetic energies responsible for the aura's power.[25] On the positive side, it resolves the contradiction, as Marcuse saw it, between the ideal essence of autonomous art, which is critical of existing reality, and its ideological function, of affirming that reality as a domain of reconciliation. Although Habermas agreed with Marcuse and Adorno that the technology of mass production could not explain the de-auraticization of art, he nevertheless expressed sympathy with the other aspect of Benjamin's analysis—the critical redemption of the secular illuminations wrought by such a process. While not subscribing to the conservative implications of

Benjamin's theory of language, which "can but comprehend itself as identification and *repetition* of emphatic experiences and utopian contents—and not as reflection in a formative process," Habermas endorsed the theory's assumption that "a semantic store of original subhuman forms of communication has found a place in human language and represents a potential [for interpreting needs] that cannot be augmented."[26] In other words, he agreed that in addition to expressing the subjectivity of the speaker, language and art imitate nature. This is as close as Habermas has ever come to acknowledging the mimetic reconciliation of man and nature. Furthermore, he subscribed to the goal of making this aesthetic experience accessible to the public and in so doing lent his support to the basic intention underwriting modern art—the restoration to everyday life of rational experiences that are ordinarily cultivated in specialized discourses. Finally, he acknowledged that communicative rationality was insufficient for achieving happiness. Also required is the redemption of those semantic energies that bespeak a reconciliation between man and nature. It is this mimetic aspect that resurfaces in Habermas's more recent formulations of aesthetic rationality.

But, as noted above, as long as the aesthetic is restricted to the domain of subjective expression, aesthetic rationalization can lead only to its own subversion. However, as we have also seen, another, more Hegelian (or Benjamian) conception of aesthetic rationality informs Habermas's recent work. The knowledge embodied in works of art, Habermas maintains, is not restricted to authentic interpretations and evaluations of subjective needs. The work of art also brings to expression an aesthetic experience that "is not simply to be transposed into judgments of taste by professional arbiters, that is not merely to circulate in the realm of art alone." Stated simply, art articulates a utopian image of "a balanced and undistorted intersubjectivity of everyday life." This aesthetic experience not only affects individually the cognitive, normative, and expressive dimensions of life; it "transforms the totality in which these moments are related to one another." What earlier appeared as a reconciliation between man and nature now appears as a mimetic correspondence between art and life. Art thus raises a special kind of validity claim concerning a "potential for truth," or, more specifically, the utopian possibilities of a fully realized life that cannot be identified with any one of the three validity claims constitutive of communicative action.

The aesthetic "validity" or "unity" that we attribute to a work refers to its singularly illuminating power to open our eyes to what is seemingly familiar, to disclose anew an apparently familiar reality. This validity claim admittedly stands for a *potential* for "truth" that can be released only in the whole complexity of life-experience; therefore this "truth-potential" may not be connected to (or even identified with) one of the three validity-claims constitutive for communicative action, as I have been previously inclined to maintain. The one-to-one relationship which exists between the prescriptive validity of a norm and the normative validity claims raised in regulative speech acts is not a proper model for the relation between the potential for truth of works of art and the transformed relations between self and world stipulated by aesthetic experience.[27]

Art communicates its "truth" in a language that belongs to everyday communicative practice, not to aesthetic criticism. This can only mean that the illumination of life situations occurs in a language that, in the words of Wellmer, metaphorically articulates the unity of a "lifeworld experience in which the three validity domains are unmetaphorically intermeshed."[28]

The importance of this conception of aesthetic rationality for the problem with which we began is apparent. That problem concerned the need to ground a holistic critique of reification in a global form of rationality. Such a rationality could not be adequately compassed by a procedural model of argumentation, no matter how far it extended over cognitive, normative, and aesthetic value spheres. For what was needed was not a form of rational argumentation that would be subordinated to one or other of the value spheres, but a form of rational teleology that would show what no form of ideal speech possibly could show—namely, complete realization of a life of freedom and happiness at the level of individual and collective life. We have now located in the corpus of Habermas's writings a conception of aesthetic rationality that satisfies this last condition.

There is much that remains problematic in this conception. Is it not, as Jean-François Lyotard has suggested, a plea for an organic unity of the sort postulated by Hegel or a synthetic unity of heterogeneous value spheres reminiscent of Kant, both of which seem to presuppose a thoroughly discredited belief in rational teleology and unified subjectivity?[29] And is it not still wedded to a traditional aesthetic of the beautiful? Modernity may well express a yearning for a lost sense of totality and harmony, Lyotard contends, but the proper category for modern art is the sublime. As described by Kant, the sublime does indeed testify to an idea of totality, but one that explodes conventions of form, frustrates the sense of harmony, escapes our capacity for representation, and in Lyotard's opinion, issues in a painful pleasure that is closer to neurosis and masochism than to Freudian sublimation. Formal boundaries are dissolved only to produce dissonance within disciplines, not harmony between them.[30] Coming from a similar position, Bürger has underscored the conflict between the rational differentiation and alienation of cultural value spheres and their reintegration with the lifeworld. He notes the difficulty, also mentioned by Habermas in his critique of surrealism, of any mediation of art and lifeworld that is not accompanied by a parallel mediation of the cognitive and practical spheres. Habermas's assumption that the three cultural spheres exhibit parallel development is belied by the resistance of modern science to mediation. Furthermore, Habermas may have underestimated the tendency of modern art to oppose any reintegration with the lifeworld.[31]

What are we to make of these criticisms? The poststructuralist fear that the desire for rational unity will issue in a totalitarian suppression of difference and autonomy is one that Habermas has repeatedly sought to lay to rest. In a recent interview with the editors of *New Left Review* he emphatically reiterated his conviction that a fully transparent, homogeneous, rationalist utopia is incompatible with the pluralism of life forms and interests, even going so far as to suggest that "compromises possess a wholly undiminished worth."[32] The rational potential for individual and social integrity implies a state of equilibrium among heterogeneous value spheres and action domains, not a harmony of interests extending beyond a general agreement over the rules of discourse. The optimal well-being of a rational society is nevertheless compatible with conflict, alienation, and suffering caused by forces other than social domination, some of which, to be sure, are inherent in the process of differentiation itself. This irrecusable fact, as well as Habermas's earlier acceptance of Benjamin's view of modern art as allegorically depicting human suffering, thus suggests that he would strongly resist Lyotard's insinuation that his is an aesthetic of the beautiful. It would also be incorrect to say that the rational teleology that it presupposes implies a necessary process or even a developmental logic. The goal of a rational society—mimetic harmony between individual, society, and nature—is contingent on the prior development of communicative rationality and takes on a specific meaning that is relative to the cultural ideals of concrete historical societies. As Jay remarks, Habermas himself expressly denies that the mimetic utopia implicit in art—which is not to be confused with a reconciliatory transcendence of suffering—is an "original reason whose place has been usurped by instrumental rationality."[33] In the final analysis, Habermas's notion of aesthetic rationality differs from its precursors in the German idealist tradition in that it is not intended to resolve the tensions in modern society. For this reason, its status

185

must remain problematic in light of the general trend toward differentiation, especially insofar as this tends to issue in a subjectivization of the aesthetic that often borders on the perverse.

The preceding discussion suggests some interesting comparisons between the work of art and the work of philosophy, not least concerning the unique kind of truth claims raised by each. How such nondescript claims are to be assessed critically if they do not fall under any distinct type of discourse remains unclear. Perhaps, as in the case of so many of our practical judgments, the mode of justification cannot be established in argumentation but must await the outcome of practice. There appears to be an affinity of sorts linking aesthetic rationality and phronēsis—not only the obvious importance of taste exercised in prudence, but also the orientation toward the good life in its entirety. Both the ethicist and the artist project (if only implicitly) a life in its integrity. In this respect, authentic art and axiology share a common structure with interpretation generally—namely, the anticipatory projection of a completion and perfection of meaning. The latter seems to transcend anything that can be articulated in criticizable utterances, in the direction of something more intuitive—the nonthematizable preunderstanding of a lifeworld. It may well be that understanding is "more being than consciousness," as Gadamer would have it, but the defense of that claim would take us well beyond the scope of this book.[34]

CONCLUDING UNSCIENTIFIC POSTSCRIPT

If what I have said above is correct, then the truth of holistic social critique, like that of truth and truthfulness in mimetic art, is circumscribed by its own preunderstanding and thus can never be grounded discursively. This means that practical reason can admit only of degrees, of being more or less appropriate, more or less convincing, more or less free from constraint. It is the denial of this nonmeritricious contextuality and relativity that seems to animate the dialectic of enlightenment. Commenting on the formalism of Kantian ethics, Adorno once remarked:

> The de-practicalization of Kant's practical reason—in other words, its rationalism—is coupled with its deobjectification; it must have been deobjectified before it can become that absolutely sovereign reason which is to have the capacity to work empirically irrespective of experience. . . . Since freedom, to Kant, amounts to reason's invariant identity with itself, even in the practical realm, it loses what in common usage distinguishes reason from the will. Due to its total rationality, the will becomes irrational.[35]

Implicit in Adorno's caveat is a Nietzschean aversion to the Platonic *ressentiment* toward time that informs all transcendental efforts at justification. This healthy aversion to nihilism does not dissolve the paradox of rationality, however. We owe it to Habermas for having at least clarified the dynamics of this modern dilemma, which pits our emancipatory and consensual ideals, as reflected in the *grands récits* of legitimation bequeathed to us by the Enlightenment, against the stubborn historicity, ethnicity, multivocity, and strategic impurity of everyday practice. This means that counterfactual conceptions of rational consensus can function as regulative ideas guiding local practices in which persons possess equal communicative competencies, but that they cannot serve as operational criteria for evaluating the justice of large-scale, complex societies without succumbing to utopian extremism. What Habermas perceives as a "pragmatic contradiction" implicit in postmodern attempts at discursive self-justification is in part attributable to the other side of this dilemma, which Lyotard has characterized as an incommensurability between the pragmatic legitimation of everyday narratives effected by the habitual and mimetic repetition of speech patterns and the decontextualizing legitimation of utterances in argumentation. But as Rorty has eloquently argued, where the Nietzschean enthusiasts of postmodernity go astray—in what is otherwise a commendable debunking of transcendental metanarratives—and where they succumb to the neoconservativism for which Habermas reproaches them, is in their sublime disregard for communication and social consensus.[36]

In their haste to distance themselves from existing social institutions and traditions that putatively stifle authentic criticism, postmodern thinkers sometimes forget that they cannot simply write off their Enlightenment heritage without falling into a kind of pragmatic contradiction, and in two senses: by tacitly affirming the validity (and by implication, rational justifiability) of their assertions, and by failing to acknowledge the complementarity of power and conflict on the one hand and reason and consensus on the other. In short, they neglect to situate surface phenomena indicative of actual fragmentation against the background of a distorted lifeworld whose ideal presuppositions, when understood from the perspective of the actor rather than the scientific observer, include solidarity and wholeness. Habermas parlays this riposte against traditionalists as well. The naive preSocratic reliance on a pure aesthetic ethos—a rhetoric of life, if you prefer—in which humanity is handed over to a fate that is at once both beautiful and tragic is no longer a real possibility for us. But neither is that equally naive confidence in the power of reason to soar above the historicity of substantive tradition. And so we return once

187

again to Weber, for to be caught up in the eternal conflict between the gods of critical reflection and those of living tradition is the only fate possible. Any attempt to extricate ourselves can only lead to nihilism. Moreover, a dogmatism that refuses to countenance a critical appropriation of tradition contributes to the annihilation of living values just as surely as a rationalism that demands universal and univocal consensus as a condition for bestowing recognition. That reason must somehow be conceived as both being and consciousness, necessity and freedom, is the Promethean legacy bequeathed to us by Hegel; to accept this contradiction is to suspend oneself in an eternal recurrence that is at once critical transcendence and living affirmation of tradition. This conclusion is inescapable, even for a rationalist like Habermas, who, in a particularly revealing moment, admits that the participants in discourse "know, or at least they are able to know, that even the presupposition of an ideal speech situation is only necessary because convictions are formed and contested in a medium which is not 'pure' nor removed from the world of appearance in the manner of Platonic ideals. Only a discourse which admits this everlasting impurity can perhaps escape the myth, thus freeing itself, as it were, from the entwinement of myth and enlightenment."[37]

ABBREVIATIONS

CD   *Habermas: Critical Debates*. Edited by J. B. Thompson and David Held. Cambridge, Mass.: MIT Press, 1982.

CES   *Communication and the Evolution of Society*. Translated and edited by Thomas McCarthy. Boston: Beacon Press, 1979. Contains selected essays from *Zur Rekonstruktion des Historischen Materialismus* and "Was Heißt Universalpragmatik."

KHI   *Knowledge and Human Interests*. Translated by J. J. Shapiro. Boston: Beacon Press, 1971. Original title: *Erkenntnis und Interesse*. Frankfurt: Suhrkamp, 1968. Also contains the inaugural address.

KK   *Kultur und Kritik: Verstreute Aufsätze*. Frankfurt: Suhrkamp, 1973.

KpS   *Kleine politische Schriften I–IV*. Frankfurt: Suhrkamp, 1981.

LC   *Legitimation Crisis*. Translated by Thomas McCarthy. Boston: Beacon Press, 1975. Original title: *Legitimationsprobleme im Spätkapitalismus*. Frankfurt: Suhrkamp, 1973.

MkH   *Moralbewusstsein und kommunikatives Handeln*. Frankfurt: Suhrkamp, 1983.

NU   *Die Neue Unübersichtlichkeit: Kleine politische Schriften V*. Frankfurt: Suhrkamp, 1985.

PDM   *Der Philosophische Diskurs der Moderne*. Frankfurt: Suhrkamp, 1985.

PP$_2$ *Philosophical-Political Profile*. Translated by Fred Lawrence. Cambridge, Mass.: MIT Press, 1984. Contains selected essays from the 1971 edition of *Philosophisch-politische Profile*, PP$_1$, (Frankfurt: Suhrkamp) and other collected writings.

SO$_1$ *Strukturwandel der Öffentlichkeit. Untersuchungen zu einer Kategorie der bürgerlichen Gesellschaft*. Neuwied: Luchterhand, 1962.

SO$_2$ Ibid., 13th ed., 1982.

TGS   *Theorie der Gesellschaft oder Sozialtechnologie—Was Leistet die Systemforschung?*, with Niklas Luhmann. Frankfurt: Suhrkamp, 1971.

TkH   *Theorie des kommunikativen Handelns*. Volume 1 subtitled *Handlungsrationalität und gesellschaftliche Rationalisierung*; Volume 2 *Zur Kritik der funktionalistischen Vernunft*. Frankfurt: Suhrkamp, 1981. Volume 1 translated by Thomas McCarthy as *The Theory of Communicative Ac-*

	tion. Volume One. Reason and the Rationalization of Society (*TCA*). Boston: Beacon Press, 1984.
TP	*Theory and Practice*. Translated by J. Viertel. Boston. Beacon Press, 1973. Contains selected essays from the 1971 edition of *Theorie und Praxis: Sozialphilosophische Studien* (Frankfurt: Suhrkamp) and *Technik und Wissenschaft als Ideologie* (Frankfurt: Suhrkamp, 1968).
TRS	*Towards a Rational Society: Student Protest, Science, and Politics*. Translated by J. J. Shapiro. Boston: Beacon Press, 1970. Contains selected essays from *Technik und Wissenschaft als Ideologie* (Frankfurt: Suhrkamp, 1968) and *Protestbewegung und Hochschulreform* (Frankfurt: Suhrkamp, 1969).
VET	*Vorstudien und Ergänzungen zur Theorie des kommunikativen Handelns*. Frankfurt: Suhrkamp, 1984. Contains published and unpublished studies that appeared prior to 1981, including the postscript, "Erläuterung zum Begriff des kommunikativen Handelns" (1982).
WT	"Wahrheitstheorien." In *Wirklichkeit und Reflexion: Walter Schulz zum 60. Geburtstag*, edited by H. Fahrenbach, pp. 211–65. Pfullingen: Neske, 1973.
ZLS$_1$	*Zur Logik der Sozialwissenschaften*. Frankfurt: Suhrkamp, 1970. Contains the title essay as well as Habermas's contributions to the *Positivismusstreit*.
ZLS$_2$	*Zur Logik der Sozialwissenschaften*. 5th ed. Frankfurt: Suhrkamp, 1982. Contains additional essays spanning the period 1970–77.
ZRhM	*Zur Rekonstruktion des Historischen Materialismus*. Frankfurt: Suhrkamp, 1976.

NOTES

PREFACE

1. For a brief summary of Habermas's academic career, see the interview in *New Left Review* 151 (May/June 1985), pp. 75–105.

1. THE HISTORICAL FOUNDATIONS OF THE THEORY OF
COMMUNICATIVE ACTION

1. F. Bacon, "New Organon," in *Bacon: Selections*, pp. 335–44.
2. F. Bacon, "De Dignitate et Augmentis Scientarum libri IX", in *Bacon: Selections*, pp. 411–16.
3. See W. Woodward, *Studies in Education During the Age of the Renaissance: 1400–1600*, chap. 7, and *Vittorino da Feltre*, pp. 93–133.
4. G. Vico, *On the Study Methods of our Time*, p. 23, and *The New Science of Giambattista Vico*, pp. 56–63. As Habermas notes (*TP* 290), Hobbes also subscribed to this maxim but used it to justify a scientization of politics (*De Corpore*, in *The English Works of Thomas Hobbes*, ed. Sir William Molesworth (London, 1839), vol. I, chap. 1, p. 9). Vico's claim that since history "cannot be more certain than when he who creates the things also describes them . . . our science proceeds exactly as does geometry . . ." (*New Science*, p. 349) is qualified by the fact that humanity does not make its history consciously. To justify the scientific status of his historical interpretation, Vico must postulate the omnipotent and omniscient force of Divine Providence, which, despite all appearances to the contrary—namely, the interminable periodicity of *corsi e ricorsi*—guarantees progress toward redemption that is perceptible to reason. However, Vico's philosophy of history, being retrospective, can only hazard a prognosis of the preordained goal of history. Kant also appealed to nature (Providence), but for him, the goal of a global, perpetual peace among nations is predictable only to the degree that humanity actively undertakes its realization. It is Marx, Habermas notes, who reconciles Vico (as sublated in Hegel) and Kant in the idea of a practical reason whose capacity to perceive the theoretical meaning of history is proportional to its emancipation from social domination (*TP* 243–49).
5. Vico, *Study Methods*, p. 19.
6. See my monograph, "The Historical Genesis of the Gadamer/Habermas Controversy," for the history of this debate.
7. ZLS_1, 15–16, 19–30, 43–64. K. Popper, *The Poverty of Historicism*, pp. 3–6, 42–45, 58–76, 122–26. The following discussion of the debate touches only on the relationship between meaningful action and historically situated understanding.

8. Hermeneutic explanations appeal to practical syllogisms that establish quasi-conceptual relationships between the intentions of agents (major premise), their beliefs about what is required for realizing them (minor premise), and intentional descriptions of already completed actions (conclusion). The inference of the action from the major and minor premises is not logically necessitated, since it is possible, albeit improbable, that an agent might intend to carry out some action, be capable of doing so, be free to do so, and yet still not do it. However, major and minor premises are logically implied by what they are supposed to explain—the action. See G. von Wright, *Explanation and Understanding*, and K.-O. Apel's attempt to situate von Wright's theory in a transcendental-pragmatic framework, in *Understanding and Explanation*.

9. *ZLS₁*, 107–13. Weber suggested on occasion that understanding a course of action involves imputing a psychological motive to the agent on the basis of an analogy between his or her behavior and patterns of behavior that the interpreter already knows, through introspection, to be causally related to motives of a certain type. But, as Habermas notes, behavioral regularities are "posited and maintained under threat of sanctions; they retain their validity in and through the conscious recognition of the subjects whose actions they direct" (*ZLS₁*, 23). Weber also distinguishes between direct understanding of a logical truth, such as $2 \times 2 = 4$, and indirect, explanatory understanding of the motivational causes underlying an action. Some philosophers, such as Alasdair MacIntyre and Peter Winch, have taken the former model to be applicable to *sinnverstehen* generally. See P. Winch, *The Idea of a Social Science*, pp. 66, 92; A. MacIntyre, "A Mistake about Causality in the Social Sciences," in *Philosophy, Politics, and Society*, ed. W. Runciman (Oxford: Basil Blackwell, 1964), p. 57; and essays by Warriner, Munch, and Wax in *Subjective Understanding and the Social Sciences*, ed. M. Truzzi. See also T. Abel, "The Operation Called Verstehen," in *Subjective Understanding*, ed. Truzzi, pp. 40–55.

10. *ZLS₁*, 32–33, 36–37, 59–64.

11. *ZLS₁*, 20–66.

12. The transition from classical political philosophy to modern social theory is examined in detail in an early essay by Habermas (*TP* 41–81). Classical political philosophy understood politics to be an extension of ethics in three senses. First, the laws of the state were held to be inseparable from the customary morality of civic life and to have as their aim the realization of human nature and civic virtue. Second, political activity was defined in terms of *praxis*, the formation and cultivation of character, rather than *technē*, the skillful mastery of objectifiable tasks. Third, political philosophy, as distinguished from apodeictic science (*epistemē*), was assigned to the status of an art whose aim was the prudential application of principles of justice to concrete circumstances. Although the Thomistic appropriation of Aristotle's *Politics* retained the notion that the goal of the state was the cultivation of the moral good of its citizens, it replaced the idea of a community of free citizens with a patriarchal hierarchy of social classes in which domestic tranquility was secured through domination (*dominium*). This new orientation is preserved in the social philosophies of Machiavelli and More, the former extolling the *realpolitik* of princely *virtù*, the latter recommending economic amelioration of conflict, crime, and poverty. Hobbes completed the transition to modern political thought by amalgamating the science of man with the prognostic science of Galileo. The natural state of humanity is now seen as a war of all against all in which what is right and just is synonymous with survival. Reason, now subordinated to desire, lawfully calculates that the interest of the individual is best served by contracting with others to mutually transfer the unlimited right to all things to an absolute sovereign. The reduction of praxis to technē is antinomial, however; Hobbes's advocacy of

noninterference by the state is contradicted by both his defense of political absolutism and his conception of natural law as deterministic.

The major source of Habermas's interpretation of the transition from classical to modern political thought is Hannah Arendt's book *The Human Condition*. But his indebtedness to her distinctions between rational political power and political violence, *vita contemplativa* and *vita activa*, politics and biological reproduction (labor) / fabrication (work), is tempered by his rejection of the neoclassical dichotomies between public and private, state and economy, liberty and welfare, that inform her work. Arendt extolled politics as the highest form of action, since it implies a communicative endeavor by a plurality of individuals of equal status who seek to reach agreement over the ends of life. As a product of mutual freedom, true political power must be distinguished from mere rulership, and the social liberation of humanity from poverty. The primary error of Marxism thus consists in its substitution of politics for the administration of society. Contesting this rigid separation of the political from the socioeconomic, Habermas argues that the narrow identification of politics with communicative action and the condemnation of the bureaucratic amortization of economic injustice as violence ignores the complexities of modern society, whose rationality depends on politically mediating the communicative sphere of the public lifeworld with the functional sphere of the combined economic-administrative system. See J. Habermas, "Hannah Arendts Begriff der Macht," in *KK*, and my article on Arendt in *Thinkers of the Twentieth Century*, pp. 16–17.

13. *SO₁*, 15–36.
14. Ibid., 38–55.
15. Ibid., 93–101.
16. Ibid., 147–52, 215–17.
17. Ibid., 218–28, 246–56.
18. Ibid., 170–98.
19. K. Marx, "The Economic and Philosophic Manuscripts of 1844," pp. 566–69; *Capital*, vol. 1, pp. 79–80.
20. K. Marx and F. Engels, *The German Ideology*, pp. 28–32, 57–62, and *Capital*, vol. 1, pp. 76–87. Regarding the relationship between Marx's theory of ideology and his theory of fetishism, see S. Moore, *The Critique of Capitalist Democracy*, chap. 3. Marx's pejorative conception of ideology postulates at least three epistemic properties that, taken singly or all together, mark a form of consciousness as ideological: the mistaken identification of the epistemic status of a belief (e.g., treating theological propositions as amenable to empirical verification), affirmation of a belief that objectifies social reality as if it were a natural process, and affirmation of a belief that mistakenly identifies the interests of some subgroup with those of society as a whole. Marx also adduces *functional* properties typical of ideological forms of consciousness (e.g., legitimating excessive repression through forms of social domination, hindering the development of productive forces, masking social contradictions, etc.) and *genetic* properties (e.g., an origin in conflicts that prevent agents from perceiving the irrationality of their motives). For further discussion of these issues, see R. Geuss, *The Idea of a Critical Theory*, pp. 4–26.
21. Marx, *Capital*, vol. 1, pp. 236–52.
22. *TP* 235–52.
23. *KHI* 25–42.
24. Ibid., 56–57; *TP* 142–69.
25. *TP* 142–69. See G. W. F. Hegel, "The Spirit of Christianity."
26. M. Heidegger, *Being and Time*, pp. 184ff.
27. Ibid., pp. 174–92.

28. Ibid., pp. 425–36. In an earlier essay he sees Heidegger, especially in his post-*Kehre* period as taking to an extreme the ontological correspondence between subject and object that he detects in Marx's early writings (*PP*₁ 67–75).

29. H.-G. Gadamer, *Truth and Method*, pp. 210ff.

30. Ibid., pp. 15ff., 265ff., 272ff., 318ff.

31. *ZLS*₁ 255–76. According to Gadamer, the traditional distinction between understanding (*subtilitas intelligendi*), interpretation (*subtilitas explicandi*), and application (*subtilitas applicandi*) cannot be sustained in light of the ontological turn; what defines ethical conduct, the reinterpretation of general principles in light of particular circumstances, also characterizes understanding, since understanding a text from the past requires reinterpreting its claim to truth so that it "applies" to the practical concerns of the interpreter. Adverting to the ontological interdependence of phronēsis and understanding, Gadamer argues that the formal ethic espoused by Kant and Habermas is too abstract. Since that exchange, Habermas has retreated from his previous invocation of application as a hermeneutic principle, on the grounds that it overemphasizes the practical relationship to the detriment of the critical; application, he now contends, is appropriate only for biblical and legal hermeneutics, in both of which a tradition is promulgated as authoritatively binding for action. Gadamer, of course, has vigorously protested this interpretation as a serious misreading of his intentions. See chap. 3 below and Gadamer, "Über die Möglichkeit einer philosophischen Ethik," as well as the following, which are critical of Gadamer's assimilation of understanding, interpretation, and application: Emilio Betti, *Die Hermeneutik als allgemeine Methodik der Geisteswissenschaften* (Tübingen: J. C. Mohr, 1967); E. D. Hirsch, Jr., *Validity in Interpretation*; and F. A. Olafson, *The Dialectic of Action*.

32. *ZLS*₂ 299ff.

33. M. Horkheimer, "Traditional and Critical Theory," in *Critical Theory*, pp. 194ff.

34. Ibid., p. 207.

35. Ibid., pp. 212–13, 216, 223.

36. *KHI* 3–65. Garbis Kortian's little book *Metacritique* contains an excellent discussion of *KHI* and German idealism. I have argued elsewhere that a more charitable reading of Hegel's *Logic* reveals that even the standpoint of absolute knowledge allows for contingency or nature-in-itself. See my "Hegel on Leibniz and Individuation," in *Kant-Studien*, vol. 4 (1985), pp. 420–35.

37. *KHI* 124ff., 308–09. See also *ZLS*₁, 27–28, 32–38, 43, 46–52.

38. For Peirce, the meaning of a factual statement of the sort "Diamonds are hard" is tantamount to a conditional prediction of the form: "Whenever certain operations are performed on diamonds under conditions *C*, the following events *E* will occur"—a statement whose operational significance bears witness to an interest in technological control. Habermas suggests that measurement, which abstracts from nonquantifiable aspects of reality, constitutes the "nature" of science. Nikolaus Lobkowicz observes that Habermas's claim that the validity of natural scientific knowledge is tied to a technical interest seems intended to answer at least three different questions, namely, why there is science at all, why there is progress in science, and why science comprehends reality the way it does ("Interest and Objectivity," p. 200). Lobkowicz's caveat, that theoretical science is disinterested, was later conceded by Habermas, but without controverting his view that the instrumental adaptability of modern science is vital to its institutionalization. See also C. Peirce, "Lectures on Pragmatism," in *Collected Papers*, vol. 5.

39. *KHI* 155–59, 162, 170, 176. See also *ZLS*₁, 64–70.

40. *TP* 22.

41. *KHI* 205–08. See J. Fichte, "Erste Einleitung in die Wissenschaftslehre," pp. 17–18.

42. *KHI* 252ff., 279ff.
43. Ibid., 226ff., 275ff.; see also *VET* 226–70.
44. S. Freud, "The Claims of Psychoanalysis to Scientific Interest," in *Complete Works*, vol. 13, p. 176.
45. See A. Lorenzer, *Sprachstörung und Rekonstruktion* and *Kritik des psychoanalytischen Symbolbegriffs*. Adolf Grünbaum has emphatically repudiated Habermas's reading of Freud on the grounds that it represents a fundamental misunderstanding of the character of natural science. This attack is three-pronged. First, he maintains that Habermas's claim that self-reflection dissolves the causal linkage between pathogen and neurosis is based on a logical confusion, for therapy eliminates the pathogenic cause but not the causal relationship between the subconscious and the conscious; in any event, Freud stressed that repression was not a sufficient cause of neurosis, since genetic factors are also implicated. Second, he accuses Habermas of ignorance of physics in his assertion that general interpretations, unlike natural laws, are context-dependent; for electrodynamic laws, for example, "exhibit context dependence with a vengeance by making the field produced by a charge dependent on the particular past history of the charge." Third, he disputes Habermas's claim that the patient has privileged cognitive access to the validation or discreditation of psychoanalytic hypotheses on the grounds of a misunderstanding of falsifiability. The falsifiability of a prediction derived from a hypothesis does not entail the falsifiability of the hypothesis itself, since the former is dependent on the proper interpretation and establishment of initial conditions, as well as on various auxiliary hypotheses. Furthermore, the weak memories and resistance of patients make their statements unreliable, so that extraclinical data, in the case of the Rat Man "supplied by the patient's mother rather than information yielded by the patient's 'experience of reflection'" may have been necessary for disconfirmation. Grünbaum is right in pointing out the overly "positivistic" conception of natural science that vitiates Habermas's attempt to defend a hermeneutic reading of psychoanalysis—a failing that need not impugn the general merits of the undertaking as such, however. His objection to Habermas's somewhat misleading description of self-reflection as dissolving pathogenic causal relations strikes me as being overly obsessive with language, but the third claim that he ascribes to Habermas is strange, particularly since he then goes on to show that Habermas himself acknowledges the very facts he cites in his rebuttal, when he says that "the interpretation of a case is corroborated only by the successful continuation of a self-formative process, that is by the completion of self-reflection, *and not in any unmistakable way by what the patient says or how he behaves*" (*KHI* 266; emphasis added). See Grünbaum, *The Foundations of Psychoanalysis*, pp. 7–43.
46. *KHI* 216–17, 259ff. Russell Keat presents a critique of *KHI* that is considerably at odds with my approach. Keat jettisons the idealistic element of critical theory (though not its appreciation of hermeneutics) in favor of a critical realism that retains the Kantian dichotomies between facts and values, 'is' and 'ought,' and so on. But he is cognizant of the ontological relationship between "world" and "language" as understood by Gadamer and sees this as a problem for his theory. Although he is right to point out the overly cognitivist aspect of Habermas's conception of emancipation and the difficulty of conceiving of a socialist community on the basis of a psychoanalytically derived concept of autonomy, he is apparently unaware of the extent to which Habermas himself, during the early seventies, was willing to accommodate himself to some of his recommendations, such as viewing critical theory as a combination of science and philosophy rather than as some third thing (*The Politics of Social Theory*).
47. *KHI* 312–13.

48. Ibid., 196.
49. McCarthy, *The Critical Theory of Jürgen Habermas*, pp. 113–25; idem, *CD* 76ff.
50. K.-O. Apel, "Wissenschaft als Emanzipation?" and D. Böhler, "Zum Problem des emanzipatorischen Interesses und seiner gesellschaftlichen Wahrnehmung." For an excellent reprise of the secondary literature on *KHI*, see Dallmayr's "Critical Epistemology Criticized" and "Reason and Emancipation" in *Beyond Dogma and Despair*.
51. *TP* 22.
52. Habermas, "A Postscript to *KHI*," p. 170.
53. M. Hesse ("Science and Objectivity") and J. B. Thompson ("Universal Pragmatics") have pointed out certain difficulties in Habermas's theory of truth as formulated in the postscript, in particular, that it cannot account for the meaning and truth of simple descriptive statements such as "This ball is red." Hesse recommends that the theory be supplemented by a correspondence theory of truth, Thompson that it be reformulated so as to allow rational discourse to include ideal experimental procedures within pragmatic contexts. Thompson also remarks that Habermas's putative identification of truth with "warranted assertibility" overlooks the fact that some predictions that are warranted empirically turn out to be false. In response, Habermas notes that the consensus theory of truth was intended to apply only to hypothetical, general, modal, counterfactual, and negative statements in which claims to truth are repeatedly raised in such a way that they can be resolved only in discourse (*CD* 275). The theory stipulates neither a criterion nor a definition of truth; it merely states what is required to redeem a truth claim. Thus something can be asserted to be true even if it later turns out to be false, as long as it is empirically warranted at the time of its utterance. Habermas readily admits that "experimental action does not lie on the same level as the instrumental action of naive or scientized practice," and that "in its function of producing data, which is always gathered with a view to testing hypothetical validity claims, experimental action is related to discourse from the start" (*CD* 273).
54. *TP* 37–40.
55. *KHI* 314.

2. RATIONALITY, REALITY, AND ACTION

1. *TkH* 1. 15ff.
2. Ibid., 8, 21ff.
3. Ibid., 25–27.
4. Ibid., 28–33.
5. Ibid., 32–33. Besides confusing successful adaptation, which is applicable to pre-conscious life, with truth, which is a complimentary title accorded justifiable factual beliefs, pragmatism ignores the internal relationship (noted by Piaget) "between the capacity of decentered perception and the manipulation of things and events on the one hand, and the capacity of intersubjective agreement over things and events on the other." Knowledge, in other words, is a linguistic phenomenon. In the words of phenomenologist Melvin Pollner (quoted by Habermas), "the anticipated unanimity of experience . . . presupposes a community of others who are deemed to be observing the same world . . . who are motivated to speak 'truthfully' of their experience and who speak according to recognizable, shared schemes of expression" ("Mundane Reasoning," *Philosophy and Social Science* 4 (1974): 140).
6. *TkH* 1. 34ff. In earlier studies by Habermas, truth, appropriateness, sincerity, and comprehensibility appeared as the four claims to validity. Following Searle, Habermas now prefers to regard comprehensibility as a condition for making claims that

are meaningful; further, Habermas's recent decision to introduce art as a symbolic medium of communication has led him to equate moral rightness (previously identified with appropriateness) with a strict claim to universality, in contradistinction to aesthetic-expressive claims to appropriateness, authenticity, sincerity, and integrity (*Stimmigkeit*).

7. Ibid., 38ff. See also K. Baier, *The Moral Point of View* (Ithaca: Cornell University Press, 1964), and K.-O. Apel, *Transformation der Philosophie*, vol. 2, pp. 358ff. Habermas's communicative ethic goes well beyond the deontological theories espoused by Kant, Rawls, and Kohlberg. See chap. 7, n. 15, and chap. 1, n. 53 for further discussion of truth and morality.

8. *TkH* 1. 68ff. Besides the transference and countertransference between patient and doctor in the clinical relationship, which in effect nullify conditions of impartiality, the doctor must resort to strategic tactics—e.g., questioning the patient's behavior, denying the sincerity of the patient's utterances, and so forth—to break down resistances hampering free association.

9. Ibid., 41ff. I am grateful to Dr. Ludwig Nagl of the University of Vienna for bringing to my attention the different senses of *appropriateness* in Habermas's work.

10. Habermas, "Questions and Counter-Questions," p. 240. Habermas rounds out his survey of forms of argumentation by introducing the concept of explicative discourse, which involves thematizing rules of grammar, syntax, and so forth.

11. *TkH* 1. 46. See S. Toulmin, *The Uses of Argument* and *Human Understanding*.

12. *WT* 243ff., 254ff.

13. See ibid., 255ff., and *MkH* 98–99. Habermas is especially concerned to refute relativists such as Wolfgang Klein, who contend that argumentative validity can be explained psychologically in terms of success (see *TkH* 1. 50–56 and W. Klein, "Argumentation und Argument," *Zeitschrift für Literatur und Linguistik* 38/39 (1980): 9ff.). Toulmin's recent attempts to examine the "strength and order" of institutionally bound arguments of the sort found in courts of law and scientific conventions are also viewed by Habermas as undermining the universalist position. Some of Toulmin's statements convey the impression that the validity of arguments is determined primarily by their context-bound institutional function, so that in adversarial settings, the validity of argumentation is a function of rhetorically achieved compromise rather than impartial consensus. Such conflict-oriented arguments do not abide by the canons of rational discourse in Habermas's view, since the ground rules—the recognition of the binding nature of legal precedent and the authoritative decision of the judge, the success orientation of the contending parties, and the emphasis on reaching a strategic compromise—presuppose neither the impartial standpoint of rational judgment nor the assumption of unconstrained agreement. See *TkH* 1. 57–63 and S. Toulmin, R. Rieke, and A. Vanik, *An Introduction to Reasoning* (New York: Macmillan, 1979), pp. 15, 28, 200, 279ff.

14. *TkH* 1. 71ff.

15. Ibid., 72ff. See E. E. Evans-Pritchard, *Witchcraft, Oracles and Magic Among the Azande*.

16. *TkH* 1. 76. In a sympathetic review of *TkH*, David Rasmussen takes exception to Habermas's pejorative depiction of mythic world views. Citing Saussure's assertion that "language is language regardless of when or where it occurs" and Levi-Strauss's belief that "the difference between archaic and modern societies is not to be found in the quality of their thought but in that to which their thought applies," Rasmussen argues that "myth is itself a resource for rational reflection," which, far from consisting in confused thinking, is "a quite legitimate and valid form of thinking with its own rubrics and properties" ("Communicative Action and Philosophy: Reflections on Habermas' *Theorie des kommunikativen Handelns*"). Habermas's recent

incorporation of aesthetic rationality into his system (see chap. 6) may be read as an attempt to salvage a poetic or dialectical dimension within critical theory.

17. *TkH* 1. 77–79.
18. Ibid., 79–85.
19. Ibid., 87–89. See S. Lukes, "Some Problems about Rationality," p. 194.
20. Winch, *The Idea of a Social Science* and "Understanding a Primitive Society," pp. 80ff.
21. *TkH* 1. 92–96.
22. R. Horton, "African Thought and Western Science," pp. 153–54; cited by Habermas, *TkH* 1. 96.
23. Winch, "Understanding a Primitive Society," pp. 92–93. See also MacIntyre, *Against the Self-Images of the Age*, pp. 252ff.
24. Winch, "Understanding a Primitive Society," p. 106; cited by Habermas on p. 101. See also *ZRhM* 339–40. Habermas's argument is indebted to the Popperian school, whose exponents include Ernest Gellner and Robin Horton. Gellner notes that in modern thought systems, categories immune to critical revision—what he calls "entrenched constitutional clauses"—are limited to a few formal principles, such as those of logic, that provide a general framework in terms of which our various beliefs about reality can be evaluated ("The Savage and the Modern Mind," pp. 162ff.). Horton puts this point slightly differently when he says that mythic world views "protect against" the possibility of dissonant experience, whereas modern world views embrace it ("African Thought and Western Science," p. 165).
25. McCarthy, *The Critical Theory of Jürgen Habermas*, p. 321.
26. *CES* 98, 140, 169.
27. *CD* 258.
28. *CES* 140ff.
29. Ibid., 102–03.
30. Ibid., 168–69.
31. Ibid., 100–02.
32. Ibid., 103–06; *TkH* 1. 103–09.
33. *TkH* 1. 145–47. See also A. C. Danto, *Analytical Philosophy of Action*. Contrary to Danto, Habermas maintains that brute physical movements (what Danto calls "basic actions") are not, properly speaking, actions at all, since they do not fall under any semantically relevant set of intentional descriptions. With the exception of actions such as those involved in exercising, one does not normally intend as one's action the performance of physical movements, but some other action, such as walking to the store, which happens to involve such movements. Likewise, Habermas objects to Wittgenstein's assimilation of linguistic meaning to a model of simple rule-following appropriate to arithmetic and grammar, on the grounds that rule-governed calculations and grammatical constructions no more refer to the world than do physical movements and therefore can at best be said to provide the material infrastructure of some intentional action, such as doing schoolwork, totaling a scorecard, and so on (*TkH* 1. 148). For further details on Habermas's discussion of intentionality and action, see *VET* 273–332.
34. *TkH* 1. 115–19. See Popper, *Objective Knowledge*, and idem and I. C. Eccles, *The Self and its Brain*.
35. I. C. Jarvie, *Concepts and Society*.
36. *TkH* 1. 121.
37. Ibid., 122–23.
38. Ibid., 123–26.
39. Ibid., 126–27, 151–52. Social action is characterized by a concerted orientation toward the achievement of goals. If the goals are strictly personal in nature, then the

coordination of efforts may involve nothing more than calculated use of another person through coercive or noncoercive means (strategic action); thus two cyclists avert a collision by signaling, warning, or threatening one another. If the goal is primarily the conformity of one's behavior to social norms or the expression of one's subjectivity, then the concerted action is qualified with respect to agreement over norms or conventional dramaturgic roles. Finally, if the goal is to reach agreement over problematic claims through communication, then the concerted action is qualified with respect to the acceptance or rejection of offers to engage in social action (communicative action).

40. Ibid., 122.
41. Ibid., 131–32.
42. Ibid., 132ff.
43. Ibid., 133.
44. Ibid., 128ff. See also E. Goffman, *Encounters* and *The Presentation of Self in Everyday Life.*
45. *TkH* 1. 139ff.
46. Ibid., 150. Anthony Giddens argues that Habermas "makes a triple reduction within the notion of interaction which involves treating action as equivalent to interaction and interaction as equivalent to communicative action" (*CD* 258). Habermas concedes that he has not always distinguished speech from communication, but his current analysis acknowledges the purely strategic use of language as a nonconsensual mechanism of coordination. Furthermore, even his earlier treatments of social action recognized that some forms of social interaction (such as dancing, ritual behavior, and so on) lack intentional reference and so are not, strictly speaking, actions at all (*CD* 263–68).

3. UNDERSTANDING AND LANGUAGE

1. *TkH* 1. 161.
2. Ibid., 163. The concept of a double hermeneutic is Gidden's; see A. Giddens, *New Rules for Sociological Method*, pp. 15ff. This distinction assumes that there is a sense in which brute observation provides the natural sciences with a data base that is prior to any theoretically determined perception of facts—an assumption that has been highly questionable ever since the discovery of the Heisenberg Uncertainty Principle in 1923. Even if the scientific perception of data were conditioned only by the pretheoretical conventions of ordinary language, it would still be twice interpreted. Without getting into a debate over whether science is doubly hermeneutic in this sense, or whether there are perceptual "givens" that remain invariant across cultures, one can simply restate Habermas's assertion to mean that, in addition to observation (linguistically conditioned or otherwise), communicative involvement with the subject matter of the social sciences is required in order to gain access to it.

Fred Alford has recently provided a detailed analysis of Habermas's philosophy of science in *Science and the Revenge of Nature: Marcuse and Habermas.* Despite the book's merits, however, it fails to do justice to the complex interweaving of hermeneutical, logical, and empirical themes in Habermas's notion of a reconstructive science. Nevertheless, it does an admirable job of tracing the evolution of Habermas's own conception of natural science from a positivistic treatment in the *Positivismusstreit* to a more hermeneutic one in *Theorie.*

3. Ibid., 152.
4. Ibid., 152–54.

5. Ibid., 154–57.

6. According to McCarthy, the hermeneutic necessity of having to relate the rationales of "native" actors to one's own and therewith the necessity of having to evaluate their rationality in relation to their culture (Weber's notion of the *Wertbezogenheit* of all sinnverstehen), is compatible with "an objectivating, hypothetical attitude in which judgment is simply bracketed" (Weber's notion of *Werturteilfreiheit*). Thus, there would seem to be a third alternative to the radically performative approach defended by Habermas and the objectivating approach of behavioristic social science (McCarthy, "Reflections on Rationalization in the Theory of Communicative Action," p. 184). Habermas has responded by claiming that this third approach is not really a neutral mode of understanding at all but is critically motivated by the realization that the rationales indigenous to some cultures are too problematic, too different from our own, to be grasped by analogy with ours. Thus, we understand mythic modes of thought "only when we can say why the participants had good reasons for their confidence in this *type* of explanation. But in order to achieve this degree of understanding, we have to establish an internal relation between 'their' sort of explanation and the kind we accept as correct. We must be able to reconstruct the successful and unsuccessful learning processes which separate 'us' from 'them'; both modes of explanation must be located within the same universe of discourse" (Habermas, "Questions," p. 239). The question remains, however, whether one could not just as well locate both modes of thought, the mythic and the modern, within a common discourse in which each is gradually relativized with respect to the other. Such a relativization could accommodate the validity and meaningfulness of both modes as expressions of distinct ways of being without requiring a critical translation or discursive confrontation between them. In his article "Holism and Hermeneutics" Burt Dreyfus suggests that once we abandon "theoretical holism," the view—held by Gadamer, Habermas, and Ricoeur among others—that the meaning of action can be captured in terms of "true beliefs," and subscribe instead to "practical holism," the view—held by Heidegger in his discussion of *Vorhabe* in *Being and Time*—that the meaning of actions refers to a prediscursive network of know-how, the problem of relativism is dissolved, since it no longer makes sense to demand justification. Habermas, of course, disagrees with this radical version of the contextuality thesis and insists, against Dreyfus and Searle, that the rationale underlying meaningful actions can be literally—that is, propositionally—transposed (*TkH* 1. 443, 449–52; 2. 332n., 421).

7. *TkH* 1. 171–72.

8. Ibid., 157–58.

9. Ibid., 163–66. See also H. Skjervheim, "Objectivism and the Study of Man," pp. 213ff., 265ff.

10. *TkH* 1. 168–71.

11. Ibid., 176–79. See A. Schütz, *Collected Papers*, vol. 1, pp. 5–6, 43–56.

12. *TkH* 1. 179–83. See P. McHugh, "On the Failure of Positivism," in *Understanding Everyday Life*, ed. J. D. Douglas (London: Aldine Press, 1971), p. 329, and A. V. Cicourel, *Method and Measurement in Sociology*, pp. 14ff.

13. See H. Garfinkel, *Studies in Ethnomethodology*, p. 33.

14. ZLS_1, 220ff.

15. *TkH* 1. 187–88.

16. Ibid., 188–92. See W. Kuhlmann, *Reflexion und Kommunikative Erfahrung*, and Gadamer, *Truth and Method*, pp. 318ff.

17. *TkH* 1. 192–93.

18. Ibid., 193–96.

200

19. See T. McCarthy and F. Dallmayr, eds., *Understanding and Social Inquiry*, pp. 53ff.
20. *TkH* 1. 377–85.
21. Ibid., 372. See K. Bühler, *Sprachtheorie.*
22. R. Carnap, "Foundations of the Unity of Science."
23. *TkH* 1. 373–76.
24. Ibid., 424–27. See M. Dummet, "What is a Theory of Meaning?," pp. 67ff., 81, 110ff., 126.
25. *TkH* 1. 376–77. See L. Wittgenstein, *Philosophical Investigations*, no. 120, and *Remarks on the Foundations of Mathematics*, p. 186.
26. *CES* 21ff. See N. Chomsky, *Aspects of a Theory of Syntax.*
27. Habermas, "Towards a Theory of Communicative Competence," p. 142. Three general classes of pragmatic universals are mentioned by Habermas: personal pronouns and their derivatives, which enable interlocutors to assume the reciprocal roles of speaker and hearer simultaneously, thereby guaranteeing intersubjective recognition of a shared meaning; deictic expressions of space and time, articles, and demonstrative pronouns, which enable them to refer to the world; and performative verbs, nonperformative intentional verbs, and modal adverbs, which enable them to draw logical distinctions and to take on certain obligations.
28. *CES* 40. See J. L. Austin, *How to Do Things with Words.* Abbreviated speech acts, such as "Hello!" and "Checkmate!," and nonverbal speech acts, such as signaling a taxi, have referential and performative meanings that can be ascertained from the context of utterance.
29. *CES* 54.
30. In fact, every speech act raises four validity claims—namely, to truth, rightness, sincerity, and comprehensibility, but Habermas now prefers to regard comprehensibility as a preparatory condition, since it does not raise a criticizable claim about objective, social, or subjective reality. Pointing out the anomalous status of poetry, humor, and salutation vis-à-vis truth, collective bargaining and play vis-à-vis sincerity, and simple factual claims vis-à-vis rightness. J. B. Thompson challenges the notion that every speech act raises all four validity claims. In response, Habermas notes that jokes, games, and multivocal (poetic) uses of language involve a deliberate and imaginative conflation of validity claims and hence occur against a background of communication involving all four claims. The same can be said about the use of perlocutionary effects in bargaining, for the escalation of demands succeeds only to the extent that such "bluffs" are taken sincerely, if only for the sake of reciprocating in kind and calling the other's bluff. As for simple sentences such as "The sky is blue this morning" and elliptical speech acts such as greetings, distinct claims to truth or rightness are discernible only from the context (*CD* 270ff., and *TkH* 1. 418ff.). See also A. Leist, "Was Heißt Universalpragmatik," in *Germanistische Linguistik* 5/6 (1977).
31. One might contest the possibility of making any sharp distinction between claims to sincerity and claims to truth in the case of first-person expressive statements. Ernst Tugendhat argues that the acceptance of the sincerity of an utterance such as "I have pain" is tantamount to the acceptance of its truth. Hence, another person is entitled to infer from the sincerity of such a first-person expression that the one making it has pain. Habermas disputes this thesis on the grounds that one can question the truth of a person's assertion that someone else is in pain without questioning the sincerity or truth of the person's own claim to be in pain.
32. Declarations of intent such as promises incur obligations for future action (*TkH* 1. 409ff., 428ff.).
33. *TkH* 1. 436 37. Habermas remarks that empirical pragmatics of the sort developed

by Wunderlich, Campbell, and Kreckel has the advantage of capturing the flexibility and creativity of natural speech, but the disadvantage of neglecting the fundamental illocutionary aims of speech in favor of the nonintentional spatial, social, and objective parameters of the context of the speech. Searle's classification of speech acts with respect to the speaker's orientation to the world in *Expression and Meaning* is more promising in this respect, though in Habermas's opinion, it remains wedded to a one-sided cognitive-instrumental approach, thereby reducing all directives to the status of strategic commands and all commissives (including declarations of intent) to the status of strategic interventions.

34. Ideally speaking, discourse is "released from the instrumental role of an action-coordinating mechanism" so that "the communicative treatment of theories itself becomes a goal of cooperation." In conversations of this sort, "the weight is shifted from purposiveness to communication" (*TkH* 1. 437–38). The difference between theoretical and practical discourse is that the former is essentially disinterested. This distinction disappears at higher levels of reflection, where the practical satisfaction of generalizable interests may become a salient consideration in deciding between two competing theoretical paradigms. See *WT* 253.

35. *TkH* 1. 440–43.

36. *Ibid.*, 449–50. Habermas concedes that an ideal model of linguistically mediated interaction must be supplemented by concrete empirical analysis in order to be sociologically fruitful. Although he stresses the contextual independence of illocutionary and locutionary meanings in order to differentiate them from perlocutionary effects, he is sensitive to Searle's and Thompson's objections to the "performative hypothesis," or the assumption that every speech act can be represented literally in standard form. As Thompson remarks, "it is not obvious what performative expression could capture the illocutionary forces involved in many indirect speech acts, such as the distinctive *mélange* of question and request in 'don't you think the rubbish is beginning to smell'?" In the final analysis, Habermas concedes that actual instances of speech are "impure," combining strategic and communicative, direct and indirect, verbal and extraverbal, institutionally bound and unbound patterns. See *CES* 45; J. Searle, *Expression and Meaning*, pp. 117ff.; J. B. Thompson, *CD* 126ff.

37. *TkH* 1. 450–52. The fruitfulness of universal pragmatics for social science resides principally in its elucidation of these structures, which explicate the mastery of speaker-listener roles (mutual recognition), the reflexive decentration of consciousness, and the achievement of individual autonomy (ibid., 444–46). See also Habermas, "Universalpragmatische Hinweise auf das System der Ich-Abgrenzungen," pp. 332ff., and "Der Universalitätsanspruch der Hermeneutik," pp. 120ff. Habermas adds that the reflexive mastery of distinct communicative types is also a necessary condition for distinguishing essence and appearance, being and illusion, is and ought, meaning and reference. Thompson has pointed out, however, that "recent research in the perceptual and communicative activities of infants seems to weigh against this view, suggesting that the child may be able to make some sort of distinction between appearance and reality before it has mastered an established system of speech-acts" (*CD* 127–28). See also T. G. R. Bower, "The Visual World of Infants," *Scientific American* 215 (December 1966), pp. 80–92.

38. "Agreement," Habermas concludes, "inheres in human speech as its telos" (*TkH* 1. 387). Communicative action coordinates in a nonstrategic way the strategic pursuit of private interests. In consensual negotiations, perlocutionary acts normally intrude. Habermas insists that this use of perlocutionary acts must be distinguished

from their use in strategic action. In the initial phase of negotiation "the participants must yield to metacommunication or otherwise find means for reaching
indirect agreement. An indirectly reached agreement proceeds along the path
delineated by the model of intentional semantics; the greeter gives the hearer to
understand, through perlocutionary effects, something that he cannot yet directly
impart" (ibid., 444). This passage is a convincing rebuttal of Allen Wood's contention that Habermas's argument in support of the priority of communicative action
fails because the distinction between perlocutionary and illocutionary acts does not
jibe with the distinction between success-oriented and agreement-oriented action.
On Wood's sympathetic but critical reading, Habermas construes the distinction
between success and agreement orientation as defining mutually exclusive ways of
acting, but a closer inspection of the text shows that Habermas not only regards
communicative action as oriented to the achievement of successful, rational agreement, but that actors engaged in communicative interaction never lose sight of the
individual goals they are trying to achieve via the coordination of their actions. The
decisive question, as Wood notes, is whether this coordination is brought about
manipulatively—i.e., whether the strategic aims of the interlocutors take prece-
dence over the need for an agreement that is equitable and legitimate. Moreover, as
the above passage shows, Habermas—contrary to Wood's assertion—acknowledges that perlocutionary acts may function within communicative action to open
up rational dialogue rather than to manipulate or deceive in a way that violates the
autonomy of the other. Wood's example of a teacher complimenting a student who
is unconvinced of the merits of her own argument illustrates well the way in which
an illocutionary (complimenting) act may be accompanied by perlocutionary effects
designed to make the other interlocutor more appreciative of her status as a rational participant in dialogue. Wood is right, of course, that the success of perlocu-
tions need not depend on their being unannounced; nonnormative imperatives,
for example, often announce the intention to persuade even if this is not explicitly
stated. Habermas's point, however, is not that perlocutionary effects and strategic
actions are never implicated in communicative action, but that they ultimately depend on the listener taking the speaker seriously. This entails that listeners presume the sincerity, truthfulness, and normative correctness of speakers as the
background context underwriting the successful pursuit of strategic actions and the
imparting of perlocutionary effects. See Allen Wood, "Habermas' Defense of Rationalism," pp. 157ff.

39. *CES* 38–40, 54ff., 60ff.

40. As Fred Dallmayr notes in *The Twilight of Subjectivity*, a quasi-Kantian trend "can
also be detected in [Habermas's] 'discursive theory of truth,' a conception which
tends to divorce rational discourse entirely from the context of practical experience,
despite the concession that some requisites of *ideal speech* (especially truthfulness)
cannot be ascertained apart from the domain of practice" (p. 292). In his more recent study, *Language and Politics*, Dallmayr draws from Michael Oakshott's essay
"The Voice of Poetry in the Conversation of Mankind" and Paul Ricoeur's *The Rule
of Metaphor* the prediscursive, poetic element of political reasoning (pp. 174–83).
The speculative identity of imagination and reason need not degenerate into subjectivistic aestheticism (Nietzsche) as Habermas seems to fear, as long as the poetic
moment is seen as a dynamic, harmonizing force within customary life forms (being). Despite his criticism of Adorno's notion of aesthetic mimesis for succumbing
to the sort of ontological conception of language and poetic thought espoused by
the late Heidegger, Habermas today seems less anxious than before to reject the validity of such thinking.

4. WEBER'S THEORY OF RATIONALIZATION

1. This aspiration is exemplified in Condorcet's "Esquisse d'un tableau historique des progrès de l'esprit humain" (1794), which proclaimed that natural science was the rational vehicle of human emancipation. Confronted with the industrial revolution and the rise of the modern state, neither the humanities nor the natural sciences provided convincing models of human progress for the nineteenth century. The functionally efficient, but rationally unorchestrated, market allocation of scarce resources favored natural selection as a more plausible explanation of social evolution. Though the turn of the century witnessed the renewed ascendance of the humanities as models of understanding, the interpretative methods of the prevailing neo-Kantian school of thought of Dilthey and Weber remained wedded to the objectivistic assumptions of the Enlightenment. The historicist critique of ethical naturalism thus issued in a Pyrrhic victory at which all cultural Weltanschauungen, including that of the Enlightenment, were stripped of validity (*TkH* 1. 210–24).
2. Weber, *From Max Weber*, p. 293.
3. Weber, *Economy and Society*, vol. 1, pp. 24–25.
4. Ibid.
5. Ibid., pp. 36–37, 655.
6. Ibid., p. 868.
7. Habermas is here following Talcott Parsons's interpretation of Weber in *The Structure of Social Action*.
8. Weber, *From Max Weber*, p. 329.
9. Ibid., p. 293.
10. Ibid., pp. 341ff., and *Economy and Society*, pp. 289–99, 809–15, 866–71.
11. Weber, *Economy and Society*, pp. 74–75.
12. Weber, *The Protestant Ethic and the Spirit of Capitalism* (hereafter cited as Weber, *Protestant Ethic*), pp. 79ff.
13. Weber's account of the rationalization of religious world views is of great interest here, because it elucidates key features of Habermas's theory of value. It has been a cardinal tenet of the neo-Kantian tradition from Rickert to Habermas that social reality is in some sense constituted by ideal values, which are understood to precede and mold the interests that motivate historical praxis. In contrast to idealism, which maintains that the dynamics of historical change are dictated by the logical progression of ideas, materialism holds that the development of ideas follows on and "reflects" constellations of social and economic interest. Although Weber is often perceived as an idealist because of his criticism of Marx's theory of historical materialism (especially the version of it associated with the "vulgar" economic determinism espoused by many German social democrats of his day), it is perhaps more accurate to say, as Habermas does, that neither Weber nor Marx can be classified in this manner, since for both the relationship between interests and ideals is reciprocal. Idealism is correct in holding that material interests become social forces only by being invested with ideal normative meaning—i.e., by becoming needs that are recognized as ones that ought to be condoned and satisfied by society. Conversely, materialism is right in holding that ideas become social forces only when their legitimacy, or normative force, resonates with existing material interests. Materialism is thus vindicated to the extent that ideas emerge as social forces in response to existing economic needs. As ideal systems of value, world views determine "the tracks along which action has been pushed by the dynamic of interest" (Weber, *From Max Weber*, p. 280).
14. Following Klaus Eder (*Die Entstehen staatlich organisierter Gesellschaften* [Frankfurt:

Suhrkamp, 1976]), Habermas speculates that the problem of suffering first emerged as a threat to society with the advent of class stratification and its attendant inequalities. See *TkH* 1. 281ff.

15. *TkH* 1. 289–94. Joseph Needham (*Science and Civilization in China*) argues that until the European Renaissance, the Chinese were more successful than their Western counterparts in developing technologies. Habermas agrees with the view espoused by Hans Blumenberg, who argues against Karl Löwith that the modern world cannot be understood as a mere secularization of Christianity. Though the radical contingency that motivates the modern, existential drive for progress is a product of medieval Christianity, the concept itself is alien to the otherworldliness of Christianity. See Blumenberg, *The Legitimation of the Modern Age*.

16. *TkH* 1. 308ff.

17. Habermas questions the assumptions underlying Weber's legal positivism—namely, that bourgeois doctrines of natural law commit a naturalistic fallacy and are incapable of formalization, that legitimacy has been replaced by statutory legality, and that modern law can function as an impartial mechanism for adjudicating conflicting substantive interests only by being purged of all ethical notions referring to justice. The first and third assumptions are untenable in light of the ideal speech situation, and the second can be defended only by presupposing what it seeks to refute, namely the legitimacy of the procedures themselves. For a good analysis of the differences between Habermas and Weber regarding the problem of legitimation, see Tony Smith, "The Scope of the Social Sciences in Weber and Habermas."

18. Weber, *From Max Weber*, p. 335.

19. Ibid., pp. 147–48.

20. Ibid., pp. 144–45.

21. Ibid., p. 357.

22. Ibid., pp. 332–34.

23. Weber, *Protestant Ethic*, p. 180.

24. Weber, *Economy and Society*, p. 988, cited from *From Max Weber*, p. 228.

25. Weber, *Economy and Society*, pp. 979–80, cited from *From Max Weber*, pp. 219–20.

26. Ibid.

27. Ibid.

28. Weber, *Protestant Ethic*, pp. 181–82.

29. Habermas by no means regards bureaucracy as totally dehumanizing, and he expresses some contempt for the early Marx's critique of *Gesellschaft* (*TkH* 2. 404–06; 454ff., 501–03).

30. *TkH* 1. 316ff.

31. Weber, *From Max Weber*, p. 328.

32. *TkH* 1. 334; translation taken from *TCA* 244–45, emphasis added.

33. Weber, *From Max Weber*, pp. 144–45.

34. *TkH* 1. 345; translation from *TCA* 252–53.

35. *TkH* 1. 339; translation from *TCA* 249.

36. *TkH* 1. 329; translation from *TCA* 240.

37. Habermas, "Questions," p. 242.

38. There seems to be some unclarity in Habermas's characterization of 2.2/3 and 3.2/3. In table 4.1, 2.2 and 2.3 are respectively labeled "obligatory relation" and "censorious relation to self"—both normative relations that must be construed as broadly constituting the moral realm; whereas in table 4.2, they are classified under distinct rationality complexes of law *and* morality. Again, in table 4.1, 3.2 and 3.3 fall under the headings "presentation of self" and "sensual-spontaneous relation to self," nei-

ther of which is directly identifiable with art, while in table 4.2 they are correlated with both eroticism and art.

39. In a recent article, McCarthy points out that the contents of moral knowledge and aesthetic sensibility do not accumulate across discontinuous paradigms in the same way as "phenomenal regularities and instrumental connections" in the natural sciences ("Reflections on Rationalization in the Theory of Communicative Action," pp. 179–80). This is especially so, as Habermas also recognizes, in the case of "authentic interpretations of needs" that "have to be renewed in each historically changed set of circumstances" ("Questions," p. 238). Habermas thus concurs with Weber and Adorno that cumulative advances in artistic technique, such as the development of modern harmony, modern musical notation, and modern musical construction or the discovery of linear and aerial perspective in representational art, need not extend to the values themselves. In the case of morality, the problem seems to be less a matter of cumulative advance than of institutionalization. Even if morality were secured in the democratic organization of the public sphere, as Habermas says it is, it could not be institutionalized in the same way as the scientific, legal, and artistic professions. Yet it is precisely such doubts about the secular institutionalization of morality that will have to be dispelled if Weber's pessimistic prognosis for individual autonomy is to be dismissed.

40. McCarthy contends that Habermas gives no justification for extruding these disciplines from the pantheon of rationalizable endeavors other than the impossibility of purely observational access to inner nature qua subjectivity. But if so, one could just as easily argue that social technologies are nonrationalizable (along with behavioral social science), since on Habermas's reading, there can be no purely observational access to social reality either.

41. Habermas is by no means opposed to incorporating such a reflection in his schema, but, in keeping with Kant's analysis of teleological judgment, he sees it as only one of several implications of a transcendental concept of nature-in-itself. A teleological reflection would interpret nature in light of the regulative idea of an organic unity, itself unfolding progressively "higher" forms of spiritual life, which could serve as a heuristic device in causal explanations of biological processes. But it could not in any way be construed as a metaphysical reenchantment or anthropomorphization of nature that might compete with science in the name of a higher, speculative knowledge. This is not enough for McCarthy, whose Hegelian proclivities lead him to question Habermas's all too Kantian expectation that knowledge of nature aspire to "the same level . . . that Newton attained in his objectivating knowledge of nature" (Habermas, *CD* 243–44, 249; and McCarthy, "Reflections on Rationalization in the Theory of Communicative Action," p. 188). See also Henning Ottmann, *CD* 79–97, and Joel Whitebook, "The Problem of Nature in Habermas."

42. *TkH* 1. 326; translation from *TCA* 328.

43. *LC* 85.

44. Habermas, "Questions," p. 236; emphasis added.

45. Habermas, "Modernity Versus Post-Modernity," pp. 10-11; *TP* 240.

46. Habermas, "Questions," pp. 237–38; emphasis added.

47. Ibid., pp. 236–37.

48. Habermas's empathy with Benjamin's redemptive critique, as opposed to the consciousness-raising ideology criticism espoused by Marcuse and Adorno, does not diminish his reservations regarding the technological de-auratization of art. If Adorno and Marcuse approach the issue from the suspect standpoint of autonomous art, whose ideal of an anticipated reconciliation perpetuates cultic enjoyment as a beautiful illusion, Benjamin's approach—and here Habermas echoes Adorno

—"can just as easily signify the degeneration of art into propagandistic mass art or into commercialized mass culture" (*LC* 86). See Habermas's critique of Benjamin in *PP*₂ 129–63. For a further discussion of Habermas's interpretation of Benjamin, see Philip Brewster and Carl Howard Buchner, "Language and Criticism: Jürgen Habermas on Walter Benjamin," and Martin Jay, "Habermas and Modernism."
49. Habermas, "Questions," p. 237; emphasis added.

5. FROM LUKÁCS TO ADORNO: RATIONALIZATION AS REIFICATION

1. *TkH* 1. 455–60.
2. Ibid., 474–75; and Georg Lukács, *Geschichte und Klassenbewusstsein*, vol. 2, p. 336.
3. Marx, *Das Kapital. Kritik der politischen Ökonomie*, vol. 1 (Alfred Kroner Verlag: Leipzig, 1929), pp. 50–51, my translation.
4. *TkH* 1. 478.
5. Ibid., 482–85; and Lukács, *Geschichte*, pp. 298–331.
6. *TkH* 1. 487. Compare Habermas's interpretation with the more sympathetic treatment of Lukács in Andrew Feenberg, *Lukács, Marx, and the Sources of Critical Theory*.
7. *TkH* 1. 505.
8. Ibid., 461. Horkheimer's substitution of *instrumental rationality* for *purposive rationality* succeeds brilliantly in highlighting the irrationality of a form of reason that is concerned only with the efficient deployment of means. Habermas remarks that for Horkheimer and other thinkers imbued with the spirit of Kantian philosophy, reason properly connotes the faculty of ideas, or transcendent ends.
9. Ibid., 462–68 and M. Horkheimer, *Zur Kritik der Instrumentellen Vernunft*, pp. 13–47.
10. Horkheimer, "The End of Reason," p. 31.
11. Herbert Marcuse, "Some Social Implications of Modern Technology," p. 154.
12. *TkH* 1. 492–94 and Horkheimer, *Zur Kritik der Instrumentellen Vernunft*, p. 119. Mommsen's catch phrase for Weber's paradoxical depiction of modern society, "the greatest possible freedom through the greatest possible domination," plays on the same dialectic (W. Mommsen, *Max Weber, Gesellschaft, Politik, und Geschichte* [Frankfurt: Suhrkamp, 1974], p. 138). Habermas cites this passage at 1. 470.
13. *TkH* 1. 495–97; T. W. Adorno, "On the Fetish Character of Music and the Regression of Listening"; T. W. Adorno and M. Horkheimer, *Dialectic of Enlightenment*, pp. 120ff. For a discussion of Adorno's disagreement with Benjamin over the radical potential of mass art, see chapters 10 and 11 below.
14. Adorno and Horkheimer, *Dialectic*, pp. xvi, 4.
15. Ibid., p. 27.
16. Ibid., p. 43. Circe, the sirens, and the lotus-eaters represent the undifferentiated stage of polymorphous erotic attachment, Polyphemus the higher, because differentiated, but equally primitive stage of rationally unmoderated hedonism.
17. Ibid., p. 63.
18. Ibid., p. 101.
19. Ibid., p. 44.
20. F. Nietzsche, *The Genealogy of Morals*, p. 194.
21. Ibid., p. 217.
22. Adorno and Horkheimer, *Dialectic*, p. 93.
23. Nietzsche, *Genealogy*, p. 221; idem, *Thus Spoke Zarathustra*, p. 140.
24. M. Heidegger, *Nietzsche IV: Nihilism*, p. 79.
25. Jean-François Lyotard, "Réponse à la question: qu'est-ce que le postmoderne?", p. 358.

26. *TkH* 1. 507–10. See also "The Entwinement of Myth and Enlightenment," in which Habermas discusses the Nietzschean roots of Adorno's and Horkheimer's book. Though there may be superficial similarities between Adorno's and Horkheimer's critique of modernity and Foucault's Nietzschean genealogical critique of it, the fact remains that, whereas the former thinkers continued to affirm enlightenment humanism *despite its contradictory elevation of "man as a transcendental-empirical doublet"* (Foucault), the latter abandoned it in favor of a "happy positivism" that equates knowledge with power. See Habermas's eulogy to Foucault, "Genealogische Geschichtsschreibung," in *Merkur* (Fall 1984). For a somewhat different estimate of the crosscurrents connecting first-generation critical theorists (especially Benjamin and Adorno) and contemporary trends in postmodern thought, see Gregory Ulmer, "The Object of Post-Criticism," in *The Anti-Aesthetic*, ed. Hal Foster, pp. 83–110; Rainer Nägele, "The Scene of the Other: Theodor W. Adorno's Negative Dialectic in the Context of Poststructuralism," in *Postmodernism and Politics*, ed. J. Arac, pp. 91–111, and my essay, "Foucault and the Frankfurt School: A Discourse on Nietzsche, Power, and Knowledge."
27. See, for example, Adorno's critique of Heidegger's notion of historicity in "Die Idee der Naturgeschichte," in *Gesammelte Schriften*, vol. 1, pp. 351–53.
28. Walter Benjamin, "Theses on the Philosophy of History," p. 264.
29. T. W. Adorno, *Eingriffe*, p. 13.
30. *TkH* 1. 512.
31. *PP*₂ 37–75.
32. Benjamin, "On Language" and "On the Mimetic Faculty." According to the early Benjamin, naming is prior to speech and communication. This theological conception of language, though eventually rejected by Benjamin, anticipated two facets of his later thought—namely, his interest in semiotics and his attitude concerning the intertranslatability of languages and sign systems as reflections of one and the same logos. As a young Hegelian, Benjamin believed that the truth content of a text was revealed to critical reflection only after enough time had elapsed to blur its connection with its original context. Later, however, he came to regard interpretations more as a confrontation between the interpreter's practical standpoint and traditional authority, in which fragments of meaning are violently wrested from their context. In the final analysis, it must be conceded that for Benjamin, it was always the isolated name and never the sentence, text, or sociohistorical environment that constituted the alpha and omega of revealed meaning.
33. Horkheimer, *The Eclipse of Reason*, p. 179.
34. Adorno and Horkheimer, *Dialectic*, p. 77.
35. Adorno, *Prisms*, p. 23.
36. The fullest account of Marcuse's thought regarding the relationship between the unconscious and art is contained in *Eros and Civilization: A Philosophical Inquiry Into Freud*, chap. 8. Unlike Horkheimer and Adorno, Marcuse always retained an interest in ontology. (See, e.g., his defense of Marx's philosophical anthropology in "Neue Quellen zur Grundlegung des historischen Materialismus.") While at Freiburg, the young Marxist was impressed with Heidegger's *Sein und Zeit*, especially its potential for amalgamating the ontological categories of historicity, concern, and resoluteness into a theory of praxis. The fruit of these early studies is contained in "Beiträge zu einer Phänomenologie des historischen Materialismus," "Das Problem der geschichtlichen Wirklichkeit," and *Hegels Ontologie und die Grundlegung einer Theorie der Geschichtlichkeit* (Frankfurt: V. Klostermann, 1932).
37. *TkH* 1. 521.
38. Ibid., 512, n. 111.

39. Ibid., 518–20.
40. See D. Henrich, "Die Grundstruktur der modernen Philosophie," and "Selbstbe-wusstsein."
41. *TkH* 1. 527.
42. Ibid., 529ff. Habermas has in mind Luhmann's interpretation of Husserl's tran-scendental ego as an impersonal system that seeks to control its own boundary by imposing meaning on a sensory environment.
43. Ibid., 525.

6. DISCOURSE ON MODERNITY: A PHILOSOPHICAL INTERLUDE

1. It was used in the late fifties by Irving Howe and Harry Levin to decry the leveling off of the modernist movement. For a more detailed discussion of this issue, see Andreas Huyssen, "Mapping the Postmodern," pp. 11ff.
2. Clement Greenberg, "Modernist Painting," pp. 101–02.
3. Hal Foster, "(Post)Modern Polemics," p. 75.
4. Huyssen, "Mapping the Postmodern," p. 25.
5. Ibid., p. 15; C. Jencks, *The Language of Postmodern Architecture*, p. 97; and R. Venturi, D. S. Brown, and S. Izenour, *Learning From Las Vegas*.
6. Fredric Jameson, "The Politics of Theory: Ideological Positions in the Postmodern-ism Debate."
7. Nancy Fraser summarizes the brief history of the French Derrideans' attempt to found a Center For Philosophical Research on the Political in her article "The French Derrideans: Politicizing Deconstruction or Deconstructing the Political?". The directors of the center, Jean-Luc Nancy and Philippe Lacoue-Labarthe, sought in vain to maintain the concentration on the political (*le politique*) to the exclusion of all politics (*la politique*). The center's study of totalitarianism, which focused on the totalitarian assimiliation of the cultural to the political, the "strong" totalitarianism of fascist and communist countries, and the "weak" totalitarianism characteristic of mass democracy, showed the imprudence of its quasi-transcendental approach once the center fell under the ideological sway of anti-Marxist, neo-liberals. Fraser provides some fascinating insights into the theoretical problems that eventually led to the center folding in 1984, not least its inability to clarify the Arendtian theme that dominated its short history—namely, whether the public realm had been ab-sorbed into the welfare state, a theme that should have been explored, Fraser be-lieves, in conjunction with the alternatives set by critical theory and Anglo-Ameri-can socialist feminism. See also P. Lacoue-Labarthe and J.-L. Nancy, *Rejouer le politique* (Paris: Galilée, 1982) and *Le retrait du politique* (Paris: Galilée, 1983).
8. Huyssen, "Mapping the Postmodern," p. 34.
9. Foster sees postmodernism and poststructuralism converging in a conservative politics, despite their differences ("(Post) Modern Polemics").
10. *PDM* 10–12.
11. Ibid., 15–19.
12. Benjamin, "Theses on the Philosophy of History," p. 263.
13. *PDM* 1. 20–26.
14. Ibid., 26–38.
15. Ibid., 39–43.
16. Ibid., 43–45.
17. Ibid., 45–49.
18. Ibid., 50–54.
19. Ibid., 54–58. In an early essay Habermas reproached Hegel for granting to Abso-

lute Spirit a practical efficacy that he denied to historical subjects: "Hegel makes revolution the heart of his philosophy in order to preserve philosophy from becoming the procurer of revolution" (*TP* 139).

20. According to Habermas, the Young Hegelians set the tone for later philosophy. The terms *fundamental ontology, critical theory, negative dialectics, deconstruction,* and *genealogy* in fact cloak the end of philosophy in the mantle of traditional philosophy (*PDM* 67).

21. As Löwith notes, the schism between Left and Right Hegelians arose from the ambiguity of Hegel's notion of *Aufhebung,* which connotes both preservation and negation, and from his dictum that the rational is what is real and the real is what is rational. The Young Hegelians stressed the critical side of the dialectic, as well as the irrationality of phenomenal existence. For them, the goal of philosophy was not the contemplative appropriation of the past but the practical realization of the reconciliation of individual and society articulated metaphysically in the Hegelian corpus (see Löwith, *From Hegel to Nietzsche,* p. 67). Habermas criticizes Löwith, who had influenced his own maturation as a critical theorist, for his pessimistic assessment of the capacity of historical consciousness to penetrate reification (*PP*₂ 79ff.).

22. Habermas argues that the Young Hegelians addressed problems associated with the legitimation of modernity that would later be of concern to Nietzschean critics: the subjectivism of modern society, the ambiguous role of intellectuals, and the antagonism between revolutionary intervention and historical continuity (*PDM* 71–75).

23. See my essay "Religion and Emancipation: Marx on the Jewish Question."

24. Ibid.

25. *PDM* 79.

26. Habermas includes under the headline "praxis philosophy" not only versions of Western Marxism stemming from Lukács and Gramsci, such as critical theory, the Budapest school, and the Yugoslavian school; the existentialism of Sartre, Merleau-Ponty, and Castoriadis; and the phenomenology of Paci, but also democratic forms of American pragmatism and analytic philosophy. In this context he cites Richard Bernstein's excellent study of Marxism, existentialism, pragmatism, and analytic philosophy, *Praxis and Action.*

27. *PDM* 82–86.

28. Habermas also discusses the praxis philosophies of Peter Berger with Thomas Luckmann, Cornelius Castoriadis, and Agnes Heller, all of which depart from phenomenological premises, the Berger-Luckmann approach taking its lead from Husserl's notion of a world-constituting transcendental subjectivity, the approach of Castoriadis and Heller from the primacy of the lifeworld. Although the latter has the advantage of avoiding the methodological problems associated with transcendental philosophy, it nevertheless conceives the lifeworld, or poetic discourse, as the product of objectifications (like Heidegger, Castoriadis collapses disclosure of meaning with validity) and is therefore incapable of providing a basis for criticizing reification. See *PDM* 95–103, 380–89; P. Berger and T. Luckmann, *Social Construction of Reality: A Treatise into the Sociology of Knowledge*; A. Heller, *Das Alltagsleben*; and C. Castoriadis, *Gesellschaft als imaginäre Institution.*

29. Rosenkranz and Haym emphasized the dialectical moment of preservation, which for them meant restoring Christian dogma to the Hegelian theodicy of Spirit. They maintained that because reality was rational—which for Rosenkranz meant that international commerce, technology, mass publicity, and so on were succeeding in

reducing the particularity of diverse nationalities and classes to the universality of a uniform civilization—ethical philosophy, understood as the moralizing of would-be reformers, was presumptuous (see K. Rosenkranz, *Neue Studien* [Leipzig: E. Koschny, 1875], vol. 1, pp. 413–64, 548ff.).

30. *PDM* 89–91 and J. Ritter, *Metaphysik und Politik* and *Hegel und die französische Revolution*. Habermas sees the recent metaphysical turn in German philosophy (Henrich, Bubner, and Theunissen) as an offshoot of neo-Aristotelian hermeneutics (Gadamer) and conservative neo-Hegelianism (Ritter), in part provoked by a conservative political climate ("Rückkehr zur Metaphysik").

31. *PDM* 91–94.

32. Ibid., 104–09 and Nietzsche, *Werke*, vol. 1.

33. According to one version of the myth, Dionysus, offspring of Zeus and the mortal Semele, was driven mad by Zeus's wife, Hera; he subsequently roamed North Africa and Asia Minor accompanied by satyrs and Bacchae until his senses were retans, and then restored to life. F. Schlegel, *Kritische Aufsätze und Briefe* (Berlin: W. Kohlhammer, 1962), vol. 2, pp. 312–17.

34. *PDM* 110–15.

35. *PDM* 115–18; *KK* 237–63.

36. *PDM* 119–20.

37. Ibid., 121–23.

38. Ibid., 169–76.

39. Ibid., 176–80.

40. Ibid., 158–65, 181–82.

41. Ibid., 162.

42. Ibid., 161–64.

43. Ibid., 167.

44. Ibid., 165–69, 182–83. Initially Habermas treats Heidegger's turn from existentialism to a theodicy of Being as if it were motivated by theoretical problems internal to the philosophy of subjectivity; but in a concluding section he suggests that it was equally motivated by Heidegger's reaction to national socialism. Only an examination of this episode, Habermas believes, can provide a clue to why Heidegger came to regard the history of Being as an event of truth somehow immune to the vicissitudes of historicism. Although in *Being and Time* Heidegger had argued that the fate of individual being was inextricably bound up with the fate of the community (§ 74), it was only after the Nazis came to power and Heidegger had been made rector of Freiburg that, as an administrative spokesman for national socialism, he expressly identified Dasein with the Dasein of a Volk, whose meaning and fate, in the case of the German people, were crystalized in the will of a *Führer*. When disappointment in national socialism finally set in, Heidegger, who had lent his philosophy to the cause, could not repudiate it without undermining his own ontological project. Continuity with *Being and Time* could be preserved only by treating the "untruth" of the Nazi movement as a manifestation of a higher event of truth, the self-concealment of Being, and not as a mistake resulting from the culpability of individuals who, in their fallen inauthenticity, had succumbed to the mass appeal of das Man. In this way, Habermas claims, Heidegger could deny responsibility for colluding with the Nazis while lumping together fascism, Americanism, and communism as equally misguided, subjectivistic phenomena of one and the same ontological event (*PDM* 184–90).

45. *PDM* 191–97 and Derrida, *Of Grammatology*.

46. *PDM* 197–203 and E. Husserl, *Logische Untersuchungen*, vol. 2, pp. 23ff.

47. *PDM* 203–11 and Derrida, *Speech and Phenomena*, chap. 5.

48. *PDM* 211–18. Habermas sees Derrida as remaining wedded to Jewish mysticism in his belief that deconstruction renews the dialogue with an absent God by breaking through the literal meaning of the text. The linking of commentary and text contrasts sharply with Christian hermeneutics, which presupposes that all things manifest literally the spiritual logos or presence of God. Habermas is indebted to Susan Handelman's essay "Jacques Derrida and the Heretic Hermeneutic," pp. 98ff., for this insight.

49. *PDM* 220–33.

50. Ibid., 234–42. A similar breakdown of the fiction-communication distinction is implicit in Roman Jakobson's privileging of the poetic over the denotative, normative, and expressive functions of language. By contrast, Richard Ohmann attributes the poetic world-disclosing, creative capacity of fiction to the use of impaired speech acts that, lacking a contextually based illocutionary power, are freed for expressive purposes ("Speech-Acts and the Definition of Literature," *Philosophy and Rhetoric* 4 [1971]: 1–19). Habermas also cites in this connection Mary L. Pratt's book *Speech Act Theory of Literary Discourse*, which contains a discussion of how fictive devices penetrate everyday communication and vice versa.

51. *PDM* 245–46. While attending a series of lectures that Habermas gave at Cornell University in September 1984, Jonathan Culler perceived a certain discomfort on Habermas's part in answering questions about the literary and rhetorical aspects of philosophical discourse—questions that Habermas now addresses. These questions, which Culler has repeated in a recent article entitled "Communicative Competence and Normative Force," cast doubt on the assumptions which he imputes to Habermas. These are that the distinction between illocutionary and perlocutionary speech acts corresponds to the distinction between strategic and communicative action, that strategic action derives from communicative action, and that consensually oriented communication is prior to, and normative for, literary communication. A reading of *TkH*—a work that Culler apparently has not studied—would show that Habermas does not make the first of these assumptions at all, and that his current defense of the second and third is a great deal more sophisticated than his earlier discussion of art and action in *CES*.

Culler maintains that Habermas's justification of the primacy of consensual norms is circular and rests on prior exclusion of "those communicative activities that do not seem to presuppose these norms" (p. 141). In a Derridean spirit, he argues that there is no reason to privilege spoken communication over literary communication, and that the literary norms of significance and unity mentioned by Pratt in her Gricean reading of literary communication (see n. 50 above) cannot be reduced to the validity claims and presuppositions of ideal speech. Pratt maintains that poetic discourse shares certain presuppositions with other types of speech action, the most important being its claim to be worthy of being told (tellability). The poetic text elaborates an exemplary experience that has been detached from its context, and in a way that is unusual or problematic, so as to elicit from its audience an intended evaluation and interpretation that is pleasurable and worthwhile. The tellability condition is somewhat analogous to the postulates of conversation mentioned by Grice but differs from the primary model of declarative speech in that it does not raise the sorts of validity claims ascribed to communicative action by Habermas. Not surprisingly, Habermas finds Pratt's advocacy of reader-response criticism more in keeping with his own view than with Culler's. Fiction, he claims, can only fulfill its poetic world-disclosing, creating function by partially, but not entirely, suspending the normative force of consensual validity claims, which continue to function as the normal background against which poetic acts are contrasted. "What grounds the superordinate rank and structure-building power of the poetic function is not the deviation of a fictive representation from the documentary reproduction of an event, but rather the exemplary treatment, which detaches the case from its context and makes it into an occasion for an innovative, world-disclosing, eye-opening representation whereby the rhetorical means of representation emerge from the communicative routine and attain a life of their own" (p. 238).

52. *PDM* 253–60 and Bataille, "The Psychological Structure of Fascism."
53. *PDM* 260–68 and Bataille, "The Notion of Expenditure."
54. *PDM* 269–78 and Bataille, *Death and Sensuality* and *La Souveraineté*.
55. *PDM* 279–312 and Foucault, *Madness and Civilization.*
56. Foucault, "Nietzsche, Genealogy, History," p. 160. In the last years of his life Foucault sought to emphasize the underlying continuity in ascetic practices linking the Greek, Roman, and Christian economies of pleasure, without obscuring their structural differences. Corresponding to this change in emphasis, we find thought playing a more important role in genealogical analysis than before. See, e.g., Foucault, *Histoire de la Sexualité*, pp. 27ff., 44ff.
57. Foucault, "Nietzsche, Genealogy, History," p. 251.
58. Nietzsche, *The Dawn*, p. 49.
59. Foucault, *The Order of Things*, p. 320.
60. Ibid., pp. 322–28.
61. Ibid., p. 334.
62. Foucault, *The Archaeology of Knowledge*, pp. 79–85. Foucault talks about a "unity" that "makes possible and governs" the discursive formation (p. 72) and the "complex group of relations that function as a rule" and "lay down [*préscrit*] what must be related" (p. 74).
63. H. L. Dreyfus and P. Rabinow, *Michel Foucault: Beyond Hermeneutics and Structuralism*, pp. 90–100.
64. M. Foucault, *Knowledge/Power*, pp. 88ff.
65. Foucault's depiction of Nietzschean genealogy as a "mere play of dominations" reminds one of Deleuze's reading of Nietzsche's interpretation of the body: "Every body lives as the 'arbitrary' product of the forces that compose it" (*The New Nietzsche* [New York: Dell, 1977], p. 80). For a criticism of Foucault's reading of Nietzsche, see R. Pippin, "Nietzsche and the Origin of the Idea of Modernism."
66. Foucault, *Knowledge/Power*, p. 39.
67. Foucault, *Discipline and Punish*, p. 226. The contrast drawn by Foucault between the personal, sovereign power of the monarch, maintained through overt displays of excessive cruelty, and the impersonal, rational power of the modern state, exercised through covert, graduated techniques of manipulation, is reminiscent of Bataille's treatment of same.
68. Foucault, *The History of Human Sexuality, Volume I: An Introduction*, pp. 9–19. Foucault's anti-Freudian stance was influenced by Deleuze and Guattari's *L'Anti-Oedipe: Capitalisme et schizophrénie* (Paris: Les Editions de Minuit, 1972), which argues that the sexual feelings of children toward their parents are not natural but are elicited and then prohibited by their parents.
69. Foucault, *Discipline and Punish*, pp. 17–19 and Otto Kirchheimer, "Criminal Law in National Socialist Germany" and "The Legal Order of National Socialism."
70. *PDM* 296–303.
71. Ibid., 394ff. In some interviews conducted in Berkeley in 1983–84 Foucault con-

ceded that similar forms of experience could well harbor similar, universal structures and that the idea of consensus, though not itself a regulative principle, was "a
critical idea to maintain at all times." He acknowledged that the aim of the social
critic was to "ask oneself what proportion of nonconsensuality is implied in such a
power relation, and whether that degree of nonconsensuality is necessary or not,
and then one may question every power relation to that extent." However, he allowed that this meant only that "perhaps one must not be for consensuality, but
one must be against nonconsensuality." More recently, he has acknowledged that
"in the serious play of questions and answers, in the work of reciprocal elucidation,
the rights of each person are in some sense immanent in the discussion." See "Politics and Ethics: An Interview with Michel Foucault" and "Polemics, Politics, and
Problemizations: An Interview with Michel Foucault," in *The Foucault Reader*, ed. P.
Rabinow (New York: Pantheon, 1984), pp. 379–81.

72. *PDM* 344ff.
73. *NU* 30–56. Norman Podhoretz, editor of *Commentary*, and Irving Kristol, editor of
Public Interest, are among the Americans identified by Habermas as New Deal liberals who have fallen into the neoconservative camp.
74. Habermas follows Rawls and Dworkin in regarding civil disobedience as a normal,
necessary feature of democracy, which deviates from routine violations of the law
in its intent and culpability. He argues that nonviolent acts of civil disobedience
perpetrated by Germans protesting the installation of nuclear missiles should not
be prosecuted as criminal acts, since they are based on an appeal to a concept of
moral legitimacy implicit in constitutional law. In his view, there would have been
no installation of missiles in Western Europe had there been no breakdown in the
democratic process; the public debate over this issue was so constrained and distorted ideologically by misinformation that the minority was left with no recourse
other than to demonstrate its conviction that not only its, but also the majority's,
rights to free, informed debate had been violated. Because there was no reason to
believe that the order to deploy missiles represented a rational consensus over
universalizable interests, the protesters could justifiably claim that, from a constitutional standpoint, the law was as much on their side as it was on the side of the civil
rights demonstrators led by Martin Luther King Jr. in the sixties (*NU* 79–116).
75. *NU* 35–39 and D. Bell, *The Cultural Contradictions in Capitalism*. According to Habermas, "Bell sees a religious revival as the only solution" to the problem of generating
new norms that "will put a brake on the levelling caused by the social welfare state,
so that the virtues of individual competition can again dominate" ("Modernity versus Postmodernity," pp. 6–7). Jonathan Arac cites this passage as just one example
of Habermas's tendentious treatment of postmodern philosophies. In fact, Bell
characterizes himself as "a socialist in economics, a liberal in politics, and a conservative in culture" ("Modernism and Capitalism," *Partisan Review* 46 [1978]: 206).
Bell does not criticize modernism per se, but only the cultural contradictions of capitalism, whose economic imperatives generate hedonism and role-fragmenta-
tion—side effects that undermine both the Protestant work ethic and the holistic
values of modern culture. Not only does Bell deny that capitalism is necessary for
preserving political liberty, but his advocacy of a religious revival constitutes a plea
for communal values that is in keeping with the spirit of Habermas's communication ethic, which also seeks to realize the emancipatory thrust of modern culture
minus its bourgeois glorification of self-interest (see J. Arac ed., *Postmodernism and
Politics*, pp. xv–xvii).
76. In his speech acknowledging the award of the Theodor W. Adorno Prize from the
city of Frankfurt, Habermas mentions an example cited in Peter Weiss's book *The*

Aesthetics of Resistance illustrating how aesthetic experience "enters into a language game that is no longer that of the aesthetic critique"—i.e., one that "is used to illuminate a life-historical situation and is related to life problems." It concerns a group of young workers attending an art class who seek to bridge the gap between art and their everyday lives: "Out of the resilient edifice of the objective mind, embodied in works of art which they saw again and again in the museums of Berlin, they started removing their own chips of stone, which they gathered together and reassembled in the context of their own milieu. This milieu was far removed from that of traditional education as well as from the then existing regime. These young workers went back and forth between the edifice of European art and their own milieu until they were able to illuminate both" (Habermas, "Modernity Versus Postmodernity," p. 112).

77. *NU* 11–23.
78. Ibid., 23–26.
79. Ibid., 26–29.
80. *PDM* 62. Arendt's *Lectures On Kant* continues this line of interpretation and provides a good starting point for understanding the political significance of the Third Critique. Her interpretation, however, vacillates between consigning judgment to the political sphere (vita activa) and relegating it to the disinterested life of the mind (vita contemplativa). See Beiner's commentary in the same volume for a fuller treatment of this issue.
81. *PDM* 63 and Schiller, *Sämtliche Werke: Säkular Ausgabe*, vol. 5, p. 593. Marcuse conceived the relationship between art and political revolution along the lines proposed by Schiller; art should not educate the soul didactically but should seek to emancipate the senses through its form alone, which transcends the moral-political, cognitive-instrumental aims of existing reality. See H. Marcuse, *Counterrevolution and Revolt*. For a further discussion of Schiller's relationship to later developments in German idealism, see Philip Kain's book *Schiller, Hegel, and Marx*.
82. *PDM* 59 and Schiller, *Sämtliche Werke: Säkular Ausgabe*, vol. 5, pp. 571ff.
83. *PDM* 60–61 and Schiller, *Sämtliche Werke: Säkular Ausgabe*, vol. 5, pp. 582–87 and 633–67.
84. *PDM* 62 and Schiller, *On the Aesthetic Education of Man*, trans. E. M. Wilkinson and L. A. Willoughby (Oxford: Oxford University Press, 1967), pp. 79–81, 107, 135–41.
85. See Culler, "Communicative Competence and Normative Force"; P. Hohendahl, "The Dialectic of Enlightenment Revisited: Habermas' Critique of the Frankfurt School," pp. 24–26; D. Misgeld, "Critical Hermeneutics Versus Neoparsonianism?," p. 56; M. Ryan, *Marxism and Deconstruction*; and J. O'Kane, "Marxism, Deconstruction, and Ideology."
86. *PDM* 64. Here one detects another link between poststructuralism and Habermas. In distinguishing the Greek economy of pleasure from the hermeneutics of the self, Foucault remarked: "What strikes me is the fact that in our society, art has become something which is related only to objects and not to individuals, or to life. That art is something which is specialized or which is done by experts who are artists. But couldn't everyone's life become a work of art? Why should the lamp or the house be an art object, but not our life?" ("On the Genealogy of Ethics: An Overview of Work in Progress," in *The Foucault Reader*, ed. P. Rabinow, p. 350). Habermas notes that there are traces of vitalism in Foucault's account of the body's experience of itself, as well as speculative passages at the end of the first volume of *The History of Human Sexuality* that suggest a visceral aestheticism. Habermas concludes, however, that Foucault's method is incompatible with any "naturalistic metaphysics" that postulates prediscursive referents. It seems to me that this reading neglects the

significance of prediscursive practice in Foucault's philosophy, an aspect stressed by Dreyfus and Rabinow, who maintain that Foucault does not dismiss the meaningfulness of practice as Habermas suggests, but only its cognitive or representational function vis-à-vis consciousness—a fact that would make his approach more amenable to an aestheticization of life than Habermas would have us believe.

7. FROM PURPOSIVE TO COMMUNICATIVE ACTION IN THE SOCIAL THEORIES OF MEAD AND DURKHEIM

1. *TkH* 2. 11–15 and George Herbert Mead, *Mind, Self and Society*, ed. C. W. Morris (Chicago: University of Chicago Press, 1934), pp. 1–41.
2. *TkH* 2. 15–18 and Mead, *Mind, Self and Society*, pp. 43–51.
3. *TkH* 2. 24–30 and Mead, *Mind, Self and Society*, pp. 65ff., 75ff., 90–100.
4. *TkH* 2. 36–39.
5. Ibid., 33ff., and Wittgenstein, *Philosophical Investigations*, p. 20. For Wittgenstein, linguistic rules do not possess the kind of universality associated with inductive generalizations, their universality being of an exemplary nature. Learning a linguistic rule involves neither abstracting common properties (forming generalizations) nor imitating past behavior. It is not like induction, since the various practices circumscribed by the rule may have no more in common with each other than a loose "family resemblance." Nor is it like imitation, since it enables one to improvise expressions in situations never encountered before. Deviation from customary linguistic behavior does not prove that an expression has changed its meaning, for linguistic rules do not refer to observed regularities or conditioned responses, but to generative competencies.
6. *TkH* 2. 39–46.
7. Ibid., 47–53 and Mead, *The Philosophy of the Act*, pp. 8–25, 103–54. Single terms, such as names, predicates, and adjectives, can assume a univocal referential role even in the absence of the objects to which they refer. By contrast, signals such as pointing, yelling, and so on are context-dependent and hence take on descriptive, expressive, and imperative functions indiscriminately.
8. Habermas distinguishes the epistemic from the practical ego, the former consisting of general cognitive and linguistic structures that every self must acquire in order to distinguish itself from an objective, social reality, the latter of a personal life history sustained by a continuous identity.
9. *TkH* 2. 160. See also *CES* 106–11. Habermas discusses D. Henrich, "Identität," in *Identität, Poetik und Hermeneutik*, ed. O. Marguard and K. Stierle (Munich: W. Fink, 1979), vol. 8, pp. 371ff., and Tugendhat, *Selbstbewusstsein und Selbstbestimmung: sprachanalytische Interpretationen* (Frankfurt: Suhrkamp, 1979), pp. 71, 284.
10. *CES* 109.
11. Ibid., 84ff., 106–10; and *TkH* 2. 161–63. Habermas admits that the distinction between role and ego identity is vague in young children, who may master the first-person role of speaker but not have the remotest idea of their role within the family. Insofar as such roles are ascribed, it would appear that not only the criteria but also the conditions of personal identity differ from those of adults.

    The symbolic interactional model developed by Mead is but one of three approaches to the study of identity formation mentioned by Habermas, the others being the psychosexual approach favored by Freud, Sullivan, and Erikson and the cognitive-developmental approach pioneered by Piaget and Kohlberg. There is little doubt in Habermas's mind that these three approaches are complementary. The formation of personal identity is a function of psychosexual (motivational) development inasmuch as a child must go through certain typical stages in order to master the conflict between its own needs and those of others. Motivational development, in turn, is dependent on the mastery of communicative roles in social interaction, a point well illustrated in Mead's theory of socialization. Finally, the formation of personal identity is dependent on the development of the epistemic ego. Habermas notes, however, that motivational development (moral action) may not keep pace with cognitive development (moral judgment). The development of conscience must go through two major crisis stages, oedipal and adolescent, in which erotic and aggressive drives come to be directed in conformity with gender roles and cultural expectations. The ability to sustain a constant threshold of interactive competence in the face of irresolvable conflicts of duty (the tragic element of human action) without succumbing to defense mechanisms and avoidance strategies is a sign of stable ego identity (*CES* 100).

12. *TkH* 2. 53ff. and Mead, *Philosophy of the Act*, pp. 149–64. Habermas uses Mead's two-stage theory of socialization to explain the transition from the stage of moral consciousness denoted by Kohlberg's "good boy" orientation to that of conventional conformity to law and order. At the level of play children learn that compliance with parental authority leads to mutual satisfaction of interests. This "I'll scratch your back if you scratch mine" stance does not require that children adopt a disinterested standpoint, but it does presuppose internalization of the concrete role model of a solicitous parent acting for the sake of mutual benefit. This orientation to a concrete role model is superseded once children learn that parental authority represents the "the generalized will of all the others." At first the capacity to perceive concrete interaction as an instance of a higher norm remains tied to reciprocal rewards and punishments; one obeys for fear of collective reprisal. Like Freud, Mead contends that the generalized other associated with a disinterested sense of moral obligation arises only when the threat of external sanctions has been internalized.

13. *TkH* 2. 63–65.

14. Ibid., 152ff. It was in a similar spirit that Anatole France once decried the injustice of a system of laws that in its majestic impartiality forbade the rich as well as the poor from begging in the streets and sleeping under bridges.

15. *TkH* 2. 144–45 and Mead, *Selected Writings*, pp. 404ff. The communicative ethic goes beyond Kohlberg's stage six, which involves ideal role taking, and beyond Rawls's notion of the veil of ignorance. The theories of Kohlberg and Rawls require that one put oneself imaginatively in the other's position in order to justify substantive principles of justice. Habermas has criticized Rawls's selection of primary goods (guided by liberty and difference principles) as representing the class biases of welfare capitalism. To guard against this bias, he advocates a procedural extension of reciprocity in which needs are not assumed to be given but are taken as subject to a collective formation of will. See *CES* 199.

16. *TkH* 2. 65–68 and Mead, *Philosophy of the Act*, pp. 173–78, 192–222. Moral autonomy and expressive creativity are themselves linked, since both involve the questioning of prejudices in light of new possibilities.

17. *TkH* 2. 92ff., 149–52.

18. *CES* 110; *TkH* 2. 167–68.

19. Adorno, *Negative Dialektik*, p. 294; cited in *CES* 72–73. Habermas adds, however, that the paradox expresses a desideratum; the reconciliation of happiness (natural spontaneity) with practical reason occurs to the extent that needs are drawn into the rational orbit of a democratic formation of the will (*TkH* 2. 168).

20. *TkH* 2. 75–80 and Émile Durkheim, "The Determination of Moral Facts," pp. 9ff.

For a more detailed analysis of the holy as *mysterium tremendum et fascinans*, see Rudolf Otto *The Idea of the Holy: An Inquiry into the Non-rational Factor in the Idea of the Divine and its Relation to the Rational*, trans. by John W. Harvey (Oxford, Oxford University Press, 1923).

21. *TkH* 2. 81.
22. Ibid., 82–83, and Durkheim, *The Elementary Forms of the Religious Life*, pp. 121–272.
23. *TkH* 2. 83–85 and Durkheim, *Religious Life*, pp. 257, 414ff.
24. *TkH* 2. 85–88.
25. Ibid., 88–94.
26. Ibid., 119–20, and Durkheim, *The Division of Labor in Society*, pp. 68–110.
27. *TkH* 2. 120–21 and Durkheim, *Leçons de sociologie, physique des moeurs et du droit*, pp. 176–77.
28. *TkH* 2. 122–26 and Durkheim, *Leçons*, pp. 198–205, and *Montesquieu et Rousseau, précurseurs de la sociologie* (Paris: M. Rivière, 1953).
29. *TkH* 2. 128–31 and Durkheim, *Division of Labor*, pp. 129–32, 290, 329, 381–88.
30. *TkH* 2. 103.
31. Ibid., 100–03. Statements of assertion that raise a knowledge claim, such as "This ball is red," possess a meaning that cannot be rendered in any other form, since "This ball should be red" and "I have a feeling that this ball is red" explicitly refer to social norms and subjective feelings, not objective facts.
32. Ibid., 104–05.
33. Ibid., 117. Habermas adds that "the binding effect of illocutionary forces ironically comes to pass in and through the fact that the participants of an interaction can say 'no' to a speech-act offer" (p. 114). Therefore it is the negativity of critical reason that guarantees the reflexivity and therewith the autonomy of the self vis-à-vis society and nature.
34. Ibid., 110 and Durkheim, *Religious Life*, pp. 484–85.

8. SYSTEM AND LIFEWORLD

1. A depressed economy, for example, is largely an unintended global consequence emanating from an aggregate of voluntary decisions.
2. Nancy Fraser argues that Habermas's assignment of the family to the lifeworld errs in the opposite direction to orthodox Marxism in ignoring the family's contribution to material production. I maintain, to the contrary, that despite Habermas's tendency to map out the lifeworld-system distinction in terms of social institutions, his analysis of the uncoupling of the two indicates a different meaning altogether. See N. Fraser, "What's Critical About Critical Theory: The Case of Habermas and Gender."
3. *TkH* 2. 189–92; ZLS_1, 240ff.
4. *TkH* 2. 182–86. Habermas asks us to consider the case of a construction worker who orders a younger colleague to get some beer so that the gang can have a "late breakfast." The situation involves a theme (late breakfast), a goal (drinking), and a plan (sending the young worker to get beer). The order explicitly raises a normative validity claim and thus refers directly to a social hierarchy based on seniority. It also raises implicit validity claims to truth and sincerity, however, and hence refers indirectly to certain states of affairs and subjective experiences (e.g., the local bar being open that morning, the desire of the workers to quench their thirst). The questioning of any of these claims would result in a redefinition of the situation and a corresponding reshuffling of references. It should be noted that less specific fields of reference radiate concentrically from the perspective of each worker. The

social space of the immediate context refers indirectly to the more distant work location, which in turn is meaningfully circumscribed by the progressively broader
horizons of family life, community, nation, and world. The plan called for by the
situation also portends a future horizon of possibilities and expectations that are
called forth by a past horizon of immediate retentions. These retentions recede
into the dim awareness of one's personal history, which itself merges with the history of others. The lifeworld, then, consists of historical sedimentations of meaning
and is therefore to be distinguished from the invariant, formal-pragmatic structures
of world and language.

5. Ibid., 206–09. Here, as in his earlier study (ZLS_2, 287ff.), Habermas cites Danto's
   Analytical Philosophy of History in support of his view that historical thought is essentially narrative in nature. Historical writing interprets the past in terms of the
   present by describing events from the evaluative standpoint of the narrator (e.g.,
   "Aristarchus anticipated Copernicus").

6. *TkH* 2. 219–23.

7. Ibid., 223–28.

8. *CES* 138–39 and Marx and Engels, "Manifesto of the Communist Party." Marx stipulates that forces and relations of production do not vary independently but normally (except during periods of crisis) correspond to one another. Habermas con-
   tests "dogmatic" versions of historical materialism that characterize the dynamics
   of development as linear, uninterrupted, and irreversible: "It is not evolutionary
   processes that are *irreversible* but the structural sequences that a society must run
   through *if* and *to the extent that* it is involved in evolution."

9. Marx, *A Contribution to the Critique of Political Economy*, pp. 20–21.

10. *CES* 143–44.

11. Ibid., 145 and *KHI* 48. Habermas cites as evidence of reductionism the passage in
    Marx's *Grundrisse*, pp. 704–06, beginning with the sentence: "To the degree that
    large industry develops, the creation of wealth depends on the general state of sci-
    ence and on the progress of industry."

12. *CES* 149, *ZRhM* 53, and *WT* 249. Habermas's reversal of Marx's formulation—his
    belief that the crisis of modern capitalism is due to the fettering of productive rela-
    tions by the expansion of productive forces—is criticized by Julius Sensat (*Haber-
    mas and Marxism: An Appraisal*) on the grounds that the division of mental and
    physical labor necessitated by productive relations stultifies problem-solving cre-
    ativity. His reply to David Held (see chap. 10) and his account of the splitting off of
    elite cultures, which acknowledges the reifying effects of this notwithstanding,
    Habermas steadfastly denies that bureaucratic hierarchies are inherently reifying.
    Sensat's contention that, for Habermas, "each stage or degree of technical rational-
    ization is conceptually (if not causally) compatible with any stage or degree of prac-
    tical rationalization" (p. 111) is surely an exaggeration. Habermas says on numer-
    ous occasions that, with few exceptions, the development of productive forces is
    dependent on the prior development of productive relations. This dependence is
    causal, with advances in social relations establishing necessary (but not sufficient)
    conditions for the implementation of cognitive potential (including abilities and re-
    sources) in productive forces.

13. *CD* 268.

14. *CES* 150–54 and *LC* 7–8. Current controversies concerning the ordering of modes
    of production tend to revolve around the following issues. First, within the cate-
    gory of primitive—i.e., communal—social formation one can distinguish appro-
    priative (hunter-gatherer) economies from producing (agricultural, livestock-
    breeding) economies. The emergence of agriculture in neolithic society introduced

stratified forms of social organizations, however, in which questions of ownership began to arise. Second, there is considerable doubt as to whether the asiatic mode of production, characterized by state ownership of land "superimposed upon the remains of village communal property" (*CES* 150), is the last stage of communal society or the first stage of class society. If the latter, as Habermas believes, then is it a universal stage of development that parallels the ancient (slave) mode of production or a mixture of ancient and feudal forms of social organization? The same can be asked of feudalism: is it a universal stage or just a phenomenon peculiar to medieval Europe? Finally, it is unclear whether the modern welfare state represents an advanced form of capitalism or a nascent form of socialism.

15. *CES* 153.

16. Ibid., 120–22 and *LC* 15–16. This has evidently been the case since the beginning of modern experimental science, which arose out of the Renaissance synthesis of Greek *theoria* and the Protestant ethic. No doubt, superior theoretical advances occurred in Greek and Chinese world views, despite their low potential for practical rationalization. Nevertheless, such advances would not have been possible without the prior institutionalization of political order, which represents a relatively higher stage of moral-legal development. Furthermore, Habermas notes that the superior cognitive potential of cosmocentric world views could not have been fully implemented and hence realized without the subsequent institutionalization of purposive-rational action in formal law.

17. *LC* 13. According to Habermas, values associated with survival, adaptability, health, and so on cannot be presumed as normative givens without committing a naturalistic fallacy. Only those inherent in the telos of communication itself—namely, truth and justice—possess such validity (*CES* 177).

18. *CES* 144. Among Marxist anthropologists, it is M. Godelier ("Infrastructures, Societies and History," in *Current Anthropology* 19 [1978]: 763ff.; and *Perspectives in Marxist Anthropology*) to whom Habermas most frequently appeals in defending the relativity of base and superstructure. Habermas adds that "the theories of postindustrial society even envision a state in which evolutionary primacy would pass from the economic system to the educational and scientific system" (*CES* 144). See A. Tourraine, *La Société post-industrielle*, and D. Bell, *The Coming of Postindustrial Society*.

19. *TkH* 2. 252. In Habermas's view, system problems are by no means invariably economic in nature but usually stem from the social base of a society. This base consists of relations of production that derive from the organizational principles of kinship, lineage, political authority, or formal law. Since it is only in capitalist society that the institutional complex of formal law permits a purely market-based mechanism for regulating access to property and distributing wealth, it is only in capitalism that system problems are rooted ultimately in economic contradictions.

20. *LC* 18.

21. *CES* 162.

22. *LC* 20.

23. Ibid., 19–21.

24. Ibid., 21–23.

25. Ibid., 24–30.

26. *CES* 163–67.

27. *TkH* 2. 173–75 and Durkheim, *Division of Labor*, pp. 111ff., 174ff. Segmentary societies are composed of a number of similar, more or less self-sufficient units held together mechanically, or externally, by their resemblance, or collective moral identity. In functionally differentiated societies there is a division of labor, with distinct,

interdependent organs arranged horizontally (in occupational roles) and vertically (in levels of power gravitating around the state as a central control). Durkheim believed that a society's size and density were proportional to its level of functional differentiation (pp. 256ff.), a view that in Habermas's opinion is valid only for tribal societies.

28. *TkH* 2. 175–77 and Durkheim, *Division of Labor*, pp. 200ff., 381ff. Habermas claims that Durkheim is confronted with a paradox similar to Weber's, for although Durkheim distinguishes "normal" forms of organic solidarity, in which contractual relations aim at moral and material equality (harmony), from "abnormal," anomic forms, exemplified by the antagonism between labor and capital (pp. 374ff.), he nowhere explains how the ethical tendencies indigenous to the division of labor can also be undermined by it.

29. The theory of evolution expounded in *KHI* combined indiscriminately the notion of a "natural history of the human species" with the idea of social development. This way of viewing human evolution was in part dictated by the aim of the book, to trace the genealogy of types of knowledge back to quasi-transcendental-natural interests. Since the early seventies, however, Habermas has come to reconsider both the theory of knowledge-constitutive interests and the corresponding concept of human evolution. He now prefers to divide human evolution into what might be described roughly as natural, natural-historical, and sociohistorical phases. He dates the origin of the "human form of life" to the break between the first and second phases (approximately four million years ago), when hominids began to distinguish themselves from other primates by procuring means of subsistence socially, through the use of simple tools. The interplay between biological and cultural mechanisms of evolution led to important changes in brain size and other morphological features, development remaining largely dependent on genetic mutations selectively conditioned by the environment. Sociocultural evolution of societies first came to the fore when the hunt, with its incipient division of labor between male hunters and female gatherers, precipitated a change from the one-dimensional rank ordering of status-dependent sexual relations by the family system, which had made possible a multidimensional assignment of social roles based on reciprocally recognized and linguistically mediated expectations. This led to a nonnatural phase of learning characterized by a heightened degree of self-awareness (*CES* 133–37).

30. *CES* 156–57.

31. Ibid., 77 and L. Kohlberg, "From Is to Ought."

32. *TkH* 2. 233–37 and M. Fortes, *Kinship and Social Order* (Chicago: University of Chicago Press, 1969), pp. 104, 234.

33. *TkH* 2. 262–64 and L. Mair, *An Introduction to Social Anthropology* (Oxford: Oxford University Press, 1972), pp. 145–48.

34. *CES* 77–81, 160; and Kohlberg, "From Is to Ought."

35. *CES* 162.

36. *TkH* 2. 250.

37. Kohlberg subdivides postconventional morality into a contractual-legalistic level, concerned with "establishing individual rights, equality, and liberty" and distinguishing values that are valid universally from those whose validity is limited to particular societies, and a universal-ethical level, concerned more with individual conscience and moral deliberation in accordance with formal canons of consistency and universalizability. A more radical level of postconventional morality is represented by discourse ethics of the sort proposed by Mead, Apel, and Habermas, which advocates the insertion of personal needs in a collective formation of the will

(*CES* 77–90; Kohlberg, "From Is to Ought." Stephen White has recently pointed out that a serious tension exists between Habermas's theory of stable ego identity, predicated on a "fictive world society" of liberated communication, and the inherently destabilizing aspects of such a society ("Habermas' Communicative Ethics and the Development of Moral Consciousness").

38. *TkH* 2. 238–40.
39. Ibid., 241.
40. Ibid., 241–46 and L. Mair, *An Introduction to Social Anthropology* (Oxford: Oxford University Press, 1972), p. 115. Habermas sees Evans-Pritchard's studies of the Nuer as particularly apposite in this regard. In order to manage tribes of up to 60,000 members, the Nuer delegate authority to aristocratic lineages that have the power to organize but lack the authority and means to exercise power. As Leach's studies of Burmese tribes and Gluckmann's studies of East African tribal revolts show, the process of segmentary differentiation and functional stratification is reversible. See E. R. Leach, *Political System of Highland Burma* (London: London School of Economics Monograph, 1964); and M. Gluckmann, *Order and Rebellion in Tribal Africa* (London: Basil Blackwell, 1963).
41. *TkH* 2. 250ff.
42. Ibid., 255ff.
43. Kinship, status, political office, and formal law condition, respectively, the four mechanisms of system differentiation: exchange, stratification, political power, and money. The first two characterize tribal societies characterized by segmentary differentiation, the last two political and economic class societies organized functionally.
44. *TkH* 2. 267–68.
45. Ibid., 268–70.
46. Ibid., 270–72.
47. Ibid., 272–75.
48. Ibid.
49. Ibid., 273, 275–76.
50. Ibid., 275–76.
51. Ibid., 276–77.
52. Ibid., 276–79.
53. Ibid., 286.
54. Ibid., 287–89. In the sacral context, symbolically mediated action has already given way to grammatical speech. The propositional differentiation of normative, expressive, and cognitive aspects is left obscure, however, in magical rites and mythical narratives. The latter shield the fragile unity of tribal societies from the potentially disruptive impact of dissonant, unpredictable, or otherwise novel experiences acquired at the level of profane action. This is accomplished by conflating internal meaning and external referent, logical and causal relations, and so on.
55. Ibid., 279–81, 289–90.
56. Ibid., 281–83.
57. Ibid., 290–92.
58. Ibid., 292–93.
59. See n. 37 above. Merleau-Ponty notes, for example, that so-called double sensations—i.e., sensations that occur whenever one part of the body touches another, initiate a kind of reflection in which "the body catches itself from outside engaged in a cognitive process" (*The Phenomenology of Perception*, p. 93). Elsewhere, he talks about a prethematic reflection, or self-awareness, by means of which the embodied self—not abstract thought—synthesizes space and sensory experience (pp. 218ff.). The body is also said to be responsible for the temporality that makes free-

dom possible (p. 453). Merleau-Ponty defends Hegel's postulation of the unity of freedom and necessity: "The fact remains that I am free, not in spite of, or on the hither side of, these (corporeal and cultural) motivations, but by means of them. For this significant life, this certain significance of nature and history which I am, does not limit my access to the world, but on the contrary is my means of entering into communication with it" (p. 455). Of course, there is the reverse danger of extinguishing the concept of reflection (and reason) in the immediacy of corporeal intuition.

60. See criticisms by Lukes, in *CD* 145ff., and the critique by William Austin in *Cognitive Development and Psychology*, ed. T. Mischel, p. 275.

61. *CD* 259–60 and Kohlberg, "The Claim to Moral Adequacy of the Highest Stage of Moral Judgement." Since the publication of *CD*, Habermas has written a more detailed analysis of the relationship between philosophical reconstruction and developmental psychology. In addition to the hermeneutic circle that obtains between philosophical and psychological levels of analysis, there is also, he notes, a hermeneutic circle between psychological theory and the data. In particular, the cross-cultural testing of psychological theory by means of story problems raises questions concerning, for example, how to translate a typical conflict situation for an American (e.g., Kohlberg's Heinz dilemma) into a comparable conflict situation for a Taiwanese. Kohlberg contends that such translations are possible, but in light of potential failures in translation and corroboration, such a postulation, Habermas contends, is premature (*MkH* 49–50).

62. *CD* 260. According to McCarthy, lower stages of cognitive and moral development can be confirmed empirically, since the competencies in question, such as the coordination of social perspectives for role taking and the ability to conceive objects as permanent and invariant through change, are undoubtedly basic to the human species. Consequently, the theoretician observing rudimentary forms of action may be said to know the structures, rules, and competencies implicit in them better than the actors themselves. When theoretician and subject possess the same reflective competence, however, the method of empirical observation must give way to dialogue (McCarthy, *CD* 72–75).

Habermas notes four problems that continue to plague Kohlberg's theory. The first concerns the failure to find test cases confirming Kohlberg's sixth stage, a failure that brings into question the naturalness of postconventional levels of moral development. The second concerns post-adolescent regression. Studies by C. Gilligan and J. M. Murphy ("The Philosopher and the Dilemma of the Fact," in *Intellectual Development Beyond Childhood*, ed. D. Kuhn [San Francisco: Jossey-Bass, 1980]) show selected women registering a preference for conventional solutions despite indications of their having reached a postconventional level of moral development. Similarly, many middle-aged test subjects prefer a relativistic ethic of responsibility that acknowledges the limits of a strict deontological ethic in dealing with the complexities of real-life situations. Though seeming to challenge the normative directionality of Kohlberg's theory, these phenomena, Habermas believes, prove that moral consciousness develops unevenly, and that the application of norms is relative to changing contexts and values. The third and fourth problems concern skepticism about values and the need to incorporate a psychodynamic model of motivational development that would account for incontinence and regression in terms of conflict avoidance strategies and repression. See *MkH* 183–200.

63. *CD* 260–61. A recent essay (*MkH* 53–125) contains Habermas's most detailed refutation of skepticism to date. The argument can be summarized as follows. Forms of ethical empiricism—intuitionism (Moore), emotivism (Stevenson), and prescriptivism (Hare)—from which theoretical skepticism derives ignore the performative

link between moral feelings and intersubjective expectations by identifying the former with nonnatural properties, subjective feelings, or groundless commands. But intersubjective expectations involve a concept of validity—analogous to truth —that refers to the idea of a discursively reached counterfactual consensus. The latter requires not only that valid judgments apply impartially, but that they instantiate universalizable interests. The universalizability principle, however, implies unconstrained public discourse, which should not be thought of as applying only to truth or as having only semantic import, independent of pragmatic meaning (Tugendhat/Tarski). Moral impartiality, therefore, is not a case of a fair compromise between competing interests. Moreover, the universalizability principle can be given an indirect (nondeductive) proof that avoids circularity by showing that any rational argument whatsoever, not just practical discourse, presupposes certain moral assumptions (the ideal speech situation) that impose counterfactual conditions of equality and freedom. Habermas accepts Apel's view that denial of the universalizability principle involves a pragmatic *contradiction*. The proof remains fallible, however, insofar as the theoretical reconstruction of intuitive knowledge, as well as the claim that there are no other alternatives, requires ongoing confirmation in dialogue. The skeptic, therefore, can deny the principle only on pain of being ostracized from the community of rational agents from which identity is procured.

64. McCarthy notes that "without an adequate understanding of the 'end-states' of development in other cultures, and thus the mode of thought and types of knowledge valued by them, we are determined before the fact to construe their performance as exhibiting a more or less deficient mastery of our competencies rather than as expressing a mastery of a different set of skills altogether" (*CD* 70).

65. Ibid., 71–72. McCarthy cites studies by P. T. Ashton ("Cross-Cultural Piagetian Research: An Experimental Perspective," *Harvard Educational Review* 45 [1975]) and others (see *Piagetian Psychology: Cross Cultural Contributions*, ed. P. R. Dasen [New York: Halsted, 1977]) showing, for example, that "children from pottery-making families in Mexico perform better on conservation of substance than do their peers from families that are not potters; that nomadic, hunting populations develop spatial concepts more rapidly than do sedentary agricultural populations, which attain concepts of conservation of quantity, weight, and volume more rapidly; that among Australian Aborigines, performance on concrete, operational tasks is directly proportional to the extent of their contact with the dominant culture"; and so on (*CD* 71).

66. For a more detailed statement of this criticism, see Michael Schmid, *CD* 173–74.

67. Ibid., 102–03.

68. The sovereignty of the modern state, like the autonomy of the ego, is predicated on mutual recognition, in this instance, recognition by other sovereign states (*CD* 114). But the identity of the state, unlike that of the ego, which is constituted through recognition by others, is constituted internally. Sometimes Habermas equates the cultural and institutional elements constitutive of social identity with just those aspects that gravitate around the organizational principle (*LC* 2–4, 7–8).

69. Schmid's essay also pinpoints difficulties with Habermas's concept of an organizational principle, which, he suggests, may be too abstract to help in differentiating types of social formation of the sort required by the theory. For Habermas to convert these abstract rules, which delimit ranges of structural variation, into useful explanatory hypotheses, he must relate them to concrete social structures. Moreover, he must do so in a way that maintains the logical distinction between *explicans* (principle of social integration) and *explicandum* (concrete patterns of ownership).

But it is not clear whether he in fact does this. He has a tendency, for example, to insert in the definition of the organizational principle of political domination the concept of class domination (see, e.g., *LC* 24). Indeed, in his earlier study of modern legitimation crises, he defined the organizational principle of capitalism in terms of nonpolitical class domination based on wage labor (*CD* 172).

70. *CES* 119.

71. Ibid., 115 and Marx, "On the Jewish Question," in *Writings of the Young Marx on Philosophy and Society*, ed. L. D. Easton and K. H. Guddat (New York: Doubleday, 1967), pp. 216–48.

9. TALCOTT PARSONS: SYSTEMS THEORY

1. *TkH* 2. 298–301.

2. B. Malinowski, *A Scientific Theory of Culture*, pp. 52, 72–75. For a critique of Malinowski's penchant for explaining cultural functions in terms of biological needs, see T. Parsons, *Social Systems and the Evolution of Action Theory* (New York: Free Press, 1977), pp. 82–99. See McCarthy's excellent summary of functionalism in *The Critical Theory of Jürgen Habermas*, pp. 213–32.

3. Malinowski, *Encyclopedia Britannica*, Supplement 1 (Chicago, 1926), p. 132.

4. A. R. Radcliffe-Brown, *Structure and Function in Primitive Societies*, pp. 179–80. See *ZLS₂* 187–89, where Habermas discusses Malinowski and Radcliffe-Brown.

5. *ZLS₂* 192–98.

6. E. Nagel, *The Structure of Science* (New York: Harcourt, Brace, and Jovanovich, 1961), pp. 421–22.

7. Ibid., pp. 527–28.

8. See R. K. Merton, "Manifest and Latent Functions." The inherent conservativism of Radcliffe-Brown's structural functionalism, which views changes greater than the standard deviation as life-threatening and leaves no room for the functionality of internal conflict, renders it highly implausible as a model for all but the most static and undifferentiated societies. Merton, Parsons, and other contemporary exponents of functionalism have subsequently modified this model to accommodate the fact that in modern society, structures that are functional for some ends (groups, interests, etc.) may be dysfunctional for others, that structural changes may enhance rather than threaten system maintenance, and that institutional practices may have latent, as opposed to manifest (intended), functions.

9. *LC* 3.

10. An animal, for example, retains its vitality only so long as it sustains a relatively constant temperature in the face of thermal fluctuations in the environment. See Parsons, *Social Systems*, pp. 101–02; Merton, "Manifest and Latent Functions"; and W. B. Cannon, *The Wisdom of the Body* (New York: Norton, 1932).

11. T. Parsons, *Societies*, pp. 2–7.

12. Ibid., pp. 10–15.

13. Parsons, "An Approach to Psychological Theory in Terms of the Theory of Action," p. 631; cited by McCarthy, *Critical Theory*, p. 216.

14. Parsons, *Social Systems*, pp. 102–04, and *Essays in Sociological Theory Pure and Applied*.

15. Parsons claims that the functions of adaptation, integration, goal attainment, and pattern maintenance are comparable in societies and organisms. As regards pattern maintenance, he notes that "what is common between the genetic code and the gene pool on the one hand and linguistic codes and other aspects of culture on the

other, is that they function as cybernetic mechanisms which, in certain fundamental respects, control life processes" *(Social Systems*, p. 113).

16. See the debate between Luhmann and Habermas in *TGS*. Habermas recognizes that Luhmann is aware of the historicity of his own position in a way that Parsons's structural functionalism is not (pp. 142–43). Whereas Parsons takes as his point of departure the analogy between organism and system, Luhmann (who, like Habermas, rejects any assimilation of social systems to either organic or mechanistic models) begins with consciousness, arguing that systems such as societies integrate themselves by imposing meaning on their environments (pp. 11, 93). Following Husserl, Luhmann holds that every intentional structuring of experience subtends a horizon of possible meaning that transcends the selected meanings *(Sinnzusammenhänge)* actually thematized. Selection involves negation of a segment of the horizon of possible meaning, thereby bringing into relief the portion relevant to the situation at hand (pp. 35ff.). In effect, selection reduces a complex and undifferentiated horizon of possible meaning to simple meanings that can be reidentified over a period of time (pp. 38, 48–61).

17. Luhmann's rejection of his original starting point, transcendental subjectivity, and his reformulation of meaning and identity in terms of a communicative paradigm have much in common with Habermas's project. Luhmann distinguishes identical meaning shared by two or more persons from the cybernetic concept of information, which denotes unexpected input (ibid., pp. 40–44). The possibility of shared meaning is said to presuppose a communicative encounter in which the subject, qua self-identical being, is itself constituted by the intersection of various subsystems of meaning (kinship, religious, political, economic, and scientific). But a reductionist tendency now sets in, for social systems are said to "consist not of concrete persons but of meaningfully identifiable actions"—understood, of course, as adaptive responses (pp. 28, 94). Habermas objects to this reduction of language to adaptive experience, noting that frustrated communications are not merely informative surprises (pp. 187–95).

18. Ibid., p. 67.

19. Ibid., pp. 97–99.

20. *TGS* 152–55.

21. The concept of a relief mechanism *(Entlastungsmechanismus)* to relieve the pressure that, as we have seen, also makes its appearance in Habermas's analysis of the differentiation of system and lifeworld, owes a great deal to the views of anthropologists such as A. Gehlen (see, for example, *Die Seele im technischen Zeitalter: Soziopsychologische Probleme in der industriellen Gesellschaft* [Hamburg: Rowohlt, 1957]). Luhmann is torn between an existential anthropology à la Sartre, which conceives of the world as an indefinite and wholly contingent field of possibilities, and an institutional anthropology of the sort proposed by Gehlen, which requires that the action system be relieved of this contingency through normative delimitation of choice. A problem then arises, Habermas observes, for the concept of reduction of complexity has come to mean two quite distinct and wholly contrary processes, both the expansion and the restriction of possible choice (ibid., pp. 155–62).

22. Ibid., pp. 162–63. Luhmann's reduction of normative categories, such as meaning, truth, and validity, to functional categories is reflected above all in his belief that the flow of information ought to be filtered through a scientifically sophisticated administrative system. Truth is then no different from communication media, such as money, power, and love, that can be used for purposes of strategically manipulating individuals and groups. Beliefs are true not because they withstand discursive criticism—criticism whose importance resides solely in the possibility of its

guaranteeing a common stock of beliefs—but because they guarantee social stability (pp. 15–17, 23, 86). This way of defining truth creates a paradox. If true beliefs are those that foster stability, and if stability requires structurification, then Luhmann's own systems theory, aspiring like all theories to a complete disclosure of its subject matter, would not itself be true—that is, conducive to functional stability. Luhmann's pragmatist theory of truth therefore leads him to advocate the replacement of democratic ideologies with an ideology of rational planning (*Soziologische Aufklärung: Aufsätze zur Theorie sozialer System* [Cologne: Westdeutscher Verlag, 1970], pp. 61–64). Restrictions on the administrative system's planning capacity are traced back to a residual dependence on public expectations—a limitation that will be entirely overcome, he believes, once science and administration, truth and power, are fused (*Demokratie und Verwaltung: 25 Jahre Hochschule für Verwaltungswissenschaften Speyer* [Berlin: Duncker und Humbolt, 1972], pp. 220–21). But for Habermas rational planning is limited by existing social relations that create insuperable barriers to crisis management. Ultimately, the issue between Luhmann and Habermas boils down to "whether the reproduction of social life is still bound to (practical) reason and, especially, whether the generation of motives is still bound to the internalization of norms that have no need of justification" (*LC* 141).

23. *ZLS*₁ 181.

24. There is a sense in which Habermas, like Parsons, advocates a normative-analytic approach when it comes to specifying ideal goal states. This is most apparent in his current reliance on a rational reconstruction of stages of moral-political development in determining principles of organizations. Such a theoretical reconstruction is quite distinct from the kind of situation-bound hermeneutic approach proposed in *ZLS*₁, which consists of projecting a philosophy of history on the basis of an understanding of culture. See *LC* 3–4 and 7–8, where Habermas vacillates between hermeneutic and rational reconstructive approaches to determining the ideal normative components of structural boundaries.

25. *TkH* 2. 305–07, 311–14; and T. Parsons, *The Structure of Social Action*, pp. 56–75, 719. According to Parsons, empiricist conceptions of action that focus only on attainment of immediate goals are confronted with a dilemma. This so-called utilitarian dilemma consists in the fact that neither pre-rational decisions motivated by heredity and environment nor rational decisions motivated by instrumental considerations can account for free choice. In the former instance the choice of ends is predetermined; in the latter, it is limited to the selection of means.

26. *TkH* 2. 310–11, 314–18; and Parsons, *Structure of Social Action*, pp. 93–101, 313, 446, 732. Hobbes believed that rationally enlightened egoists in a state of nature would voluntarily contract with one another to transfer their unlimited right to survival to a sovereign authority whose commands would be recognized as morally binding. Parsons finds this solution implausible for two reasons. First, the social contract already presupposes a mutual willingness to refrain from violating an oath, even though it might be individually advantageous to do so. Locke's account of the social contract avoids this difficulty by investing natural law (practical reason) with a noninstrumental content involving recognition of universal equality and freedom. Second, as Durkheim notes, social bonds that rest exclusively on personal convenience are ineffectual in compelling lasting obedience among hostile competitors, since the latter will find it to their advantage to break them whenever the perceived assets outweigh the liabilities.

27. *TkH* 2. 319–22.

28. "The evaluative mode involves the cognitive act of balancing out the gratification-deprivation significances of various alternative courses of action with a view to

maximizing gratification in the long run" (Parsons and Shils, eds., *Toward a General Theory of Action*, p. 71).

29. *TkH* 2. 327–30. Parsons concludes that "unlike need dispositions and role expecta-tions, the symbols which are the postulated controlling entities in this case are not internal to the system whose orientations they control. Symbols control systems of orientations, just as do need dispositions and role expectations, but they exist not as postulated internal factors but as objects of orientations (seen as existing in the external world alongside of the other objects oriented by a system of action" (*The Social System*, p. 160). Habermas remarks that Parsons by no means underestimates the importance of language and communication for cultural reproduction, social in-tegration, and socialization (see, e.g., *The Social System*, pp. 33–35). The problem is that Parsons does not develop this insight in the direction of a theory of communi-cative action.

30. Parsons, *The Social System*, pp. 58ff., and *Toward a General Theory of Action*, pp. 78ff.

31. *TkH* 2. 334–38. Habermas sees evidence that Parsons's table of pattern variables may have been influenced by Ferdinand Tönnies's masterpiece *Gemeinschaft und Gesellschaft*. But the theory of pattern variables fails, for "*without the brace (Klammer) of a lifeworld centered in communicative action, culture, society, and personality fall apart from one another.*" Subsequently, "Parsons gives up trying to explain *in action-theo-retical terms* the idea that cultural values become embodied in society and personal-ity through channels of institutionalization and internalization. Instead, the model of reciprocally *penetrating, analytically separated systems* pushes its way to the fore" (p. 338).

32. Parsons, *Toward a General Theory of Action*, p. 173, and "Some Problems of General Theory in Sociology," p. 35.

33. Parsons, *Toward a General Theory of Action*, p. 203.

34. Ibid., pp. 173–78.

35. *TkH* 2. 345–51.

36. Habermas cites R. Dubin's assessment that "Parsons's model I essentially 'looks out' to the social system from the vantage point of the actor; his model II 'looks down' at the individual actor from the perspective of the social system. . . . In model I the social act is seen as the product of the actor's evaluations of objects and his orientations toward them. . . . In model II the social act is viewed as a *product of the role definitions peculiar to the four presumably universal social system problems*" ("Par-sons' Actor: Continuities in Social Theory," p. 530). Habermas formulates the change in Parsons's epistemology accordingly: "Statements concerning the analyti-cal relations between values, norms, goals, and resources are transformed . . . into statements about empirical relations between system components. . . . What was once understood as a constructive projection of the scientist now possesses the connotation of a self-structuring action system" (*TkH* 2. 356).

37. Parsons, *Societies*, pp. 7, 9, 28.

38. Ibid., pp. 11, 12, 17.

39. *TkH* 2. 362.

40. T. Parsons and M. Platt, *The American University* (Cambridge, Mass.: Harvard Uni-versity Press, 1973), pp. 10–11.

41. *TkH* 2. 370 and Parsons and Smelser, *Economy and Society*, p. 36. On the second model, the integration function ostensibly compels actors to evaluate the particular factors of a given situation in light of an interest that is at once global, diffuse, and intuitive. Habermas finds this arbitrary, noting that in the case of integration, it would be just as plausible to stipulate a universalistic evaluation of the object.

42. *TkH* 2. 372–73; Parsons, *Social Systems and the Evolution of Action Theory* (New York:

Free Press, 1977), p. 181; and Parsons and Platt, *The American University*, p. 32. Habermas adds that the telic system cannot serve the function assigned to it, since it is wholly external to the empirical control factors operative within the self-regulating social system.

43. *TkH* 2. 373–84. Whether Habermas himself succeeds in eluding the neo-Kantian impasse encountered by Parsons is a good question. To what extent do the presuppositions of the ideal speech situation actually govern concrete social life? The assumption that we are accountable for all aspects of our conduct and that it must be possible to justify them argumentatively runs counter to the facts of practical life. The totality of competencies, habits, and prejudices that comprise our preunderstanding of life and moderate our conduct is a realm that cannot be entirely thematized. To assume that the aspects of conduct for which we are rationally accountable can be so thematized is to confuse the preconditions of rational conduct — the concrete substantive virtues underlying phronēsis — with the formal, objectifiable preconditions of rational discourse. See chap. 11 for further discussion of this difficulty.

44. Parsons, *Sociological Theory and Modern Society* (New York: Free Press, 1967), p. 307.

45. *TkH* 2. 400–03 and Parsons, *Sociological Theory and Modern Society*, pp. 264ff., 318.

46. *TkH* 2. 404–06.

47. Ibid., 398. During the sixties Parsons introduced influence and value commitment into the interchange paradigm along with power, thereby extending the media concept to cover social, cultural, and political subsystems. Later still he added intelligence, efficiency, emotion, and interpretation (corresponding to the behavioral, personality, social, and cultural action subsystems), followed by yet more media pertaining to the human condition (the total number at the time of *TkH*'s publication being sixty-four). Habermas sees this attempt as futile, since it neglects the peculiar properties, exemplified above all in the case of money, that enable it to function as a proxy for consensual communication. Some of Parsons's statements appear to anticipate the kind of distinction between steering media (money and power) and generalized communication media of the sort that Habermas makes (see Parsons, *Sociological Theory and Modern Society*, p. 361). However, Parsons interprets "having an effect on alter's intentions" through "some kind of communicative operation" as a form of empirical motivation involving rewards and punishments (*TkH* 2. 408–19).

48. *TkH* 2. 420–27 and Parsons, *Societies*, pp. 21ff.

49. *TkH* 2. 427–31; *LC* 121; and Parsons, *Action Theory and the Human Condition*, pp. 240ff., 309, 320ff.; Parsons and Platt, *The American University*, p. 1; and "Religion in Postindustrial America: The Problem of Secularization," pp. 300–22.

50. Parsons, *Societies*, pp. 109ff.

51. *TkH* 2. 421–22, 426, 431–33, and Parsons, *The System of Modern Societies* (Englewood Cliffs, N.J.: Prentice-Hall, 1971), p. 116.

52. *TkH* 2. 434. The remainder of Habermas's discussion of Parsons is devoted to examining various attempts by R. C. Baum and R. Münch to accommodate his functionalism to the realities of social conflict and pathology. Baum observed that the materialistic world view prevalent in our affluent society has led to the pathological extension of fully institutionalized steering media, especially money, into areas of life governed by less institutionalized media (power, influence, or value commitment) for purposes of solving problems pertaining to social integration — urban renewal, delinquency, and so on ("On Societal Media Dynamics," in *Explorations in General Theory in Social Science: Essays in Honor of Talcott Parsons*, ed. J. J. Loubser et al. [New York: Free Press, 1976], pp. 604ff.). However, in Habermas's view, only a

re-Kantianization of Parsons of the sort undertaken by Münch can restore the normative dimension necessary to account for social pathology ("Über Parsons zu Weber, von der Theorie der Rationalization zur Theorie der Interpenetration," in *Zeitschrift für Sozialwissenschaft* 10 [1980]: 30ff.).

53. Habermas notes that biological paradigms for social evolution have difficulty coming up with equivalents for mutation, survival, and progress. "Natural evolution leads to a more or less homogeneous repertoire of behavior among members of a species, whereas social learning (through 'cultural' mutation) results in accelerated diversification of behavior. . . . Whereas the mutation process produces chance variations, the ontogenesis of structures of consciousness is a highly selected and directional process" (*CES* 171–72).

10. FROM PARSONS TO WEBER AND MARX

1. *TkH* 2. 488.
2. Ibid., 452.
3. Ibid., 458ff.
4. Ibid., 473.
5. Ibid., 485–86.
6. Ibid., 472–76.
7. Ibid., 476.
8. Ibid., 476–84.
9. Ibid., 494–98. Habermas interprets the theory of value as providing rules whereby theoretical statements about concrete class relationships and interests at the level of the lifeworld (TL) can be translated into theoretical statements about abstract functional laws of capital realization (*Kapitalverwertung*) pertaining to the economic system (TS) and rules whereby objective descriptions of system breakdown (DS) can be translated into hermeneutic observations of subjectively experienced social pathologies, class identifications, and revolutionary inclinations on the part of oppressed classes (DL). The transition from TL to TS (which relates to the impact of lifeworld on system) is made possible by that aspect of the labor theory which explains the generation of surplus value. The reverse transition, from system (DS) to lifeworld (DL), is established by empirical hypotheses connecting, for example, the socializing effects of cost-efficient factory production (necessitated by the laws of competition) with the rise of democratic worker solidarity (militant labor organizations) and the tendency for the rate of surplus value to fall (necessitated by the cost-efficient replacement of labor with machine-intensive production) with growth of an unemployed reserve of discontented, impoverished workers, and so on. The labor theory also specifies rules for correlating observational with theoretical statements within each level of analysis. A well-known correlation problem is the relationship between the objectively ascribed situation of a class (the class as it exists "in itself") and the empirically identifiable attitudes and actions of its members (the class as it exists "for itself"); a famous example of a transformation problem involves the transformation of values into prices.
10. Ibid., 498–501.
11. Ibid., 501–04. This criticism ignores Marx's later recognition of the rationality of specialization and administrative hierarchy in communist society—a moment of "alienated labor" (as the term is understood prior to the *Grundrisse*) that is mitigated by job rotation.
12. *LC* 33–34. Habermas has in mind J. O'Connor's three-sector model, which was de-

veloped primarily with the United States in mind. See *The Fiscal Crisis of the State* (New York: St. Martin's Press, 1973).

13. *LC* 34–36.

14. Ibid., 37–39.

15. *TkH* 2. 514–15.

16. *LC* 40–44.

17. The law of value states that the rate of profit is proportional to the exploitation of labor. The latter is limited by the length of the work day, the cost of replenishing the work force, and so on. These absolute limits can be relativized, however, by increasing the productivity of labor through new technologies. Marx thought that the introduction of labor-saving devices, after initially increasing the production of surplus value by reducing the cost per unit of production of materials, machinery, etc. and hence the cost of reproducing labor power, would lead to a gradual reduction in the labor component of the production process, thereby depriving the capitalist of his sole source of surplus value. The growing mass of displaced and unemployed workers, coupled with a sharp reduction of wages, would then precipitate an economic and political crisis. But in Habermas's opinion the orthodox position neglects the extent to which "labor applied to itself with the aim of increasing the productivity of labor"—indirectly contributes to the production of surplus value in a way that counteracts the tendency for the rate of profit to fall by cutting the cost of production. See K. Marx, *Capital*, vol. 3, pp. 41ff. Sensat argues that Habermas misunderstands the law concerning this tendency as originally formulated by Marx; for the law purports to show that a fall in the rate of profit would occur eventually *regardless* of the "external" introduction of productivity-increasing innovations (*Habermas and Marxism: An Appraisal*, p. 217, and Marx, *Capital*, vol. 3, p. 240). Marx believed that replacement of workers by technological innovation was inherent in the capital-accumulation process. Increases in productivity tend to induce increases in real wage rate insofar as laborers' "necessary wants" depend upon the "degree of civilisation" attained by society, which depends on productivity, and insofar as their level of education rises as the financial and technical aspects of production and consumption become more complicated. Moreover, intensification of labor, which results in workers expending more psychological and physical energy per hour of labor, leads to demands for more compensation (*Capital*, vol. 1, chap. 15, § 9). The tendency for real wages to rise, as well as the threat of worker noncompliance, thus depress the rate of profit (Sensat, *Habermas and Marxism*, pp. 150–53).

18. *LC* 57.

19. Ibid., 59–60. Habermas finds the systems-theoretical model developed by Claus Offe particularly useful in that it "distinguishes between the structure of an administrative system, on the one hand, and the processes of conflict resolution and consensus formation, of decision and implementation on the other" (*Strukturprobleme des Kapitalistischen Staates*, pp. 60ff., 78ff.

20. *LC* 62–64. According to one theory, the welfare state incurs chronic rationality deficits because administrators are beholden to special interest groups for information and planning expertise. This hampers the freedom of the state to implement policies that are detrimental to those groups, however necessary they may be for averting economic collapse. The above diagnosis might be disputed on the grounds that "the state *can* make visible to its negotiating partners how the generalizable interests of the population differ from organized individual interests as well as from the collective-capitalist interest in the continued existence of the system." In other words, there may not be any logical incompatibility between administrative global

planning and freedom of investment, since a compromise between competing claims might allow for the requisite organizational rationality.

21. Ibid., 66.

22. Ibid., 66–68 and C. Offe, *Strukturprobleme*, pp. 27ff.

23. *LC* 70. Habermas elaborated on the separation of politics from demands for legitimation in his earlier study of the public realm. Under conditions of class compromise, the public realm is "refeudalized." Symbolic shamming of democracy is achieved by manipulating public opinion and restructuring the bureaucracy of the parliamentary system. Once the parliamentary system ceases to function as a forum in which conflicting class interests can be discussed openly, it becomes no more than a vehicle for consolidating the power of mass parties. Unlike the class parties of the nineteenth century, mass parties effect an "ideological integration" of widely varying social strata and interest groups that succeeds in obscuring the lines of social conflict behind the veneer of a united front. Competing parties do not question the basic assumptions underlying the economic system. Because they must promote platforms of the most vague, general, and often contradictory sort in order to garner mass support, the differences between them end up having less to do with the substance of their programs than with the images conveyed by their leaders. Hence, in place of a rational debate between alternatives, one finds a purely cosmetic display that pits the charisma and patriotic fervor of one slate of candidates against those of another. The role of the electorate is reduced to passive acclamation of candidates and platforms that, by and large, have been preselected by a party bureaucracy. Quite aside from the segmentation of the electoral process, the general impotence of local party organizations vis-à-vis the central committee, and the tendency of the electorate to vote on the basis of party loyalty, the capacity to make informed, rational decisions is blunted; the choices themselves are either vague or inconsistent, and the mass media serve up only images with an immediate, subconscious impact (SO_2 215–63).

24. *LC* 71–74.

25. Ibid., 75–77.

26. Ibid., 80–84.

27. Ibid., 84–89. The evidence adduced by Habermas to support his contention that communicative ethical and countercultural elements have become significant motivational factors in some segments of society includes studies by Kenneth Keniston showing that the crisis of adolescence has entered a new phase of self-questioning. The problems facing adolescents are no longer those of adjusting to the system, for, thanks to changes in education and child rearing (lengthier periods of improved formal education, egalitarian family structures, the loosening of sexual prohibitions, etc.), possibilities of social experimentation and identity formation have expanded, with results that are often incompatible with the privatistic needs of the system, and hence the prevalence of withdrawal and protest among today's youth. See K. Keniston, *Young Radicals* (New York: Harcourt, Brace and World, 1968) and *Youth and Dissent* (New York: Harcourt, Brace, Jovanovich, 1971).

28. *LC* 93.

29. Ibid., 122–30.

30. Ibid., 80, 121.

31. *CD* 278–81. Habermas now admits that in his earlier diagnosis of advanced capitalism, "there were in fact obscure points in the conceptual demarcation between legitimation crisis and motivation crisis, as I could not clearly connect the paradigms of 'life-world' and 'system'." He still holds that economic crisis and rationality crisis refer to *"deficits* in the reproduction of economic values and in the state's organiza-

tional achievements" that are generated within the combined system of functional interconnections. Although these deficits have their ultimate source in productive relations—above all, the relation between labor and capital—which are legally anchored in the cultural lifeworld, they can nonetheless be analyzed independently of it as manifestations of contradictory steering imperatives. Unlike these intersystemic crisis phenomena, legitimation crisis, motivation crisis, and the pathological disorders associated with colonization of the lifeworld reflect contradictions between competing imperatives of system and social integration. Legitimation and motivation crises refer to "deficits that inflexible structures of the lifeworld can give rise to in maintaining the economic and political subsystems" (the withdrawal of motivation affecting the occupational system and of legitimation affecting the system of domination). The catch phrase "motivation crisis" also denotes "deformations of the lifeworld which make themselves felt in modern societies as the destruction of traditional forms of life, as attacks on the communicative infrastructure of lifeworlds, (and) as the rigidity of one-sidedly rationalized everyday practice —pathological disturbances which he now classifies under the separate rubric of colonization and cultural fragmentation" (*CD* 280–81).

32. *TkH* 2. 565–66.
33. Ibid., 522–30. Habermas's earlier treatment of the transformation of the public realm, in SO_1, did not clearly distinguish between the first two stages of legal formalization. This may be attributed to a failure to distinguish between lifeworld and system, the salient distinction there being that between state and civil society. Since the family and public domain constitutive of civil society acquire their autonomy as independent sources of legitimation only by being secured in a system of private property, there is a sense in which the freedom acquired during the first stage of formalization is directly related to the second (SO_1 58–68, 86ff.).
34. *TkH* 2. 531–34.
35. Ibid., 534–35. In this he disputes his earlier analysis in SO_1, which focuses precisely on this conflict (pp. 43–45). He now argues that neither the freedom of association, press, and personal opinion nor the principle of universal suffrage under conditions of modern mass communication is responsible for restricting civil liberties, since these are its consummate expression and guarantee.
36. *TkH* 2. 535–38. It is important to distinguish between statutory laws, whose function is to organize media-steered subsystems (law as steering medium), and normative laws, which regulate and enforce legitimate orders within the lifeworld (law as institution). The former, exemplified by civil law, give rise to new domains of action by condensing economic and political relations into money- and power-steered transactions. The latter, exemplified by constitutional and criminal law, regulate and enforce preexisting codes of conduct. Legal media are evaluated functionally—i.e., on the basis of how well they expedite economic and political transactions. Because they pertain to nonnormative contexts of action and therefore do not require direct legitimation, they need be promulgated only in accordance with proper legal procedure. The most that can be said of legal media is that, being dependent on constitutional law, they are indirectly grounded in the normative bedrock of the lifeworld. Legal institutions, by contrast, require legitimation.
37. Stated simply, Habermas's argument demonstrates that the moral pillars of liberalism—the theory of entitlements (bourgeois property rights) and the theory of citizenship (democratic social rights)—are incapable of satisfying the notion of universal equality and freedom intrinsic to the modern concept of right. This line of argument has been developed by Gerald Doppelt in a powerful attack on the political theories of Nozick and Rawls. Although the Rawlsian "theory of citizenship,"

which guarantees equal civil liberty and opportunity in conjunction with economic policies that maximize the income of the worst-off classes, appears to resolve the contradiction inherent in the Lockean theory of property rights defended by Nozick—namely, that not all persons in a market society can realize their freedom as buyers and sellers—it does not satisfy its own Kantian assumptions regarding the derivation of principles of justice, Doppelt claims. These assumptions require that principles of justice accord with a conception of society that would be "stable," "well-ordered," and freely supported by its members because they gain "equality in the bases of self-respect" (Rawls, *A Theory of Justice*, pp. 177, 180–82, 440–42, 453–54). The liberty and maximin principles that Rawls proposes, however, condone a form of social welfare that would prevent people from gaining equality in self-respect—at least insofar as self-respect is related to widespread cultural expectations concerning earning a living for oneself and being treated as an equal. Social democratic theories, of the sort advanced by Markovic and Gould, Doppelt notes, satisfy only some of these expectations, since they still affirm the division of labor and its support of technical elites. Similar objections have been leveled against Habermas's communicative ethic by Sensat, Held, Miller, and Gouldner, just to name a few, yet Habermas's willingness to yield on this score is demonstrated by his apprehension concerning the splitting off of elite subcultures, the impoverishment of the lifeworld caused by the division of mental and physical labor, and the reifying tendencies associated with the segmentation of the labor process and the lack of job rotation. In the final analysis, one possible advantage of Doppelt's dialectical critique of liberalism over Habermas's is his use of a method of internal criticism which does not appeal to speculative assumptions regarding the universal structure of communication. However, the drawback of such an approach, as Habermas points out, is that it relies too heavily on the unreliable hermeneutic standpoint of historical agents; thus, Doppelt's belief that the bourgeois ideal of justice as entitlement implies a valid notion of freedom that must be brought to bear on the redistributive economics advocated by Rawls. This method of critique, which involves playing one conception of freedom off against another equally one-sided conception, would be rejected by Habermas as both insufficiently grounded and lacking in radicalness. In any case, Habermas would have a hard time accepting Doppelt's assumption that the achievement ideology undergirding the capitalist state is as viable as he thinks it is. See G. Doppelt, "Conflicting Social Paradigms of Freedom and the Problem of Justification."

38. *TkH* 2. 538–40. Habermas concentrates on the effects of bureaucratization on families and schools in West Germany. Child custody cases are notorious examples of the kinds of self-defeating measures undertaken by the state to guarantee the welfare of minors. The evidence legally permissible in custody hearings is often restricted so as to exclude questions concerning the psychological well-being of the child. Even when such cases are farmed out to social agencies, the supervision by state-appointed therapists and social workers does nothing to promote the interests of the child as regards becoming a self-sufficient adult. Similarly, in education, the state fiercely resists attempts by parents to exercise control over the curriculum, the development, implementation, and use of tests, the disciplining of children, and so forth. But the legal capacity of school boards to adjudicate conflicts between parents and faculty is often inadequate, given the complexity of the issues involved. Finally, the goal of pedagogical practice is vitiated once it becomes a mechanism for occupational selection. The emphasis on competition and achievement often runs counter to the purpose of nurturing a sense of social responsibility. Likewise, in requiring teachers to act as disciplinarians, pedagogical interests are sacri-

ficed, as well as opportunities for the self-realization of the students (pp. 540–47). Once again, it is instructive to compare the analysis of social pathology presented here with Habermas's earlier discussion in *SO*$_1$. There, Habermas traced the dissolution of the public sphere to its subsumption under the imperatives of occupational and familial privatism (pp. 193ff.). Conversely, the dissolution of the family was attributed to the colonization of the household by television and radio, the structuring of leisure and consumption around public entertainment, and so on.

39. *TP* 197–98.
40. *TGS* 266.
41. *CES* 152, 158.
42. *LC* 69.
43. *TkH* 2. 564ff. Arato disputes Habermas's contention that existing forms of bureaucratic socialism have attained the same degree of legal rationalization as advanced capitalist societies (see *CD* 196–218).
44. *CD* 282.
45. Arato adds that it is necessary to distinguish between the party, the aspect of the "prerogative state" that symbolizes and legitimates "the arbitrary mode of political action unchecked by any legal limits," and the state bureaucracy, which exercises this function. See C. Offe, *Strukturprobleme*.
46. *CD* 205–07.
47. Ibid., 283. The extent to which communicative processes inherent in the lifeworld are capable of being bureaucratically appropriated and shammed within the democratic centralist structures of the one-party state is far from clear. Arato's assessment, which Habermas finds plausible, focuses on the possibility of a "negative subordination"—Offe's term for the functional priority of a dominant system permitting a high degree of autonomy for subsystems—of economy to state within the Soviet Union, as opposed to a "positive subordination," in which such autonomy is not permitted. The uncoupling of economic planning functions (administration) from ideological planning functions (politics) would open up competition between sectional lobbies, thereby shattering the ideology of the state as the representative of unified interests. To avert a legitimacy crisis that could affect both party and state, while restricting the expansion of legally constituted economic freedom within collectivist limits, the state could draw on a mixture of cultural resources including rationalistic formal legalism (New Economic Policy ideology, liberal residues within Marxist-Leninism, and so on) and conservative traditions (authoritarian technocratic ideology and nationalism) (*CD* 204–17). In Arato's judgment, the possibility of maintaining a complementary relationship between a rationally organized legal system and a more traditionalist form of social identity runs counter to Habermas's view that legal rationalization is incompatible with cultural institutions based on dogmatic tradition and a prerogative state. He concludes that the civil-familial privatism built into the Soviet system, as well as the "slightly rationalized welfare-statist version of traditional Russian autocracy" gravitating around Russian nationalism, with its attendant indifference to political participation, may produce a dual state combining emancipatory and authoritarian elements (*CD* 218).
48. *TkH* 2. 567–68. The communicative competencies fostered by nonpatriarchal families are not conducive to the promotion of the authoritarian behavioral patterns that are required by the occupational system. Yet families today are expected to assume increasing responsibility for initiating adolescents into that system. Imposition of contrary functions of social and system integration on the family has the net effect of prolonging and exacerbating what is otherwise a normal, temporary identity crisis to the point where it assumes pathological proportions. This explains the

pronounced shift in clinically observed phenomena noted by Christopher Lasch and other psychologists, from hysteria, symptoms associated with compulsive neurosis, and syndromes related to the oedipal complex to those reflecting disturbances of a narcissistic nature. It would also account for reverse strategies of coping whereby absorption into the system is resisted either by trying to change it through active protest or by rejecting it in favor of a countercultural life-style.

49. Ibid., 571–75.

50. Ibid., 575–78.

51. Ibid., 578–83. A discussion of Habermas's analysis of contemporary protest movements would not be complete without a glance back to his earlier examination of the student protest movements of the late sixties. Although he was severely critical of revolutionary posturing, deploring what he perceived as regressive, narcissistic hostility toward all forms of organizational discipline ("the Great Refusal"), postponed gratification ("the New Immediacy"), and cultural tradition, he took seriously the rational potential underlying the protest as a vehicle for democratizing universities and encouraging a greater degree of public accountability on the part of scientific and administrative professions (*TRS* 46–48).

52. In effecting the transition from Kant to Rousseau, from conceiving freedom as a function of personal morality to conceiving it politically, Habermas makes it abundantly clear that he is not advocating the totalitarian suppression of particular interests or the tyranny of public opinion. See his earlier critique of Rousseau, *SO*₁ 94.

53. *NU* 152ff, 245ff.

54. See McCarthy, "Complexity and Democracy, or the Seducements of Systems Theory," pp. 32ff.; W. Buckley, "Society as Complex Adaptive System," in *Modern Systems Research For the Behavioral Scientist*, ed. W. Buckley, (Chicago: Aldine, 1968); E. Bittner, "The Concept of Organization"; D. Misgeld, "Critical Hermeneutics Versus Neoparsonianism?," pp. 71ff. The ensuing two paragraphs follow McCarthy's exposition closely.

55. McCarthy, "Complexity and Democracy," pp. 43–45.

56. Ibid., pp. 45ff. Curiously, after pointing out the seemingly insuperable difficulties attendant on a hermeneutically enlightened systems theory modeled on a general interpretative framework analogous to that of psychoanalysis, McCarthy goes on to suggest that some such functionalist approach may be viable after all. If I understand Misgeld correctly, he does not share this view, though he has nothing in principle against combining objectifying and interpretative methodologies, as long as the latter retain a privileged place.

57. Fraser, "What's Critical About Critical Theory?" Fraser cites the work of Linda Nicholson (*Feminism and Social Theory* [New York: Columbia University Press, forthcoming]) as a more positive assessment of the potential of Habermas's lifeworld-system distinction for feminism. Nicholson argues that Habermas's "dual systems" theory has the advantage over orthodox Marxist theories of historical materialism that it permits women's unpaid child-rearing activity to enter history as a form of social reproduction and learning.

58. Fraser, "What's Critical About Critical Theory?," pp. 111–23, and "Women, Welfare, and the Politics of Need Interpretation," *Hypatia* (forthcoming).

59. Fraser, "What's Critical About Critical Theory?" Despite her objections to Habermas's lifeworld-system distinction, Fraser acknowledges her indebtedness to those aspects of Habermas's thought that concern the sociocultural, interpretative character of human needs and his contrast between dialogical and monological processes of need interpretation.

60. *CD* 188–89 and M. Mann, *Consciousness and Action Among the Western Working Class* (London: Macmillan, 1973).

61. *CD* 190–91. This fragmentation is reflected above all in the technical division of labor, capital, and state and in the diversions, distractions, and escapist gratifications proffered by the culture industry. As production becomes increasingly mechanized, standardized, and differentiated, there are fewer chances for reflection. "With the development of the capitalist division of labor, knowledge and control of the whole work process are absent from daily work situations. . . . Centralised control mechanisms and private and public bureaucracies then appear as agencies which are necessary for, and guarantee, 'a rational course and order.'" The creation of occupational hierarchies based on ethnicity, race, sex, education, and seniority also undercut working-class solidarity. In conjunction with bureaucratically encrusted labor organizations that suppress militant rank-and-file demands for worker control in favor of nonthreatening salary negotiations, the state's disperson of wage scales and inflationary-recessionary side effects over disparate groups further contributes to the diffusion of class opposition. See H. Marcuse, "Some Social Implications of Modern Technology"; H. Braverman, *Labor and Monopoly Capital: The Degradation of Work in the Twentieth Century* (New York: Monthly Review Press, 1974); and S. Aronowitz, *False Promises: The Shaping of American Working Class Consciousness* (New York: McGraw-Hill, 1973).

62. *CD* 281. Held concludes that the capacity to penetrate reified social relations "depends less on factors affecting social identity and more on economic and political crisis tendencies in capitalism." In particular, he criticizes Habermas for concentrating his analysis of economic crisis on the nation-state, thereby ignoring global crisis tendencies centering on the disparate economic development between advanced industrialized nations and Third World countries, which transcend the management capabilities of parochial institutions (*CD* 193).

11. THE THEORY-PRACTICE PROBLEM REVISITED

1. R. Bernstein, ed., *Habermas and Modernity*, p. 17. Assuming that there has been a transformation, it is not clear to which, if either, of the two likely value spheres—normative or aesthetic-expressive—the emancipatory interest and correlative form of critical knowledge correspond, though the interest would appear to be generated within communicative action rather than within any of the other action modalities. The difficulty is compounded by the ambiguity both of the distinction between practical and emancipatory interests, as Habermas originally conceived it, and of communicative action, which is sometimes regarded as structurally foundational for normative and dramaturgic action, despite the latter being occasionally associated with strategic action! See Anthony Gidden's discussion of this problem in ibid., pp. 112–14.

2. Marx and Habermas see bourgeois ideologies as the first to do this, in that they criticize traditional ideologies of inherited privilege and natural hierarchy in terms of the universal rights of man. Science-based ideologies, by contrast, effect a critique of traditional authority while sanctioning a "refeudalization" of the political hierarchy. Habermas also classifies as ideological movements such as fascism, anarchism, and certain varieties of utopian socialism that advocate the auratic absorption of the system into the lifeworld, or the subordination of formal law to the imperatives of heroic nihilism, ethical-religious hegemony, or totalitarian democracy (*TkH* 2. 519–20).

3. Because bourgeois natural law affords only a partial political emancipation compat-

ible with social domination, Marx saw the rational basis of universal human emancipation as residing in the class interests of the proletariat—the class denied everything but its humanity. But, following the decline in working-class militancy and the blurring of class distinctions through class compromise, this option no longer seemed viable to Marxists.

4. Habermas objects to two contradictory strands in critical theory: the historicism of *Kulturkritik* and the ontologism implicit in the theory of instincts. The latter objection must be assessed in light of first-generation critical theory's tendency to both historicize and dehistoricize Freud's metapsychology (the Marcuse-Fromm debate in the fifties revolved primarily around this issue). The former must be evaluated with respect to Habermas's qualification of the transcendental status of his own theory, especially in view of his frank admission of the fallible hermeneutic status of rational reconstructions.

5. The method involves imagining the parties in question as participants in a rational discourse in which their real interests are made known to them in light of economic scarcities. The requirement that the parties be perfectly rational has been objected to by Steven Lukes, who argues that there is no a priori guarantee that the interests of ideally rational persons would coincide with those of actual historical agents (*CD* 139). As Habermas remarks, this objection comes from transforming a methodological problem—that of separating true and false interests—into an ontological one—in this case concerning the identity of persons.

6. Habermas concluded that the dogmatism of everyday life warranted the questioning of any de facto consensus as potentially ideological. This suspicion justified a refusal to participate in routine social interaction. Gadamer, on the contrary, found this deployment of the ideal speech situation paradoxical, for it seemed to condone just the opposite of what it mandated—namely, recognizing others as rationally accountable, taking them seriously, and participating in one's community. See Habermas, "Der Universalitätsanspruch der Hermeneutik," pp. 153–54., and Gadamer, "On the Scope and Function of Hermeneutical Reflection," pp. 41–42.

7. Gadamer, "Über die Planung der Zukunft," pp. 40–41.

8. *PP*₂ 158.

9. *TCA* 73–74. In a recent article, "Die Neue Unübersichtlichkeit: Die Krise des Wohlfahrtsstaates und die Erschöpfung utopischer Energien," *Merkur* (Winter 1985), pp. 1–14, Habermas says that "even the expression 'ideal speech situation' invites misunderstanding insofar as it suggests a concrete form of life" (p. 14); he thereby emphatically underscores the extremely tenuous relationship between necessary communicative conditions and the possible social alternatives that might emerge therein.

10. *TkH* 2. 522.

11. Ibid., 269. Despite his intention to combat the elitist specialization of modern culture, Habermas's political agenda is far removed from the populist, boundary-shattering praxis advocated by many left-leaning poststructuralists. The idea that social evolution is teleologically oriented toward an ideal speech situation in which unconstrained individual and group identity are attained does not adequately address the poststructuralist deconstruction of identity, meaning, subjectivity, and history. The ideal speech situation would require univocity of meaning vis-à-vis rigorously determined contexts of communication, as well as rationally consistent transparent self-consciousness. By exposing the contextuality and alterity of all meaning qua repetition complex, poststructuralism undermines the binary oppositions of identity/difference, consciousness/unconsciousness, that underwrite the possibility of a pure communication purged of displacement, distortion, and mis-

understanding. Because signification is here understood as an effect of contingent relations of power, structuralists from Althusser to Foucault have been inclined to de-emphasize, if not dismiss altogether, the critique of ideology as a holdover from idealism; and some, such as Deleuze and Guattari, have positively reveled in the emancipatory possibilities of a schizoid reinvestment of unconscious processes in the ego. Thus, one of the problems that Habermas's ideal speech situation poses for poststructuralists is that it demands precisely the sort of pure agreement regarded as repressive by those who have been excluded from the academic discourse of rationality. In my opinion, the poststructuralist policy of combating cultural hegemony is valid insofar as it proceeds from an analysis of actual linguistic constraints and fragmentations—impurities that even Habermas himself acknowledges. These impurities, however, do not impugn the liberal, social democratic ideals of personal integrity and social harmony that inform Habermas's political philosophy, for these remain an abiding part of our traditional self-understanding, albeit one that conceals genuine possibilities behind a façade of ideological distortion. The political goal of rational consensus must therefore be qualified. Among contemporary writers, Fredric Jameson has articulated a position that comes closest to this view insofar as he attempts to retrieve the idea of totality, or meaningful historical narrative, from a Marxist perspective (see *The Political Unconscious: Narrative as a Socially Symbolic Act*). However, as Cornel West notes, Jameson succumbs all too easily to the poststructuralist temptation to transcend the ethical dimension in the direction of the political ("Ethics and Action in Fredric Jameson's Marxist Hermeneutics," in *Postmodernism and Politics*, ed. J. Arac). For a good summary of the poststructuralist case against Habermas, see M. Ryan, *Marxism and Deconstruction: A Critical Articulation*, pp. 112–16. For a critical rejoinder see my essay on Lyotard, "Legitimacy and the Postmodern Condition" (unpublished).

12. *TCA* 74.
13. *TkH* 2. 585–86.
14. Unlike empirical-analytic explanations in the exact sciences, rational reconstructions are said to "systematically reconstruct the intuitive knowledge of competent (speaking and acting) subjects," thereby requiring an interpretative explication of meaning. In contrast to straightforward hermeneutic paraphrase or translation, however, rational reconstruction explicates the "deep structures," or rules, by means of which expressions are generated in the first place. More precisely, rational reconstruction attempts to make propositionally explicit through questioning and systematically ordered examples a prior, theoretically proved capacity to speak and act competently. Thus, the formal nature of the rules ostensibly guarantees a level of generality sufficient to justify a claim to universal validity. Although Habermas denies that rational reconstructions rely on personal phenomenological reflections, insisting that "the procedures employed in constructive proposals, in gathering and selecting data, are in some ways like the procedures used in the nomological sciences," a cursory reading of his writings, as McCarthy has shown, indicates that the formulation of hypotheses relies much more on personal reflection, conceptual analysis, and hermeneutic appropriation of philosophical traditions than the above would lead one to believe. See *CES* 8–20; *CD* 259.
15. Habermas and Gadamer agree that everyday language functions as the ultimate metalanguage, mediating formally specialized discourses with each other and with the lifeworld; hence the priority of hermeneutic reflection in critically mediating different spheres. Habermas maintains, nevertheless, that the priority of a participatory understanding over a distancing ideology critique or psychotherapeutic depth interpretation must be reversed whenever social theory is confronted

with systematically distorted communication. Compare Gadamer, "On the Scope and Function of Hermeneutical Reflection" and "Replik," with Habermas, "Der Universalitätsanspruch der Hermeneutik."

16. *PDM* 245–46.
17. *MkH* 114–19, 189–94. Critics such as Seyla Benhabib and Joel Whitebook question the enlightenment pretensions of a theory in which "progress in morality and justice does not preclude the reification of the lifeworld." If there *is* a utopian break between critical theory's conception of morality and the contractual and utilitarian models bequeathed to us by the Enlightenment, it resides, Benhabib believes, in the extension of procedural justice to include a stage of "universalized need interpretation." On this model, rationally accountable moral agents must move beyond abstract considerations of reciprocity, rights, and entitlements to ask whether their needs are compatible with forms of association free from domination. A truly just society—one that is humanly as well as politically emancipated in Marx's sense—presupposes the transformation of antisocial, acquisitive, and aggressive needs into needs for solidarity, love, and friendship. Or, as Benhabib puts it, "conceptions of justice and the good life flow into each other"; moral responsibility entails aesthetic-expressive authenticity and vice versa.

Albrecht Wellmer has argued that, despite the dissociation of the ideal speech situation from any concrete, organizationally specified utopia, there remains the idea of an "idealized lifeworld," which "would no longer be subjected to the imperatives of system maintenance" but "would rather subject the systemic mechanisms to the needs of the associated individuals." However, this attempt to reconnect the utopian aspirations of critical theory with the emancipatory rationalism of the Enlightenment is too abstract, not because it contradicts some of Habermas's disclaimers about advocating the reabsorption of the system back into the lifeworld, but because it is still compatible with a life without meaning and virtue. In my opinion, no moral philosopher has discussed the above crisis in ethical theory with more perspicuity and insight than Alasdair MacIntyre. See J. Whitebook, "Reason and Happiness: Some Psychoanalytic Themes in Critical Theory"; S. Benhabib, "The Utopian Dimension of Communicative Ethics"; A. Wellmer, "Reason, Utopia, and the *Dialectic of Enlightenment*," in *Habermas and Modernity*, ed. R. Bernstein; R. Bubner, "Rationalität als Lebensform: Zu Jürgen Habermas' *Theorie des kommunikativen Handelns*"; and A. MacIntyre, *After Virtue: A Study in Moral Philosophy*.
18. This is how Habermas currently understands the argument advanced in *Theorie*. See "Questions," p. 235.
19. *TCA* 20.
20. "Questions," p. 237.
21. *TCA* 20.
22. "Questions," p. 236.
23. Ibid.
24. *LC* 78.
25. Ibid., 86.
26. *PP*₂ 48–49. Philip Brewster and Carl Buchner question Habermas's reading of Benjamin's theory of language on the grounds that it overestimates the extent to which the theory is based on a model of communication rather than "representational construction" ("Language and Criticism: Jürgen Habermas on Walter Benjamin").
27. "Questions," p. 237. For Huyssen, the utopian vision of an integrated experience informs even avant-garde art, thereby rendering it vulnerable to a totalizing tendency that menaces the autonomy of gay, feminist, and other countercultures ("The Search for Tradition: Avant-garde and Post-modernism in the 1970's"). Rep-

resenting a more sympathetic viewpoint, Peter Bürger questions whether the trenchant resistance of cognitive-instrumental rationality to reintegration and the bourgeois opposition between autonomous and useful art do not pose insuperable barriers to the sort of nonselective rationalization envisioned by Habermas ("Avant-garde and Contemporary Aesthetics: A Reply to Jürgen Habermas"). Although Martin Jay also eschews the deconstructionist critique of rationalization and defends Habermas against Lyotard's accusation that he favors an aesthetics of beauty, he nonetheless hesitates to embrace as rational that "critique of the false wholeness of affirmative culture" which proceeds by redeeming "the semantic potentials that Benjamin saw preserved in art as a residue of its original mimetic-expressive relationship with nature." Given that Habermas himself warns against attributing to mimesis "the role of representative of an original reason, whose place has been usurped by instrumental rationality" (*TkH* 1. 512), Jay can only conclude that "there may even be a contradictory relationship between increased artistic rationalization and its redemptive function" ("Habermas and Modernism"). But in light of Habermas's more recent pronouncements regarding the peculiar global nature of aesthetic "truth," the views expressed in Jay's extremely useful essay may have to be modified somewhat.

28. "Questions," p. 238.
29. "My question is to determine what sort of unity Habermas has in mind. Is the aim of the project of modernity the constitution of socio-cultural unity within which all the elements of daily life and thought would take their places as an organic whole? Or does the passage that has to be charted between heterogeneous language games—those of cognition, of ethics, of politics—belong to a different order from that? . . . The first hypothesis, of Hegelian inspiration, does not challenge the notion of a dialectically totalizing *experience*; the second is closer to the spirit of Kant's *Critique of Judgment*, but must be submitted, like the *Critique*, to that severe examination which postmodernity imposes on the Enlightenment, on the idea of a unitary end of history and of a subject" (J. F. Lyotard, *The Postmodern Condition: A Report on Knowledge*, p. 73). I discuss Lyotard's philosophy in an unpublished paper entitled "Legitimacy and the Postmodern Condition."
30. Lyotard, *The Postmodern Condition*, pp. 77–78.
31. Bürger, "Avant-garde and Contemporary Aesthetics," pp. 20–22.
32. *NU* 241.
33. *TkH* 1. 512.
34. See Gadamer, *Truth and Method*. In his debate with Gadamer during the sixties and seventies Habermas renewed the Frankfurt school's attack on the ontological philosophizing of the Heideggerian school. However, the key assumption of the former—namely, that practical life and everyday language are the ultimate, prereflective (in a thematizing sense) basis of all critical reflection (consciousness) and meaningful world (Being)—is not only consonant with Marx's early and later thought, as Habermas himself recognized in an early critique of Heidegger, but is also compatible with some assertions made by Horkheimer, Adorno, and, of course, Habermas himself, despite all their talk about "autonomous art," "transcendent critique," and "the non-identity of subject and object." Along with Ricoeur and Bubner, I have argued that there is no absolute opposition between an ontological hermeneutics of appropriation and an epistemological, or methodological, hermeneutics of suspicion. This compatibility in principle should not, of course, obscure the very real differences in emphasis between the two positions. See my dissertation "Truth, Method, and Understanding in the Human Sciences: The Gadamer/Habermas Controversy" (University of California at San Diego, 1980)

and the following essays: "Habermas, Gadamer, and Bourdieu on Discourse: A Communicative Ethic Reconsidered"; "The Historical Genesis of the Gadamer/ Habermas Controversy"; and "Hermeneutics and Truth."

35. Adorno, *Negative Dialectics*, pp. 236–37.

36. See Rorty's article comparing Lyotard and Habermas, "Habermas and Lyotard on Post-Modernity," p. 34. For his part, Habermas lumps Rorty together with other pragmatic-minded thinkers—Heidegger, Marx, Wittgenstein, and Nietzsche— who bid us take leave of philosophy. Habermas takes issue with Rorty's refusal to accord philosophy any truth value whatsoever, arguing that the "edifying function" that Rorty assigns to philosophy during periods of scientific upheaval itself implies possession of such a value. Although I am inclined to side with Rorty's critique of foundationalism, his interpretations of Gadamer and Habermas as representatives of historicism and transcendentalism are caricatures. Gadamer describes his philosophy as transcendental (in an ontological sense), and Habermas underscores the fallibility of his supposed grounding of morality. Finally, Rorty fails to acknowledge the extent to which tolerance of cultural pluralism is a value for Habermas as well, one that is implicated in communicative action. See *MkH* 20–21; Rorty, *Philosophy and the Mirror of Nature*, pp. 315–16, 377; and my critique of him in "Hermeneutics and Truth."

37. Habermas, "The Entwinement of Myth and Enlightenment," p. 30.

BIBLIOGRAPHY

Adorno, T. W. *Eingriffe*. Frankfurt: Suhrkamp, 1963.

———. *Negative Dialektik*. Frankfurt: Suhrkamp, 1973. Translated by E. B. Ashton as *Negative Dialectics*. New York: Seabury Press, 1973.

———. "On the Fetish Character in Music and the Regression of Listening." In *The Essential Frankfurt School Reader*, edited by A. Arato and E. Gebhardt, pp. 270–99. New York: Continuum, 1982.

———. *Prisms*. Translated by Samuel and Sherry Weber. Cambridge, Mass.: MIT Press, 1981.

Adorno, T. W., and Horkheimer, M. *Dialectic of Enlightenment*. Translated by John Cumming. New York: Herder and Herder, 1972.

Alford, C. F. *Science and the Revenge of Nature: Marcuse and Habermas*. Gainesville: University Presses of Florida, 1985.

Allison, D., ed. *The New Nietzsche*. New York: Dell, 1977.

Apel, K.-O. "Das Apriori der Kommunikativensgemeinschaft und die Grundlagen der Ethik." In *Transformation der Philosophie*, vol. 2, pp. 358–436. Frankfurt: Suhrkamp, 1973.

———. *Understanding and Explanation: A Transcendental-Pragmatic Perspective*. Translated by Georgia Warnke. Cambridge, Mass.: MIT Press, 1984.

———. "Wissenschaft als Emanzipation? Eine kritische Würdigung der Wissenschaftskonzeption der Kritischen Theorie." In *Zeitschrift für allgemeine Wissenschaftstheorie*, pp. 73–95. Frankfurt: Suhrkamp, 1970.

Arac, J., ed. *Postmodernism and Politics*. Minneapolis: University of Minnesota Press, 1986.

Arato, A. "Critical Sociology and Authoritarian State Socialism." In *CD* 196–218.

Arendt, H. *The Human Condition*. Chicago: University of Chicago Press, 1958.

———. *Lectures On Kant*. Edited by Ronald Beiner. Chicago: University of Chicago Press, 1982.

Austin, J. L. *How to Do Things with Words*. Oxford: Oxford University Press, 1962.

Bacon, F. *Bacon: Selections*. Edited by S. Warhaft. New York: Odyssey, 1965.

Bataille, G. *Death and Sensuality*. New York: Walter, 1962.

————. *La Souveraineté*. In *Oeuvres complètes* 8. Paris: Gallimard, 1957.

————. "The Notion of Expenditure." In *Visions of Excess: Selected Writings*, edited by A. Stoekl, pp. 116–29. Minneapolis: University of Minnesota Press, 1985.

————. "The Psychological Structure of Fascism." In *Visions of Excess: Selected Writings*, edited by A. Stoekl, pp. 137–60. Minneapolis: University of Minnesota Press, 1985.

Bell, D. *The Coming of Postindustrial Society*. New York: Basic Books, 1973.

————. *The Cultural Contradictions in Capitalism*. New York: Basic Books, 1976.

Benhabib, S. "Epistemologies of Postmodernism: A Rejoinder to Jean-François Lyotard." *New German Critique* 33 (Fall 1984): pp. 103–26.

————. "The Utopian Dimension of Communicative Ethics." *New German Critique* 35 (Spring/Summer 1985): 83–96.

Benjamin, Walter. "Theses on the Philosophy of History." In *Illuminations*, translated by H. Zohn, edited by H. Arendt, pp. 255–66. New York: Harcourt, Brace, and World, 1968.

————. "On Language as Such and on the Language of Man." In *Reflections: Walter Benjamin: Essays, Aphorisms and Autobiographical Writings*, edited by P. Demetz, pp. 314–32. New York: Harcourt, Brace, Jovanovich, 1979.

————. "On the Mimetic Faculty." In *Reflections: Walter Benjamin: Essays, Aphorisms and Autobiographical Writings*. Edited by P. Demetz, pp. 333–36. New York: Harcourt, Brace, Jovanovich, 1979.

Berger, P., and Luckmann, T. *Social Construction of Reality. A Treatise into the Sociology of Knowledge*. Garden City, N.Y.: Doubleday, Anchor Books, 1966.

Bernstein, R. *Beyond Objectivism and Relativism: Science, Hermeneutics, and Praxis*. Philadelphia: University of Pennsylvania Press, 1983.

————, ed. *Habermas and Modernity*. Cambridge, Mass.: MIT Press, 1985.

————. *Praxis and Action*. Philadelphia: University of Pennsylvania Press, 1971.

Bittner, E. "The Concept of Organization." *Social Research* 32 (1965): 239–55.

Blumenberg, H. *The Legitimation of the Modern Age*. Cambridge, Mass.: MIT Press, 1982.

Böhler, D. "Zum Problem des emanzipatorischen Interesses und seiner gesellschaftlichen Wahrnehmung." *Man and World* 3 (1970): 26–53.

Bourdieu, P. *Outline of a Theory of Practice*. Translated by R. Nice. New York: Cambridge University Press, 1977.

Brewster, P., and Buchner, C. H. "Language and Criticism: Jürgen Habermas on Walter Benjamin." *New German Critique* 17 (1979): 15–29.

Bubner, R. "Habermas's Concept of Critical Theory." In *CD* 42–56.

————. "Rationalität als Lebensform: Zu Jürgen Habermas' *Theorie des kommunikativen Handelns*." *Merkur* 4 (April 1982): 341–51.

Bühler, K. *Sprachtheorie*. Stuttgart: Gustav Fischer, 1934.

Bürger, P. "Avant-garde and Contemporary Aesthetics: A Reply to Jürgen Habermas." *New German Critique* 22 (1982): 19–22.

Carnap, R. "Logical Foundations of the Unity of Science." In *Readings in Philosophical Analysis*, edited by H. Feigle and W. Sellers, pp. 408–21. New York: Appleton Century Crofts, 1949.

Castoriadis, C. *Gesellschaft als imaginäre Institution.* Frankfurt: Suhrkamp, 1984.

Chomsky, N. *Aspects of a Theory of Syntax.* Cambridge, Mass.: MIT Press, 1965.

Cicourel, A. V. *Method and Measurement in Sociology.* Glencoe, Ill.: Free Press, 1964.

Connerton, P. *The Tragedy of Enlightenment: An Essay on the Frankfurt School.* Cambridge: Cambridge University Press, 1980.

Coward, R., and Ellis, J. *Language and Materialism.* London: Routledge, 1977.

Crews, F. "In the Big House of Theory." *The New York Review of Books,* 33, no. 9 (29 May 1986): 36–42.

Culler, J. "Communicative Competence and Normative Force." *New German Critique* 35 (Spring/Summer, 1985): 133–44.

Dallmayr, F. *Beyond Dogma and Despair.* Notre Dame: University of Notre Dame Press, 1981.

———. *Language and Politics.* Notre Dame: University of Notre Dame Press, 1984.

———. *Materialen zu Habermas's 'Erkenntnis und Interesse'.* Frankfurt: Suhrkamp, 1974.

———. "Pragmatism and Hermeneutics." *Review of Politics* 47, no. 3 (July 1985): 411–30.

———. *The Twilight of Subjectivity: Contributions to a Post-Individualist Theory of Politics.* Amherst: University of Massachusetts Press, 1981.

Danto, A. C. *Analytical Philosophy of Action.* Cambridge: Cambridge University Press, 1973.

———. *Analytical Philosophy of History.* Cambridge: Cambridge University Press, 1965.

Derrida, J. *Of Grammatology.* Translated by G. Spivak. Baltimore: Johns Hopkins University Press, 1974.

———. *Speech and Phenomena.* Translated by D. Allison. Evanston: Northwestern University Press, 1973.

Doppelt, G. "Conflicting Social Paradigms of Human Freedom and the Problem of Justification." *Inquiry* 27 (1984): 51–86.

Dreyfus, B. "Holism and Hermeneutics." *Review of Metaphysics* 34 (1980): 3–23.

Dreyfus, H. L., and Rabinow, P. *Michel Foucault: Beyond Hermeneutics and Structuralism.* Chicago: University of Chicago Press, 1982.

Dubin, R. "Parsons' Actor: Continuities in Social Theory." In *Sociological Theory in Modern Society,* edited by T. Parsons, pp. 456–66. Glencoe, Ill.: Free Press, 1967.

Dummet, M. "What is a Theory of Meaning?" In *Truth and Meaning,* edited by G. Evans and J. McDowell, pp. 16–137. Oxford: Basil Blackwell, 1976.

Durkheim, E. "The Determination of Moral Facts." In *Essays on Sociology and Philosophy,* by E. Durkheim et al., pp. 35–62. New York: Free Press, 1964.

———. *The Division of Labor in Society.* Translated by G. Simpson. New York: Macmillan, 1933.

————. *The Elementary Forms of the Religious Life.* Translated by J. W. Swain. New York: Free Press, 1965.

————. *Leçons de sociologie physique des moeurs et du droit.* Paris: Presses Universitaire de France, 1969.

Evans-Pritchard, E. E. *Witchcraft, Oracles and Magic Among the Azande.* Oxford: Clarendon Press, 1937.

Feenberg, A. *Lukács, Marx, and the Sources of Critical Theory.* Totowa, N.J.: Rowman and Littlefield, 1981.

Fichte, J. "Erste Einleitung in die Wissenschaftslehre." In *Werke,* vol. 3, pp. 419–79. Berlin: Veit, 1895.

Foster, H., ed. *The Anti-Aesthetic: Essays in Modern Culture.* Port Townsend, Wash.: Bay Press, 1983.

Foster, H. "(Post)Modern Polemics." *New German Critique* 33 (1984): 68–78.

Foucault, M. *The Archaeology of Knowledge.* Translated by A. M. Sheridan Smith. New York: Pantheon, 1972.

————. *Discipline and Punish: The Birth of the Prison.* Translated by A. Sheridan. New York. Pantheon, 1979.

————. *Histoire de la sexualité: l'usage des plaisirs.* Paris: Gallimard, 1984.

————. *The History of Human Sexuality, Volume I: An Introduction.* Translated by R. Hurley. New York: Pantheon, 1979.

————. *Knowledge/Power: Selected Interviews and Other Writings by Michel Foucault, 1972–1977.* Edited by Colin Gordin. New York: Pantheon, 1980.

————. *Madness and Civilization. A History of Insanity in the Age of Reason.* Translated by R. Howard. New York: Random House, 1973.

————. "Nietzsche, Genealogy, History." In *Language, Counter-Memory, Practice,* edited by D. F. Bouchard. Ithaca: Cornell University Press, 1977: 139–64.

————. *The Order of Things.* New York: Random House, 1973.

Fraser, N. "The French Derrideans: Politicizing Deconstruction or Deconstructing the Political?" *New German Critique* 33 (1984): 127–54.

————. "What's Critical About Critical Theory?: The Case of Habermas and Gender." *New German Critique* 35 (1985): 97–111.

Freud, S. *The Complete Psychological Works of Sigmund Freud.* 24 vols. London: Hogarth Press, 1967.

Gadamer, H.-G. "On the Scope and Function of Hermeneutical Reflection." In *Philosophical Hermeneutics,* edited by D. Linge, pp. 18–43. Berkeley: University of California Press, 1976.

————. "Replik." In *Hermeneutik und Ideologiekritik,* edited by K.-O. Apel, pp. 283–317. Frankfurt: Suhrkamp, 1971.

————. *Truth and Method.* Translated by J. Cumming. New York: Seabury, 1975.

————. "Über die Möglichkeit einer philosophischen Ethik." In *Kleine Schriften,* vol. 1, pp. 179–91. Tübingen: J. C. Mohr, 1967.

————. "Über die Planung der Zukunft." In *Kleine Schriften,* vol. 1, pp. 161–78. Tübingen: J. C. Mohr, 1967.

Garfinkel, H. *Studies in Ethnomethodology.* Englewood Cliffs, N.J.: Prentice-Hall, 1967.

Gellner, E. "The Savage and the Modern Mind." In *Modes of Thought*, edited by R. Horton and R. Finnegan, pp. 168–81. London: Basil Blackwell, 1973.

Geuss, R. *The Idea of Critical Theory.* Cambridge: Cambridge University Press, 1981.

Giddens, A. "Habermas's Critique of Hermeneutics." In *Studies in Social and Political Theory*, edited by Richard Bernstein, pp. 135–64. London: Hutchinson, 1977.

———. "Labor and Interaction." In *CD* 149–61.

———. *New Rules for Sociological Method.* London: Hutchinson, 1976.

———. "Reason without Revolution? Habermas' *Theorie des kommunikativen Handelns.*" In *Habermas and Modernity*, edited by R. Bernstein, pp. 95–121. Cambridge, Mass.: MIT Press, 1985.

Godelier, M. *Perspectives in Marxist Anthropology.* Cambridge: Cambridge University Press, 1976.

Goffman, E. *Encounters.* Indianapolis: Bobbs-Merrill, 1961.

———. *The Presentation of Self in Everyday Life.* New York: Doubleday, Anchor Books, 1959.

Görtzen, R. and van Gelder, F. "Jürgen Habermas: The Complete Oeuvre: A Bibliography of Primary Literature, Translations and Reviews." *Human Studies*, 2 (1979).

Gould, C. "Socialism and Democracy." *Praxis International* 1, no. 1 (1981): 49–69.

Gouldner, A. *The Dialectic of Ideology and Technology.* New York: Seabury Press, 1976.

Greenberg, C. "Modernist Painting." *Art and Literature* 4 (Spring 1965): 193–201.

Grünbaum, A. *The Philosophical Foundations of Psychoanalysis.* Berkeley: University of California Press, 1984.

Habermas, J. "The Analytical Theory of Science and Dialectics." In T. W. Adorno et. al., *The Positivist Dispute in German Sociology.* Translated by G. Adey and D. Frisby, pp. 131–62. London: Heinemann, 1976.

———. "Conservatism and Capitalist Crisis." *New Left Review* 115 (1979): 33–84.

———. "Der Universalitätsanspruch der Hermeneutik." In *Hermeneutik und Ideologiekritik*, pp. 120–59. Frankfurt: Suhrkamp, 1971.

———. "The Entwinement of Myth and Enlightenment." *New German Critique* 26 (1982): 13–30.

———. "History and Evolution." *Telos* 39 (1979): 5–44.

———. "Modernity Versus Post-Modernity." *New German Critique* 22 (1981): 3–14.

———. "On Social Identity." *Telos* 19 (1974): 91–103.

———. "On Systematically Distorted Communication." *Inquiry* 13 (1970): 205–18.

———. "The Place of Philosophy in Marxism." *Intransigent Sociologist* 5 (1975): 41–48.

———. "A Positivistically Bisected Rationalism." In T. W. Adorno et. al., *The*

Positivist Dispute in German Sociology. Translated by G. Adey and D. Frisby, pp. 198–275. London: Heinemann, 1976.

———. "A Postscript to Knowledge and Human Interest." *Philosophy of the Social Sciences* 3 (1973): 157–89.

———. "Questions and Counter-Questions." *Praxis International* 4, no. 3 (1984): 229–50.

———. "A Reply to my Critics." In *CD* 219–83.

———. "Rückkehr zur Metaphysik—Ein Tendenz in der deutschen Philosophie." *Merkur* 432 (October 1985): 898–905.

———. "Theory and Politics: A Discussion with Herbert Marcuse, Jürgen Habermas, Heinz Lubasz and Telman Spengler." *Telos* 38 (1978–79): 124–54.

———. "Toward a Theory of Communicative Competence." In *Recent Sociology*, no. 2, edited by H. Dreitzel, pp. 115–48. New York: Macmillan, 1970.

———. "Universalpragmatische Hinweise auf das System der Ich-Abgrenzungen." In *Kommunikation, Interacktion, Identität*, edited by M. Auwarter, E. Kirsch, and M. Schroter, pp. 332–47. Frankfurt: Suhrkamp, 1976.

———. "Why More Philosophy?" *Social Research* 38 (1971): 633–54.

Handelman, S. "Jacques Derrida and the Heretic Hermeneutic." In *Displacement, Derrida and After*, edited by M. Krupnick, pp. 98–129. Bloomington: Indiana University Press, 1983.

Hegel, G. W. F. "The Spirit of Christianity." In *Early Theological Writings*, edited by T. M. Knox, pp. 224–36. Philadelphia: University of Pennsylvania Press, 1968.

Heidegger, M. *Being and Time.* Translated by J. Macquarrie and E. Robinson. New York. Harper and Row, 1962.

———. *Nietzsche IV: Nihilism.* Translated by Frank Capuzzi. Edited by David Krell. New York: Harper and Row, 1978.

Held, D. *Introduction to Critical Theory: Horkheimer to Habermas.* Berkeley: University of California Press, 1980.

———. "Crisis Tendencies, Legitimation and the State." In *CD* 181–95.

Heller, A. *Das Alltagsleben.* Frankfurt: Suhrkamp, 1978.

———. "Habermas and Marxism." In *CD* 21–41.

Henrich, D. "Die Grundstruktur der modernen Philosophie." In *Subjektivität und Selbsterhaltung*, edited by H. Ebeling, pp. 97–121. Frankfurt: Suhrkamp, 1967.

———. "Selbstbewusstsein: Kritische Einleitung in einer Theorie." In *Hermeneutik und Dialektik*, edited by R. Bubner, K. Cramer, and R. Wiehl, pp. 259–89. Frankfurt: Suhrkamp, 1970.

Hesse, M. "Science and Objectivity." In *CD* 98–115.

Hirsch, E. D. *Validity in Interpretation.* New Haven: Yale University Press, 1967.

Hohendahl, P. "The Dialectic of Enlightenment Revisited: Habermas' Critique of the Frankfurt School." *New German Critique* 35 (Summer/Spring 1985): 3–26.

Hollinger, R., ed. *Hermeneutics and Praxis*. Notre Dame: University of Notre Dame Press, 1985.

Honneth A. "Communication and Reconciliation. *Telos* 39 (1979): 45–61.

Horkheimer, Max. *Critical Theory*. Translated by J. O'Connel. New York: Continuum, 1972.

———. *The Eclipse of Reason*. New York: Seabury Press, 1973.

———. "The End of Reason." In *The Essential Frankfurt School Reader*, edited by A. Arato and E. Gebhardt, pp. 373–77. New York: Continuum, 1982.

———. *Zur Kritik der Instrumentellen Vernunft*. Frankfurt: Suhrkamp, 1967.

Horton, R. "African Thought and Western Science." In *Rationality*, edited by B. R. Wilson, pp. 131–71. Oxford: Basil Blackwell, 1970.

Husserl, E. *Logische Untersuchungen*. 2 vols. Tübingen: J. C. Mohr, 1980.

Huyssen, A. "Mapping the Postmodern." In *New German Critique* 33 (Fall 1984): 5–52.

———. "The Search for Tradition: Avant-garde and Post-modernism in the 1970's." *New German Critique* 22 (1981): 23–40.

Ingram, D. "Arendt." In *Thinkers of the Twentieth Century*. Detroit. Gale Publishers, 1983, pp. 16–17.

———. "Foucault and the Frankfurt School: A Discourse on Nietzsche, Power and Knowledge." *Praxis International* (October 1986).

———. "Habermas, Gadamer, and Bourdieu on Discourse: A Communicative Ethic Reconsidered." *Man and World* 15 (1982): 149–61.

———. "Hermeneutics and Truth." *Journal of the British Society for Phenomenology* 15, no. 1 (1984): 62–78. Reprinted in *Hermeneutics and Praxis*, ed. R. Hollinger, pp. 32–53.

———. "The Historical Genesis of the Gadamer-Habermas Controversy," *Auslegung* 10, nos. 1, 2 (1983): 86–151.

———. "Philosophy and the Aesthetic Mediation of Life: Weber and Habermas on the Paradox of Rationality." *The Philosophical Forum* (forthcoming).

Jameson, F. *The Political Unconscious: Narrative as a Socially Symbolic Act*. Ithaca: Cornell University Press, 1981.

———. "The Politics of Theory: Ideological Positions in the Postmodernism Debate." *New German Critique* 33 (1984): 53–65.

Jarvie, I. C. *Concepts and Society*. London: Routledge and Kegan Paul, 1972.

Jay, M. "Habermas and Modernism." *Praxis International* 4, no. 1 (1984): pp. 1–13.

———. *Marxism and Totality*. Berkeley: University of California Press, 1984.

Jencks, C. *The Language of Postmodern Architecture*. New York: Rizzoli, 1977.

Kain, P. *Schiller, Hegel, and Marx: State, Society, and the Aesthetic Ideal of Ancient Greece*. Montreal: McGill-Queens University Press, 1982.

Keat, R. *The Politics of Social Theory*. Chicago: University of Chicago Press, 1981.

Kirchheimer, O. "Criminal Law in National Socialist Germany." *Studies in Philosophy and Social Science* 8, no. 3 (1939): 444–63.

———. "The Legal Order of National Socialism." *Studies in Philosophy and Social Science* 9, no. 3 (1941). 456–75.

Kohlberg, L. "From Is to Ought." In *Cognitive Development and Epistemology*, edited by T. Mischel, pp. 151–236. New York: Academic Press, 1971.

———. "The Claim to Moral Adequacy at the Highest Stage of Moral Judgement." In *Journal of Philosophy* 70 (1973): 630–46.

Kortian, G. *Metacritique*. Cambridge: Cambridge University Press, 1980.

Kuhlmann, W. *Reflexion und Kommunikative Erfahrung*. Frankfurt: Suhrkamp, 1975.

Kuhn, T. *The Essential Tension: Selected Studies in Scientific Tradition and Change*. Chicago: University of Chicago Press, 1977.

———. *The Structure of Scientific Revolutions*. 2d ed. Chicago: University of Chicago Press, 1970.

Lobkowicz, N. "Interest and Objectivity." *Philosophy and Social Science* 2 (1972): 193–210.

Lorenzer, A. *Kritik des psychoanalytischen Symbolbegriffs*. Frankfurt: Suhrkamp, 1970.

———. *Sprachstörung und Rekonstruktion*. Frankfurt: Suhrkamp, 1970.

Löwith, K. *From Hegel to Nietzsche*. Garden City: Doubleday, Anchor Books, 1967.

Lukács, Georg. "Geschichte und Klassenbewusstsein." *Werke*, vol. 2. Neuwied: Luchterhand, 1968.

Lukes, S. "Of Gods and Demons: Habermas and Practical Reason." In *CD* 134–48.

———. "Some Problems about Rationality." In *Rationality*, edited by B. R. Wilson, pp. 194–213. Oxford: Basil Blackwell, 1970.

Lyotard, J.-F. *The Postmodern Condition: A Report on Knowledge*. Translated by Geoff Bennington and Brian Massumi. Minneapolis: University of Minnesota, 1984.

MacIntyre, A. *After Virtue: A Study in Moral Philosophy*. Notre Dame: University of Notre Dame Press, 1981.

———. *Against the Self-Images of the Age*. Notre Dame: University of Notre Dame Press, 1971.

Malinowski, B. *A Scientific Theory of Culture*. Chapel Hill: University of North Carolina Press, 1944.

Marcuse, H. "Beiträge zu einer Phänomenologie des historischen Materialismus." *Philosophische Hefte* 1 (1928): 45–68.

———. *Counterrevolution and Revolt*. Boston: Beacon Press, 1972.

———. *Eros and Civilization: A Philosophical Inquiry Into Freud*. Boston: Beacon Press, 1962.

———. "Neue Quellen zur Grundlegung des historischen Materialismus." *Die Gesellschaft* 9, no. 8 (August 1932): 136–74.

———. "Das Problem der geschichtlichen Wirklichkeit Wilhelm Dilthey." *Die Gesellschaft* 4 (April 1931): 350–67.

———. "Some Social Implications of Modern Technology." In *The Essential Frankfurt School Reader*, edited by A. Arato and E. Gebhardt, pp. 138–62. New York: Continuum, 1982.

Marković M. "New Forms of Democracy and Socialism." *Praxis International* 1 no. 1 (1981): 23–39.

Marx, K. *Capital.* 3 vols. New York: International, 1967.

──────. *A Contribution to the Critique of Political Economy.* Edited by M. Dobb. New York: International, 1970.

──────. *Grundrisse.* Translated by Martin Nicolaus. New York: Vintage Books, 1973.

──────. "Paris Manuscripts." In *Marx/Engels Collected Works,* vol. 3, pp. 229–326. New York: International, 1975.

──────, and Engels, F. "The German Ideology." In *Marx/Engels Collected Works,* Vol. 5, pp. 15–539. New York: International Publishers, 1976.

──────, and Engels, F. "Manifesto of the Communist Party." In *The Marx-Engels Reader,* 2d ed., edited by R. C. Tucker, pp. 469–500. New York: Norton, 1978.

McCarthy, T. "Complexity and Democracy, or the Seducements of Systems Theory." *New German Critique* 35 (Spring/Summer 1985): 27–53.

──────. *The Critical Theory of Jürgen Habermas.* Cambridge, Mass.: MIT Press, 1978.

──────. "Reflections on Rationalization in the Theory of Communicative Action." *Praxis International* 4, no. 2 (1984): 77–91.

──────, and Dallmayr, F., eds. *Understanding and Social Inquiry.* Notre Dame: University of Notre Dame Press, 1981.

Mead, G. H. *The Philosophy of the Act.* Edited by C. W. Morris. Chicago: University of Chicago Press, 1934.

──────. *Selected Writings.* Edited by A. J. Reck. Indianapolis: Bobbs-Merrill, 1964.

Merleau-Ponty, M. *The Phenomenology of Perception.* Translated by C. Smith. London: Routledge and Kegan Paul, 1962.

Merton, R. K. "Manifest and Latent Functions." In *Social Theory and Social Structure,* pp. 19–84. Glencoe, Ill.: Free Press, 1957.

Mischel, T., ed. *Cognitive Development and Psychology.* New York: Academic Press, 1971.

Misgeld, D. "Critical Hermeneutics Versus Neoparsonianism?" *New German Critique* 35 (1985): 55–87.

Moore, S. *The Critique of Capitalist Democracy.* New York: Paine-Whitman, 1957.

Needham, J. *Science and Civilization in China.* 4 vols. Cambridge: Cambridge University Press, 1954.

Negt, O. *Die Linke antwortet Jürgen Habermas.* Frankfurt: Europäische Verlagsanstalt, 1968.

Nietzsche, F. *The Dawn.* New York: Random House, 1967.

──────. *The Genealogy of Morals.* Translated by F. Golffing. Garden City, N.Y.: Doubleday, Anchor Books, 1956.

──────. *Thus Spoke Zarathustra.* Translated by W. Kaufmann. New York: Modern Library, 1954.

──────. *Werke: Kritische Ausgabe sämtlicher Schriften und nachgelassenen Fragmente.* 30 vols. Berlin: de Gruyter, 1967.

Offe, C. *Strukturprobleme des kapitalistischen Staates.* Frankfurt: Suhrkamp, 1972.

251

O'Kane, J. "Marxism, Deconstruction, and Ideology: Notes Toward an Artic-ulation." *New German Critique* 33 (Fall 1984): 219–47.

Olafson, F. A. *The Dialectic of Action*. Chicago: University of Chicago Press, 1979.

O'Neill, J., ed. *On Critical Theory*. New York: Seabury, 1976.

Ottmann, H. "Cognitive Interests and Self-Reflection." In *CD* 79–97.

Parsons, T. *Action Theory and the Human Condition*. New York: Free Press, 1978.

———. "An Approach to Psychological Theory in Terms of the Theory of Ac-tion." In *Psychology: A Study of a Science*, edited by S. Koch. 6 vols. New York: Free Press, 1959.

———. *Essays in Sociological Theory Pure and Applied*. Glencoe, Ill.: Free Press, 1949.

———. *The Social System*. New York: Free Press, 1951.

———. *Societies: Evolutionary and Comparative Perspectives*. Englewood Cliffs, N.J.: Prentice-Hall, 1966.

———. "Some Problems of General Theory in Sociology." In *Theoretical Soci-ology*, edited by J. C. McKinney and E. A. Tiryakan. New York: Free Press, 1970.

———. *Structure of Social Action*. New York: McGraw-Hill, 1937.

———, and Shils, E., eds. *Toward a General Theory of Action*. Cambridge, Mass.: Harvard University Press, 1963.

———, and Smelser, N. J. *Economy and Society*. New York: Free Press, 1956.

Peirce, C. "Lectures on Pragmatism." In *Collected Papers*, vol. 5, edited by C. Hartshorne and P. Weiss, pp. 13–131. Cambridge, Mass.: Harvard Uni-versity Press, 1960.

Pippin, R. "Nietzsche and the Origin of the Idea of Modernism." *Inquiry* 26 (1983): 151–80.

Popper, K. *Objective Knowledge*. Oxford: Oxford University Press, 1972.

———. *The Poverty of Historicism*. New York: Harper and Row, 1957.

———, and Eccles, J. C. *The Self and its Brain*. New York: Springer Interna-tional, 1977.

Pratt, M. L. *Speech Act Theory of Literary Discourse*. Bloomington: Indiana Uni-versity Press, 1977.

Radcliffe-Brown, A. R. *Structure and Function in Primitive Societies*. London: Oxford University Press, 1952.

Radnitzky, G. *Contemporary Schools of Metascience*. Chicago: Regnery, 1973.

Rasmussen, D. "Communicative Action and Philosophy: Reflections on Habermas' 'Theorie des kommunikativen Handelns.'" *Philosophy and So-cial Criticism* 9, no. 1 (1982): 3–28.

Rawls, J. *A Theory of Justice*. Cambridge, Mass.: Harvard University Press, 1971.

Ricoeur, P. "Hermeneutics and the Critique of Ideology." In *Hermeneutics and the Human Sciences: Essays on Language Action and Interpretation*, edited and translated by J. B. Thompson, pp. 63–100. Cambridge: Cambridge Uni-versity Press, 1981.

Ritter, J. *Hegel und die französische Revolution*. Frankfurt: Suhrkamp, 1965.

───── . *Metaphysik und Politik.* Frankfurt: Suhrkamp, 1969.

Rorty, R. "Habermas and Lyotard on Post-Modernity." *Praxis International* 4, no. 1 (April 1984): 32–44.

───── . *Philosophy and the Mirror of Nature.* Princeton: Princeton University Press, 1979.

Ryan, M. *Marxism and Deconstruction: A Critical Articulation.* Baltimore: Johns Hopkins University Press, 1982.

Schiller, F. *Sämtliche Werke: Säkular Ausgabe.* 16 vols. Berlin: Cotta, 1904–05.

Schmid, M. "Habermas's Theory of Social Evolution." In *CD* 162–80.

Schütz, A. *Collected Papers,* vol. 1. Edited by M. Natanson. The Hague: Nijhoff, 1967.

Searle, J. *Expression and Meaning.* Cambridge: Cambridge University Press, 1979.

Sensat, J. *Habermas and Marxism: An Appraisal.* Beverly Hills: Sage, 1979.

Shroyer, T. *The Critique of Domination.* New York. Braziller, 1973.

Skjervheim, H. "Objectivism and the Study of Man." *Inquiry* 17, no. 2 (1974): 213–39.

Smith, T. "The Scope of the Social Sciences in Weber and Habermas." In *Philosophy and Social Criticism* 1 (1981): 69–83.

Thompson, J. B. *Critical Hermeneutics: A Study in the Thought of Paul Ricoeur and Jürgen Habermas.* Cambridge: Cambridge University Press, 1981.

───── . "Universal Pragmatics." In *CD* 116–33.

Toulmin, S. *Human Understanding.* Princeton: Princeton University Press, 1972.

───── . *The Uses of Argument.* Cambridge: Cambridge University Press, 1958.

Tourraine, A. *La Société post-industrielle.* Paris: Gallilée, 1969.

Truzzi, M., ed. *Subjective Understanding in the Social Sciences.* London: Addison-Wesley, 1974.

Venturi, R., Brown, D. S., and Izenour, S. *Learning from Las Vegas.* Cambridge, Mass.: MIT Press, 1972.

Vico, G. *The New Science of Giambattista Vico.* Translated by T. G. Bergin and M. H. Fisch. Ithaca: Cornell University Press, 1970.

───── . *On the Study Methods of our Time.* Translated by E. Gianturco. Indianapolis: Bobbs-Merrill, 1965.

von Wright, G. *Explanation and Understanding.* Ithaca: Cornell University Press, 1971.

Watson, S. "Jürgen Habermas and Jean-François Lyotard: Post-Modernism and the Crisis of Rationality." *Philosophy and Social Criticism* 2 (Fall 1984): 1–24.

Weber, M. *Economy and Society.* Edited by G. Roth and C. Wittich. 2 vols. Berkeley: University of California Press, 1970.

───── . *From Max Weber.* Edited by H. H. Gerth and C. W. Mills. Oxford: Oxford University Press, 1969.

───── . *The Protestant Ethic and the Spirit of Capitalism.* New York: Scribner, 1958.

Wellmer, A. *Critical Theory of Society.* Translated by J. Cumming. New York: Seabury, 1974.

White, S. "Habermas' Communicative Ethics and the Development of Moral Consciousness." *Philosophy and Social Criticism* 2 (Fall 1984): 25–48.

Whitebook, J. "The Problem of Nature in Habermas." *Telos* 40 (1979): 41–69.

———. "Reason and Happiness: Some Psychoanalytic Themes in Critical Theory." *Praxis International* 4, no. 1 (April 1984): 15–31.

Winch, P. *The Idea of a Social Science.* London: Routledge and Kegan Paul, 1958.

———. "Understanding a Primitive Society." In *Rationality,* edited by B. R. Wilson, pp. 78–111. Oxford: Basil Blackwell, 1970.

Wittgenstein, L. *Philosophical Investigations.* New York: Macmillan, 1953.

———. *Remarks on the Foundations of Mathematics.* Oxford: Basil Blackwell, 1956.

Wood, A. "Habermas' Defense of Rationalism." *New German Critique* 35 (Spring/Summer, 1985): 145–64.

Woodward, W. *Studies in Education During the Age of the Renaissance: 1400–1600.* New York: Teachers College Press, 1967.

———. *Vittorino da Feltre.* New York: Teachers College Press, 1963.

INDEX

Action: meaningful and intentional, 3–4, 28–30, 32, 39, 105; instrumental, 12, 24, 73, 84, 119, 129–30, 139–40; and discourse, 16, 186; rational, 19–22, 32–33; four types of, 30–32; Weber's theory of, 37, 43–44; and systems theory, 104–05, 115–17, 139–46, 168, 172; domains of, 115–16, 149, 164, 168, 172, 178, 180, 185–86

Adorno, T. W., 6–7, 57, 73–74, 78, 110, 119, 164, 182; on dialectic of enlightenment, 65–66, 75, 96, 186–87; *Negative Dialectics*, 67, 69, 91, 96. *See also* Frankfurt school

Alienation, 154, 176, 185. *See also* Marx, K.

Apel, K.-O., 15

Appropriateness, 20–21, 58

Arac, J., 214n75

Arato, A., 163

Architecture, 76–77, 100–01

Arendt, H., 193n12, 215n80

Argumentation, 92, 103, 117–18, 170, 178, 181, 184. *See also* Discourse

Arguments, types of, 20, 22, 54

Aristotle, 4, 22, 42, 79, 102

Art, 42, 65, 69–71, 74–87 passim; and rationality, 21–22, 56–59, 180–81;

modern, 56–57, 76, 79, 85, 159, 178, 181–83, 185; and mediation, 101–03, 178–86

Arts and sciences, 30, 44–45, 52, 101, 130, 175, 178

Attitudes, 29–30, 34–35, 39, 55–57, 118, 130–31

Austin, J. L., 37–38

Authenticity, 21, 58, 88, 180–84

Autonomy, personal, 98, 106, 110–14, 131–32, 139, 150, 159, 175

Bacon, F., 1, 71

Bataille, G., 58, 75, 87, 92–94, 111

Baudelaire, C., 69, 79

Behaviorism, 4, 28–29, 34, 105

Bell, D., 100, 214n75

Benhabib, S., 240n17

Benjamin, W., 57–59, 66–69, 79–80, 164, 175, 182–85

Berger, P., 210n28

Bühler, K., 37

Bureaucracy, 46, 50–51, 64–65, 82, 98, 147, 166–67

Bureaucratic elites, 5, 151, 159

Bürger, P., 185

Capitalism, 4–5, 46, 83, 95, 115, 127, 133, 177; and social pathology, 48–54, 60–65, 146–47, 151–71 passim

Surrealism, 57–59, 76, 100, 182, 185
Symbolic interactionism, 71, 105–07, 109–10

Teleology, 56, 184–85
Therapeutic relationship, 21, 45, 97
Thompson, J. B., 196n53, 201n30, 202
Totalitarianism, 62, 185
Totality, 59, 79, 102, 152, 175, 183–84
Toulmin, S., 22
Truth: and hermeneutics, 2, 9; and intersubjective validity, 16, 62, 114, 172; as rational ideal; 53, 114, 130–31, 178–81; aesthetic, 58, 103, 183–84, 186; and critical theory, 68, 74; and poststructuralism, 77, 94, 96; and German philosophy, 81, 86–90, 152; and morality, 114, 180
Truth claims, 29–30, 114, 178, 181
Tugendhat, E., 201n31

Understanding: ethical aim of, 2, 4; Heidegger's notion of, 7–8, 87–88; hermeneutic theory of, 7–10, 36; Gadamer's notion of, 8–9, 186; phenomenological theory of, 34–35; narrative, 117, 131
Universalizability, 21, 44, 85, 109–10, 178, 180
Universal pragmatics, 38–39
Utopia, 58–59, 160, 174, 178–79, 183–84, 185, 187

Validity, domains of, 93, 178–79, 183–84
Validity claims: types of, 20, 183–84; relationship to language, action, and world, 22–23, 30; and meaning, 38, 99; counterfactual status

of, 98–99, 114, 141, 180; poetic conflation of, 201n30
Value generalization, 127–28, 146
Values, 86, 136, 139–44, 149, 158–59, 176, 181–82, 188; conflict between, 49, 52–54
Value spheres: differentiation of, 44–45, 73, 114, 117–18, 130–31, 148, 176, 184; mediation of, 54–55, 101–03, 178–79, 184–85; subjectivization of, 63–64, 101
Vico, G., 2
Vocational ethic, 100, 112, 124. *See also* Protestant work ethic

Weber, M., 72–73, 140–54 passim, 173, 180, 188; on understanding action, 3; and romantic hermeneutics, 8; and types of action, 36–37; on rationality and rationalization, 43–44; on religion, 46–48; and critical theory, 60–65 passim; and value freedom, 200n6
Wellmer, A., 58, 184, 240n17
Whitebook, J., 56, 240n17
Will to power, 66–67, 78, 86–87, 89
Winch, P., 24–26
Wittgenstein, L., 25, 37–38, 106
Wood, A., 203n38
World(s): as referential contexts, 22, 28–30, 116–18, 130; cross-tabulated with basic attitudes, 55–56. *See also* Lifeworld
World views: mythic versus modern, 23–28, 176; religious and metaphysical, 26–28, 46–47, 114, 117, 122, 133–34, 159; development of, 27; rationalization of, 44, 114, 148, 154, 178

Young Hegelians, 82, 85